THE PSYCHOSOCIAL WORK ENVIRONMENT:

Work Organization, Democratization and Health

Essays in Memory of Bertil Gardell

**JEFFREY V. JOHNSON and
GUNN JOHANSSON, Editors**

POLICY,
POLITICS,
HEALTH AND
MEDICINE
Series
Vicente Navarro, Series Editor

Baywood Publishing Company, Inc.
Amityville, N.Y. 11701

Library of Congress Catalog Number: 90-19713
ISBN: 0-89503-077-2 (Paper)
ISBN: 0-89503-078-0 (Cloth)

Library of Congress Cataloging-in-Publication Data
  Main entry under title:

The Psychosocial work environment : work organization,
  democratization, and health : essays in memory of Bertil Gardell /
  Jeffrey V. Johnson and Gunn Johansson, editors.
      p. cm. -- (Policy, politics, health and medicine series)
  Includes bibliographical references and index.
  ISBN 0-89503-078-0. -- ISBN 0-89503-077-2 (pbk.)
  1. Work--Social aspects. 2. Work--Psychological aspects.
  3. Management--Employee participation. 4. Gardell, Bertil.
  I. Gardell, Bertil. II. Johnson, Jeffrey V. III. Johansson, Gunn.
  IV. Series.
RC963.3 P79 1991
658.3'8--dc20   90-19713
                                                        CIP

DEDICATION

This book is dedicated to the memory of Bertil Gardell,
scientist, teacher, activist and friend, whose life inspired this volume,
and whose work continues to provide direction to our own.

ACKNOWLEDGMENTS

We would like to take this opportunity to thank our friends and colleagues who have reviewed and edited the 18 manuscripts appearing in this book. In this regard we would especially like to acknowledge the work of Ellen M. Hall. We would also like to gratefully acknowledge the role of the Swedish Work Environment Fund for its interest in this book, and its financial support for the editorial work involved. A special note of appreciation is due Vicente Navarro, the editor-in-chief of the *International Journal of Health Services*, who was involved in the initial conception of this tribute to Professor Gardell, and who lent his support to this project during the period in which the chapters in this book were published as a special series of articles in the Journal throughout 1988 and 1989. We would also like to acknowledge the many contributions of Linda Hansford, the technical editor of the *International Journal of Health Services*, who has helped guide both the authors and editors through the difficulties posed by language, meaning, and method.

TABLE OF CONTENTS

6 / Contents

INTRODUCTION

Work Organization, Occupational Health, and Social Change: The Legacy of Bertil Gardell

Jeffrey V. Johnson and Gunn Johansson

In the last two decades the field of psychosocial work environment research and practice has grown and matured. It now spans the disciplines of social psychology, psychobiology, organizational and historical sociology, epidemiology, and health policy. The nucleus of this varied research effort is the work process—specifically those aspects of work organization that are detrimental to mental and physical health. With the rise in office and service occupations and the parallel decline in manufacturing industries, concerns with work organization and stress are becoming more central to the field of occupational health (1). One indication of the growing importance of this area is that at the present time stress-related disability claims are the most rapidly growing form of occupational illness within the Worker's Compensation system in the United States (2).

Although significant advances have been made in the psychosocial work environment field in North and South America, Australia, and Western Europe, researchers and practitioners continue to look to the Scandinavian countries for scientific and program-matic leadership. Within Scandinavia, the sustained research programs of the late Professor Bertil Gardell and of his colleagues at the University of Stockholm have played a decisive role in the development of the scientific agenda for this field (3). They have greatly advanced the formation of policy and legislation which today influences the structure of the work environment in Sweden and elsewhere. Moreover, Bertil Gardell's scientific work has contributed to the development of a multilevel strategy for workplace reform which is presently being pursued by a number of groups throughout the world.

It is therefore with both pleasure and sorrow that we present this book dedicated to the memory and work of the late Professor Gardell who died in 1987 at the age of fifty-nine. Shortly before his death we agreed to develop this collection of articles from his colleagues that would articulate some of the major themes that he helped to place on the scientific agenda. For those who are unacquainted with Bertil Gardell, his contributions to the field of work environment research were personal, scientific, and political. At the personal level Bertil touched the lives of many working people—nurses, mail personnel, factory workers, chemical process workers, miners, bus drivers, and forestry workers. From this experience he developed a deep and abiding conviction that working people had the capacity to conceptualize, change, and ultimately control the nature of their own working life.

At another personal level, Bertil Gardell had a profound influence on his students and colleagues. He was a man who appreciated human companionship and developed lasting friendships all over the world. As many of the authors in this volume would acknowledge—for many of us were once his students—although demanding much (sometimes too much it seemed at the time), he also gave much—of his time, of his faith, and perhaps most importantly by providing an open and creative context in which individuals could pursue their own vision within the framework of a larger humanistic perspective. Anyone who heard him speak remembers how elegantly he could bring together seemingly diverse concepts and experiences into a larger synthesis. This ability to provide a scientific and political context for those of us working in this field was one of his greatest gifts.

Gardell believed that work is one of the most important sources of social and psychological well-being and that it provides much of the meaning and structure in adult life (4). Grounded in this broad and humanistic view, he encouraged others to investigate both sides of this issue—the ways in which work can kill the human spirit, and the ways in which it can encourage the development of full human potential. This interest in the daily life concerns of working people grew out of a set of particular historical experiences. Gardell was involved in numerous practical work reform and change efforts throughout the 1950s and 1960s. Initially trained as an experimental psychologist at the University of Uppsala, after a short period in academia he turned to what was to become his life's work: the problems of work organization and alienation. Throughout the 1950s Gardell "got his hands dirty" in countless small shops and large factories throughout Sweden where he was called in to "trouble-shoot" in instances where major stress-related problems had emerged. This experience provided him with both an understanding of the importance of the psychosocial aspects of working life as well as a "human touch"—that is, the ability and willingness to connect with and learn from the workers themselves.

Later, in the 1960s, Gardell returned to an academic setting and performed a series of studies on alienation and mental health which placed his earlier practical knowledge within a scientific context. Operating at both an empirical and a political level, Gardell, together with his colleagues, studied a series of work settings and found that deskilling, loss of freedom, passivity, social isolation, and related aspects of alienation had an impact, not just on psychological and physiological functioning but in other, heretofore unsuspected areas. He and his colleagues found, for example, that work which socializes people to be passive on the job carries over into nonworking life. A phenomenon that he investigated in Sweden—one which deserves greater consideration—was that those who have little control over their jobs continue to be passive in other aspects of their life as well (5). Alienation at work contributes to larger political and social alienation. By contrast, workers with a greater degree of self-determination and control in their work demonstrate greater interest and involvement in addressing and changing the problems they encounter in their workplace (6). This work of Gardell's also provides a useful counterpoint to the idea that it is psychologically demanding work that is uniquely deleterious to the body and the psyche. His observations point to the importance of boredom, dehumanization, and the other host of small dissolutions that occur when human beings do not continue to learn and to grow in work, regardless of the pace at which the work is performed.

The linkage that Gardell made between work psychology on the one hand and occupational health on the other helped to create the new field of psychosocial work environment research. Up to the late 1960s there continued to be a theoretical focus on the degree of pressure or load placed on the individual worker by the demands of the production system. This model of workplace stress was analogous to the way an engineer would view the structural integrity of a bridge: how much load can it bear, and when does damage occur? However, this relatively simplistic stimulus–response model had little success in explaining disease related to work exposure. As a consequence researchers began to examine aspects of the individual worker and the psychosocial environment which might serve to explain the differences observed in stress responses and disease rates within the working population. Two rather distinct approaches were, and presently are, being taken. The first has focused primarily on the individual worker and his or her predispositions, attributes, and skills— an orientation that might be considered congruent with the political and cultural values that predominate in the United States. On the other hand, European researchers, particularly those in Sweden and Norway, have tended to emphasize the structural characteristics of the work setting itself, and have focused their attention on the resources available to individuals or groups to meet demands for production and performance.

One of the major structural resources now considered to be essential to psychosocial health is the ability to *control* the planning and execution of work tasks. The current centrality of the control concept in the work environment field is, to a significant degree, one of the legacies of the research of Bertil Gardell (3). Gardell's most important early work was "Alienation and Mental Health" (7) which compared different types of production systems in terms of the major psychosocial determinants of mental health status. He hypothesized that rationalized forms of production "come into conflict with fundamental needs of self esteem, such as to have influence and control over one's work situation" (7, p. 148). Throughout the 1970s, and until his death in 1987, the Research Unit for the Social Psychology of Work at the University of Stockholm, under his leadership, investigated the importance of control in a variety of occupational groups, such as bus drivers, computer operators and programmers, hospital workers, nuclear power plant operators, factory employees, child care workers, and salaried employees (8, 9). Gardell summarized the major findings of the group in the following way (10, p. 22):

> This research makes it sufficiently clear that industrial production systems can be organized in a way that is incompatible with the broadened concept of health and safety and with the social goals of a democratic working life. Among the critical factors in technology and organizational design special emphasis is laid on workers

lack of control of pace and working methods, severely impoverished job content and socially isolated jobs. It is shown first that these conditions lead to stress in both a physiological and a psychological sense and to different signs of ill health. Second, that people cope with these conditions by nonparticipation and by holding back of human resources.

Gardell's research was deeply influenced by a system of values characteristic of the progressive aspects of Swedish social democracy. In a sense his work was an expression of a broader social movement directed at the democratization of working life (3, 11). Björn Gustavsen, one of Gardell's long-time colleagues, discusses in this volume (Chapter 13) the connection between the empirical research on control and the development of occupational health legislation in Norway and Sweden. From this chapter one can gain a sense of the Scandinavian value system and research tradition, which is rather distinct from that found in North America, or even much of Western Europe.

In Sweden many problems, especially those having to do with equality and fairness, are socially, rather than individually, resolved. In fact, a major task for researchers is to investigate economic, social, and political inequality. In social and political life there are strong sanctions against both economic extremes of poverty and wealth. This emphasis on equality also influences labor market policies. Social policy establishes that employment and health are both rights and resources that should be available to all people, even those who are physically or psychologically handicapped (see 12).

This widespread emphasis on social equality explains the structural orientation characteristic of Scandinavian research on working life. However, until the 1960s, trade unions, employees, and social scientists had adopted an "American" perspective which combined scientific management with elements of the human relations school (13). During the period of labor unrest and intellectual ferment in the late 1960s, radical changes in work organization, legislation, and social research orientation occurred (14). During the earlier 1960s, national productivity declined and there were labor shortages. This meant not only that women and immigrants were encouraged to enter the work force in increasing numbers, but that industrial workers were in a position to refuse alienating and stressful work (14). Of particular importance were the famous wildcat strikes in Sweden's northern mines where the miners protested piece work, unhealthy conditions, and speed-ups. There were numerous instances of formal and informal protest against the dominant production system of "methods-time-measurement" and piece rate pay (3). There was also a concurrent public debate concerning the contradiction between the Swedish orientation toward humanistic values, and the alternative commitment to industrial efficiency as the means of achieving general national prosperity (3, 15).

Gardell was active during this period, and in 1966, at the request of the blue-collar trade union federation, published an influential work, *Technological Change and Adaptation to Work*, with his colleague Edmund Dahlstrom (16). This book examined the human consequences of rationalized production systems and discussed the relationship between machine-paced, deskilled work and psychological dissatisfaction. Gardell and Dahlstrom concluded that psychological and political advances in Sweden were contingent upon alternative forms of work organization. Based on the research that took place during the 1960s and early 1970s it was established that machine pacing, isolation, piece rate pay, and authoritarian management systems had negative social and psychological consequences for working people (7, 8).

These themes continued to influence the work of Gardell and his group. One of the practical features of this research was Gardell's unusual talent for bridging gaps between disciplines (see, for example, 17). He initiated dialogues and instituted collaborations involving social, biobehavioral, and medical scientists as well as engineers and architects. He eloquently integrated and communicated ideas generated as a result of these cross-disciplinary efforts to those concerned. A distinctive feature in this approach was to combine several lines of research that are often mutually exclusive or even mutually suspect (17). He knit together psychosocial and medical concerns and further synthesized these with a political perspective that emphasized the potential for change (3, 11, 17).

This capacity to transform working life, he claimed, was inherent in the individual under conditions of autonomy and control. Readers from the non-Scandinavian countries, perhaps, can appreciate the great challenge of combining the efforts of physicians, social scientists, rank and file workers, and industrial leaders in the practice of transforming working life. Gardell attempted to break from the conventional view which cast the worker in the role of a relatively passive "object" without voice or defense who could be acted upon by others—be they researchers, managers, or politicians. Gardell viewed workers as inherently "subjects" who not only responded to their environment, but acted formally and informally to change it. The role of the research investigator, as he saw it, was to affirm this essential "subject nature" by acting in concert with working people to examine and ultimately change the nature of the work process.

All of the contributors to this book have either worked together with or been deeply influenced by Professor Gardell. However, this effort is intended to be more than a traditional festschrift. We hope that this volume also makes a substantive contribution to the understanding of the psychosocial work environment by examining those aspects of work organization that are of particular concern from the standpoint of health and by suggesting strategies for improving the nature and content of the work process. Throughout many of the chapters the concept of individual and collective control is of central importance. Not only is control regarded as a necessary means for individuals and groups to regulate their rhythm and methods of work, it also provides opportunities for individual and collective involvement in improving work conditions "from below," and it provides improved opportunities for learning and for variation in work.

The book is organized into four overlapping thematic areas. We begin, in Part 1, by looking at the basic relationship between psychosocial work environment and health. The first three chapters examine the epidemiological and psychobiological evidence concerning the link between adverse work organization, neurohormonal arousal patterns, and the manifestation of chronic disease. The next three chapters elaborate, expand, and suggest new approaches to research in this area. Part 2 addresses issues of work organization from different disciplinary perspectives using distinctive levels of analysis: psychological, social, organizational, historical, and political. In Part 3 we examine the experience of transforming work through a democratization strategy oriented toward the participation of rank and file workers—specifically, the strategy of "action research." In Part 4 the authors discuss the diffusion and development of psychosocial work environment research and practice in the United States, Australia, and Canada.

Part 1 begins with a chapter by Syme, who demarcates a clear contrast between individual as opposed to structurally oriented prevention strategies and discusses the implication of these opposing views for a social epidemiology of work. Syme takes issue with the conventional emphasis on individual health behavior evident in many health promotion programs, and articulates an alternative *social* epidemiology that examines those socially determined structures of daily life to which populations are systematically exposed. A more fruitful intervention strategy, according to Syme, would begin by pinpointing and changing certain critical aspects of the social environment, such as a lack of control and social isolation in the work place, which could influence the health of populations.

As Syme suggests, the organization of work determines to a significant degree the daily life experiences of most working people by imposing a relatively constant pattern of structured activities. Unlike many occupational health hazards, matters such as work-related stress cut across numerous occupational groups. However, aspects of work that are associated with stress are not randomly distributed in the working population. The second chapter, by Marmot and Theorell, points out that class differences in work organization may account for a significant proportion of the well-documented class gradient in cardiovascular disease. According to these authors lower social class groups are exposed to greater psychosocial stress and have fewer resources with which to cope with them. Marmot and Theorell suggest that the psychosocial work environment may be linked to cardiovascular risk either through influencing established risk factors, such as smoking intensity, or through other neuroendocrinal pathways.

These potentially pathophysiological neuroendocrinal mechanisms linking adverse work organization to chronic disease are discussed in the next two chapters. Frankenhaeuser (Chapter 3) presents a summary of the concepts and methods that have guided her research group's efforts for the past two decades. She presents a "biopsychosocial model" which focuses on the connection between the psychosocial work environment and the human biological organism as mediated through neuroendocrine responses. Her conceptual model is based on an even more fundamental evolutionary perspective which points out that it is the slowness of environmental change throughout human history that has made adaptation possible. However, with the advent of the industrial revolution, the rate of change has accelerated. According to Frankenhaeuser: "It is this mismatch between our old biology and the demands of the new socio-technical world that has made stress such an important issue of our time." Physiological stress reactions, such as high levels of catecholamines and cortisol, may provide us with valuable warning signals, indicating that "the human limits of adaptation" have been reached. If this biological "wear and tear" continues indefinitely, structural changes in the blood vessels, and eventually increases in cardiovascular disease, may occur. For this reason, physiological stress reactions, according to Frankenhaeuser, ". . . may play a key role in early intervention, monitoring and prevention." Finally, Frankenhaeuser presents the "effort-distress" model which links epidemiologically oriented models, such as those discussed by Marmot and Theorell, with a specifically defined set of biological effects that are quite different in high and low control conditions.

Johansson (Chapter 4) addresses another aspect of work organization in the modern era: monotony. Monotony has been acknowledged as a major aversive factor in traditional industrial jobs, and through the introduction of office automation, similar elements now appear in administrative work. Johansson analyzes the difference between repetitive and uneventful monotony. The purpose of this analysis is twofold: first, to evaluate psychoneuroendocrine activation in response to the two types of monotony; second, to specify differences in organizational conditions surrounding the two types of monotony. The first part of this analysis reveals distinct differences between the two conditions in terms of biological and psychological reactions. The second part concludes that the strategy for redesign of monotonous work must be adjusted to the type of organizational framework, and that repetitive work and uneventful work call for different types of action.

Lennerlöf (Chapter 5) discusses a very different type of linkage between work and health—learned helplessness. He suggests that passivity and depression may be a consequence of chronic exposure to environments characterized by ". . . scant opportunities for influence and personal development." Workers in these types of jobs are at a greater risk of what he refers to as "helplessness learning"—and ultimately, may have a greater risk for depression and suicide as well. Although Lennerlöf is critical of the way in which the helplessness concept has been used to date, he argues that it is critical to understand ". . . how people learn about influence and control; i.e., how they learn about those forces that act upon their lives."

In Chapter 6, Hall also looks at the importance of work control—but from a gender perspective. She begins with a critique of the present research on work stress, pointing out that the vast majority of studies to date have examined male populations. The unintended consequence of this has been that most models, concepts, and instruments in this field have been standardized on men. Although the call for research on work stress in women has been heard since the 1970s, the bulk of the studies, according to Hall, have focused thus far on physical health in men, and emotional or mental health among women. In effect, a double standard has existed for some time, and continues to influence thinking in this field. Hall's position can be summarized in the following way: How can we hope to generalize and make definitive conclusions concerning the relationship between work organization and health without explicitly dealing with the psychosocial working conditions of women? She then presents original empirical data on work control, as a means to further examine points raised in her theoretical critique.

Each of the five chapters in Part 2 also addresses the control concept, but from different analytical viewpoints: Aronsson concentrates on the psychological; Johnson on the social; Westlander on the organizational; Gustavsson on the historical; and Karasek on the political-economic.

Both Aronsson and Johnson take a similar starting point—a critique of conventional job design theories, particularly those that embody "Taylorism" or "scientific management" (18, 19). Both authors recognize that this management philosophy—with its emphasis on work fragmentation, deskilling, and the separation of conception from execution—is at the root of much that is stressful in the modern workplace. Aronsson (Chapter 7) warns us that these Tayloristic principles are now being transferred from the shop floor to the office. He specifically addresses the linkage between power and work control. According to this author, those who have power to change the rules governing the work situation ultimately have control over it. When considering the issue of power in the workplace, Aronsson emphasizes the importance of distinguishing between two types of control: horizontal-level, "control in," from vertical-level, "control over." He uses this distinction to examine the managerial response to the political pressure that has arisen to make work more democratic in Sweden. The difficulty he identifies is that although workers might find their individual "control in" the workplace expanded, management continues to maintain a monopoly over knowledge through increasing its overall power or "control over" the work organization.

Johnson (Chapter 8) also deals with the issue of power in the workplace, but with an emphasis on the strategies developed by workers to counteract managerial authority. He suggests that in many work situations where the possibility for individual-level control is limited, collective control mechanisms are particularly important in relation to stress and health. He discusses the need to link the concept of individual work control with that of social support, thereby redefining the meaning of both concepts, in a more active, collective direction. Johnson also distinguishes the social forms created by workers' collectivities from those engineered by management, and urges health professionals to be aware of the difference.

Westlander (Chapter 9) deals implicitly with issues of power by emphasizing the distinction between organizational change initiated from "within and below" from that initiated from "outside and above." Her emphasis is on outcomes in terms of occupational mental health, and she notes how this type of outcome, if considered at all, is usually regarded as secondary to production goals in the reorganization process. The examples used—primarily administrative work—demonstrate how changes initiated at a low level in the organization, although initially associated with strain and effort, may prove vital and successful in a long-term perspective, especially in terms of mental health outcomes.

In Chapter 10, Gustafsson points out that work environment research involves more than the study of work-related problems such as stress, social support, etc. He examines the historical roots of occupational structures and administrative hierarchies in what Gardell and he have referred to as the "acute care model" of medical care (20). By taking a historical sociological approach, he is able to trace the roots of current work environment problems in the Swedish health care sector, locating the structure of medical administration as well as the internal structure of the work situation in pre-medical and extra-medical influences.

The last chapter in Part 2, by Karasek (Chapter 11), takes us to the political and economic level and represents an ambitious effort to develop a new psychosocial model of class. He argues that psychosocial measures are better able to explain the adversity associated with working-class experience than more traditional economic criteria. His model of class emerges out of a critique of Taylorism and the "existing political economic synthesis," and is based on a new concept of production output value. Karasek uses this "New Value" concept to examine the political and economic prerequisites for the development and utilization of skills and creative resources.

Part 3 begins with Bertil Gardell's 1982 report articulating a multilevel strategy for transforming and democratizing the workplace (Chapter 12). After reviewing fifty years of experience with worker participation efforts in Sweden he concludes: "Today the main problem is not to state the requirements of a more humane organization—these have been put forward in much the same terms by many—but to develop strategies for bringing about such a work organization as a living and growing reality." Gardell reviews the limited success of field experiments using the autonomous work group approach and discusses why the diffusion of these experiments has met with considerable resistance. The main problem, he suggests, was that they tended to focus on the individual companies as primary units of change. In addition, trade unions were often left out of the picture in these work reform efforts, and tended to be rather more interested in worker influence at all levels of the organization. The multilevel strategy that Gardell proposes combines a two-pronged approach: representative influence in formal bodies, referred to as codetermination in Sweden, with increased control and influence by the rank and file over their daily work. To illustrate this approach he presents the Almex case as an example of a trade union–based strategy for the development of a democratic work organization where autonomous work groups are combined with forms of representative democracy.

Gustavsen (Chapter 13) expands on the theme of what he refers to as "ameliorative action"—democratization efforts designed to improve the work environment. He reviews the history of legislative initiatives and workplace interventions over the past fifteen years in Norway and Sweden. He is critical of relying on a more conventional approach based on research and protective legislation as the major components of a reform strategy. The problem, according to Gustavsen, is that work organization is a *meta-condition*: "The way work is organized can be seen as the factor that decides exposure to *all* work environment hazards since it is the organization of work that determines who is to do what for how long." The powerful generalized effect of work organization makes it very difficult to establish a legal structure of protection based on defining exposure limits and enforcing these through labor inspectors. Rather, he suggests that the key agent for successful change efforts in the workplace is the knowledgeable worker, acting in concert with others, on their own behalf. He discusses the obstacles to this type of activation and his experience with this participative approach in Norway.

Svensson, who collaborated with Bertil Gardell in the Almex case study noted above (21), touches on some of the same themes discussed by Gardell and Gustavsen by presenting a strategy for the introduction and development of workplace democracy "from within and below" that is derived from action-oriented research in the private and the public sector (Chapter 14). Action research is based on the notion that means must be consistent with the goal, i.e., democratic forms for work organization should be achieved through a democratic process involving those directly affected by their change. In accordance with this conception, the strategy presented in Svensson's chapter regards the mobilization of the employees and local trade unions as a central element in reform work. But the strategy for change must involve more than one organizational level. Neither legislation nor shop-floor struggle for democracy is enough in itself for successful organizational change. Only an interaction between the two can prevent failure to reach the goal. Referring to better opportunities for work reform in the public than in the private sector in Sweden, and to women's stronger preferences for informal, collective, and solidaristic solutions to work problems, Svensson suggests that female employees in the public sector might emerge as an "avant-garde" in a union-based struggle for the democratic organization of work.

Israel, Schurman, and House, in Chapter 15, also address action research in their study of a large, sustained intervention effort in a U.S. factory. The authors begin with a critique of the conventional orientation toward occupational stress interventions which focus primarily on the modification of individual behavior rather than altering organizational and environmental factors that are often beyond the individual's ability to control. They also criticize much of the current literature on work stress as assuming an unjustified and impractical "value neutrality" which views workers as relatively passive research "objects." Moreover, they note that researchers and organizational development specialists are often met with suspicion by employees who consider these "outsiders" as representatives of management and the existing hierarchical structure. This essentially paternalistic view toward workers may explain the failure of many planned change programs, which do not engage workers in the planning and implementation, and ultimately in control over the reform efforts (22). By contrast *action research*, according to Israel, Schurman, and House, is a joint process of workers and researchers based on principles of mutual participation, collaboration, and co-learning. It is fundamentally a process of empowerment, whereby workers gain increased understanding and control over their own working life. The authors suggest that action research, as a strategy for preventive psychosocial interventions, by expanding the participation and control of employees, "may be considered health enhancing in and of itself."

If these concerns and activities were restricted to Scandinavia this book would be of limited interest to many readers. However, as the chapters in Part 3 indicate, lessons drawn from the Scandinavian experience are being applied in other countries as well. Part 4 begins with Deutsch's warning that it is not possible to simply reproduce these policies without taking into consideration the divergent social and political forces one encounters within different national contexts (Chapter 16). In the United States, unlike Sweden and Norway, decentralized unionization and collective bargaining have been the major avenues used to increase the decision-making authority of workers, as opposed to the Scandinavian legislative reforms. Deutsch considers that collective bargaining constitutes ". . . the first line of action in the United States," and reviews some of the recent coalition efforts between unions, health professionals, and environmental groups to promote new protective standards governing video display terminal use.

Deves and Spillane (Chapter 17) point to an inherent danger in the use of occupational health legislation as a sole strategy to achieve work reform. Their review of the Repetition Strain Injury phenomenon in Australia shows how a rapid growth of the incidence of this musculoskeletal disorder and the application of a primarily medical perspective led to strong reliance on litigation and compensation. Although stress-related psychosocial factors are likely to have affected the incidence and persistence of the complaints, and although stress research has provided guidelines for work reform that emphasize autonomy, participation, and control at work, the strong emphasis on legislation became an obstacle to constructive solutions at the work site. The account of the Repetition Strain Injury phenomenon underscores the problems that arise when social conflicts are interpreted as medical problems.

Sass's contribution (Chapter 18) is based on his earlier experience of formulating and implementing occupational health policy in the Canadian province of Saskatchewan under the New Democratic Government. During this period Sass was deeply influenced by the research of Gardell and his colleagues in Sweden. Taking the broader concept of the *work environment* as a starting point, Sass and his co-workers considered that the democratization of workplace decision making would enable workers to influence their work environment and was the key component in a long-term occupational health strategy. This policy, however, encountered a great deal of resistance from management, and ultimately stalled following the political victory of conservatives in Saskatchewan and throughout Canada. These advances and retreats, played out in the field of legislation and in the workplace, have provided Sass with experiences that have led him to question a simple legislative approach, since it is "based on utilitarian concepts which trade worker health and safety for economic considerations." Sass calls for a new ethics of the work environment based on egalitarian principles that recognize the importance of the workplace as a community with the capacity to shape the nature of its own work environment.

In constituting this book we have been mindful of one of Gardell's central concerns: that research should be formulated so as to permit generalized knowledge, as the basis for collectively determined changes in technology and work organization. In his last book *Work Organization and Human Nature*, published shortly before his death, Gardell spoke of the need to develop a strategy for preventive psychosocial work. He noted the danger of focusing primarily on the individual level ". . . since this would be to transform social problems in the working environment into private problems" (4, p. 51). Rather, as he indicated in some of his last written words (12, p. 51):

> It is also necessary and perhaps in the long term even more important to try to counteract the continued impoverishment of job content and the coercion of the individual. Thus stress and stress-induced illness must be prevented by a different kind of work organization in which self-determination, social interaction, and professional responsibility are central concepts.

REFERENCES

1. Bezold, C., Carlson, R. J., and Peck, J. C. *The Future of Work and Health.* Auburn House, Dover, Mass., 1986.
2. McCarthy, M. Stressed employees look for relief in worker's compensation claims. *Wall Street J.,* April 7, 1988, p. 21.
3. Gardell, B. Scandinavian research on stress in working life. *Int. J. Health Serv.* 12(1): 31–41, 1982.
4. Gardell, B.. *Work Organization and Human Nature.* The Swedish Work Environment Fund, Stockholm, 1987.
5. Gardell, B. Autonomy and participation in work. *Hum. Relations* 30(6): 515–533, 1977.
6. Gardell, B., and Johansson, G. Strategies for reform programmes on work organization and work environment. In *Working Life: A Social Science Contribution to Work Reform,* edited by B. Gardell and G. Johansson, pp. 3–13. Wiley, London, 1981.
7. Gardell, B. Alienation and mental health in the modern industrial environment. In *Society, Stress and Disease,* Vol. 1, edited by L. Levi, pp. 148–180. Oxford University Press, Oxford, 1971.
8. Gardell, B. Psychosocial aspects of industrial production methods. In *Society, Stress and Disease, Vol. 4: Working Life,* edited by L. Levi, pp. 65–75. Oxford University Press, Oxford, 1981.
9. Gardell, B., Aronsson, G., and Barklof, K. *The Working Environment of Local Transport Personnel.* Swedish Work Environment Fund, Stockholm, Sweden, 1982.

10. Gardell, B. Psychosocial aspects of industrial production methods. *Department of Psychology Research Report* 47. University of Stockholm, Stockholm, 1979.
11. Gardell, B., and Gustavsen, B. Work environment research and social change: Current developments in Scandinavia. *J. Occup. Behav.* 1: 3–17, 1980.
12. Levi, L., et al. The psychological, social and biochemical impacts of unemployment in Sweden: Description of a research project. *Int. J. Mental Health* 13(1): 18–34, 1984.
13. Sandberg, T. *Work Organization and Autonomous Groups.* CWK Gleerup, Lund, Sweden, 1982.
14. Forseback, L. *Industrial Relations and Employment in Sweden.* The Swedish Institute, Stockholm, 1976.
15. Zetterberg, H. The rational humanitarians. *Daedalus: J. Am. Acad. of Arts Sci.* 113(1): 75–92, 1984.
16. Dahlstrom, E., et al. *Teknisk forandring och arbestsanpassning. (Technological Change and Adaptation to Work.)* Prisma, Stockholm, 1966.
17. Frankenhaeuser, M., and Gardell, B. Overload and underload in working life: Outline of a multidisciplinary approach. *J. Hum. Stress* 2(3): 35–46, 1976.
18. Braverman, H. *Labor and Monopoly Capital.* Monthly Review Press, New York, 1974.
19. Taylor, F. W. *Principles of Scientific Management.* Harper Brothers, New York, 1947.
20. Gardell, B., and Gustafsson, R. A. *Sjukvard pa lopande band. (Hospital Care on the Assembly Line.)* Prisma, Stockholm, 1979.
21. Gardell, B., and Svensson, L. *Medbestammande och sjalvstyre. (Codetermination and Autonomy.)* Prisma, Stockholm, 1981.
22. Elden, M. Sociotechnical systems ideas as public policy in Norway: Empowering participation through worker-managed change. *J. Appl. Behav. Sci.* 22: 239–255, 1986.

PART 1

Psychosocial Work Environment and Health

CHAPTER 1

Social Epidemiology and the Work Environment

S. Leonard Syme

A central theme in virtually all of Bertil Gardell's work is that a person's position in the social and work environment affects health and well-being. This concern with the environment has been a major influence in the development of a new area of research increasingly being referred to as social epidemiology. Epidemiology may be defined as the study of the distribution of disease in the population and of the factors that influence that distribution. *Social* epidemiology may be defined as the study of social factors as they affect these distributions. Much of Bertil Gardell's work is a dramatic and compelling demonstration that a person's position in the work environment "gives rise in most people to certain types of reactions which are harmful to the individual as a biological and social being and thus are of profound importance for him personally as well as for the whole of industrialized society" (1).

Gardell's focus on the job environment as a factor in biological and social pathology represents an important departure from the view taken in most epidemiologic research. In most of this work, risk factors for disease are sought in the individual. Thus, individuals are studied in terms of their eating, drinking, smoking, and exercise behavior to see whether these characteristics increase disease risk. Similarly, study is made of the individual's height and weight, medical history, and physiologic status. The goal of this work is to identify risk factors so that changes can be recommended to lower risk.

While Gardell's focus on the social and work environment does not ignore these individual characteristics and behaviors, it tends to concentrate more on the importance of structural elements and concludes therefore with structural rather than individual interventions for improvement.

The purpose of this chapter is to emphasize the importance of this environmental approach to disease prevention and to argue that study of social factors in the *work* environment is of strategic and timely importance.

THE CASE FOR AN ENVIRONMENTAL APPROACH

It is clear that the way we behave as individuals affects both the occurrence of disease and the outcome of treatment. However, a disease prevention program focused only on individual behavior is seriously limited, for at least two reasons.

The Difficulty of Changing Behavior

The first reason an individual approach is limited is that people have such a difficult time changing their behavior. It is reasonably simple to inform someone that they are at risk for disease because of their eating, smoking, drinking, or driving behavior; however, this information will not necessarily result in a change in that behavior. Exhaustive efforts to help people make such changes have shown clearly that it is extremely difficult to bring about a behavior change and even more difficult to maintain those changes once achieved.

Even in the Multiple Risk Factor Intervention Trial (MRFIT) where optimal conditions existed for such change, many people were unable to follow recommendations for dietary change and smoking cessation (2). This occurred in spite of the fact that MRFIT included an informed and highly motivated group of participants, an excellent behavioral intervention plan, an excellent staff in sufficient numbers, and enough time to work with each participant. In the general population, we have even greater difficulty in inducing people to change high-risk behavior. Most people who try to quit smoking fail (3). We have had little success in getting people to lower the fat or salt in their diet (4). The vast majority of people who try to lose weight and maintain losses do not succeed.

This is a difficult and challenging problem. One of the reasons for failure in intervention programs such as MRFIT is that we have viewed these behaviors almost exclusively as problems of the individual. In fact, the behavior of individuals occurs in a social and cultural context. These behaviors are neither random nor idiosyncratic but exhibit patterned consistencies by age, race, sex, occupation, education, and marital status. Indeed, by focusing on individual motivations and perceptions, we may be neglecting some of the most important influences on behavior (5).

The Magnitude of the Problem

Even if we were completely successful in getting people to change their risk behavior, this could have only a very limited impact on the prevalence of disease in the community. The reason for this is that most of the diseases of concern today in industrialized society are so prevalent that a one-to-one approach simply is not efficient or effective. While it may be of value to friends and family, an individual approach does little to alter the distribution of disease in the population because new people develop disease even as sick people are cured and because new people enter the "at-risk" population as others leave it. Thus, an individual approach exhausts substantial medical care resources but does little to address those environmental factors that have initiated the problem. In this circumstance, an environmental approach to prevention obviously is needed and is likely to be more efficient than one-to-one approaches.

TOWARD THE DEVELOPMENT OF AN ENVIRONMENTAL
AND COMMUNITY FOCUS

Population groups often have a characteristic pattern of disease over time even though individuals come and go from these groups. If groups have different rates of disease over time, there may be something about the groups that either promotes or discourages disease among individuals in those groups. Everyone is aware of the fact that patterned regularities in disease rates exist for socioeconomic status, race, sex, marital status, religious groups, geographic areas, and so on. In spite of this awareness, we have a very imperfect understanding of the reasons for these patterns. Indeed, most epidemiologic research "holds constant" these "background" factors so that other, more interesting, variables can be studied. This is done because it is tacitly recognized that if these factors were not statistically removed from analysis, they are so powerful that they would overwhelm everything else being studied. In consequence, these factors are rarely studied in their own right.

This is a remarkable phenomenon. Historically, we have had in public health a long experience in preventing and controlling many infectious diseases from a community and environmental perspective. We have long known that it is better to assure clean water supplies at the community level than it is to teach people, one at a time, to boil their household water. The same is true for milk supplies, other foodstuffs, and even air. More recently, we have seen that it is more effective in reducing highway fatalities to design safer cars, build safer roads, and lower speed limits than it is to teach people, one at a time, to drive more safely. None of these problems can be seen in an either/or manner: we need people to drive more safely and to look after their food supply in a hygienic manner. It clearly is crucial, however, that we not rely on these individual initiatives to deal with the problem.

What a difference it makes when we turn our attention to such diseases as coronary heart disease, stroke, arthritis, and cancer, and to such behaviors as smoking, drinking, and eating. With regard to these matters, we tend not to look to the environment but rather to see these as problems that affect individuals and that individuals must deal with.

In the control of infectious diseases, public health workers developed a disease classification system that was environment and community specific and not simply based on a one-to-one clinical model. They used such disease classification categories as water-borne, food-borne, air-borne, and vector-borne diseases. This classification scheme grouped together different clinical entities in terms of their modes of transmission and it pointed to aspects of the environment as being relevant to intervention and disease prevention. In the study of the noninfectious diseases of concern today, we have no such categories. Instead, we still use a set of terms that may be useful in clinical practice, but these terms do not suggest anything about etiology and they do not point us toward prevention strategies.

The reason for this is not clear. It may be easier to think of infectious diseases in terms of a contaminated environment and to therefore take action at that level. It may be more difficult to think of diseases such as coronary heart disease and cancer as having environmental and community origins. About as close as we come is to bring an environmental focus to the study of some aspects of the *physical* environment.

Thus, we have been able to identify disease agents and toxic exposures in the workplace, and we have identified environmental contaminations in the community. We have, in consequence, been able also to develop at least limited prevention programs aimed toward those aspects of the physical environment. In contrast, we have done little work directed toward the development of a disease classification scheme relevant to the social environment. Nevertheless, several clues are now available from existing research that might be of value in such an effort.

RISK FACTORS IN THE SOCIAL ENVIRONMENT: THE CHALLENGE OF BEING PRECISE

Many patterned differences in disease rates exist but few have been studied carefully and little is known about the reason for their consistency. Without a better idea of the factors that account for such patterns over time and place, these observations are of little value except as interesting curiosities.

Socioeconomic Status

One of the most persistent disease patterns observed in public health research is that people in the lowest socioeconomic groups have the highest rates of morbidity and mortality. In a comprehensive review of 30 studies on this topic, Antonovsky (6) noted the consistency of this finding dating from the 12th century. Further, this differential has been observed throughout the world, regardless of whether the dominant diseases causing premature death and disability were attributed to infectious or noninfectious causes, and regardless of the specific methods used to assess socioeconomic status (7).

In a massive nationwide survey of mortality in the United States, Kitagawa and Hauser (8) found that mortality rates varied dramatically among socioeconomic groups for both men and women, whether socioeconomic status was studied in relation to education, income, or occupation: the lower the socioeconomic level, the higher the death rate. In addition, Kitagawa and Hauser found that those in lower socioeconomic groups had higher death rates for every cause of death except, among women, cancer of the breast and motor vehicle accidents. Higher rates of morbidity also have been observed among those in lower socioeconomic groups. These higher morbidity rates include virtually every disease as well as mental illness and conditions such as schizophrenia, depression, unhappiness, worry, anxiety, and hopelessness (7).

These higher rates of morbidity and mortality cannot simply be attributed to poverty. The lower ranks of many of the hierarchies studied have included people earning relatively substantial incomes; in spite of this relative affluence, the disease rates of these people nevertheless are higher than the rates of those higher in status. For example, Marmot and associates (9) have shown in the United Kingdom that those in top administrative civil service positions have the lowest rate of coronary heart disease and that this rate increases progressively as one descends the civil service hierarchy. Similarly, Lee and Schneider (10) have observed that those in top management positions have the lowest blood pressures and that blood pressures rise progressively as one moves down the occupational ladder. The question, then, is not simply to explain why poor people have higher rates of disease but why even those fairly high up in a rank ordering have higher rates of disease than those above them.

An important study recently conducted by Haan and associates (11) provides an example of the difficulty we have in explaining socioeconomic differentials in disease incidence in a simple or straightforward way. These investigators compared death rates among persons living in defined poverty and nonpoverty areas in Oakland, California, from 1965 to 1974. As might be expected, persons living in poverty areas had death rates 50 percent higher than those living in nonpoverty areas. A long list of factors that might have explained this difference was examined, but none could account for it. Thus, after removing the effect of income, lack of medical care, unemployment, race and ethnicity, health practices, and such psychological factors as depression and personal uncertainty, rates in the poverty area were still 50 percent higher than in the nonpoverty area. The explanation for these findings is not clear. It is possible that the measurement of such factors as income and medical care was not sufficiently accurate in this study or, as Haan and associates note, other as yet unidentified factors may be involved (such as quality of the physical environment and higher levels of social stressors).

Marital Status

It has been known for many years that people who are not married—whether single, separated, widowed, or divorced—have higher mortality rates than married people (12-14). These differences in rate cannot be explained by an increase in any one cause of death. Ortmeyer (13), using national data, has reported that divorced and single white men have higher mortality rates for virtually every major cause of death (except leukemia for divorced men and genital cancer for single men). Similarly, divorced and single white women, compared with those who are married, have higher death rates for almost all causes of death. Although these differences conceivably could be accounted for by socioeconomic factors, three studies now have shown that the effect of marital status is independent of socioeconomic status.

In an effort to account for the fact that single, widowed, and divorced persons have more disease than married persons, Weiss (15) compared these groups in terms of a variety of disease risk factors. Using data from the U.S. Health Examination Survey, he studied a sample of 6,672 adults with and without coronary heart disease and found that such risk factors as serum cholesterol, systolic and diastolic blood pressure, and obesity did not diminish the differences observed for marital status.

Considerable attention is now being given to this issue, especially to the effect of different types of work on women in various marital circumstances and to the way in which these relationships are affected by variations in socioeconomic status. The effect of marital status on health, however, remains largely unexplained.

Gender

One of the most well-established facts among students of health and disease is that men have higher mortality rates than women (16). In 1980 in the United

States, men had an age-adjusted death rate 80 percent higher than women and, as would be expected, men live about 7.5 years less than women. This excess of male deaths occurs at every age and for every major cause for which comparison is possible. The largest male excess occurs for suicide and homicide (age-adjusted ratios of 3.33 and 3.86, respectively) and the lowest for diabetes (age-adjusted ratio of 1.02). These patterns are generally similar in all of the developed nations of the world.

Wingard and co-workers (17, 18) have examined two proposed explanations for this differential: a biological explanation (women are biologically more "fit" than men) and a social or lifestyle explanation (men behave in ways more damaging to their health). After a detailed review of such possible lifestyle explanations as marriage, parenthood, employment, hard-driving behavior, cigarette smoking, and physical activity, Wingard concluded that none of these, singly or together, eliminated the sex differential in mortality. In fact, in one study, multivariate adjustments for all known risk factors actually increased the sex differential. Once again, a major factor known to influence rates of disease remains largely unexplained.

These examples of patterned consistency of disease rates among socioeconomic, marital, and gender groups emphasize the importance of environmental factors in the study of disease etiology and also illustrate how little is known about these major issues.

It is not clear why we have not studied these patterns more enthusiastically. One explanation may be that we cannot easily see what we could *do* about them to prevent disease. What good is it, we might ask, to identify a risk factor that cannot readily be changed? Since it is not easy to think about introducing changes in socioeconomic status, marital status, age, religion, and geographic location, what benefit is there in studying them?

This line of argument suffers from two defects. One is the implicit assumption that it is easier to change smoking, drinking, and eating behavior than to change "the world." Based on our experience in these matters over the last 10 or 20 years, this assumption may be open to serious challenge. The second defect is that it presupposes that essential and crucial components of such factors as socioeconomic status, marital status, and so on are known and that they cannot be changed. With reference to socioeconomic status, for example, perhaps the crucial component is money and it might be reasonable to assume that there is nothing we can easily do to change the income distribution in society. On the other hand, the crucial ingredient in socioeconomic status distributions might be education or nutrition or sanitation and these may be far more amenable to intervention. Indeed, it may be more realistic to think about changing these characteristics than deeply entrenched behaviors and beliefs. In any case, it certainly seems reasonable to study this issue in some detail before rejecting the matter without thought.

RELEVANCE OF THE WORK ENVIRONMENT

While it is of importance to study those forces in the environment that increase or decrease the risk of disease, it is very difficult to think concretely about how this might be done. These issues are so vast, the complexities so great, our concepts so vague, and our methods so weak that this seems a meritorious but futile mission. Whether or not things are as bad as that, it would certainly be desirable if we could first study more manageable "mini-environments" with the hope of sharpening our conceptual and methodologic tools. The work environment seems ideally suited to this challenge.

Marmot and associates (9) have described research on coronary heart disease carried out in London among British civil servants. These investigators have shown a striking difference in coronary heart disease rates between those at the bottom and those at the top of the civil service grade hierarchy. Civil servants at the lowest grade (mainly unskilled manual workers) have coronary heart disease rates four times higher than those in the top (administrative) grade. After adjustment for the effects of such coronary heart disease risk factors as serum cholesterol, smoking, blood pressure, physical activity, obesity, and glucose tolerance, the difference in rate between the top and bottom grades was reduced to three times. About 60 percent of the difference in coronary heart disease rates among civil service grades, however, remained unexplained after this adjustment for risk factors. So, whatever is causing this difference in disease rate among civil service grades is a mystery and is not explained by the well-established and well-known risk factors for coronary heart disease.

As noted earlier, the most interesting aspect of these data from London is that a *gradient* exists in coronary heart disease rates. Thus, professionals and executives in the second highest grade have rates of coronary heart disease twice that of administrators; clerical workers have higher rates than professionals and executives. Professionals, executives, and clerical workers hardly can be considered to be poor, and yet they have higher rates of disease than those even higher in the civil service grade. This gradient of disease is not limited to civil service workers but has been seen also in almost all studies of socioeconomic status and disease, and it poses a very difficult problem that is not easily explained. Thus, while it is reasonably simple to come up with possible explanations for the fact that those at the bottom have higher rates than those at the top, these explanations do not account for the fact that those in relatively affluent positions also have higher rates of disease. Factors such as inadequate medical care, unemployment, low income, racial factors, poor nutrition, poor housing, and poor education perhaps account for high rates of disease among those in the very lowest of socioeconomic levels, but they do not account for the fact that disease rates progressively increase from the highest to the lowest ranks of the socioeconomic status hierarchy.

There are probably many hypotheses that could be formulated to explain these findings. One concept is particularly interesting in this regard because it seems to be relevant in accounting for so many sets of unexplained data and because it has been, in one form or another, discussed and thought about by so many other investigators. For want of a better term, I have referred to this concept as "control of destiny." This concept would apply to the civil servant data as follows: the lower people are in the socioeconomic status hierarchy, the less chance they have to do what they need to do to live as they wish to live and the less chance they have to command the events that affect their lives. The lower down people are, the fewer opportunities and options they have for controlling their lives. This is a complex idea that includes not only structural limitations because of people's position in the social structure but also the fewer resources and less training that people have to take advantage of opportunities and options.

Of course, this concept is not new. Other investigators have suggested the importance of such related concepts as mastery (19), self-efficacy (20), locus of control (21), learned helplessness (22), sense of permanence (23), sense of coherence (24), hardiness (25), and others. If this notion, or something like it, was in fact supported by research evidence, an avenue for intervention would become available that is more precise and understandable than simply to suggest that we change "socioeconomic status." While there are many forms this intervention might take, it clearly would involve interventions not simply at the individual level, but more importantly, at the community level as well.

We currently are pursuing these ideas in a research project on San Francisco bus drivers. Several previous studies have noted that bus drivers, compared with workers in other occupations, have a higher prevalence of hypertension, as well as diseases of the gastrointestinal tract and of the musculoskeletal system. These results have been obtained from studies in different transit systems, under different conditions, and in several countries (26-31). Based on these findings, it has been suggested that certain aspects of the bus drivers' occupation may create an increased risk for disease among these workers.

From a clinical viewpoint, it is valuable to identify drivers with disease in order to treat them. To help drivers, it also would be of value to teach them about better posture, more healthful eating habits, and alternative ways of dealing with job stress. However, from an environmental perspective, to prevent disease it would perhaps be more useful to identify characteristics of the job itself that are associated with increased disease risk in order to change them.

In our study of bus drivers, we are monitoring such environmental factors as exposure to noise, vibration, and carbon monoxide fumes, but we also are paying particular attention to the drivers' social environment (32, 33). For example, in preliminary studies of bus drivers, the "tyranny of the schedule" has been forcefully brought to our attention. Drivers must keep to a specific schedule, but, in almost every instance, this schedule is arranged without realistic reference to actual road conditions and, in fact, cannot be met. The instant bus drivers sit in the bus, they are behind schedule. Further, they are continually reprimanded for being behind schedule. We also have been struck by the social isolation and loneliness of drivers. Most work a very long shift without much opportunity to talk to other people all day long. In spite of this long and lonely work day, many drivers do not immediately go home after work, but remain instead at the bus yard for one to three additional hours to "wind down." By the time they do get home, it is very late and they usually go directly to bed. Many drivers with whom we have talked have indicated that they have very limited interactions with their spouses, children, or friends. In addition to loneliness, we have observed that driving a bus often provokes inappropriate coping responses. In particular, we have observed hostile and impatient behavior being stimulated and provoked in situations that involve limited personal control, unpredictability, deadlines, and tight schedules.

If in this research we can identify characteristics of the job of bus driving that are associated with disease, we may be able to introduce interventions, not merely among bus drivers, but directly on those environmental factors associated with the job. For example, it may be that by changing the way in which schedules are arranged, the bus company will be able to earn more money than it loses because of reduced rates of absenteeism among drivers as well as lower rates of sickness, accidents, and in particular, turnover. The way in which schedules are changed is an issue that quite properly ought to centrally involve the drivers themselves. As matters now stand, the schedule is made by administrators with little input by drivers.

In addition, rest stops might be located in or near central cities so that the drivers would be more likely to meet other drivers from time to time instead of the current practice of locating rest stops at remote and lonely places on the outer edges of the city. Increased interaction with other drivers provides an opportunity for the exchange of emotional support, advice, and encouragement—things that increase the likelihood that one can control both work and nonwork impingements. Another improvement would be the initiation of a campaign to inform the public of the difficult circumstances faced by drivers. At present, drivers feel themselves the objects of considerable negative affect from passengers, car drivers, and the media and they feel blamed for problems that are not of their making. Feeling victimized and helpless cannot help but evoke a sense that one has little control over one's life.

While the concept of "control over one's destiny" was suggested by difficulties in explaining socioeconomic differentials in disease, it turns out to be very closely related to another set of concepts developed in studies of the workplace itself. For several years, Gardell (34), Karasek and associates (35), and Theorell and associates (36), among others, have been generating an impressive body of research evidence suggesting that occupational stressors have consequences for health, primarily when workers do not have sufficient latitude and discretion for coping with these stressors. The work of these investigators is discussed in detail in other chapters and will not be dealt with further here. In essence, these investigators have found that when workers have little control over work pace and methods, higher levels of catecholamines are seen as well as higher rates of mental strain, coronary heart disease, and other health problems.

It is quite possible, of course, that the concept of control is not the right one to explain disease occurrence in the workplace. The important point is that differentials in disease rates observed at work provide a powerful starting point for testing hypotheses about the impact of the environment on health. The hope is that the ideas developed here will have applicability beyond the workplace. The concepts that currently are being explored regarding work design, worker participation, and worker control certainly seem relevant and promising for such extrapolation.

CONCLUSIONS

Bertil Gardell's writings on the importance of worker control and participation in the organization of work are of crucial significance for anyone interested in the health and well-being of workers. The impact of his studies beyond the workplace, however, is now clearly becoming evident. The research of Theorell, Karasek, and others on decision latitude, for example, may be of relevance in helping to shed light on one of the most persistent, challenging, and complex issues in public health—socio-economic gradients in disease. In addition to this major contribution, Gardell's work compellingly emphasizes the central role of the social environment in determining the health of individuals. This view is increasingly being recognized and is, in fact, one of the major factors in the development of a new area of research referred to as social epidemiology. It is evident from the foregoing that the true scope of Bertil Gardell's contribution to public health cannot be discerned at this time. While his work already has had important impact throughout the world, much of it will yield results only in the years to come. His writings have stimulated and enriched a whole generation of researchers, and it is from their accumulated work that his influence will be fully realized. The challenge he set down is clear, and the rest is now up to us, his students.

REFERENCES

1. Gardell, B. Psychosocial aspects of industrial product methods. In *Society, Stress and Disease, Vol. IV, Working Life*, edited by L. Levi, pp. 65-75. Oxford University Press, London, 1980.
2. Multiple Risk Factor Intervention Trial Research Group. The Multiple Risk Factor Intervention Trial. *Prev. Med.* 10: 387-553, 1981.
3. Syme, S. L., and Alcalay, R. Control of cigarette smoking from a social perspective. *Annu. Rev. Public Health* 3: 179-199, 1982.
4. Kirscht, J. P., and Rosenstock, I. M. Patients' problems in following recommendations of health experts. In *Health Psychology: A Handbook*, edited by G. C. Stone, F. Cohen, and N. E. Adler, pp. 189-215. Jossey-Bass, San Francisco, 1979.
5. Leventhal, H., and Cleary, P. D. The smoking problem: A review of the research and theory in behavioral risk modification. *Psychol. Bull.* 88: 370-405, 1980.
6. Antonovsky, A. Social class, life expectancy and overall mortality. *Milbank Mem. Fund Q.* 45: 31-73, 1967.
7. Syme, S. L., and Berkman, L. F. Social class, susceptibility and sickness. *Am. J. Epidemiol.* 104: 1-8, 1976.
8. Kitagawa, E. M., and Hauser, P. M. *Differential Mortality in the United States*. Harvard University Press, Cambridge, Mass., 1973.
9. Marmot, M. G., et al. Employment grade and coronary heart disease in British civil servants. *J. Epidemiol. Community Health* 3: 244-249, 1978.
10. Lee, R. E., and Schneider, R. F. Hypertension and arteriosclerosis in executive and non-executive personnel. *JAMA* 167: 1447-1450, 1958.
11. Haan, M. N., Kaplan, G. A., and Camacho, T. Poverty and health: Prospective evidence from the Alameda County study. *Am. J. Epidemiol.* 125(6): 989-998, 1987.
12. Carter, H., and Glick, P. C. *Marriage and Divorce: A Social and Economic Study*. Harvard University Press, Cambridge, Mass., 1970.
13. Ortmeyer, C. F. Variations in mortality, morbidity, and health care by marital status. In *Mortality and Morbidity in the United States*, edited by L. L. Erhardt and V. E. Berlin, pp. 159-188. Harvard University Press, Cambridge, Mass., 1974.
14. Thiel, H. G., Parker, D., and Bruce, T. Stress factors and the risk of myocardial infarction. *Psychol. Res.* 17: 43-57, 1973.
15. Weiss, N. S. Marital status and risk factors for coronary heart disease: The United States Health Examination Survey of Adults. *Br. J. Prev. Soc. Med.* 27: 41-43, 1973.
16. Wingard, D. L. The sex differential in morbidity, mortality, and life-style. *Annu. Rev. Public Health* 5: 433-458, 1984.
17. Wingard, D. L. The sex differential in mortality rates: Demographic and behavioral factors. *Am. J. Epidemiol.* 115: 205-216, 1982.
18. Wingard, D. L., Suarex, L., and Barrett-Connor, E. The sex differential in mortality from all causes and ischemic heart disease. *Am. J. Epidemiol.* 117: 165-172, 1983.
19. Pearlin, L., et al. The stress process. *J. Health Soc. Behav.* 22: 337-356, 1981.
20. Bandura, A. Self-efficacy mechanisms in human agency. *Am. Psychologist* 37: 122-147, 1982.
21. Rotter, J. B. Generalized expectancies for internal versus external control for reinforcement. *Psychol. Monogr. Gen. Applied* 80(609), 1966.
22. Abrahamson, L. Y., Seligman, M., and Teasdale, J. D. Learned helplessness in humans: Critique and reformulation. *J. Abnorm. Psychol.* 87: 49-74, 1978.

23. Boyce, W. T., Schaefer, C., and Uitti, C. Permanence and change: Psychosocial factors in the outcome of adolescent pregnancy. *Soc. Sci. Med.* 21: 1279-1287, 1985.
24. Antonovsky, A. The sense of coherence as a determinant of health. In *Behavioral Health: A Handbook of Health Enhancement and Disease Prevention*, edited by J. D. Matarazzo, pp. 114-129. Wiley, New York, 1984.
25. Kobasa, S. C., Maddi, S. R., and Kahn, S. Hardiness and health: A prospective study. *J. Pers. Soc. Psychol.* 42: 168-177, 1982.
26. Berlinguer, G. *Maladies and Industrial Health of Public Transportation Workers* (Translation). U.S. Department of Transportation, UMTA-VA-06-0034-82-2, Washington, D.C., 1962.
27. Garbe, C. *Health and Health Risks among City Bus Drivers in West Berlin* (Translation). U.S. Department of Transportation, UMTA-VA-06-0034-3, Washington, D.C., 1980.
28. Morris, J. N., et al. Incidence and prediction of ischemic heart disease in London busmen. *Lancet* 1: 533-559, 1966.
29. Netterstrom, B., and Laursen, P. Incidence and prevalence of ischemic heart disease among urban bus drivers in Copenhagen. *Scand. J. Soc. Med.* 2: 75-79, 1981.
30. Pikus, V. G., and Taranikova, V. A. Hypertensive disease in drivers of passenger motor transport. *Ter. Arkh.* 47: 135, 1975.
31. Winkleby, M. A., et al. Excess risk of sickness and disease in bus drivers: A review and synthesis of epidemiologic studies. *Int. J. Epidemiol.* 17: 255-262, 1988.
32. Ragland, D. R., et al. Prevalence of hypertension in bus drivers. *Int. J. Epidemiol.* 16: 208-213, 1987.
33. Winkleby, M. A., Ragland, D. R., and Syme, S. L. Self-reported stressors and hypertension: Evidence of an inverse association. *Am. J. Epidemiol.* 27: 124-134, 1988.
34. Gardell, B. Worker participation and autonomy: A multilevel approach to democracy at the workplace. *Int. J. Health Serv.* 12(4): 527-558, 1982.
35. Karasek, R., et al. Job decision latitude, job demands, and cardiovascular disease: A prospective study of Swedish men. *Am. J. Public Health* 71: 694-705, 1981.
36. Theorell, T., et al. On the interplay between socioeconomic factors, personality and work environment in the pathogenesis of cardiovascular disease. *Scand. J. Work Environ. Health* 10: 373-380, 1984.

CHAPTER 2

Social Class and Cardiovascular Disease: The Contribution of Work

Michael Marmot and Tores Theorell

One of the dominant features of the epidemiology of cardiovascular diseases is their relation to social class. One of the dominant themes of recent research on psychosocial factors and cardiovascular disease is the importance of working life. In this chapter we attempt to put these together; first by reviewing the evidence and implications of the social class distribution of cardiovascular disease; second by placing the findings on work characteristics and cardiovascular diseases in the context of other psychosocial factors and other biomedical risk factors for cardiovascular disease. We then consider the extent to which the psychosocial characteristics of lower status jobs might account for the higher rates of cardiovascular disease in people of lower social status. We conclude with a justification of our focus on work in terms of both research and public health action.

To anticipate: our conclusion gives a rationale for singling out work characteristics from the other features that characterize the differences between social classes in modern industrialized societies. Our focus is not, however, to "explain away" social class differences in disease occurrence. We do not seek to show that social class differences in disease can be accounted for by differences in the characteristics of individuals. Much of the work on psychosocial factors has attempted to accord these factors the status of another individual risk factor, analogous to plasma cholesterol, smoking, or blood pressure level. This is not our intention. We acknowledge that it is of interest to know if people who are hostile or display type A behavior or lack a hardy personality are at increased risk of coronary heart disease (CHD). If this were the case, these could be considered individual risk factors. This fits into a clinical approach to disease—find individuals and treat them. It lacks a social/causal perspective. Why are individuals hostile, type A, or nonhardy? Our concern is with the links between social position and disease occurrence. To concentrate only on individual characteristics ignores the powerful social influences that are reflected in social class differences in disease rates.

It is not our intention to discuss all of the literature linking social class to cardio-vascular disease but to articulate a specific research program that has examined this subject over the last decade. This program has been built up in an international collaborative effort based upon epidemiological population registers and psycho-physiological stress research in Sweden, sociological expertise in the United States and West Germany, and medical epidemiological research traditions in Great Britain.

PERSISTENCE OVER TIME AND PLACE

In British national data, social class has traditionally been based on occupation using the Registrar-General's classification into classes from I (professional) to V (unskilled manual). In Figures 1 and 2, classes are grouped into nonmanual and manual since this diminishes the possible effects of changes over time in classification (1). The data come from successive Registrar-General's reports, 1970-72 and 1979-83, on mortality according to occupation around the 1971 and 1981 censuses. All-cause mortality has declined, over the decade, in men and women and in manual and nonmanual classes, but the gap between manual and nonmanual that existed in 1970-72 has increased. For CHD there has actually been an increase in mortality for manual and a decline in mortality for nonmanual groups. Tracing mortality further back to the 1930s confirms the impression that, although mortality rates have declined, the relative disadvantage of lower social classes has increased (2).

Great Britain is not alone in having such social class differences. It is true in Scandinavia (3), other Western European countries (4), North America (5), and Japan

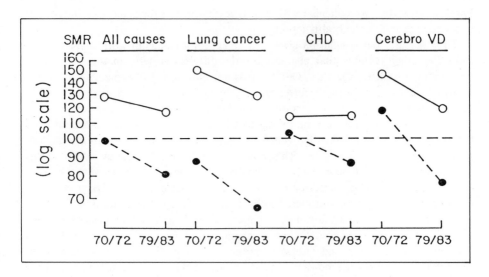

Figure 1. Standardized mortality ratios in men aged 20–64 for death due to all causes, lung cancer, coronary heart disease (CHD), and cerebrovascular disease (Cerebro VD) in Great Britain, 1970-72 and 1979-83, for manual (o—o) and nonmanual (•—•) groups.

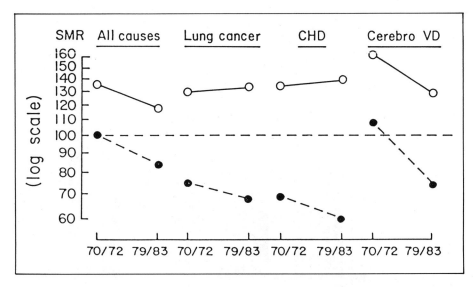

Figure 2. Standardized mortality ratios (SMRs) in married women aged 20–54, classified by husband's occupation, for death due to call causes, lung cancer, coronary heart disease (CHD), and cerebrovascular disease (Cerebro VD) in Great Britain, 1970–72 and 1979–83, for manual (o–o) and nonmanual (•–•) groups. (For each cause the SMR in 1979–81 is 100.)

(6). Data are not readily available on social class and cardiovascular disease in developing countries. That the picture may be different is shown by the experience of immigrants to England and Wales (7) (Figure 3). Among immigrants from European countries, the familiar inverse association is seen: lower class–higher mortality; but there is no association among immigrants from the Indian subcontinent, and higher mortality in nonmanual classes among immigrants from the Caribbean.

Pathways Linking Social Class to Cardiovascular Disease

In the Whitehall study of British civil servants, we have had the opportunity to investigate the links between social position and disease rates. As indicated in Figure 4, there is a steep inverse association between grade (level) of employment and mortality from CHD and a range of other causes (8). This gradient is steeper than that seen nationally when mortality is compared across the Registrar-General's social classes. The Whitehall gradient has therefore been dismissed as somehow atypical (9). It is instructive to ask what "atypical" might mean. The Whitehall population consisted of all office-based civil servants, overwhelmingly of one ethnic group, with one employer, in one geographical district, in stable employment, not exposed to the physical environmental hazards of factory and outdoor work. Why then should the gradient in mortality between administrators and clerks be so large?

It is this type of question that we will discuss in the remainder of this chapter. It may be the very homogeneity of the civil service that allows the social gradients

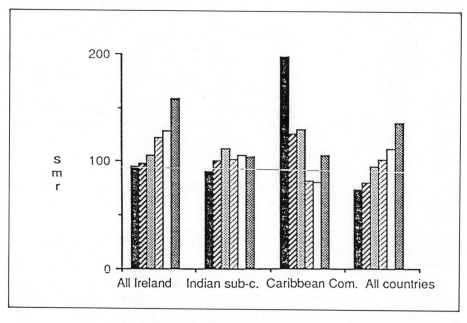

Figure 3. All-cause mortality in England and Wales, 1970–72, by country of birth (Ireland, Indian Subcontinent, Caribbean Community, and all countries) and Registrar-General's social class; standardized mortality ratios (SMRs) for men aged 20–69.

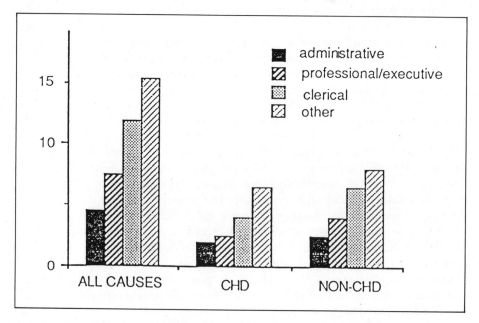

Figure 4. Percentage of men dying in 10 years from all causes, from coronary heart disease (CHD), and non-CHD, by grade in the British Civil Service (age-adjusted figures).

to emerge so starkly. Administrative grade civil servants are likely to have more in common with each other than do the diversity of occupations that make up social class I in the country as a whole. They are largely university-educated (a high proportion of them have studied at the most prestigious British universities at Oxford and Cambridge) in stable, highly responsible, well-paid, and relatively fulfilling jobs. Before the explosion of high-paying jobs in the City of London (the financial sector), the administrative grades of the civil service were seen as a highly favored option by the elite of the country's graduates.

The clerical grades of the civil service differ sharply from this, but there is likely to be greater homogeneity within the clerical grades than within social class III nonmanual in the country as a whole. This homogeneity within and heterogeneity between grades makes the civil service population appropriate for the investigation of social class differences.

There are clear differences between the grades in risk-related behaviors and biological risk factors (Table 1). These "explain" a part, but not the large part, of the social gradient in cardiovascular and other diseases (8). Here we must clarify what we mean by "explain." It is incomplete to state that differences in the prevalence of smoking are partly the reason for the social differences in the rate of occurrence of CHD, lung cancer, or chronic obstructive airways disease. We must ask why there are social class differences in smoking. Thus two types of questions emerge—why are there social class differences in risk-related behaviors and biological risk factors such as blood pressure, and what may account for the link between social position and disease that acts independently of these risk factors?

To what extent might the link between social position and disease be a result of the influence of psychosocial factors? The social classification is based on occupation. Does this suggest that circumstances at work, as discussed in one of the sections below, might be responsible? Or should we be inquiring after other social differences among people in these occupations?

Interpretation of Social Class Differences

Social class is a complex concept. It arose in Marxist analysis (10) which pointed out that owners of financial resources had the power of buying work and that they tended to buy it at the least expensive price. This would, of course, mean that there was always a risk of unreasonable exploitation of workers whenever they had too little to say in the bargaining process. When industrial development expanded, the situation of workers became influenced increasingly by the process of selling their labor power. For instance, workers often lived in special areas built for them and shops grew up to serve this special market. Thus, the effect of the industrial process was not limited to work but extended to the whole of life. Our concept of social class must evolve, but it is still likely to be associated not only with work situations—which is the basis of social class allocation—but also with living conditions, upbringing of children, eating habits, leisure activities, etc. Therefore, it is difficult to separate the effects of work conditions from effects of other conditions of life in epidemiological analysis. It is also obvious that there may be strong intergenerational effects of social class; i.e., the children are strongly influenced by their parents with regard to dietary habits, physical

Table 1

Major risk factors in different grades: age-adjusted means and percentage
showing increased value

	Grade			
Variable	Administrative	Professional/ Executive	Clerical	Other
Systolic blood pressure				
Mean (SEM) (mm Hg)	133.7(0.67)	136.0(0.19)	136.8(0.42)	137.9(0.64)
Percentage ⩾ 160 mm Hg	10.7	12.2	13.8	16.5
Plasma cholesterol				
Mean (SEM) (mmol/liter)	5.20(0.04)	5.13(0.01)	5.08(0.03)	4.96(0.04)
Percentage ⩾6.72 mmol/liter	12.6	10.2	10.5	7.8
Smoking (%)				
Smokers	28.8	37.3	53.0	60.9
Never smoked	33.0	23.2	17.0	14.8
Ex-smokers	38.1	39.6	29.9	24.3
Body mass index (weight/height^2)				
Mean (SEM) (kg/m^2)	24.5(0.09)	24.8(0.03)	24.6(0.07)	25.0(0.10)
Percentage ⩾28 kg/m^2	9.9	11.8	13.8	17.4
Leisure, physical activity				
Percentage inactive	26.3	29.5	43.0	56.0
Height				
Mean (SEM) (cm)	178.5(0.20)	176.3(0.05)	174.0(0.13)	173.2(0.23)
Percentage >183 cm (6 ft)	21.1	12.8	7.6	8.7
Family history				
1st-degree relatives with heart-disease (%)	21	16	10	7

activity, and many psychological reaction patterns. For instance, a father coming home from a boring job that gives him no pride and provides no possibilities to learn new things—a situation that could be assumed to be more common in lower social classes than in higher ones—may release his feelings of frustration and tension at home, with his children as spectators. Therefore, social class should preferably not be studied as a one-generational phenomenon.

There has been much criticism of the Registrar-General's classification based on occupation. It has even been suggested that occupations were ranked by standard mortality ratios and social classes artificially constructed to fit the data (11) and that social class has outlasted its usefulness.

However valid these criticisms, the striking consistency of the inverse association between social class and cardiovascular disease in industrialized countries suggests that social class continues to be worthy of attention. The countries listed in which social class differences have been reported vary in culture and their position along various spectra: capitalist/socialist, more/less egalitarian, oriental/Western. Yet all show a similar social class–CHD pattern. What can account for this consistency in different countries and historical periods? It may, of course, reflect material conditions of life. Housing, nutrition, child care facilities, physical working conditions, and possibilities for recreation are all likely to follow people of higher socioeconomic status in different countries and at different times. The undoubted importance of inequalities in material conditions in generating social inequalities in health was emphasized by the Black Report in the United Kingdom (12).

Regrettably, material poverty is still in evidence in wealthy countries. This is unlikely, however, to be the complete explanation. It is arguable that the decline in mortality in England and Wales, for example, is the result of improvement in material conditions. Yet at the same time, the relative difference in mortality between social classes has increased. This might reflect increased relative differences in material conditions, but clearly in the lower grades of the civil service we are not dealing with poverty in any absolute sense. Compared with social classes IV and V in the 1930s, 40s, and 50s, a clerical officer is not poor. What may be at issue is inequality. Certainly a civil service executive officer is not poor but he has a higher mortality risk than an administrator although a lower risk than a clerical officer.

Syme (13) suggests that, above a threshold of poverty, position on the social hierarchy per se may be a more important determinant of health and disease than material conditions. We must then ask what is it about position in the social hierarchy that is important? One clear possibility is psychosocial conditions. These are considered in the next section, which tries to bring the psychosocial work conditions into a social class perspective.

PSYCHOSOCIAL WORK CONDITIONS IN RELATION TO CORONARY HEART DISEASE

Initially, when psychosocial factors were explored in relation to CHD, the common wisdom was that demands and psychological "load" would be the main problem. The assumption was that "stress" would increase with increasing demands, and consequently stress diseases would be more common in more demanding occupations. Most researchers seemed to assume that the most demanding occupations were upper-class occupations (14). Thus, great confusion arose when epidemiological studies of occupations started to show that cardiovascular mortality, presumably "stress dependent," is lower in upper-class occupations than in other occupations (15-16).

In more recent stress research, it has been considered necessary to relate psychological demands in the work situation to the resources that are available to the worker. This relates to our discussion concerning social class, since most kinds of resources are more readily available in the upper classes than in the lower classes. The resources may determine whether the worker will be able to cope effectively with the demands made upon him or her (17). We will confine this analysis to psychological resources, following the hypothesis introduced by Syme (13) that in the present period of history in the Western countries, psychological conditions may be more important than material ones to health. Research on psychological resources at work has a long tradition. At present, three basic psychological dimensions describing resources at work summarize the literature, namely, skill discretion (use of skills and development of new skills), authority over decisions, and social support. Each one of these dimensions has several synonyms, but it would reach far beyond the limits of this review to describe them in detail.

One concept that has been extensively studied in this research and has a close relationship to social class is "decision latitude," which was introduced by Karasek. The first measure of decision latitude was constructed on the basis of the American Quality of Employment Surveys (18). A series of factor analyses were performed which indicated that decision latitude had two components: "skill discretion" and "authority over decisions." These were closely related statistically, and in most studies the two dimensions have been added to one another. It could be assumed, on theoretical grounds, that skill discretion may be a more basic dimension than authority over decisions. When workers have the possibility to learn new skills they can also master unpredicted future situations in a much better way, and since they feel more secure in their role they may be ready and able to make more and more decisions on their own, which, of course, means increasing decision latitude. Fellow workers and supervisors will also know that such workers can make more decisions and will therefore allow them to do so. Almost by definition, both skill discretion and authority over decisions decrease with descending social class.

Social support at work has been illuminated by several research groups, which have shown that different aspects of support are central to health (19). A good support may mean emotional support as well as feedback from superiors and fellow workers. Most studies of social support at work indicate that low social class is associated with poor social support at work (20). Thus, those who work in low status jobs are likely to be on the low end of all three basic dimensions of psychological resources. The obvious question will then be whether part of the association between social class and cardiovascular disease may be due to this unequal distribution of psychological resources at work. Karasek (21), Karasek and associates (22), and Johnson (17) have developed theoretical models for analyzing the possible joint effects of demands, lack of decision latitude, and lack of social support at work on the pathogenesis of CHD. Several epidemiological studies, cross-sectional as well as prospective, have tested these models (23-26). Such studies have been performed by means of two different methods:

1. *Individual-based* in which subjects have described their own psychological work situation. These descriptions have subsequently been related to the prevalence or incidence of cardiovascular disease or cardiovascular risk factors in the same individuals. The psychological dimensions have been constructed by means of factor analyses in the United States (21)—demands and decision latitude—and in Sweden—demands, decision latitude (17, 25), and social support (17).

2. *Group-based* ("aggregated") in which representative samples of the working population have been interviewed. On the basis of response distributions in each

occupation, all occupations were characterized with regard to demands and decision latitude. In the analysis of health outcome, all workers in an occupation were assumed to have the same work conditions. In the U.S. version of this classification (18, 27), it is possible to adjust the individual's occupational scores with regard to age, race, and education. Men and women were analyzed separately. The occupation classification score was treated like a cardiovascular risk factor. In a simplified Swedish classification system, occupations were classified with regard to each one of a number of single questions regarding "monotony," "rush," etc. on the basis of the Swedish Survey of Living Conditions (23). In a later version adjustment was made for the individual's age (24).

The estimates of associations given by these two methods—individual-based and group-based—are complementary. The individual method may be vulnerable to personality traits; for instance, a "hostile" person may be more likely to describe the social support as poor and habitually denying subjects may underreport all psychosocial problems. The group-based method, on the other hand, is less vulnerable to these "subjective" measurement problems but may provide crude estimates and require large samples.

The individual method was used in a follow-up study of working men in Sweden (25). This showed that working men who described their job as demanding and reported a low level of decision latitude were more likely than others to develop cardiovascular symptoms and to die cardiovascular deaths during follow-up. Another study using similar questionnaires (28) showed that men who had developed a myocardial infarction before age 45 and who were interviewed within three months after the disease onset regarding their pre-infarction job situation described less skill discretion than men without myocardial infarction. This held true even when the relevant biomedical factors, as well as education and type A behavior, had been taken into account. In multivariate analysis, job monotony was a significant discriminator between "cases" (myocardial infarction men) and "controls" (noninfarction men). Hahn (29) has made an individual prospective study of male Finnish industry workers. This study showed a clear-cut association in the predicted direction between high work demands and a low decision latitude at work on the one hand and elevated risk of developing angina pectoris or myocardial infarction during follow-up. Another individual-based study was made on the Framingham cohort (26). This study showed results in the predicted direction both for women and for men, although the results were statistically significant only for the female participants—the more demands and the less decision latitude, the more angina pectoris and myocardial infarction during follow-up. Both these latter studies showed that the association persisted even after adjustment for biomedical risk factors.

Group-based analyses of myocardial infarction prevalence in U.S. working men (18) showed that the prevalence was higher in high demand/low decision latitude occupations than in other occupations, even when biomedical factors and education had been taken into account. Two Swedish prospective group-based studies have shown that occupations with a high frequency of monotony and nonlearning have a higher myocardial infarction incidence than other occupations, particularly when the "rush" is reported to be common. These findings were true even when a number of socioeconomic factors had been taken into account.

Table 2 shows an analysis based upon three-digit occupation titles of all working men and married women classified according to their husband's job in the British Census in 1971 and the corresponding information at the time of death for all working men and married women who died in Great Britain during the years 1970 to 1972. Since there is no British occupation classification system, both the simplified Swedish (23) and the U.S. system (27) were tested. The findings were quite similar. Men working in occupations classified as "nonlearning" or "monotonous" were more likely to die from cardiovascular disease than other men. In this study, it did not make any difference whether workers commonly reported "hectic work" or not. Adjusting for social class decreased the magnitude of the association but the relationship was still clear. For women classified according to their husband's occupation, similar findings were made, but in this case controlling for social class made the association disappear completely. Thus, there is substantial evidence that a low level of decision latitude—in particular the skill discretion component—is associated with increased cardiovascular disease risk.

An analysis of all components (demands–lack of control; demands–lack of support; lack of control–lack of support; demands–lack of support–lack of control) performed by Johnson (17) showed that all three psychological main dimensions, as well as interactions between them, add to the cardiovascular health predictions. Thus, it is likely that psychological work conditions constitute an important part of the association between social class and cardiovascular disease risk. The multivariate analyses

Table 2

Mortality from coronary heart disease, expressed as standardized mortality ratio (SMR) in men aged 15–64, by occupation, in England and Wales. Occupations are classified according to the Swedish system of work characteristics[a]

Job characteristic	SMR	SMR adjusted for social class
Monotony		
Yes	113	104
No	102	102
Possibility of learning new things		
"Poor"	114	106
"Good"	98	98
Hectic work		
Yes	104	102
No	112	104

[a]Some occupations were excluded because the Swedish and British occupational codes differed.

taking social class indicators into account show that there is a partial but not complete overlapping between social class and psychological work conditions. Furthermore, the observation has been made that the psychosocial work descriptions have stronger predictive power in lower social classes than in upper ones.

Psychosocial Factors at Work and Cardiovascular Risk Factors

The psychological work environment may relate to cardiovascular illness in two different ways. Either it may influence known cardiovascular risk factors such as blood lipids, blood pressure, smoking habits, and leisure time physical activity, or it may have more direct effects via known physiological stress mechanisms. Smoking habits and blood pressure have been shown to have important relationships with the psychosocial work environment. Research regarding blood lipoproteins has produced more ambiguous results so far. However, according to Siegrist and associates (30), blue-collar workers working under psychosocially stressful conditions have adversely affected lipoproteins. A few examples will be described that relate to this discussion.

Pieper and co-workers (31) have recently examined four U.S. data bases: the Health Examination Survey, the Health and Nutrition Examination Survey, the Exercise Heart Study, and the Western Collaborative Group Study. These examinations of large groups of American men were linked to a U.S. occupation descriptive system based upon the American Quality of Employment Surveys. Occupation title was available in the data base, and this job title was then tied to the occupation descriptive system assuming, for instance, that bakers in general have similar conditions. For each individual, data on biomedical risk factors were available. In three of the data bases there was a significant association between a low level of decision latitude (so-called "strain") in an occupation and average systolic blood pressure at rest in the same occupation. For diastolic blood pressure the associations were less convincing. In each data base there was a significant inverse association between decision latitude and smoking habits—the lower the decision latitude in an occupation, the higher the proportion of smokers. For serum cholesterol no clear pattern was observed.

A study of 28-year-old men in Sweden showed that young men working in "nonlearning occupations" were more likely to have high levels of plasma adrenaline at rest and high systolic blood pressure at rest than others (32). A high plasma adrenaline at rest was associated not only with a job classified as boring but also with a poor social network in general. In the same analysis, the other biomedical factor of great importance to elevated systolic blood pressure at rest—overweight—was significantly associated with "lack of employment security," a dimension constructed on the basis of factor analysis. Lack of employment security is also more common in lower social classes than in others.

Variations in Blood Pressure (As an Indicator of Arousal) in Relation to Psychosocial Work Conditions

There have also been studies of longitudinal blood pressure changes that are relevant to the discussion on psychosocial work environment, its association with social class, and its effect on cardiovascular health. In the study of young Swedish men mentioned above, those who had a high blood pressure at the age of 18 (and had thus shown a tendency to react with blood pressure elevation) and who were now working in occupations characterized as "strain" occupations (such as waiter and driver) were more likely to have a marked systolic blood pressure elevation at work than others (33). Furthermore, in a recent study, men and women in different occupations were followed four times during a year. When self-perceived demands rose in relation to self-reported decision latitude, average systolic blood pressure during work hours also rose. This occurred particularly among subjects with a positive family history of hypertension and in low decision latitude jobs (baggage handlers and waiters) (34). In a recent study, fully automated 24-hour recordings of blood pressure were made in widely different occupations in New York. The results showed that occupations with a low decision latitude had a much higher proportion of hypertensive men than other occupations (35).

Psychosocial Conditions at Work and at Home in Relation to Blood Pressure Variations

In a study of civil servants in Great Britain, participants were instructed to measure their own blood pressure at work and at home. The findings were related both to social grade and to job conditions. Both systolic and diastolic blood pressure at work increased with increasing "job stress"—a score that was combined, after factor analysis, from dimensions describing "lack of skill utilization" (which relates to the long-term development of decision latitude discussed above), "tension," and "lack of clarity" in tasks. Thus, men with a combination of these three factors had higher blood pressure than others. For each one of the job stress factors there was a rising systolic and diastolic blood pressure with rising level of stress, but the combination of factors was particularly damaging. The rise in blood pressure from the lowest to the highest job stress score was much larger among low-grade men than among upper-grade men—a finding that supports the epidemiological cardiovascular illness finding described above. Blood pressure at home, on the other hand, was not related to job stress level. The interesting observation was made that men in upper and lower grades had the same average blood pressure levels in the clinic and at work but marked differences in blood pressure at home; upper-grade men had much lower systolic and diastolic blood pressure at home than had low-grade men. All the blood pressure levels in the study of civil servants had been adjusted for age, reported alcohol consumption, body mass index, serum high density lipoprotein level, and hemoglobin (5) (Figure 5). These findings indicate that different social domains may affect different physiological reactions; the work conditions are likely to affect the physiological states during working hours—exactly as we would expect.

Although several studies point to an association between psychosocial job factors and the "accepted" cardiovascular risk factors, this does not mean that all of the association between psychosocial job factors and heart disease is due to these associations. The previously mentioned study of men who had suffered a myocardial infarction before the age of 45 in Stockholm showed that in multivariate analysis, "lack of

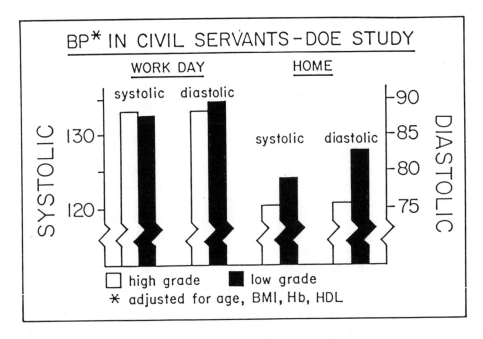

Figure 5. Blood pressure (BP) in male British civil servants recorded at work and at home, according to grade of employment, adjusting for age, body mass index (BMI), hemoglobin (Hb), and high density lipoproteins (HDL).

variety at work" explained as much of the (retrospectively recorded) early myocardial infarction risk as family history of early coronary heart disease and almost as much as excessive tobacco smoking habits. Lipoprotein patterns explained more of the total risk than the other recorded factors. Several factors that were more common among the patients than in a healthy matched group of men did not appear to be significant in the multivariate analysis, such as type A behavior pattern, disturbed carbohydrate metabolism, and level of education (28). Other biomedical mechanisms have been proposed to be of importance in this association. For instance, in a study of civil servants, Marmot (36) showed that men who reported a low level of decision latitude were likely to have high fibrinogen levels in the blood. Since fibrinogen is important in coagulation and coagulation is important in atherosclerosis, increased production or lack of breakdown of fibrinogen may be a mechanism of importance.

Studies of occupation and smoking (31, 37) have indicated that occupations characterized in national surveys as low on decision latitude have a higher proportion of cigarette smokers than other occupations. The explanation of such findings may simply be that boredom and lack of skill discretion may make the workers feel that they need to smoke in order to stay awake. Another mechanism that may be operating is that smoking may have a social role. In some occupations, in particular the "caring" occupations, taking a pause with smoking colleagues may be one way of releasing tension.

Our review of the cardiovascular risk factors shows that psychosocial work conditions may indeed influence the risk factors directly. Thus, it is likely that psychosocial work conditions are an important link between social class and heart disease.

THE CONTRIBUTION OF WORKING CONDITIONS TO SOCIAL INEQUALITIES IN CARDIOVASCULAR DISEASE

In cardiovascular epidemiology, there has been a tendency to pose questions that take the form: how much of the variance in disease occurrence can be attributed to a given set of risk factors? For example, it is commonly asserted that about half the international variation in rates of occurrence of CHD can be explained on the basis of the main coronary factors: serum cholesterol, blood pressure, and smoking. This approach has value in focusing attention on what is known and what is not. It has two limitations in addressing the topic of this section: measurement problems and failure to proceed in the light of a causal model.

Parametric statistical techniques, such as analysis of covariance, are used because they are convenient in sorting through intercorrelated variables. We should be wary, however, of the precise quantitative measures they give us. Assuming that a relationship exists, the strength of the association between social class and CHD will depend on both the validity and the precision of the social class measurement. As long as uncertainty exists as to the concept and definition of social class, we shall be uncertain if we have a valid measure. An observed association with disease may therefore yield a spuriously low (or high) quantitative estimate. Whatever the validity of the measure (systematic error), the less precise it is (more random error) the weaker will be the apparent association. Hence the difficulty in attempting to quantify the degree to which work characteristics could account for social class differences. We have imprecision on measures of both social class and work characteristics. If, for example, the measure of smoking is more precise, other things being equal, it will appear to have a stronger association with disease. Hence the difficulty in deciding the relative importance of different factors.

Quite apart from measurement difficulties, to ask whether smoking or blood pressure rather than work characteristics "explain" social class differences in CHD may be the wrong way to pose the question. Similarly, it may be inappropriate to ask whether work characteristics are related to disease risk, independent of social class. An appropriate causal model is needed. As indicated in the previous sections, social position (social class) may be related to cardiovascular disease risk through the association with behaviors such as smoking or diet, or physiological factors such as blood pressure. If this is the case, we could not conclude, comfortably, that these risk factors account for social class differences, but ask why there is the link between social position and risk.

Psychosocial characteristics such as working conditions may be in part responsible for the higher cardiovascular risk in lower social classes, because they may influence established risk factors or act via other, neuroendocrinal pathways. To control statistically for social class in an analysis of the relation between working conditions and disease may, therefore, be to control out the variation of interest. The causal model might be, in turn: social class → low skill utilization at work → smoking and physiological changes in homeostasis such as blood pressure and endocrine secretions → cardiovascular disease.

Given the imprecise nature of the social class concept, and the large variety of ways by which people in the lower social strata differ from those in the higher, why have we focused on working conditions? Among the answers we might give is the possibility of translating research findings into social change. One response to evidence of persisting social inequalities in health and disease is that little can be done about it without fundamental political change. As Bertil Gardell showed, working conditions *can* be influenced. Research findings on the health consequences of certain types of work have the potential to influence decisions on the design of work. It therefore represents one possible way of breaking the nexus between low social position and higher disease risk.

REFERENCES

1. Marmot, M. G., and McDowell, M. E. Mortality decline and widening social inequalities. *Lancet* 2: 274–276, 1986.
2. Pamuk, E. R. Social class inequality in mortality from 1921 to 1972 in England and Wales. *Population Studies* 39: 17–31, 1985.
3. Valkonen, T. Social inequality in the face of death. *Central Statistical Office of Finland*, pp. 201–261. Helsinki, 1987.
4. Derriennic, F., Ducimetiere, P., and Kritsikis, S. Cardiac mortality among working middle-aged Frenchmen according to their socio-economic class and geographic region. *Rev. Epidemiol. Sante Publ.* 25: 131–146, 1977.
5. Buring, J. E., et al. Occupation and risk of death from coronary heart disease. *JAMA* 258(6): 791–793, 1987.
6. Kagamimori, S. Occupational life tables for cerebrovascular disease and ischaemic heart disease in Japan compared with England and Wales. *Jpn. Circ. J.* 45: 195–201, 1981.
7. Marmot, M. G., Adelstein, A. M., and Bulusu, L. Immigrant mortality in England and Wales 1970–78. *OPCS Studies of Medical and Population Subjects*, No. 47. Her Majesty's Stationery Office, London, 1984.
8. Marmot, M. G., Shipley, M. G., and Rose, G. Inequalities in death—specific explanations of a general pattern? *Lancet* 1: 1003–1006, 1984.
9. Pocock, S. J., et al. Social class differences in ischaemic disease in British men. *Lancet* 1: 197–201, 1987.
10. Marx, K. *Capital,* Vol. I. International Publishers, New York, 1967.
11. Jones, I. G., and Cameron, D. Social class analysis—an embarrassment to epidemiology. *Community Med.* 6: 37–46, 1984.
12. Department of Health and Social Security. *Inequalities in Health: Report of a Research Working Group.* DHSS, London, 1980.
13. Syme, S. L. Strategies for health promotion. *Prev. Med.* 15: 492–507, 1986.
14. Kasl, S. V. The challenge of studying the disease effects of stressful work conditions (editorial). *Am. J. Public Health* 71(7): 682–684, 1981.
15. Antonowsky, A. Social class and the major cardiovascular diseases. *J. Chronic Dis.* 21: 65–106, 1968.
16. Lehman, E. W. Social class and coronary heart disease: A sociological assessment of the medical literature. *J. Chronic Dis.* 20: 381–391, 1967.
17. Johnson, J. V. The Impact of Workplace Social Job Demands and Work Control upon Cardiovascular Disease in Sweden. Department of Psychology, Report No. 1, University of Stockholm, 1986.
18. Karasek, R. A., et al. Job characteristics in relation to the prevalence of myocardial infarction in the U.S. HES and HANES. *Am. J. Public Health* 78: 910–918, 1988.
19. Johnson, J. V., and Hall, E. M. Social support in the work environment and cardiovascular disease. In *Social Support and Cardiovascular Disease,* edited by S. Shumaker and S. Czajkowski. Plenum Publishing Corporation, New York, in press, 1990.

20. Orth-Gomer, K., Unden, A. L., and Edwards, M. E. Social isolation and mortality in ischemic heart disease: A ten year follow-up study of 150 middle aged men. *Acta Med. Scand.* 224: 205-215, 1988.
21. Karasek, R. A. Job demands, job decision latitude and mental strain: Implications for job redesign. *Administrative Sci. Q.* 24: 285-308, 1979.
22. Karasek, R. A., Russell, R., and Theorell, T. Physiology of stress and regeneration in job related cardiovascular illness. *J. Hum. Stress* 3: 29-42, 1982.
23. Alfredsson, L., Karasek, R. A., and Theorell, T. Myocardial infarction risk and psychosocial work environment: An analysis of the male Swedish working force. *Soc. Sci. Med.* 16: 463-467, 1982.
24. Alfredsson, L., Spetz, C. L., and Theorell, T. Type of occupation and near-future hospitalization for myocardial infarction and some other diagnoses. *Int. J. Epidemiol.* 14: 378, 1985.
25. Karasek, R. A., et al. Job decision latitude, job demands and cardiovascular disease: A prospective study of Swedish men. *Am. J. Public Health* 71: 694-705, 1981.
26. La Croix, A. Z. Occupational Exposure to High Demand/Low Control Work and Coronary Heart Disease Incidence in the Framingham Cohort. Dissertation, University of North Carolina, Chapel Hill, 1984.
27. Schwartz, J. E., Pieper, C. F., and Karasek, R. A. A procedure for linking psychosocial job characteristics data to health surveys. *Am. J. Public Health* 78: 904-909, 1988.
28. Theorell, T., et al. Psychosocial work conditions before myocardial infarction in young men. *Int. J. Cardiol.* 15: 33-46, 1987.
29. Hahn, M. Psychosocial Work Conditions and Risk of Coronary Heart Disease. Academic thesis, Department of Sociology, University of California, Berkeley, 1986.
30. Siegrist, J., et al. Atherogenic risk in men suffering from occupational stress. *Atherosclerosis* 69: 211-218, 1986.
31. Pieper, C., LeCroix, A., and Karasek, R. A. The relation of psychosocial dimensions of work with coronary heart disease risk factors: A meta-analysis of five United States data bases. *Am. J. Epidemiol.* 129: 483-494, 1989.
32. Knox, S., et al. The relation of social support and working environment to medical variables associated with elevated blood pressure in young males: A structural model. *Soc. Sci. Med.* 21: 525-531, 1985.
33. Theorell, T., et al. Blood pressure variations during a working day at age 28: Effects of different types of work and blood pressure level at age 18. *J. Hum. Stress* 11: 36-41, 1985.
34. Theorell, T., et al. Changes in job strain in relation to changes in physiological state—a longitudinal study. *Scand. J. Work Environ. Health* 14: 189-196, 1988.
35. Schnall, P. L., et al. The relationship between 'job strain,' workplace diastolic blood pressure, and left ventricular mass index. *JAMA* 263: 1929-1935, 1990.
36. Marmot, M. Does stress cause heart attacks? *Postgrad. Med. J.* 62: 683-686, 1986.
37. Alfredsson, L. Myocardial Infarction and Environment: Use of Registers in Epidemiology. Academic thesis from Department of Social Medicine, Karolinska Institute and National Institute for Psychosocial Factors and Health, Stockholm, Sweden, 1983.

CHAPTER 3

A Biopsychosocial Approach to
Work Life Issues

Marianne Frankenhaeuser

It is our good fortune to live in a time when environments can be molded to suit people. The demands and pressures facing people today are largely human-made, which means that they are not as unchangeable as were the demands confronting our ancestors. The human nervous system allows for considerable plasticity, but there are limits beyond which people cannot be pushed without being damaged. In contrast, new technology seems infinitely flexible. Technology, depending upon how it is used, can make people grow, or it can make people shrink. A major task for biobehavioral and social scientists is helping to clarify when technological solutions can be relied upon to improve the quality of life, and when technical solutions may, in fact, deprive people of crucial sources of growth and development.

Among the external influences that shape us, the work we do is probably the most powerful one in adult life. The workplace is the site of dramatic transitions brought about by technological advances. The benefits of new technology in terms of increased productivity and reduction of physically dangerous jobs are well recognized. Today, there is increasing awareness of negative side effects on both physical and mental health of automation and computerization. Some of the negative side effects can be eliminated if sufficient attention is paid to job content and job design. To date, we have hardly begun to exploit the enormous opportunities to adapt jobs to the workers' psychological and social needs.

In principle, work stress and work dissatisfaction can be dealt with in two ways: by changing people or by changing jobs (1). Changing people's behavior may involve education, training, counseling, behavior therapy, or psychotherapy. Corporate health promotion programs generally focus on changing the employees' lifestyle by discouraging risk behaviors such as smoking and overeating, and encouraging behaviors such as

This work was supported by grants from the Swedish Work Environment Fund, the J. D. and C. T. MacArthur Foundation Network on Health and Behavior, and the Swedish Medical Research Council.

exercise, relaxation, and adequate rest. Such interventions tie easily into traditional medical models. They are a valuable part of a corporation's campaign to reduce the harmful effects and costs of stress. However, the individual-oriented programs need to be supplemented by organization-wide changes that may involve altering the conditions under which people work, the tasks they perform, and the rewards they obtain. Approaches involving changes at the structural level are much more controversial and complex than are changes at the level of the individual (2). The aim of our biopsychosocial approach to working life is to provide a broad scientific base for redesigning jobs and modifying work organization in harmony with human needs, abilities, and constraints. These ambitions receive support in the Swedish Work Environment Act, effective since 1977, which states that "working conditions shall be adapted to the mental and physical capacity of human beings," and "jobs shall be designed so that the employees themselves can influence their work situation."

THE EVOLUTIONARY PERSPECTIVE

The mismatch between people and their environment that we experience today should be viewed in an evolutionary perspective. We are so firmly anchored in the present that it is difficult to comprehend how new our world really is in evolutionary terms. Our ancestors evolved into the present species over millions of years, when conditions for survival were entirely different. They adapted gradually to an environment that changed very slowly, and it was the slowness of the change that made adaptation possible. With the industrial revolution the rate of change began to increase, and in the electronic era it keeps accelerating.

In striking contrast, the human brain and body have remained essentially the same over several thousands of years. Thus we are faced with two seemingly incompatible phenomena: the standstill of genetic evolution and the accelerating pace of social evolution. For our ancestors, adaptability to physical hazards such as heat, cold, and starvation was a prerequisite for survival. Thanks to the body's ingenious mechanisms of adaptation, referred to by Walter B. Cannon (3) as "the wisdom of the body," our ancestors survived the unchangeable and uncontrollable hardships that were part of their everyday existence.

While today's demand are generally psychological rather than physical in nature, they trigger the same bodily stress responses that served our ancestors by making them "fit for fight." These bodily responses may, of course, be totally inappropriate for coping with the pressures of life today. There is nothing in the history of humankind to prepare us for the high-technology environment that we have so rapidly created for ourselves. It is this mismatch between our old biology and the demands of the new sociotechnical world that has made stress such an important issue of our time. For this mismatch we pay a price in terms of coronary heart disease, hypertension, psychosomatic disturbances, and distress.

STRESS RESEARCH

Stress research has become a meeting place for psychology and medicine. The progress in biomedical recording techniques has been a powerful stimulus. These techniques allow bodily responses to be monitored under real-life conditions, even at the workplace, without interfering with the people's ordinary activities. Using ambulatory monitoring techniques, one can find out what makes the blood pressure rise, the heart beat faster, the muscles tense up. In this way one can identify aversive aspects of the psychosocial environment as well as protective factors, buffers that protect people against potentially harmful influences. It is an exciting task for stress research to identify those factors in the work environment that evoke physiological responses, and then to determine when these responses are adaptive and health promoting and when they are maladaptive and potentially health damaging.

Recent advances in understanding how the brain regulates endocrine functions has brought about a reorientation of psychobiological research on human stress and coping. Until recently, the brain and the endocrine system were generally viewed as separate entities. The brain was seen as mediating the organism's relation to the external environment. The endocrine system, on the other hand, was regarded as oriented toward the body's internal environment, regulating growth, metabolism, and reproduction. New insights have been gained into the pathways and neuroendocrine mechanisms by which the brain controls the endocrine system. We are beginning to grasp the coordinated functioning of the nervous system and the endocrine system in the adaptation of the whole human being to the environment (4).

THE BIOPSYCHOSOCIAL MODEL

The biopsychosocial model (Figure 1) provides a strategy for locating stress-inducing environmental factors and analyzing their consequences at the individual level (5, 6). Adding biological aspects to the psychosocial perspective helps us understand the mechanisms linking environmental demands to the individual's health, well-being, and efficiency.

When we are challenged by different demands, their nature and strength are appraised by the cortex of the brain. The cognitive appraisal process involves weighing the importance and the severity of the external demands against one's own coping abilities. Any situation that is perceived as a threat to something we value, or a challenge requiring effort, takes signals from the brain's cortex to the hypothalamus, and via the autonomic nervous system to the adrenal medulla (Figure 2). This gland responds by putting out adrenaline and noradrenaline. These two catecholamines, often referred to as stress hormones, mobilize our bodily resources and make us "fit for fight or flight." In the event that the situation induces feelings of distress and helplessness, the brain sends messages also to the adrenal cortex, which secretes another stress hormone, cortisol, which plays an important part in the body's immune defense. This route is more complex and involves the release of adrenocorticotropic hormone (ACTH) from the pituitary gland. The stress hormones can be determined in blood and in urine, and these measurements help to assess the load that a particular environment exerts on a person.

Generally speaking, stress hormones facilitate both mental and physical adjustment to acute environmental demands. Hence, in the short term, a rise in stress hormones is often beneficial and seldom a threat to health. In the longer term, however, a high arousal level may include damaging effects. Evidence is now

A biopsychosocial model

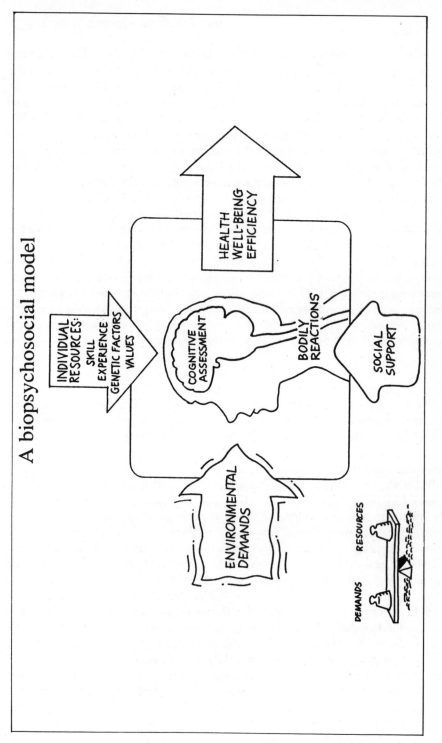

Figure 1. A biopsychosocial model of stress-health interactions.

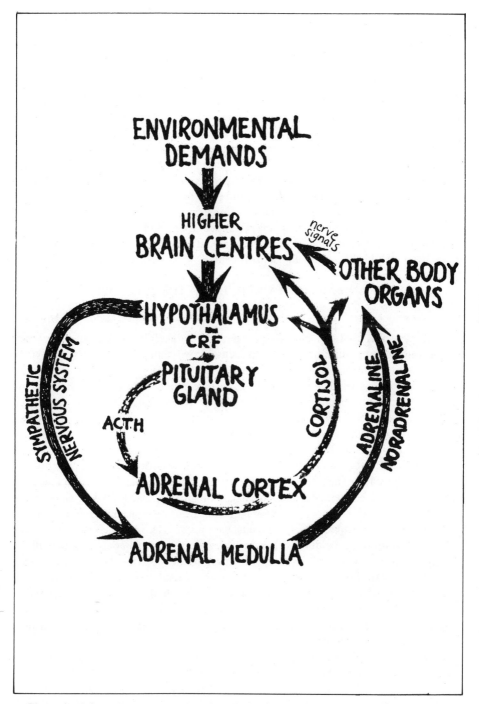

Figure 2. Schematic representation of pathways from the brain to the adrenal systems involved in stress, showing the sympathetic–adrenal medullary system and the pituitary–adrenal cortical system. *ACTH*, adrenocorticotropic hormone; *CRF*, corticotropin releasing factor.

accumulating that frequent and long-lasting elevations of stress hormone levels in the course of daily life may result in structural changes in the blood vessels which, in turn, may lead to cardiovascular disease. Hence, consistently high levels of catecholamines and cortisol should be regarded as warning signals of long-term health consequences.

In short, bodily stress reactions are important both because they allow monitoring of the impact of the environment on the individual, pinpointing aversive as well as protective factors, and because they serve as early warnings of long-term risks. For both these reasons physiological stress responses play a key role in early intervention and prevention of health damage at the workplace (7, 8).

As shown in the model (Figure 1), stress responses are modified by individual characteristics involving values, attitudes, and personality patterns, whether genetically determined or shaped by social influences. Moreover, stress responses are modulated by social support systems, which may dampen them and serve as buffers against harmful influences. The interaction of all these influences determines the total impact on each person's health, well-being, and efficiency.

EFFORT AND AFFECT: A MODEL FOR THE PSYCHOBIOLOGY OF WORK

Work demands that are perceived differently induce different bodily responses. A large number of studies have led us to focus on two dimensions of the stress experience: an activity dimension, ranging from a passive to an active state, and an affective dimension, ranging from a negative to a positive mood state (9). The active state involves effort, engagement, and determination to reach a goal. It is often associated with a positive mood state. A passive state is characterized by negative affects, distress, helplessness, and giving up.

In our studies at different work sites (10, 11), we have identified specific characteristics of work processes that promote active, positive attitudes versus passivity and negative mood states. The interesting point is that activity versus passivity and negative versus positive affect tend to be associated with different neuroendocrine response patterns (5, 12). The neuroendocrine relationships can be conceptualized as follows:

1. *Effort and positive affect* is a joyous, happy state. This is experienced when one is doing something demanding with a high degree of personal control, which allows using one's creativity and getting deeply involved in the job. This state is accompanied by increased catecholamine secretion, whereas cortisol is generally low and may even be suppressed. Examples of occupations in which these individuals are found are craftsmen, artists, scientists, and entrepreneurs. We find them also among top executives. In other words, these individuals are in occupations that allow a high degree of autonomy and personal control.

2. *Effortless positive affect* implies feeling pleasantly relaxed. Both mind and body are at rest, and stress-hormone output remains low.

3. *Effort and negative affect* is a state characteristic of the pressure to produce while having low control over the situation. This is a state typical of the hassles of everyday life. In working life this state is common among people engaged in repetitious, machine-paced jobs. This type of work demands effort, which is accompanied

by increased catecholamine secretion. It evokes negative affects, which tend to increase the secretion of both catecholamines and cortisol.

4. *Effortless negative affect* implies feeling helpless, lacking control, giving up. This is the prisoner's situation. The unemployed are at risk, and so are people in extremely coercive jobs. Feelings of helplessness are likely to develop when people experience that events and outcomes are independent of their actions. Helplessness is accompanied by an outflow of stress hormones, particularly cortisol. It is interesting that among fighting animals, the losers display the same endocrine pattern as the helpless human beings, whereas the endocrine stress profile of the winners resembles that of the active, determined individual (for a review, see 6).

UNDERSTIMULATION: A THREAT TO SAFETY

When work demands are too repetitious, the human brain is undernourished, and when people's skills are underutilized, their performance deteriorates (13). Then stress is not only a threat to health, but to safety as well. This is a problem confronting operators in the control rooms of large industrial plants. Control-room operators carry responsibility for safety under conditions in which temporary inattention and intrinsically slight errors may have extensive economic and other disastrous consequences. Monitoring a process calls for acute attention and readiness to act throughout a monotonous period of duty, a requirement that does not match the brain's need to be stimulated in order to maintain optimal alertness (14). In a monotonous environment the ability to detect signals starts to decline in less than half an hour. Yet the job calls for unfailing attentiveness and preparedness. Should something go wrong, the operator must switch instantaneously from passive, routine monitoring to active problem-solving. He or she must quickly form a picture of the alarm signals, interpret their overall message, decide which measures to take, and carry them out.

In a crisis situation, the control-room operator has to act under strong emotional pressure, with the brain at a high level of arousal, when the risk of committing errors increases and judgment is impaired. Ability to make decisions may even suffer a temporary paralysis under conditions such as these. In a brief critical interval, the operator may be incapable of making use of the information available to him or her. This seems to have been the case during the Three Mile Island incident, when about a hundred alarms sounded within the first few minutes (14).

The fact that operators work in shifts means that their attention-demanding jobs have to be performed even when the operator is out of step with his or her biological rhythm. Particularly during night shifts, the adrenaline level is likely to be low, which means that alertness and ability to concentrate are reduced. Under such conditions the threat to safety will increase. When people make mistakes that lead to accidents, it is customary to refer to "the human error." I would argue that when human beings are expected to perform beyond the limits imposed by basic biological and psychological constraints, the "fault" lies in the situation. There is nothing wrong with the person who does not cope with such requirements.

The risk of becoming a victim of understimulation is particularly great when opportunities for socialization are also poor. Hence, it is completely consistent with basic biological principles that getting rid of the traditional assembly line should bring success, not only in terms of workers' health and satisfaction, but also in terms of increased productivity. This is what we have witnessed following the radical changes in production technology, pioneered in the early 1970s, at one of Volvo's plants in Sweden, and followed by similar changes at several other factories in many countries (15).

While new production technology has made it possible to get rid of the traditional assembly line, the computerized office has taken on the characteristics of a "mental assembly line." This is the "deskilling" that we witness in routinized coding in the computerized office work. Accordingly, the neuroendocrine stress profile is similar for assembly line workers and those white-collar workers who hold intellectually undemanding routine jobs and spend the greater part of their work day feeding data into the computer. These office workers and their assembly line counterparts tend to have more psychosomatic symptoms and more sick leaves than their fellow workers in less constrained jobs (8).

PERSONAL CONTROL: A BUFFER AGAINST HARMFUL STRESS EFFECTS

The chance of exercising control may "buffer" stress in two ways: first, by decreasing job dissatisfaction, thus reducing bodily stress responses; second, by helping people develop an active, participatory work role. A job that allows the worker to use his or her skills to the full will increase self-esteem. Such jobs, while demanding and taxing, may help to develop competencies that aid in coping with problems and crises.

Epidemiological as well as experimental studies support the notion that personal control and influence are important "buffering" factors, helping people to achieve a state of effort paired with positive affect (7, 16, 17). When demands are experienced as a stimulus rather than as a burden, the balance between stress hormones changes: adrenaline output is typically high, whereas the cortisol-producing system is put to rest. This means that the total load on the body, the "cost of achievement," will be lower than during less demanding but tedious work (6).

The role of personal control in achieving a positive state has been demonstrated in a laboratory experiment in which subjects were exposed to performance demands in both low-control and high-control situations (18). The low-control situation induced effort and negative affect. Accordingly, both adrenaline and cortisol increased. The high-control situation induced effort and positive affect. Accordingly, adrenaline increased, but cortisol was suppressed. Similar results were obtained in real-life work situations differing with regard to the level of control.

A possible mechanism for the favorable health effects of work conditions allowing personal control could be the catecholamine/cortisol balance typical of controllable situations. There is evidence that damage to the myocardium requires the simultaneous release of catecholamines and cortisol (19). Hence, the fact that cortisol tends to be low in controllable situations could account for the buffering effects of personal control. Such a neuroendocrine mechanism could explain the epidemiological data (16) from national surveys in Sweden and the United States, which show that high job demands and work overload have adverse health consequences only when combined with low control over job-related decisions. According to the Karasek (16) model, the combination of work overload and low decision latitude is dangerous to the cardiovascular system, whereas the risk that work overload will lead to heart disease is reduced when people are given a high degree of personal control over their heavy workload.

It is interesting to note the similarities and differences between our effort-affect model and Karasek's job strain model. Personal control and workload are key concepts in both models. Karasek's model builds on the external work situation, characterized in terms of workload and personal control, and the relationship of these job characteristics to health outcomes. Our effort-affect model adds a psychological and a physiological dimension. It emphasizes the experience of effort and positive versus negative affect induced by different work demands as the determinants of the physiological-hormonal responses evoked. These stress responses, in turn, influence health outcomes. In this model, personal control is seen as a mediator of the quality of the affect experienced, high control inducing positive and low control negative affect.

THE WORK–LEISURE RELATIONSHIP

Another mechanism by which personal control might exert its positive influence on health outcomes has to do with the duration of the stress response: the ability to unwind after stressful encounters. This takes us to the after-effects of a day at work. While we are immersed in work, the body's "stress machinery" tends to stay in full gear. This may be seen as the price we pay for good achievement. But when the work is over, how quickly do we unwind? This depends on the type of task and the type of person.

Repetitive and machine-paced jobs tend to slow down unwinding (8). As to individual differences, "rapid unwinders" tend to be mentally better balanced and more efficient in achievement situations (20). It is significant that the time for unwinding varies predictably with the individual's state of general well-being. Thus, when rested and in good trim after a vacation period, a group of industrial workers were able to unwind more quickly. In contrast, excessive overtime at work induced slow unwinding (21).

The issue of unwinding after a day's work is crucial for the wider issue of the work-leisure relationship. The prevailing view until a decade ago was that one could compensate for a dull, boring job by rich and stimulating activities in the free time. We now know that this is not so. There is a "spillover" from job experience to leisure (22). In other words, those who hold boring and constricted jobs are not likely to engage in leisure activities requiring effort and planning. Those whose job is interesting are much more likely to be active in their leisure, too. This is not due mainly to personal characteristics that lead active people to select exciting jobs. A longitudinal study of a Swedish national sample showed that workers whose job changed over a six-year period to a richer job content and more autonomy and control also became more active outside working hours, participating in more educational activities, and in union and cultural activities (for a review, see 22).

An interesting aspect of this spillover from job to leisure is that people holding stimulating jobs might be more likely to engage in physical activity and other health behaviors. In traditional corporate health-promotion programs, the focus is on teaching the individual employees healthy lifestyles. One conclusion from stress research is that improving psychosocial work conditions may, in fact, be the most effective means of motivating people to engage in health behaviors in their free time (23). According to this way of reasoning, investing in improving job content and work organization would enhance the employees' personal efforts to improve their lifestyle.

Unwinding is a key concept in health promotion, and the most important obstacle to unwinding after work is "the second job," which a large part of the employees take up when they return home, i.e., demands related to the family, children, household, and a number of home-management duties. In a recent study of male and female white-collar workers at Volvo in Göteborg, Sweden, we introduced the concept of "total workload," taking into account, separately, the load exerted by the paid work and the load exerted by other demands (24). In collaboration with American colleagues we constructed a questionnaire by which to measure and analyze the total workload of the male and female participants in our study.

According to our results the group of female managers showed no sign of unwinding in the evenings as assessed by measurements of blood pressure, heart rate, catecholamine secretion, and self-reports. During working hours there were no marked sex differences in stress responses, whereas after work, sex differences were pronounced, particularly between male and female managers. While the males' noradrenaline level dropped markedly after 5 p.m. when they returned home from work, the female managers' noradrenaline continued to rise. For blood pressure the picture was the same: a decrease after 5 p.m. in males, but not in females. Hence, our results suggest that winding down after work is a male privilege.

So far, stress research has tended to focus on men. Therefore the workplace has been identified as the primary stressor. In contrast, the home has been viewed as an environment in which one recovers from the stress at work. If we are to come to grips with the sources of stress in both males and females, it will be necessary to take their total workload into account. Moveover, we will have to consider how work role and family role interact. These problems will be given priority in our future research.

PLEA FOR DIALOGUE

The main message of this chapter is that research-based knowledge about human motives, abilities, and constraints provides guidelines for adapting work to people. To make effective use of such knowledge we need to increase the dialogue between the scientific community and the world of work. In Swedish work life there is an openness for the view that the psychosocial environment needs to be corrected and cultivated. However, even when there is agreement on fundamental human issues, the communication gap remains wide. As long as the gap is not bridged, a wealth of knowledge and ideas on both sides will remain unutilized.

These are challenges to biobehavioral and social scientists to present their research results in such a way that they affect conditions at the workplace. To what extent has this been accomplished? A major achievement, so far, has been to increase awareness among the groups concerned of the importance of psychosocial problems and their health consequences. This is the first step. Moreover, biopsychosocial research has provided the employees and their organizations with arguments for the discussions that now take place at many work sites. Physiological "hard data" have been shown to strengthen the arguments by providing "visible evidence" of frustration, conflicts, and maladaptation.

The dialogue between the worlds of science and of work takes time to develop. There are no shortcuts for a productive exchange of ideas and competencies between researchers and their speaking partners in the workplace. Researchers need an input from the employees, their unions, and management. Such inputs will widen the researchers' field of vision so that they have a better chance to contribute constructively to the process of development and implementation. Insofar as researchers become partners in this process, it will reduce the risk that their findings remain isolated fragments, which may not even touch base with the problems that stimulated the research in the first place.

The opportunities for constructive dialogue are particularly good in some areas. This is true for the field of stress and health at the workplace, where corporate health care departments function as bridges from research laboratories to management, personnel departments, safety committees, and unions. As more such bridges are built, we will be better equipped to translate research findings into practical measures.

REFERENCES

1. Kahn, R. L. *Work and Health.* Wiley, New York, 1984.
2. Levi, L., Frankenhaeuser, M., and Gardell, B. The characteristics of the work place and the nature of its social demands. In *Occupational Stress and Performance at Work,* edited by S. Wolf and A. J. Finestone, pp. 54–67. PSG Publishing Co., Littleton, Mass., 1986.
3. Cannon, W. B. *The Wisdom of the Body.* Norton, New York, 1932.
4. Hamburg, D. A., Elliott, G. R., and Parron, D. L. *Health and Behavior: Frontiers of Research in the Biobehavioral Sciences.* National Academy Press, Washington, D.C., 1982.
5. Frankenhaeuser, M. Psychobiological aspects of life stress. In *Coping and Health,* edited by S. Levine and H. Ursin, pp. 203–223. Plenum, New York, 1980.
6. Frankenhaeuser, M. A psychobiological framework for research on human stress and coping. In *Dynamics of Stress,* edited by M. H. Appley and R. Trumbull, pp. 101–116. Plenum, New York, 1986.
7. Frankenhaeuser, M. Coping with stress at work. *Int. J. Health Serv.* 11(4): 491–510, 1981.
8. Frankenhaeuser, M., and Johansson, G. Stress at work: Psychobiological and psychosocial aspects. *Int. Rev. Appl. Psychol.* 35: 287–299, 1986.
9. Lundberg, U., and Frankenhaeuser, M. Pituitary-adrenal and sympathetic-adrenal correlates of distress and effort. *J. Psychosom. Res.* 24: 125–130, 1980.
10. Frankenhaeuser, M., and Gardell, B. Underload and overload in working life: Outline of a multidisciplinary approach. *J. Hum. Stress* 2: 35–46, 1976.
11. Johansson, G., Aronsson, G., and Lindström, B. O. Social psychological and neuroendocrine stress reactions in highly mechanized work. *Ergonomics* 21: 583–599, 1978.
12. Frankenhaeuser, M. The sympathetic-adrenal and pituitary-adrenal response to challenge: Comparison between the sexes. In *Biobehavioral Bases of Coronary Heart Disease,* edited by T. M. Dembroski, T. H. Schmidt, and G. Blumchen, pp. 91–105. S. Karger, Basel, 1983.
13. Johansson, G. Job demands and stress reactions in repetitive and uneventful monotony at work. *Int. J. Health Serv.* 19(2): 365–377, 1989.
14. Frankenhaeuser, M. To err is human: Nuclear war by mistake? In *Breakthrough: Emerging New Thinking,* edited by A. Gromyko and M. Hellman, pp. 53–60. Walker, New York, 1988.
15. Frankenhaeuser, M. Stress at work: Threat, challenge, opportunity. In *Dignity at Work,* edited by B. Ekman, pp. 128–139. Streiffert, Stockholm, 1985.
16. Karasek, R. A. Job demands, job decision latitude and mental strain: Implications for job redesign. *Administr. Sci. Q.* 24: 285–308, 1979.

17. Gardell, B. Effectiveness and health hazards in mechanized work. In *Work Stress: Health Care Systems in the Workplace,* edited by J. C. Quick et al., pp. 50–71. Praeger Scientific Publishers, New York, 1987.
18. Frankenhaeuser, M., Lundberg, U., and Forsman, L. Dissociation between sympathetic-adrenal and pituitary-adrenal responses to an achievement situation characterized by high controllability: Comparison between Type A and Type B males and females. *Biol. Psychol.* 10: 79–91, 1980.
19. Steptoe, A. *Psychological Factors in Cardiovascular Disorders.* Academic Press, London, 1981.
20. Johansson, G. Subjective wellbeing and temporal patterns of sympathetic-adrenal medullary activity. *Biol. Psychol.* 4: 157–172, 1976.
21. Rissler, A. A psychobiological approach to quality of working life: Costs of adjustment to quantitative overload. In *Satisfaction in Work Design: Ergonomics and Other Approaches,* edited by R. G. Sell and P. Shipley. Taylor and Francis, London, 1979.
22. Gardell, B. Scandinavian research on stress in working life. *Int. J. Health Serv.* 12(1): 31–41, 1982.
23. Johansson, G., Johnson, J. V., and Hall, E. M. Smoking and sedentary behavior as related to job design. *Soc. Sci. Med.,* 1990, in press.
24. Frankenhaeuser, M., et al. Stress on and off the job as related to sex and occupational status in white-collar workers. *J. Organization. Behav.,* 1989, in press.

CHAPTER 4

Job Demands and Stress Reactions in Repetitive and Uneventful Monotony at Work

Gunn Johansson

Ever since Tayloristic principles were introduced into manufacturing industries, monotony and boredom have presented an industrial problem. Research on monotonous work has emphasized several aspects of monotony. One line of research has focused on monotonous work as related to work motivation, alienation, job satisfaction, general life satisfaction, job socialization, and life outside work (e.g., 1-4). Within a traditional ergonomic framework, psychological analyses have concentrated on information processing and means to optimize individual work output (e.g., 5, 6), while medical research has emphasized the development of musculoskeletal disorders as a result of repetitive body movements (7). Finally, monotonous work has been subject to research concerning psychosocial stressors in the work environment. Among the stressors that have traditionally been acknowledged in the work site are, for instance, high physical and mental demands, excessive work, and time pressure. But more recent research has identified psychosocial stressors of a different kind. When factors such as understimulation, underutilization of skills, few opportunities to learn new things on the job, and lack of autonomy and social support were brought into focus, they were also found to be associated with perceived strain, heightened sympathetic nervous system activity, and morbidity (e.g., 8-10).

"Monotony," however, is an ambiguous term. One sense of the word refers to frequent repetition of stimuli, sequences of events, and body movements, etc. This kind of *repetitive monotony* is found in work on the assembly line and also in clerical work such as data entry tasks. The most adequate single measure of repetitive monotony is the duration of work cycles. Extremely repetitive tasks, e.g., along an assembly line, may consist of cycle times of five to ten seconds. In another sense, monotony refers to almost constant stimulus conditions, with few and/or hardly

This work was supported by the Swedish Work Environment Fund and the Swedish Council for Research in the Humanities and Social Sciences.

61

noticeable events or changes. Such *uneventful monotony* is mainly found in the control rooms of process industries, where operators supervise complex technical systems producing electrical power, chemical and petrochemical products, paper and pulp, gas, etc. The work situation is characterized by long periods of uneventful monitoring of the process while it is in a normal and stable state. These periods are interrupted unexpectedly, at irregular intervals, by demands for operator intervention when process failures occur (11-13).

When the two types of monotony appear in industrial work they represent entirely different work conditions. Work on the assembly line of a car factory and process monitoring in a nuclear power plant, for example, differ in terms of demands for training and education, in terms of physical environment, consequences of human error, etc. However, the differences between repetitive and uneventful are often over-looked, and even the most comprehensive reviews of monotony and boredom have failed to make a clear distinction between the two (e.g., 14-16). In this chapter I will attempt to clarify the distinction between repetitive and uneventful monotony in terms of health-relevant psychological demands and psychoneuroendocrine stress reactions. The purpose of the analysis is to show that the character of stressors in the two work conditions is different, and that they therefore require different actions and strategies for the improvement of occupational health and well-being.

JOB DEMANDS ASSOCIATED WITH REPETITIVE AND UNEVENTFUL MONOTONY

Table 1 is a summary of some of the most obvious differences between repetitive and uneventful monotonous work. Whereas assembly-line workers are physically con-strained to their place on the line, and often cannot leave their place even for ten minutes without someone relieving them, control-room workers are usually free to move about in the control room. Temporarily they may also be expected to attend to certain tasks outside the control room. Social interaction is often hindered or prevented on the assembly line. The reason may be noise that prevents conversations, or a combination of physical distance and physical constraint. Social interaction is restricted to rest breaks, and the growth of social support and networks on the job may be obstructed. The control room operator, on the other hand, especially in the highly automated plant, can often interact freely with other individuals in the control room. If the control room is located in a plant with noise and other unpleasant environmental conditions, it sometimes becomes a natural point of interaction for larger groups of workers than those working in the control room. This forms an impor-tant precondition for increased collective control in the work situation, which is usually lacking in machine-controlled repetitive work.

One of the most apparent differences between repetitive and uneventful monotony lies in the complexity of the tasks. The supervision of production in process industries is often a highly complex task, in which the operator needs an elaborate and accurate "mental model" of a production process (e.g., manufacturing of paper and pulp; production of energy, chemicals, or food). In modern plants the mental model must include not only a complex production process, but also the functions of a com-puterized system for control of the process. Furthermore, the individual operator

Table 1

Typical psychosocial work conditions distinguishing work characterized by
repetitive monotony (e.g., work on the assembly line or clerical data entry work)
from that characterized by uneventful monotony (e.g., supervisory monitoring of
automated technical processes).

Work condition	Repetitive monotony: "assembly line"	Uneventful monotony: "control room"
Possibilities for:		
Physical mobility	Restricted	Good
Social interaction	Poor	Good (within control room)
Social support	Restricted	Good
Collective control	Poor	Good
Task complexity	Low	High
Predictability	High	Moderate
Control over work pace	Low, machine-paced	Usually high, but occasionally paced by technical system
Physical work environment	Multiple exposures	Comfortable
Physical work load	Light to moderate	Light
Night work	Unusual	Common
Payment	Piece-rate	Salary

usually controls only a specific section or subprocess of the production. The operator
therefore also needs an understanding of how his or her own subprocess relates to
preceding and subsequent phases of the entire process. This complexity is in sharp
contrast to the simple tasks on the assembly line, where the individual performs
identical and simple operations of short duration hundreds or thousands of times
during a work shift.

Despite the similarities in terms of monotony, repetitive and uneventful conditions
differ distinctly in terms of predictability of events. Assembly work, by definition, is
preplanned and almost perfectly predictable. The process operator often supervises
a highly automated process, which may be stable most of the time, but the operator's
primary task is to interfere when unpredicted failures or disturbances occur. The
assembly-line worker can seldom control his or her work pace, which most often is
machine-controlled, but work cycles or work rhythms cannot even be clearly
distinguished in the process operator's work situation. Instead, long periods of passive
monitoring are unexpectedly interrupted by process failures, and the operator is

expected to select relevant information, make decisions, and act efficiently in order to minimize material damage and loss. In this way, the variability of the operator's work load becomes extremely large, with sudden shifts between monotonous monitoring and demanding, sometimes hectic, work during process disturbances. The physical work environment is another distinguishing aspect of repetitive and uneventful monotony. Workers on the assembly line are often exposed to noise generated by machinery. Fumes and dust may also affect the worker, as well as heat, cold, and vibrations. Such conditions are unusual in the control room, where the worker is protected from most aversive environmental impacts. Finally, the responsibility resting on the individual worker is in certain respects less for workers on the assembly line than for process operators. In the former case, human error may result in faulty products and limited damage to the machinery, etc. In the latter case, however, human error may result in large batches of deficient production, in extremely expensive damage to technical systems, and in risky situations for fellow workers in the plant as well as for the population in the surrounding area. Thus, responsibility for economic values and other people's safety is often more pronounced for the process operator.

A study by Caplan and associates (17) is probably the only field study providing an empirical basis for a direct comparison of assembly-line workers and process operators in terms of job satisfaction and occupational stress. Using a survey technique, Caplan and his coworkers studied 2,010 men of 23 different occupations with regard to stress, strain, and health. Two of the occupations, "assembler, machine paced" (n = 79) and "continuous flow monitor" (n = 101), resemble the two work conditions compared here: repetitive and uneventful monotony. Neuroendocrine measures were obtained for a subsample but did not allow a comparison between assembly-line workers and continuous flow operators. It should be emphasized that, judging from indicators of job complexity, monitoring in this study was probably not representative of today's most automated process production methods. It is reasonable to assume that the industry concerned had not reached an advanced level of computerization, and therefore the role of the operator may have been less passive than is common today. Another reservation concerns the difference in average age between the two groups: workers on the assembly line were about 30 and continuous flow monitors about 45 years of age. Keeping these facts in mind, cautious comparisons are still of interest.

Both groups rated perceived boredom above the general average for all occupations, and assemblers reached a significantly higher level than monitors. Both groups reported high levels of general job dissatisfaction. Almost all other differences were to the disadvantage of the assembly-line workers. They reported more anxiety, depression, and irritation and more work-load dissatisfaction. Although both groups suffered "underutilization of abilities," this was more pronounced in work on the assembly line. The same group was also the highest of the 23 occupational groups in reports of somatic complaints, and reported more dispensary visits in the most recent time.

The assembly-line group included more smokers (60 versus 50 percent) and fewer ex-smokers (15 versus 38 percent) than the continuous flow monitors, and smokers in the former group tended to smoke more than those in the latter group (25 versus 16 cigarettes per day). In two respects, unfavorable conditions were reported for the continuous flow operators. They consumed considerably more coffee and somewhat more other caffeine-containing drinks than the assembly-line workers. In fact, in these respects the monitors were higher than any other group in the study. Finally, they also displayed a higher and above-average percentage of individuals reporting cardiovascular disease (11.9 versus 1.3 percent; average for the total group, 7.3 percent). Although the low level of incidence within groups did not allow effective age-adjustment, this is a very notable difference between the two groups exposed to repetitive and uneventful monotony.

STRESS REACTIONS IN MONOTONOUS WORK

Job Stress and Health

In the evaluation of stress and health consequences of monotonous work, the psychobiological mechanisms involved are of primary interest. It is generally agreed (e.g., 18-20) that adrenal hormones—e.g., adrenaline, noradrenaline, and cortisol—respond to demands and challenges in the psychosocial environment, and that, under certain circumstances, they may play an important role as precursors of pathological states. The risk for disease is considered to increase when the sympathetic–adrenal medullary system and the pituitary-adrenal cortical systems are frequently and intensely activated, when they are activated for extended periods of time, and when the output of adrenaline, noradrenaline, and cortisol is associated with perceived distress (21). Psychobiological stress reactions can be modified by situational factors. One of the most important modifying factors is the individual's possibility for exerting control in a stressful situation (8, 9, 18, 21). Autonomy and job discretion not only attenuate the strength of acute stress reactions. Several studies (e.g., 9, 22) have shown that individuals who can control their work process run a smaller risk for cardiovascular disease and mortality.

Adrenal hormones can be measured in blood and in urine. For studies of individuals in their regular work conditions, urinary estimates are particularly useful, since the collection of samples can take place with little interference in regular work routines. Urinary estimates of excretion rates are obtained as integrated measures for one or several hours. A limited number of studies of monotonous work have employed psychoneuroendocrine measurements, usually measures of adrenaline and noradrenaline excretion. The findings of such investigations are reviewed in the next section. All of these measures have used urinary estimates, and for each individual, hormone measurements were obtained for a period of work as well as for baseline or resting conditions. Tables 2 and 3 present information on sympathetic-adrenal medullary activity reported in studies on monotonous work. In order to facilitate comparisons between studies, simple quotients of work over baseline measures were calculated from data reported in tables or graphs of each research report. The character of the baseline condition determines the level of relaxation that can be achieved, and thereby the work/baseline quotient. Therefore, the circumstances under which baseline measures were obtained are also reported in the tables.

Table 2

Investigations of repetitive work reporting urinary catecholamine excretion:
The character of baseline condition, sex of subjects, work/baseline quotient for
adrenaline and noradrenaline, and subjective states most commonly
associated with the task

Study (reference)	Baseline condition	Sex	Work/baseline quotient[a]		Subjective evaluation[a]
			A	NA	
Field studies					
(23) Metal industry	Nonrepetitive work	M	3.4*	3.1*	—
(25) Light repetitive work (average of group piece-rate and individual piece-rate condition)	Leisure at home	F	2.4	3.0	—
(26) Mechanized sawmill	Leisure at home	M	1.9*	2.1*	Rushed, irritated
(24) Metal industry					
1st occasion	Nonrepetitive work	M	5.1*	2.3*	—
6 months later	Nonrepetitive work	M	4.7*	2.2*	—
Laboratory studies					
(27)					
Simple motor task	Nonrepetitive work	M	1.4*	—	Bored, drowsy
Discrimination	Nonrepetitive work	M	1.7*	—	Tense
Counting	Nonrepetitive work	M	1.5*	—	Bored, drowsy
(28) Machine-paced reaction-time task	Relaxation in lab	M	1.8*	1.2*	Rushed, tense, irritated
(29)					
Loading	Night rest	F	3.8	1.0	—
Sorting	Night rest	F	3.0	0.9	—
Loading	Relaxation in lab	F	1.3	1.5	—
Sorting	Relaxation in lab	F	1.2	1.4	—

[a]A, adrenaline; NA, noradrenaline; dash indicates data not available.
*Work-baseline difference statistically significant at or beyond the 5 percent level.

Repetitive Monotony

Timio and Gentili (23) studied the output of catecholamines and 11-hydrocortico-steroids by assembly-line workers in a metal industry, and found significantly increased excretion levels for periods of assembly-line work compared with work off the line. Perceived arousal was not recorded. Later, Timio and coworkers (24) reported catecholamine excretion of metal workers to be significantly higher on the assembly line than in work off the line. The results were replicated six months later in the same group of workers. In a study of light repetitive work, Borsch-Galetke (25) found pronounced activation of the sympathetic–adrenal medullary system in women being paid by piece-rate. Urinary excretion of adrenaline and noradrenaline was more pronounced when work was paid by individual than by group piece-rate. In this study no self-reports were collected. Johansson and associates (26) reported self-ratings as well as hormone output by sawmill workers in highly repetitive tasks. These workers secreted considerably larger amounts of catecholamines and reported more irritation on the job than fellow workers in nonrepetitive jobs. In this case, repetitiveness was associated with machine pacing, physical constriction, and higher frequencies of psychosomatic disorders.

In real life, the monotony dimension can seldom be isolated from other psychological aspects of work. Repetitive tasks, especially in manufacturing industries, are always associated with physical constraint and often with underutilization of human resources, with machine pacing, and with piece-rate remuneration. Therefore, laboratory studies, in which repetitiveness can be isolated from other conditions, provide a useful complement to field studies. In one such laboratory experiment Weber and associates (27) compared repetitive discrimination and counting tasks with a simple motor task. They obtain measures of self-reports as well as neuroendocrine reactivity and indicators of cortical arousal such as critical flicker fusion and EEG recordings. They concluded that repetitive work resulted in depressed alpha activity, elevated heart rate, and elevated adrenaline excretion rates. In a laboratory experiment on machine-paced versus self-paced repetitive work (complex reaction-time task), Johansson (28) recorded self-reports and urinary catecholamine excretion rates. Heart rate, as well as adrenaline and noradrenaline excretion, were significantly increased during performance of the machine-paced task compared with a control session. Self-paced work resulted in a similar, but less pronounced reaction. In addition, machine-paced—but not self-paced—repetitive work was followed by delayed recovery of adrenaline and noradrenaline excretion to baseline levels. Finally, Cox and coworkers (29) designed a laboratory study simulating two repetitive tasks that were chosen to reflect various aspects of unskilled repetitive work. The results showed a pronounced increase of adrenaline output during work compared with night rest, and a less dramatic increase between day-time relaxation in the laboratory and work.

Although comparisons between studies should be made with great caution, it may be concluded that real-life work situations tend to give rise to larger increases in catecholamine output than laboratory settings. A reasonable explanation would be that field data reflect the totality of the work situation, including factors such as machine pacing, piece-rate payment, and exposure to environmental stressors such as noise. Another circumstance to take into consideration is that subjects in a laboratory study endure the experimental condition for a limited number of hours, whereas workers on the assembly line are exposed to repetitive conditions during entire work shifts and on a regular basis. Thus, in this respect, most laboratory data can be assumed to represent under- rather than over-estimations of sympathetic–adrenal medullary activity during repetitive work. Again, the impact of the character of baseline situations on the work/baseline quotient must be considered. High quotients should be expected in cases for which baselines were obtained during night rest. However, it is worth noting that some of the highest quotients reported in Table 2 were obtained in real-life situations and with baselines recorded during other, nonrepetitive work conditions.

Uneventful Monotony

Work characterized by uneventful monotony has not attracted much interest in occupational stress research. The majority of empirical studies on uneventful monotony have concerned either perceived boredom or "human reliability," i.e., the quality of work performance (for reviews, see 14–16). The focus on performance is due to the severity of potential consequences of human error in industrial operations such as nuclear power generation, gas production, chemical and petrochemical production, etc. A considerable part of this research has studied so-called vigilance tasks, in which attention is directed to an information display over long, unbroken periods of time, for the purpose of detecting infrequent changes in the state of the display that are difficult to discriminate (15). The first studies by Mackworth (30) were modeled on military radar monitoring, and an important purpose was to establish an optimal length of watch for radar operators. A major finding in these studies was that vigilance deteriorates rapidly over time, in particular during the first half hour of a watch period. This decline of performance has been explained in terms of insufficient environmental stimulation and a slowing down of cortical processes (e.g., 31, 32).

The combination of uneventful monotony and demands for sustained mental preparedness imposes severe demands on the worker (14). A limited number of studies have evaluated the impact of uneventful monotony on neuroendocrine stress responses. Five of these studies, selected according to the criteria used for Table 2, are summarized in Table 3.

There is at least one field study of supervisory monitoring work that includes urinary measures of catecholamines (33). Process operators supervising oxygen production, power generation, and the flow of cooling and heating water were studied during typical morning shifts and during work-free days spent at home. The work situation was perceived as boring, with the operators sometimes having a vague, uneasy feeling that was most pronounced during night shifts. Adrenaline excretion was significantly increased during work. Self-reported health did not differ between the process controllers and operators performing more hectic work in control rooms.

The majority of studies on uneventful monotony that include psychoneuroendocrine measurements are laboratory experiments of fairly short duration, usually no more than a few hours. One such study was carried out by Frankenhaeuser (34). The subjects performed a three-hour vigilance task that caused a 50 percent increase of adrenaline and noradrenaline excretion. The experimental situation was associated

Table 3

Studies of uneventful monotony reporting urinary catecholamine excretion:
The character of baseline condition, sex of subjects, work/baseline quotient for
adrenaline and noradrenaline, and subjective states most commonly
associated with the task

Study (reference)	Baseline condition	Sex	Work/baseline quotient[a] A	NA	Subjective evaluation[a]
Field studies					
(33) Process monitoring	Leisure at home	M	1.2*	1.1	Boredom, uneasy feeling
Laboratory studies					
(34) Three-hour vigilance task	Relaxation in lab	M	1.5	1.5	Distress, effort
(6) Two-hour vigilance task	Relaxation in lab	M/F	1.0	1.3*	–
(35) 70-minute vigilance task	Relaxation in lab	M	1.4	1.0	–
		F	1.4	1.0	–
(36)					
Passive monitoring	Relaxation in lab	M	1.1*	1.4*	Monotony, boredom
Active monitoring	Relaxation in lab	M	1.8*	1.3*	Monotony, boredom

[a]A, adrenaline; NA, noradrenaline; dash indicates data not available.
*Work-baseline difference statistically significant at or beyond the 5 percent level.

with perceived distress and effort. In a study of simulated radar monitoring behavior of men and women, only noradrenaline excretion was significantly increased above baseline levels (6). Mood and arousal were not recorded in this study. Lundberg and Frankenhaeuser (35) studied vigilance performance as one of several experimental conditions and reported a 40 percent increase of adrenaline among male and female subjects. Finally, Johansson and coworkers (36) performed a study of two uneventful monitoring conditions that differed in terms of the amount of activity required by the subjects. In active as well as passive monitoring, adrenaline excretion was significantly increased above baselines, and the increase of hormonal activity was associated with an increase of perceived monotony and boredom.

To conclude, empirical evidence on psychoneuroendocrine reactions to uneventful monotony is scarce, especially with regard to real-life investigations. The data available indicate that, although prolonged uneventful monotony is associated with cortical deactivation and a perceived difficulty to remain alert (32), the excretion of adrenaline tends to increase in relation to baselines, and occasionally the increase reaches statistical significance.

The reviews presented above suggest a difference of degree in reactions to repetitive and uneventful work conditions. Repetitive monotony tends to be more potent in activating the sympathetic-adrenal medullary system and in increasing the production of adrenaline. This difference does not in itself indicate that repetitive work is a more severe threat to health than uneventful monotony. Rather, it is the combination of psychoneuroendocrine activation on the job and various other adverse factors, such as perceived strain, job dissatisfaction, somatic complaints, and absenteeism (2, 17, 26, 37), that makes repetitive work stand out as more hazardous to health and well-being than uneventful monotony as experienced in supervisory monitoring of industrial processes. In the case of uneventful monotony in the work situation, the stress and health aspects have not yet been thoroughly investigated. The moderate activation of adrenal hormones reported above can be interpreted as reflecting the mental effort required for sustained attention and mental preparedness, and does not seem to be associated with somatic complaints (33).

IMPLICATIONS FOR WORK REFORM

A major issue in the improvement of monotonous work will be the increase of workers' control over the work process. However, the difference in character between repetitive and uneventful work conditions calls for different strategies. In the case of repetitive work, severe criticism has been formulated in several, by now classical accounts (e.g., 1, 37). Experiments have been introduced aiming at a profound change of manufacturing processes and the restructuring of assembly work to offer greater flexibility of work routines, increased worker influence, better psychosocial and physical work environments, and better feedback on results (38, 39). Reports indicate that considerable improvement can be achieved without loss of efficiency and production level.

These interesting experiments cannot overshadow the fact that repetitive, coercive, machine-paced work is still a reality for large groups of workers. Official Swedish records published in 1986 show that 27 percent of the female and 24 percent of the male labor force reported that their work was monotonous and offered little variation (40). The same survey presented data on work in which identical tasks and movements are repeated many times per hour during the major part of the work day, and in which these conditions are combined with low demands for skill and qualifications. This category, in which the most repetitive tasks will be found, included 23 percent of the female and 14 percent of the male labor force. This information points to the trend for repetitive work to become primarily a problem for female workers. One reason may be that increasing numbers of women are employed in manufacturing industries and are assigned to unattractive jobs such as light, repetitive tasks formerly carried out by male workers. Another reason may be the increase of repetitive clerical work that tends to accompany the introduction of office automation. Simple data entry work is a modern example of fragmented, specialized, short-cycle tasks bearing a close resemblance to industrial work on the assembly line.

In uneventful process monitoring, biological reactions tend to be secondary to more direct effects on worker well-being that occur at the psychological and social levels. The infrequency with which operators who supervise highly automated processes get to exercise their skills may influence their work situation in at least two respects (cf. 13). Job motivation may be negatively affected since effective monitoring performance is associated with little or no feedback. Furthermore, the nonuse of skills eventually makes the operator uncertain about his or her capacity to handle unexpected and unfamiliar disturbances, and this, in turn, may contribute to perceived strain. For the process monitor, worker control over the work process has to do with the operator's understanding of the production process, appropriate design of computer software, and the organization of work (13). Various measures can be taken in order to avoid long periods of passive monitoring and to improve and help maintain operator skill. Operator participation in the improvement of computer software as well as process simulation could be used for these purposes, but application, or even serious consideration, of such procedures is unusual except in high-risk and high-cost operations (e.g., aviation, nuclear power generation). Improvement at the organizational level is another possibility. Most investigations of error detection, information processing, and decision-making in the control room have concerned individual behavior rather than group performance. Exploration of alternative and group-based modes of organizing the supervision of complex technical production might provide a better basis for individual and collective worker control and facilitate growth of occupational skill.

REFERENCES

1. Walker, C. R., and Guest, R. H. *Man on the Assembly Line*. Harvard University Press, Cambridge, Mass., 1952.
2. Gardell, B. Alienation and mental health in the modern industrial environment. In *Society, Stress and Disease*, Vol. I: *The Psychosocial Environment and Psychosomatic Diseases*, edited by L. Levi, pp. 148-180. Oxford University Press, London, 1971.
3. Volpert, W. Psychische Regulation von Arbeitstätigkeiten. (Mental regulation of work behavior.) In *Enzyklopädie der Psychologie*, edited by J. Rutenfranz and U. Kleinbeck. Hogrefe, Göttingen, 1986.
4. Kohn, M., and Schooler, C. *Work and Personality*. Ablex, Norwood, N.J., 1983.
5. Conrad, R. Letter sorting machines—paced, "lagged" or unpaced? *Ergonomics* 3: 149-157, 1960.
6. O'Hanlon, J. F., and Beatty, J. Catecholamine correlates of radar monitoring performance. *Biol. Psychol.* 4: 293-303, 1976.
7. Hagberg, M. *Occupational Shoulder and Neck Disorders*. The Swedish Work Environment Fund, Stockholm, 1987.
8. Frankenhaeuser, M., and Gardell, B. Underload and overload in working life. A multidisciplinary approach. *J. Hum. Stress* 2: 34-46, 1976.
9. Johnson, J. V. The Impact of Workplace Social Support, Job Demands and Work Control upon Cardiovascular Disease in Sweden. Doctoral dissertation. Reports from the Division of Environmental and Organizational Psychology, Department of Psychology, University of Stockholm, 1986.
10. Theorell, T. Stress at work and risk of myocardial infarction. *Postgrad. Med. J.* 62: 791-795, 1986.
11. Edwards, E., and Lees, F. P. (eds.). *The Human Operator in Process Control*. Taylor and Francis, London, 1974.
12. Bainbridge, L. The process controller. In *The Analysis of Practical Skills*, edited by W. T. Singleton, pp. 236-292. MTP Press, Lancashire, 1978.
13. Johansson, G. Stress, autonomy and the maintenance of skill in supervisory control of automated systems. *Appl. Psychol. Int. Rev.* 38: 45-56, 1989.
14. Thackray, R. I. The stress of boredom and monotony: A consideration of the evidence. *Psychosom. Med.* 43: 165-176, 1981.

15. Davies, D. R., Shackleton, V. J., and Parasuraman, R. Monotony and boredom. In *Stress and Fatigue in Human Performance*, edited by G. R. J. Hockey, pp. 1-32. Wiley, Chichester, 1983.
16. O'Hanlon, J. F. Boredom: Practical consequences and a theory. *Acta Psychol.* 49: 53-82, 1981.
17. Caplan, R., et al. *Job Demands and Worker Health*. National Institute for Occupational Safety and Health, HEW Publication No. (NIOSH), 75-160, Washington, D.C., 1975.
18. Appley, M. H., and Trumbull, R. (eds.). *Dynamics of Stress. Physiological, Psychological, and Social Perspectives*. Plenum, New York, 1986.
19. Elliott, G. R., and Eisdorfer, C. (eds.). *Stress and Human Health. Analysis and Implications of Research*. A study by the Institute of Medicine/National Academy of Sciences. Springer, New York, 1982.
20. Quick, J.-C., et al. (eds.). *Work Stress. Health Care Systems in the Workplace*. Praeger, New York, 1987.
21. Frankenhaeuser, M. A psychobiological framework for research on human stress and coping. In *Dynamics of Stress. Physiological, Psychological and Social Perspectives*, edited by M. H. Appley and R. Trumbull, pp. 101-116. Plenum, New York, 1986.
22. Karasek, R., et al. Job decision latitude, job demands and cardiovascular disease: A prospective study of Swedish men. *Am. J. Public Health* 71: 694-705, 1981.
23. Timio, M., and Gentili, S. Adrenosympathetic overactivity under conditions of work stress. *Br. J. Prev. Soc. Med.* 30: 262-265, 1976.
24. Timio, M., Gentili, S., and Pede, S. Free adrenaline and noradrenaline excretion related to occupational stress. *Br. Heart J.* 42: 471-474, 1979.
25. Borsch-Galetke, E. Katekolaminausscheidung bei Feinwerkerinnen mit und ohne Akkordarbeit. *Zentralbl. Arbeitsmed.* 27: 53-58, 1977.
26. Johansson, G., Aronsson, G., and Lindström, B. O. Social psychological and neuroendocrine stress reactions in highly mechanized work. *Ergonomics* 21: 583-599, 1978.
27. Weber, A., et al. Psychophysiological effects of paced and repetitive tasks. *Ergonomics* 23(11): 1033-1046, 1980.
28. Johansson, G. Psychoneuroendocrine correlates of unpaced and paced performance. In *Machine Pacing and Occupational Stress*, edited by G. Salvendy and M. J. Smith, pp. 277-286. Taylor and Francis, London, 1981.
29. Cox, S., et al. Effects of simulated repetitive work on urinary catecholamine excretion. *Ergonomics* 25: 1129-1141, 1982.
30. Mackworth, N. H. *Researches on the Measurement of Human Performance*. Medical Research Council Special Report, No. 268. Her Majesty's Stationery Office, London, 1950.
31. Frankenhaeuser, M., and Johansson, G. On the psychophysiological consequences of understimulation and overstimulation. In *Society, Stress, and Disease*, Vol. IV: *Working Life*, edited by L. Levi, pp. 82-89. Oxford University Press, Oxford, 1981.
32. Davies, D. R., and Parasuraman, R. *The Psychology of Vigilance*. Academic Press, London, 1982.
33. Johansson, G., and Sandén, P.-O. Mental load and job satisfaction of control room operators. Reports from the Department of Psychology, University of Stockholm, Stockholm, 1989.
34. Frankenhaeuser, M. The role of peripheral catecholamines in adaptation to understimulation and overstimulation. In *Psychopathology of Human Adaptation*, edited by G. Serban, pp. 173-191. Plenum, New York, 1976.
35. Lundberg, U., and Frankenhaeuser, M. Pituitary-adrenal and sympathetic-adrenal correlates of distress and effort. *J. Psychosom. Res.* 24: 125-130, 1980.
36. Johansson, G., Cavalini, P., and Pettersson, P. Psychobiological reactions to unpredictable performance stress in a monotonous situation. Reports from the Department of Psychology, No. 646. University of Stockholm, Stockholm, 1986.
37. Braverman, H. *Labor and Monopoly Capital*. Monthly Review Press, New York, 1974.
38. Agurén, S., and Edgren, J. *New Factories*. The Swedish Employers Confederation, Stockholm, 1980.
39. Agurén, S., et al. *Volvo Kalmar Revisited: Ten Years of Experience*. Efficiency and Participation Development Council, SAF/LO/PTK, Stockholm, 1985.
40. Kvinno- och mansvärlden. (The World of Women and Men 1986. Equal Opportunity in Sweden.) Statistics Sweden, Stockholm, 1986.

CHAPTER 5

Learned Helplessness at Work

Lennart Lennerlöf

THE PARADIGMATIC FINDING

The phrase "learned helplessness" was first used by Overmier, Seligman, and Maier (1, 2) to represent certain unexpected features in the behavior of dogs after they had been given inescapable shocks in learning experiments (Pavlovian conditioning). To quote a later text by Seligman (3): "After this experience the dogs were placed in a shuttle box, a two-sided chamber in which a dog jumping from one side to the other side turns off or *escapes* shock. Jumping can also prevent or *avoid* shock altogether if the jump occurs before the shock begins." A dog that has not had the experimental treatment with unavoidable shocks learns within a few trials to escape and soon also to avoid the shocks. However (3, pp. 21-22):

> A dog that has first been given inescapable shock showed a strikingly different pattern. This dog's first reactions to shock in the shuttle box were much the same as those of the naive dog: it ran around frantically for about thirty seconds. But then it stopped moving; to our surprise, it lay down and quietly whined. After one minute of this we turned the shock off; the dog had failed to cross the barrier and had not escaped from shock. On the next trial, the dog did it again; at first it struggled a bit, and then, after a few seconds, it seemed to give up and to accept the shock passively. On all succeeding trials, the dog failed to escape. This is the paradigmatic learned-helplessness finding.

This experiment became the starting point for a fast-growing new field of research. During the last decade, the concept of learned helplessness has also begun to appear in the public debate about various social problems. The theory of learned helplessness should also be of interest to behavioral scientists engaged in work environment research. Although the concept has been referred to in the literature, there is a paucity of empirical research.

This chapter is meant to arouse interest in this subject among my colleagues. I will review developments in learned helplessness theory and research and take up some critical issues. I will then present some empirical data and discuss the potential usefulness of the learned helplessness model in work environment research.

EARLY RESEARCH

In 1975, the first 10 years of research on learned helplessness were summed up in a book by Seligman that has already become a classic: *Helplessness—On Depression, Development and Death* (3). Although the theory has since been revised and elaborated, it is still important to note its origin.

The "paradigmatic" experiments with dogs were followed by several experiments with other infrahuman species. The results were mostly similar; in some instances they were quite spectacular. Older experiments were also reinterpreted, for instance Richter's (4) dramatic study of wild rats (3, p. 169):

> He had found that if a wild rat was placed in a large vat of warm water from which there was no escape, the rat would swim for about 60 hours before drowning in a state of exhaustion. Other rats were held in the investigator's hand until they stopped struggling, and then they were put in the water. These rats swam around excitedly for a few minutes, then suddenly sank to the bottom and drowned without resurfacing.

The hypothesis that this was a result of learned helplessness was strengthened by the finding that if the rats were released several times from the hand of the researcher, they did not behave in a helpless way: "These immunized wild rats swam for 60 hours" (3, p. 170).

Early research also included experiments with the human species. "What are the laboratory effects of inescapable trauma in *Homo sapiens*? Like the dog, cat, rat, fish, and non-human primates, when a man is faced with noxious events that he cannot control, his motivation to respond is drastically undermined" (3, p. 30). A typical example described by Seligman (5) has been used often as a paradigm of research on human helplessness (3, p. 30):

> Donald Hiroto replicated our findings on dogs, quite exactly, in college students. His escape group received loud noise, which they learned to turn off by pushing a button; the yoked group received the same noise, but independently of any response; a third group received no noise. Each subject was then taken to a finger shuttle box: in order to escape noise the individual had only to move his hand from one side to the other. Both the no-noise group and the escape group learned readily to shuttle with their hands. As with other species, however, the human yoked group failed to escape and avoid; most sat passively and accepted the aversive noise.

I shall have more to say later about Seligman's claims that this replicated the dog experiment and that this kind of experience in the laboratory was an "inescapable trauma" for human beings.

Seligman did not proceed, however, from experimental evidence only. His book begins with five cases, two concerned with depression, one with anxiety, one with childhood failure in school, and one with sudden psychosomatic death. In the following chapters of his book we find several more such cases from "real life," some taken from Seligman's own clinical work and some from other sources. Together, these case studies are quite convincing. Seligman was a little ambivalent, however; he seemed dubious of their value by academic standards.

THE ORIGINAL THEORY

The original model of learned helplessness was founded in learning theory, especially operant conditioning with partial or intermittent reinforcement: "Not only can an organism learn that its responding produces an outcome with a certain probability, and that refraining from responding produces an outcome with a certain probability; it can also put these two together . . . to come up with an overall estimate of contingency" (3, p. 18); and "When the probability of an outcome is the same whether or not a given response occurs, the outcome is *independent* of that response. When this is true of all voluntary responses, the outcome is *uncontrollable*" (3, p. 16). Or more generally: "When an organism can make no operant response that controls an outcome, I will say the outcome is *uncontrollable*" (3, p. 12).

Learned helplessness has motivational, cognitive, and emotional consequences (3, pp. 55–56):

> The expectation that an outcome is independent of responding (1) reduces the motivation to control the outcome; (2) interferes with learning that responding controls the outcome; and, if the outcome is traumatic, (3) produces fear as long as the subject is uncertain of the uncontrollability of the outcome, and then produces depression.

The emotional consequences thus presuppose a traumatic event (3, pp. 53–54):

> When a traumatic event first occurs, it causes a heightened state of emotionality that can loosely be called fear. This state continues until one of two things happens: if the subject learns that he can control the trauma, fear is reduced and may disappear altogether; or if the subject finally learns he cannot control the trauma, fear will decrease and be replaced with depression.

Fear has motivational effects. Seligman referred to White's (6) well-known concept of "competence motivation": "In a classic exposition R. W. White . . . argued that the basic drive for control had been overlooked by learning theorists and psychoanalytic thinkers alike. The need to master could be more pervasive than sex, hunger, and thirst in the lives of animals and men" (3, p. 55). For Seligman, the existence of such a drive followed directly from the emotional premises of his theory: "Since being helpless arouses fear and depression, activity that avoids helplessness thereby avoids these aversive emotional states. Competence may be a drive to avoid the fear and depression induced by helplessness" (3, p. 55).

Seligman's laboratory experiments indicated that helplessness was generalized across situations (3, pp. 36–37):

> Man and animals are born generalizers. I believe that only in the rarest circumstances is a specific, punctate response or association learned. The learning of helplessness is no exception: when an organism learns that it is helpless in one situation, much of its adaptive behavioral repertoire may be undermined. On the other hand, the organisms must also discriminate those situations in which it is helpless from those in which it is not, if it is to continue to behave adaptively. . . . Those factors that provide limits to generalization of helplessness [are] immunization, discriminative control, and significance of the uncontrollable event.

Immunization is an effect of a past history in which the individual has been able to control outcomes. By differential learning in different situations the individual learns to discriminate between controllable and uncontrollable circumstances. "The final factor that may limit the transfer of helplessness from one situation to another is the relative significance of the two situations: helplessness may generalize readily from more traumatic or important events to less traumatic or important ones, but not vice versa" (3, p. 61).

Seligman set out to demonstrate the similarities between the effects of learned helplessness as a laboratory phenomenon on the one hand and depression on the other hand. More than that, he claimed that at least certain kinds of reactive depressions were caused by learning to be helpless (3, p. 93):

> Learned helplessness is caused by learning that responding is independent of reinforcement; so the model suggests that the cause of depression is the belief that action is futile. What kind of events set off reactive depressions? Failure at work and school, death of a loved one, rejection or separations from friends and loved ones, physical disease, financial difficulty, being faced with insoluble problems, and growing old. There are many others, but this list captures the flavour.

"What is the meaning of job failure or incompetence at school? Often it means that all of a person's efforts have been in vain, that his responses have failed to achieve his desires" (3, pp. 93-94). Seligman referred also to depression therapies that were congruent with the learned helplessness theory, e.g., Beck's cognitive therapy (7; see also 8).

My selective review has left out large and interesting parts of Seligman's book; for instance, separate chapters on anxiety and unpredictability, on emotional development and education, and on learned helplessness and death (e.g., in institutions and among old people).

THE REFORMULATED THEORY

A few years after the publication of Seligman's book, the learned helplessness theory was reformulated in an attributional frame of reference. The revision was presented in a comprehensive article by Abramson, Seligman, and Teasdale (9). The reformulation was designed to bring the theory in line with current knowledge of depression: "When helplessness theory proved unable to account for the generality and chronicity of depressive symptoms or for self-esteem loss in depression, it was revised along attributional lines" (10, p. 347). The reformulation was based mainly on clinical observations and real-life experiences. Earlier scientific studies were also reanalyzed.

The revised theory applies to human beings. "We do not know whether the conditions apply to infrahumans. In brief, we argue that when a person finds that he is helpless, he asks *why* he is helpless. The causal attribution he makes then determines the generality and chronicity of his helplessness deficits as well as his later self-esteem" (9, p. 50). It is, however, the expectation of future noncontingency that is the crucial determinant of the symptoms of learned helplessness. The sequence leading from objective noncontingency to learned helplessness can be summarized as follows (9, p. 52): (*a*) objective noncontingency, (*b*) perception of present and past noncontingency, (c) attribution of present or past noncontingency, (d) expectation of future noncontingency, and (e) symptoms of helplessness.

The attributions were described in three dimensions, which in turn characterized different kinds of helplessness: internal versus external (personal versus universal helplessness), specific versus global (specific versus general helplessness), and unstable versus stable (transient versus chronic helplessness). The authors regarded their "attributional framework" as a refinement of the attribution theories of, among others, Heider (11) and Weiner (12). In this connection they also examined Rotter's concept "locus of control." According to Rotter (13), beliefs about causality could be described in terms of internal versus external attributions. An internal locus of control denotes a belief that an outcome is caused by a person's own behavior, whereas an external locus denotes a belief that the outcome is determined by external factors, e.g., other people, chance, or fate.

The interaction between locus of control and learned helplessness research makes it important to note the two quite different meanings of the terms *internal* and *external*. In the revised helplessness theory, "when people believe that the outcomes are more or less likely to happen to themselves than to relevant others, they attribute these outcomes to internal factors. Alternatively, persons make external attributions for outcomes that they believe are as likely to happen to themselves as to relevant others" (9, p. 52). Thus, when an individual cannot control an aversive outcome, but believes that other relevant people can, the individual has to take the blame: the fault is attributed to internal factors. In terms of locus of control, the attribution would in this case be called external: it is factors other than the individual's own behavior that control the outcome. In the original helplessness theory it was also this kind of external uncontrollability that seemed to be harmful (cf. 14).[1]

In the revised as well as in the original theory, learned helplessness was followed by motivational, cognitive, and emotional effects; now, lowered self-esteem was added. Even positive outcomes were believed to produce the two first-mentiond effects. "Recent evidence bears this out: uncontrollable positive events produce the motivational and cognitive deficits in animals . . . and in humans . . . but probably do not produce sad affect" (9, p. 54). Only negative outcomes are followed by sad feelings and, if the attribution is internal ("it's my fault"), by lowered self-esteem as well. The intensity of the affect depends on the importance of the outcome: "When highly desired outcomes are believed improbable or highly aversive outcomes are believed probable, and the individual expects that no response in his repertoire will change their likelihood, (helplessness) depression results" (9, p. 68).

Universal as well as personal helplessness could result in depressed affect. The authors referred to different types of depression in psychoanalytical theory. On the other hand, "those people who typically tend to attribute failure to global, stable, and internal factors should be most prone to general and chronic helplessness depressions with low self-esteem" (9, p. 68). "Our model predicts that [this] attributional

---

[1] Lefcourt (15) published an extensive review in 1976 of the early "locus of control" research that in many respects paralleled Seligman's 1975 publication (3) (see also the many articles in 16). Research within this frame of reference has also expanded during the last decades. It has many similarities with the study of learned helplessness but there are also some notable differences.

style will produce depression proneness, perhaps the depressive personality" (9, p. 68). Thus, people's various attributional styles were described almost as personality traits.

Once more, laboratory research was used to explain the mechanisms by which events in people's real lives are followed by real depressions. It is only a matter of degree (9, pp. 67-68):

> The attributions subjects make for helplessness in the laboratory are presumably less global and less stable than attributions made by depressed people for failure outside the laboratory. Thus, the laboratory-induced depressions are less chronic and less global and are capable of being reversed by debriefing, but, we hypothesize, they are not different in kind from naturally occurring helplessness depressions. They differ only quantitatively, not qualitatively, that is, they are mere "analogs" to real helplessness depressions.

EARLY CRITICISM OF THE REFORMULATED MODEL

The "reformulation" article appeared in a special issue of the *Journal of Abnormal Psychology* devoted to learned helplessness as a model of depression (9). The authors of the other articles expressed mainly favorable but occasionally critical opinions on theoretical as well as empirical grounds, especially concerning the interpretation of the laboratory findings on humans. Thus, the assumption that laboratory experiments with college students mirrored the process underlying depression was criticized, as was the practice of equating sad states measured by a questionnaire with real depressions. Costello, for instance, argued that "one's assumption of the relevance of laboratory experiments to natural events becomes somewhat strained. Only with a major stretch of imagination does inescapable noise in the laboratory model incurable illness" (17, p. 27; cf. 18, 19). In addition, in the reformulated theory, controllability was given less attention than in the original theory, in which this concept was central. This was also criticized, e.g., by Wortman and Dintzer: "We feel that assessments of the controllability of the causal factor may be of the utmost importance in predicting the nature and magnitude of subsequent deficits" (20, p. 82).

In a separate article in the same issue of the journal, Seligman (21) dealt with this criticism. He argued that the learned helplessness model of depression was supported by earlier studies. The findings on college students were of interest even if there were important differences between "mild" and clinical depression: "Mild depression is an enormously widespread and significant problem; its cost in misery and loss of productivity is untold" (21, p. 177). But the findings had significance for a clinical population, too: "Learned helplessness is a theory that suggests there may be a subclass of depression caused by the expectation that important events are uncontrollable" (21, p. 166). "This subclass may cut across the usual ways of classifying clinical depression, and it should be found in the nonclinical population as well' (21, p. 169).

In a later article by Abramson, Garber, and Seligman, the authors stated, however: *"Only those cases, in which the expectation of response-outcome independence is about the lack or loss of a highly desired outcome or about the occurrence of a highly aversive outcome, are sufficient for the emotional component of depression"* (22, p. 18).

FURTHER RESEARCH AND DEBATE

The hypothesis on the importance of cognitive factors for depression was, during the late 1970s and the early 1980s, the subject of much empirical research and theoretical debate, as is evidenced by several reviews (e.g., 10, 23-25; see also various articles in 26). Furthermore, the question of learned helplessness (and related constructs) appeared in many articles and books that reviewed other areas: attributional theory (14, 27-29), uncontrollability (30, 31), motivation (32, 33), health-related behaviors (34), clinical theory and methods (8, 35-37), control and stress (38), role theory and depression (39), and social and cultural influences on psychopathology (40). Here I will quote some comments from the four reviews first mentioned (10, 23-25).

The review by Silver and associates (23) appeared in an issue of the *Journal of Personality* that contained three other articles (41-43) presenting results of empirical research indicating that real uncontrollability rather than attribution might have effects on later behavior (23, p. 481):

> In fact, one conclusion that might be drawn from the foregoing papers in this issue . . . is that attributional and cognitive mediators of the learned helplessness phenomenon are less important than originally hypothesized; . . . one might even suggest (as Oakes and Curtis explicitly do) [41] that learned helplessness is simply a learning effect among humans as well as infrahuman species, obviating the need to invoke cognitive mediators to explain the resulting performance decrements.

After a more comprehensive survey of available research, however, the authors were more cautious. The conclusion that cognitive factors are unimportant would be unfortunate: "It ignores the many studies that have demonstrated the importance of cognitive mediators of helplessness effect" (23, p. 505).

Silver and associates as well as Brewin (25) were critical of many attempts to design experiments with humans that closely paralleled the original animal studies. "In our opinion, such traditional laboratory helplessness studies place subjects in an artificial situation that may make little phenomenological sense" (23, p. 496). "Abramson et al. (1978) pointed to the importance of 'current concern,' that is, the relevance of the uncontrollable outcome to the person concerned. There must remain considerable doubt as to whether laboratory tasks are sufficiently relevant to the concerns of depressed patients to justify their use" (25, p. 299). "In an attempt to refine the phenomenon under study and establish precise experimental control investigators may ultimately study problems that do not relate to real world concern" (23, p. 497). The laboratory experiments with humans even lacked "experimental realism"; subjects were unlikely to accept them at face value.

Coyne and Gotlib (24) admitted that subjects from clinical and inpatient samples were being used more frequently (24, p. 476):

> Nonetheless, for reasons that likely have more to do with the isolation of researchers from clinical populations than with the viability of the continuity hypothesis, the bulk of the literature examining cognition and depression currently involves the study of mildly depressed college students, and will probably continue to do so.

Thus, sampling problems "necessitate a qualification of any statements concerning the relationship between cognition and depression that are based on the current empirical literature" (24, p. 477). The postulation of bias or distortion in the attributional style of depressed individuals could, according to Coyne and Gotlib, be an unnecessary stipulation: "What people think probably depends more on what their external circumstances provide than these models assume" (24, p. 500). Depression could thus come from an entirely accurate conceptualization, the "fault" lying in the environment rather than in the person.

The authors of these reviews advocated that researchers should move out of the laboratory. So far this has seldom been the case. "Few investigators have explored the impact of repeated uncontrollable life stressors on the motivations, cognitions, and emotions of individuals who encounter them. It is of course possible to conduct theory-based research in real world settings" (23, p. 501).

The review by Peterson and Seligman (10) was written in defense of the revised theory. Their core prediction was formulated in the following way: "*If this [attributional] style invokes internal, stable, and global causes, then the person tends to become depressed when bad events occur*" (10, p. 255).

The authors reviewed laboratory experiments, cross-sectional correlation studies, some longitudinal investigations, "experiments of nature," and "case studies" (based on content analysis of written material). They conclude that (10, pp. 369, 370):

> Taken together, these five lines of research support the predictions of the attributional reformulation of learned helplessness model of depression. Each type of research is open to criticism on several grounds, but the convergence of results across different strategies of investigation, different operationalizations, and different populations argues strongly for the validity of the reformulation. . . .
>
> Although we believe explanatory style is traitlike, we do not believe it is invariant. Future investigations should adopt a more sophisticated view of explanatory style. It should be treated as a dependent variable that can be modified by life events, as well as an independent variable that modifies future events.

The causal role of attributional style, however, was questioned by Brewin (25) in his later review. Even if associations between attributional patterns and depression had been found, Brewin found no reliable empirical evidence showing that a certain attributional style made people more prone to depressions.

LABORATORY EXPERIENCES AND HELPLESSNESS IN REAL LIFE

The "paradigmatic learned-helplessness finding" (3, p. 22) came from experiments with animals followed by laboratory experiments with human beings. Seligman and his coworkers maintained that the experiments with animals and with human beings were similar, the latter being replications of the former. But there are differences, as many critics have pointed out. The most important difference has to do with the reality of the laboratory setting. For an animal, the laboratory is its present world in a very real sense; for a human being, the experience of a few hours in the laboratory is something artificial, usually without any deeper significance for his or her "real" life. We should also note that the consequences for the animals are often grave while the manipulated effects on humans are rather trivial. The animal and the human situations are, of course, from a psychological point of view, very different.

The main criterion used to prove that learned helplessness has been induced in the laboratory is that the effects carry over from one situation (inducing) to another (testing). For example, human beings who have experienced an uncontrollable situation tend afterwards to make fewer attempts when facing other problems. But what and how do people learn in the laboratory? Surely not only by simple conditioning. People can also interpret the situation and draw conclusions about what to expect; e.g., the first task was uncontrollable and the next one probably will be, too, so there is no use trying too hard. Seligman described experiments showing that "a person can become helpless without being exposed to the contingency as such: he can merely be told that he is helpless" (3, p. 48; cf. pp. 31, 61). Even if the effects of these experiments are still called learned helplessness, they differ in many respects from what we can witness in the animal laboratory. The human experiences in the laboratory are also far removed from the "traumatic" experiences that Seligman himself said laid the ground for helplessness that led to depression. In my view, only the laboratory experiments on animals are truly analogous to such "traumatic" experiences in humans. Seligman seemed to mean, however, that we really can induce symptoms of depression in the laboratory (3, p. 93; cf. 21):

> Preeminent among these are the depressive symptoms that cannot be investigated in animals: dejected mood, feelings of self-blame and self-dislike, loss of mirth, suicidal thoughts, and crying. Now that learned helplessness has been reliably produced in man it can be determined whether any or all of these states occur in helplessness. If such studies are undertaken, the investigator must take great care to undo any effect that the laboratory manipulations produce.

I dare not guess what kind of experiments Seligman had in mind; fortunately for the subjects, I have not found any examples in his reports. It is of course very valuable if we can find mechanisms in the laboratory that help us to understand people's reactions in "real life." But there is a risk of believing that the experiences in a laboratory and in real life are similar and have similar effects when we try to study the graver effects of learned helplessness.

In research on depression, it is of course necessary to study persons who are diagnosed as depressed. A growing field of research is now studying depressed patients from the helplessness point of view. There are many similarities between the assumed effects of learned helplessness and depressive symptoms. But there are few attempts to investigate whether learned helplessness can be seen as a cause of depression (cf. 25). Here is a clear need for more longitudinal research.

Yet another potential area for learned helplessness research exhibits a paucity of investigations: field studies in "normal" life. The "everyday" implications of the learned helplessness theory are discussed in research reports as well as in more popular media. Are people made helpless in old-age institutions, in hospitals, and in prisons? Do the unemployed learn helplessness? Is modern society organized in a way that fosters the learning of helplessness? And how about working life? What, for instance, is the impact of computerization and automation? And if people learn to be helpless in their daily lives, what are the consequences of this for them and for the society in which they live? But we find few, if any, empirical studies. When researchers in learned helplessness have tried to find support for the theory in people's lives, they usually have given examples from so-called "life events," i.e., rather dramatic single occurrences (e.g., the death of a relative, being told about an incurable disease, failing in an examination, loss of money). General circumstances may, however, be of greater long-run importance than single events.

The fact that people learn helplessness in uncontrollable situations is central to the theory of learned helplessness in its original as well as its revised version. If this learning is to have more serious consequences, the outcomes must be important and the individual must expect that they will continue to be uncontrollable. Having to live in a situation in which you cannot control important aspects of your daily life and in which you have little influence over future events may, therefore, have serious effects. At least in our Western society, working life is of central importance to many people. If they cannot control significant aspects of their work and work situation, there is a risk of learned helplessness. As a matter of fact, it was experiences from work environment research that stimulated the interest of our research group in the learned helplessness phenomenon.

SOME EMPIRICAL FINDINGS

In one research project, we used consecutive case studies to investigate the work environment consequences of automation in the engineering industry. Elsewhere, I have summarized our first two cases in the following way (44; see also 45):

> In both cases, the lack of opportunities for influencing working conditions and of acquiring new skills plays a dominant role. The stress observable in the first study was primarily a result of the discrepancy between responsibility and competence. In both studies, the scant opportunities for influence and personal development appear to lead to passivity, lack of interest in problem-solving and depressed mood (resignation, absence of pleasure in work).

As we continued with further case studies in other companies, I hunted for epidemiological data that could be used to test the suggested connection between work and symptoms of learned helplessness. Among the various analyses on working conditions made by or in cooperation with the Swedish Central Bureau of Statistics (SCB), I found two studies that shed light on the problem.

In data from the so-called "Low-Income Survey" (of a large representative sample of the Swedish population), I thus came across some interesting indications (46). Women and men working in "heavy" (hectic and monotonous) jobs stated, respectively, two and four times more frequently than those doing "light" (neither hectic nor monotonous) work that they were prey to moods of deep dejection and depression. Monotonous and hectic work can be assumed to leave little scope for control; it is likely that the worker has few opportunities to influence his or her conditions. Thus, the results were in agreement with the hypothesis. Unfortunately, the data were unsatisfactory in several respects. For example, statements about working conditions as well as various forms of distress were obtained from the same interviews, and no efforts had been made to check for other variables likely to affect the outcome.

The other material was more satisfactory and I will describe it in more detail. The data had been collected and analyzed by Alfredsson, Spetz, and Theorell (47) for the

Government Commission on Medical and Health Care Services for the Nineties. The survey covered persons, 20 to 65 years old at the time of the 1975 population and housing census, who stated that they had some form of occupation and were registered in Stockholm, Uppsala, or the counties of Kopparberg, Gävleborg, and Jämtland (in all, 958,000 persons). Each type of work or occupation was described in a number of variables according to work characteristics extracted from surveys on living conditions made by the SCB between 1977 and 1981 (known as the ULF studies; approximately 10,000 interviews per year).

A follow-up was done to establish which individuals had been inpatients in hospitals during 1976 (inpatient statistics). The occurrences of various diseases among individuals employed in the 50 percent of occupations with the highest ULF-variable values were compared with expected occurrences calculated for the remaining 50 percent (job-variable combinations: individuals in occupations with high values in both variables were compared with those with low values in both). A standard morbidity rate (SMR) was derived by expressing the number of inpatients with a certain diagnosis in the "high-exposure" group as a percentage of the expected value (the number 100 thus meaning that the figures were identical).

Ages were standardized by dividing the sample into five-year intervals. The researchers also analyzed the combined influence of age and 12 other variables (county, type of municipality, civil status, nationality, work period, occupational status, cohabitation, children at home, accommodation, disposable income, smoking, and whether work involved heavy lifting). The data presented in diagrams in the report were limited to variables that, in these analyses of confounding factors, still gave significant differences.

Using the stress paradigm as their basis, the authors of the original report were especially interested in diagnostic groups such as those with cardiac, stomach, and intestinal diseases. The report also contained other diagnoses, for instance, attempted suicide. The authors noted the many high SMR values for this diagnosis but offered no interpretation.

My hypotheses can be summarized as follows. Jobs that are characterized by little control, influence, learning, and development entail risks of helplessness learning. If this is the case, there will be an overrepresentation of depression among the workers concerned. Thus, there will be an overrepresentation of attempted suicides. (This does not imply that all people in these jobs learn helplessness, or that all learned helplessness is followed by depression, or that all depressions are caused by learned helplessness, or that all attempted suicides are caused by "helplessness depressions.") Thus, I extracted from the report the job variables with the highest SMR values for attempted suicides and ranked them as shown in Table 1. The column for men is headed by the variable "little scope for learning." Here the SMR is as high as 244; i.e., the frequency of attempted suicide in the "exposed" group is 2.44 times higher than expected. Ranked third through sixth for men are "hectic work and little scope for learning," "little influence over own planning," "monotonous work," and "few opportunities of attending courses." This sounds very much like a job description implying major risks of helplessness learning. The other two variables in the column for men are indicative of physically demanding jobs. For women, we find high SMR values for "hectic and monotonous work," "hectic and sweaty work," "hectic work and heavy

Table 1

Inpatient treatment for attempted suicide
(highest SMR values for various work characteristics)[a]

Work characteristics (ULF)[b]	SMR value	
	Men	Women
Little scope for learning	244	–
Hectic and monotonous work	–	234
Heavy lifting	225	–
Hectic work and little scope for learning	215	–
Little influence over own planning	212	–
Monotonous work	198	151
Few opportunities of attending courses	195	–
Hectic work and heavy lifting	190	162
Hectic and sweaty work	–	178

[a]Source: reference 47. SMR, standard morbidity rate.
[b]Extracted from surveys on living conditions conducted by the Swedish Central Bureau of Statistics between 1977 and 1981 (the ULF studies).

lifting," and "monotonous work." Physically demanding work may be a very heavy burden to women doing a lot of housework, but I will refrain from further speculation (outside my original hypothesis) on the SMR values for women.

Although the material used here is of considerably higher quality for my purpose than that of the Low-Income Survey, it may nevertheless contain unknown sources of error (e.g., selection effects), and it may be open to other interpretations. At the very least, there is a noteworthy indication that the learned helplessness hypothesis may apply to men in working life. If the results are valid, the high SMR rates are alarming. There is a strong need for further research.

CONCLUSIONS

Learned helplessness research during the last few decades has made important contributions to our understanding of the influence of learning on the interaction between humans and the environment. The theories have implications for many problems in our society, examples of which are sometimes cited by researchers. Apart from clinical studies, however, empirical research has usually been confined to traditional laboratory experiments. This is perhaps natural, considering the "paradigmatic" roots. But significant aspects of people's lives cannot be simulated in the laboratory. Attempts to devise more and more refined laboratory designs may lead to a situation in which we move farther and farther away from real-world concerns. If we are to gain better knowledge about learned helplessness in the real world, we must design and do field research. Future research must move back to reality.

The theory of learned helplessness was first formulated in terms of learning. The reformulation shifted the emphasis to attribution. These two processes are of course related. But the reformulation also meant that individual instead of environmental factors came into focus. If we are engaged in applied research with the aim of producing knowledge about the conditions (e.g., in work) that are favorable to human beings, I believe that we should move this focus back to learning (human learning, not only conditioning). Important work environment questions will then follow. What circumstances in the work situations entail risks for helplessness learning? How can we counteract these risks with environmental measures? And how about favorable conditions for mastery effects?

In research on the conditions of working life, such questions as learning, development, autonomy, and influence (i.e., controllability) have long been of interest to many researchers. I need only mention Maslow's hierarchy of needs (48), the two-factor theory of Herzberg and associates (49), Argyris's organizational mix (50), Kornhauser's studies of the relations between working conditions and mental health (51), French's theory of self-esteem and health (52), McGregor's theory X and theory Y (53), and, in Sweden, Gardell's and Westlander's studies of the impact of working conditions (54, 55). All of these showed the significance of work content and organization for learning and development, and for well-being and health. These conditions were also of central importance in the Scandinavian experiments with new forms of work organization beginning around 1970; the corresponding research was often based on alienation theories (56) and on sociotechnical designs (57-59). In this connection, we may also note the similarities between learned helplessness and the alienative feelings of powerlessness and meaninglessness (cf. 60).

In psychological research on the work environment, stress theories have had a central position during the late 1970s and the early 1980s. This research is based on a strain paradigm. But the importance of controllability (freedom of action and influence) has also been amply demonstrated by this research (61-67). During the 1980s, the so-called "qualification research," mainly by German researchers, has attracted growing interest (68, 69). Here, the cognitive content of work has been given special attention in the theories of mental regulation (70, 71). These theories start with the premise that all work operations have a cognitive aspect. Different jobs, however, afford the worker varying opportunities (work content, freedom of decision) to use and develop his or her abilities. In the United States, the same conclusion has been drawn by Kohn (72) on the basis of his long and extensive research on work and secondary socialization. In Kohn's terminology, the substantive complexity of work is of vital importance to personality development.

These research traditions all have implicit connections to theories of learned helplessness (cf. 44, 73). This concept, however, is rarely mentioned by work environment researchers. There are some exceptions (74-77), but the learned helplessness model is not used in empirical research.

The main criticism in this chapter bears upon some features of the revised theoretical formulations and, above all, upon the restricted empirical tradition. In my view, research in working life should be well suited to the testing of learned helplessness hypotheses. And, more important, the theory of learned helplessness could generate valuable research if applied and adapted to the work environment field. The conditions at work that are thought to be favorable to development and personality growth are usually described as the antithesis of those assumed to imply a risk of learned helplessness (competence learning versus helplessness learning). It is important that future research take into account both negative and positive factors. We need more research on how people learn about influence and control; i.e., how they learn about those forces that act upon their lives and about how they can gain control over present and future circumstances and thus avoid helplessness. As I have suggested elsewhere (44), perhaps we need a new generic term to cover this whole area, for example, research about influence learning.

REFERENCES

1. Overmier, J. S., and Seligman, M. Effects of inescapable shock upon subsequent escape and avoidance learning. *J. Appl. Comp. Physiol. Psychol.* 63: 23–33, 1967.
2. Seligman, M., and Maier, S. F. Failure to escape traumatic shock. *J. Exp. Psychol.* 74: 1–9, 1967.
3. Seligman, M. *Helplessness–On Depression, Development and Death.* Freeman, San Francisco, 1975.
4. Richter, C. P. On the phenomenon of sudden death in animals and man. *Psychosom. Med.* 19: 191–198, 1957.
5. Hiroto, D. S. Locus of control and learned helplessness. *J. Exp. Psychol.* 102: 187–193, 1974.
6. White, R. W. Motivation reconsidered: The concept of competence. *Psychol. Rev.* 66: 297–333, 1959.
7. Beck, A. T. *Depression–Clinical, Experimental, and Theoretical Aspects.* Harper & Row, New York, 1967.
8. Beck, A. T., et al. *Cognitive Therapy of Depression.* Guilford, New York, 1979.
9. Abramson, L. Y., Seligman, M., and Teasdale, J. D. Learned helplessness in humans: Critique and reformulation. *J. Abnorm. Psychol.* 87: 49–74, 1978.
10. Peterson, C., and Seligman, M. Causal explanations as a risk factor for depression: Theory and evidence. *Psychol. Rev.* 91: 347–374, 1984.
11. Heider, F. *The Psychology of Interpersonal Relations.* Wiley, New York, 1958.
12. Weiner, B. *Theories of Motivation: From Mechanism to Cognition.* Rand McNally, Chicago, 1972.
13. Rotter, J. B. Generalized expectancies for internal vs. external control of reinforcement. *Psychol. Monographs* 80: 609, 1966.
14. Försterling, F. Attributional retraining: A review. *Psychol. Bull.* 98: 495–512, 1985.
15. Lefcourt, H. M. *Locus of Control–Current Trends in Theory and Research.* Wiley, New York, 1976.
16. Lefcourt, H. M. (ed.). *Research with Locus of Control Construct.* Academic Press, New York, 1981.
17. Costello, C. A critical review of Seligman's laboratory experiments on learned helplessness and depression in humans. *J. Abnorm. Psychol.* 87: 21–31, 1978.
18. Depue, R. A., and Monroe, S. M. Learned helplessness in the perspective of the depressive disorders: Conceptual and definitional issues. *J. Abnorm. Psychol.* 87: 3–20, 1978.
19. Buchwald, A. M., Coyne, J. C., and Cole, C. S. A critical evaluation of the learned helplessness model of depression. *J. Abnorm. Psychol.* 87: 180–193, 1978.
20. Wortman, C. B., and Dintzer, L. Is an attributional analysis of the learned helplessness phenomenon viable?: A critique of the Abramson-Seligman-Teasdale reformulation. *J. Abnorm. Psychol.* 87: 75–90, 1978.
21. Seligman, M. Comment and integration. *J. Abnorm. Psychol.* 87: 165–179, 1978.
22. Abramson, L. Y., Garber, J., and Seligman, M. Learned helplessness in humans: An attributional analysis. In *Human Helplessness–Theory and Applications*, edited by J. Garber and M. Seligman, pp. 3–34. Academic Press, New York, 1980.
23. Silver, R. L., Wortman, C. B., and Klos, D. S. Cognitions, affect, and behavior following uncontrollable outcomes: A response to current helplessness research. *J. Personality* 50: 480–514, 1982.
24. Coyne, J. C., and Gotlib, I. H. The role of cognition in depression: A critical appraisal. *Psychol. Bull.* 94: 472–505, 1983.
25. Brewin, C. R. Depression and causal attribution: What is their relation? *Psychol. Bull.* 98: 297–309, 1985.

26. Garber, J., and Seligman, M. (eds.). *Human Helplessness–Theory and Applications.* Academic Press, New York, 1980.
27. Kelley, H., and Michela, J. Attribution theory and research. *Ann. Rev. Psychol.* 31: 457–501, 1980.
28. Lund, L. G. *Mind and Reasoning.* Uppsala University, Uppsala, 1983.
29. Harvey, J., and Weary, G. Current issues in attribution theory and research. *Ann. Rev. Psychol.* 35: 427–459, 1984.
30. Pasahow, R. J., West, S. G., and Borota, D. R. Predicting when uncontrollability will produce performance deficits: A refinement of the reformulated learned helplessness hypothesis. *Psychol. Rev.* 89: 595–598, 1982.
31. Mineka, S., and Henderson, R. W. Controllability and predictability in acquired motivation. *Ann. Rev. Psychol.* 36: 459–529, 1985.
32. deCharms, R., and Muir, M. S. Motivation: Social approaches. *Ann. Rev. Psychol.* 29: 91–113, 1978.
33. Weiner, B. An attributional theory of achievement motivation and emotion. *Psychol. Rev.* 92: 548–573, 1985.
34. Strickland, B. R. Internal-external expectancies and health-related behaviors. *J. Consult. Clin. Psychol.* 46: 1192–1211, 1978.
35. Krumboltz, J., Becker-Haven, J., and Burnett, K. Counselling psychology. *Ann. Rev. Psychol.* 30: 555–602, 1979.
36. Phillips, J., and Bierman, K. Clinical psychology: Individual methods. *Ann. Rev. Psychol.* 32: 405–438, 1981.
37. Rosenhan, D. L., and Seligman, M. *Abnormal Psychology.* Norton, New York, 1984.
38. Fisher, S. Control and blue collar work. In *Job Stress and Blue Collar Work,* edited by C. L. Cooper, pp. 19–48. Wiley, Chichester, U.K., 1985.
39. Oatley, K., and Bolton, W. A social-cognitive theory of depression in reaction to life events. *Psychol. Rev.* 92: 372–388, 1985.
40. Strauss, J. S. Social and cultural influences on psychopathology. *Ann. Rev. Psychol.* 30: 397–415, 1979.
41. Oakes, W. F., and Curtis, N. Learned helplessness: Not dependent upon cognitions, attributions or other such phenomenal experiences. *J. Personality* 50: 387–408, 1982.
42. Tennan, H. et al. Learned helplessness and detection of contingency: A direct test. *J. Personality* 50: 426–442, 1982.
43. Tennan, H., Gillen, R., and Drum, P. E. The debilitating effect of exposure to noncontingent escape: A test of the learned helplessness model. *J. Personality* 50: 409–425, 1982.
44. Lennerlöf, L. Learning at work. In *Learning and Socialization at the Workplace,* edited by H. Kornbluh and H. Leymann, 1989.
45. Lennerlöf, L. *Automatisering och Människor.* Liber, Stockholm, 1984.
46. Sundbom, L. *De Förvärvsarbetandes Arbetsplatsförhållanden.* Allmänna förlaget, Stockholm, 1971.
47. Alfredsson, L., Spetz, C. L., and Theorell, T. *Arbetsmiljö–yrke–utnyttjande av sluten vård.* SOU,41. Liber, Stockholm, 1984.
48. Maslow, A. H. *Motivation and Personality.* Harper, New York, 1954.
49. Herzberg, F., Mausner, B., and Snyderman, B. *The Motivation to Work.* Wiley, New York, 1959.
50. Argyris, C. *Integrating the Individual and the Organization.* Wiley, New York, 1964.
51. Kornhauser, A. *Mental Health of the Industrial Worker.* Wiley, New York, 1965.
52. French, J. The conceptualization and measurement of mental health in terms of self-identity theory. In *The Definition and Measurement of Mental Health,* edited by S. B. Sells, pp. 136–159. U.S. Department of Health, Education and Welfare, Washington, D.C., 1968.
53. McGregor, D. *The Professional Manager.* McGraw-Hill, New York, 1967.
54. Gardell, B., and Westlander, G. *Om Industriarbete och Mental Hälsa.* PArådet, Stockholm, 1968.
55. Westlander, G. *Arbete och Livssituation.* PArådet, Stockholm, 1976.
56. Blauner, R. *Alienation and Freedom.* Chicago University Press, Chicago, 1964.
57. Thorsrud, E., and Emery, F. *Medinflytande och Engagemang i Arbetet.* Utvecklingsrådet, Stockholm, 1969.
58. Gardell, B. *Produktionsteknik och Arbetsglädje.* PArådet, Stockholm, 1971.
59. Hansson, R. *Advances in Work Organization.* Organization for Economic Cooperation and Development, Paris, 1973.
60. Seeman, M. Alienation motifs in contemporary theorizing: The hidden continuity of the classical themes. *Soc. Psychol. Q.* 46: 171–184, 1983.

61. Frankenhaeuser, M. Coping with job stress: A psychobiological approach. In *Working Life*, edited by B. Gardell and G. Johansson, pp. 213-233. Wiley, Chichester, U.K., 1981.
62. Karasek, R. A. Job socialization and job strain: The implications of two related psychosocial mechanisms for job design. In *Working Life*, edited by B. Gardell and G. Johansson, pp. 75-94. Wiley, Chichester, U.K., 1981.
63. Levi, L. *Preventing Work Stress.* Addison-Wesley, Reading, Mass., 1981.
64. Levi, L. Work, stress and health. *J. Work Environ. Health* 10: 495-500, 1984.
65. Johansson, G. Computer technology: Stress and health relevant transformation of psychosocial work environments. In *Human-Computer Interaction*, edited by G. Salvendy, pp. 347-354. Elsevier, Amsterdam, 1984.
66. Aronsson, G. (ed.). *Arbetets Krav och Mänsklig Utveckling.* Prisma, Stockholm, 1983.
67. Aronsson, G. *Arbetsinnehåll–Handlingsutrymme–Stressreaktioner.* Stockholm University, Psychology Department, Stockholm, 1985.
68. Kern, H., and Schumann, M. *Industriarbeit und Arbeiterbewusstsein.* Europäischer Verlagsanstalt, Frankfurt AM, 1970.
69. Haug, F., et al. *Theorien über Automationsarbeit.* Argument-Verlag, Berlin, 1978.
70. Hacker, W., Volpert, W., and von Cranach, M. (eds.). *Kognitive und motivationale Aspekte der Handlung.* Huber, Bern, 1983.
71. Volpert, W. Psychische Regulation von Arbeitstätigkeiten. In *Enzyklopädie der Psychologie, Arbetspsychologie*, edited by J. Rutenfranz and U. Kleibeck. Hogrefe, Göttingen, 1986.
72. Kohn, M. Work complexity and the adult personality. In *Themes of Work and Love in Adulthood*, edited by N. Smelser and E. Erikson, pp. 193-210. Harvard University Press, Cambridge, Mass., 1980.
73. Lennerlöf, L. Psychology at work–Behaviour science in work environment research. *Int. Rev. Appl. Psychol.* 35: 79-99, 1986.
74. Frese, M. Partialisierte Handlung und Kontrolle; Zwei Theman der industrieller Psychopathologie. In *Industrielle Psychopathologie*, edited by M. Frese, S. Greif, and N. Semmer, pp. 159-183. Huber, Bern, 1978.
75. Peterson, B. *Psykiska Störningar hos Arbetare–utifrån Seligmans Teori om Kontroll.* Stockholm University, Psychology Department, Stockholm, 1982.
76. Peterson, B. Mänsklig hjälplöshet i arbetslivet. *Kritisk Psykologi* 82: 45-56, 1982.
77. Peterson, B. Arbetslöshet och inlärd hjälplöshet. *Kritisk Psykologi* 83: 23-36, 1983.

CHAPTER 6

Gender, Work Control, and Stress: A Theoretical Discussion and an Empirical Test

Ellen M. Hall

What does working mean to women? Do women have the same types of experiences as men do when they enter the world of work? Is job stress the same for both sexes? What sort of patterns of stress and illness might be observed if we examined class and sex simultaneously? Although this chapter will address these questions, it cannot fully answer them. However, by focusing on a critical facet of the psychosocial work environment for both men and women—work control—I hope to shed light on the gender differences in the relationship between occupational stress and health. By looking at control we may understand something of the larger structures of power and the patterns of individual efficacy that are present in blue- and white-collar, male and female workers. If it is evident that both the availability of work control and the opportunities for occupational selection are not similarly accessible to members of both sexes, then we might have reason to expect differential patterns of response, *including* mental and physical health effects, which reflect this differential exposure to the comparative deprivation or abundance of social resources. Heretofore most research on occupational control and stress has been confined to male subjects; in fact, a great deal is known about the stress and health of men of several different nationalities and occupations, while remarkably less is known about these matters in women.

The first part of this chapter evaluates—in the context of the scientific literature on work stress—why and how the research on women and work has been, and continues to be, supernumerary to that on men. Furthermore, we address why this deficiency may pose important challenges to etiological inference and to the various conclusions that have been drawn by the mainstream of stress research. Next, we will empirically

This work was supported by the Swedish Work Environment Fund and the U.S. National Heart, Lung and Blood Institute.

examine a large representative sample of the total Swedish workforce. This sample provides an empirical basis to examine the differential distribution of work control as a function of gender, class, and sex-segregation within an advanced, socially progressive, industrial society. For example, we can observe what has been reported by those women who work in jobs that are traditionally occupied by men, as well as learn what men report who work as nurses and maids. We will further evaluate the truth of the conventional wisdom that women will replicate the occupational stress patterns of men merely by entering the labor force.

OCCUPATION AND GENDER

The research on women and work stress is dichotomized between the larger literature that emphasizes gender or role and a handful of studies that feature occupational concerns. This pattern is consistent with that found in most of the literature on women's occupational health. With some notable exceptions (1-3), women have been neglected as subjects in the mainstream of occupational health research, *except* as relevant to those particular areas where women differ from men, such as different levels of endurance and strength, different reproductive systems, and so forth (4). Likewise, investigations of women's working lives have been used in deeply contradictory ways: to argue for protection and to impose exclusion; to agitate for more and better child care, or to keep women at home to "meet their family responsibilities"; to emphasize or to disregard reproductive capability; to suggest that the workplace should treat every employee fairly, and to insist that women cannot expect the same rewards as men. A frequently heard argument of the 1960s and 1970s used as a rationale for not permitting women into the labor market was: "you are taking a job away from a man who has a family to support and you women don't have this responsibility." Now, ironically, a reason proposed by some for not promoting or advancing women is that women *do* have families to support and therefore cannot be taken seriously as workers, because they are "on the Mommy track" (5).

Much of the literature on gender and stress is part of a larger tradition that is based on the often unconscious assumption that as regards matters pertaining to employment, males are the "gold standard" against which women are to be compared. Women are investigated in relation to their biological, structural, and psychosocial differences relative to men. The unconscious logic of this comparison serves to perpetuate the subordinate position of women. One is tempted, given the number and the biological hardiness of women, to wonder what sort of science and policy would exist if we assumed that women were the norm, and men were defined as atypical. Unions, employers, and policy makers might then have cause to debate whether it was time for occupational standards that took men's "particular problems" into account—such as a higher rate of mortality in every age group compared with women. We might provoke a heated social debate about the need for a "Daddy track," and so forth.

One example of how women are evaluated in terms of their ability to measure up to men is the current scientific debate on the question: will the increased entry of women in the labor force mean that the favorable mortality rates observed in women change as a result of this new exposure to occupational stress? Several troubling assumptions are implied in the way in which this inquiry is posed:

1. Occupational stress is assumed to be synonymous with *men's* stress.
2. Disease-producing stress is presumed to be largely confined to men's work experiences.
3. It is exposure to workplace stress that accounts for the higher mortality (notably from cardiovascular disease) observed in men than in women.
4. Women who are not engaged in paid employment are not subject to disease-producing stress.
5. By entering the labor market women will have a similar experience to that of men, and presumably women who are now engaged in paid employment are subject to the same stresses as men.
6. This similarity in occupational experience will produce a *new* pattern of disease in women, which is comparable with that observed in men.

In fact, the scientific evidence suggests that women have not yet succumbed to "men's stress" through their entry into the workforce. A widely cited study by Passannante and Nathanson (6) on the increasing involvement of women in the labor force and male and female mortality differentials in the Wisconsin labor force (1974-84) indicates that the mortality differential is not negatively affected by female labor force participation. Only among single labor force participants (aged 55-59) and single clerical workers (aged 55-59) were the female death rates found to be higher than for males and significantly different. Relative to housewives, the death rates for female labor force participants due to heart disease were higher for laborers and sales workers. These findings were essentially confirmed by Kotler and Wingard (7) who found that neither employment status, nor type of employment, nor increasing number of children among employed women predicted elevated mortality risk, although increasing children in the home did elevate the risk in single working mothers.

Exceptions to the more general neglect of women's occupational stress are the various studies performed by Haynes, LaCroix, Feinleib, and Kannel (8-11) who have used the Framingham Heart Study to evaluate the impact of women's work on cardiovascular disease. Although other researchers have looked at mixed and female populations (12-14), the Framingham data represent the major study to date that has used a prospective as opposed to cross-sectional design and has focused on a physical health outcome. These investigators have compared employed women with housewives and have found that there is more type A behavior, more daily stress, and more marital dissatisfaction in employed women than in housewives. However, housewives and working women were found to have the same incidence of coronary heart disease (CHD). In comparing white-collar professionals with blue-collar workers, no elevation in risk was observed. The occupation at greatest risk was found to be female clerical workers with major domestic responsibilities and a punitive or restrictive psychosocial work environment. The facets of home and work that were associated with higher rates of CHD were decreased job mobility, repressed hostility, and having the combination of a nonsupportive boss, children, and a blue-collar husband. None of the usual risk factors (smoking, age, blood pressure, serum cholesterol) were associated with CHD in these clerical workers. In short, several studies that are specifically concerned with the physical health of working women indicate that working does not appear to be *in and of itself* harmful to women.

The majority of related research studies have focused on questions of the psychological impact of the increasing number of roles that many women are now occupying (15-20). Although there is an extensive literature on the issue of multiple roles and psychological health, few studies have linked "role stress" to major physical health outcomes, such as CHD (14, 20). Similarly, attitudinal research also includes studies of how husbands and children experience or react to having a wife or mother who is also a working person (21-26). One critical reason why this type of stress research is predominantly performed within a psychological context is discussed by Aneshensel and Pearlin (27, pp. 75-76):

> Research on gender and stress has evolved largely from attempts to account for differences between women and men in psychological distress . . . the investigation of the stress process among women has been entered into through the back door. Starting with the presumed outcome—gender differences in psychological distress—stress researchers have sought to identify differences in the stress producing circumstances of men's and women's lives that might account for the differences in their distress.

By contrast, occupational stress research on men has involved markedly different methods and has, moreover, a rather different set of intellectual *origins*. The preponderance of studies have been generated by biomedically oriented researchers who have concentrated on physiological responses and physical health outcomes. Since the early work of Cannon (28) in the 1920s, this research tradition spans much of the 20th century and has involved the investment of tremendous intellectual, technical, institutional, and financial resources to address the problems of defining and elaborating the influence of stress on health and disease. Studies that are particularly relevant to occupational stress are voluminous and include clinical, laboratory, field, and large-scale epidemiological investigations as well as cross-cultural research. From this research we discover that male subjects have been evaluated in almost exhaustive detail, such that scientists can delineate the importance of any number of different variables (independent, intervening, and dependent) that might occur in a variety of occupational settings. The literature on men spans a wide variety of *occupations*, such as medicine and bus driving; *class characteristics,* such as civil service grade and blue-/white-collar; *physical stressors,* such as noise and temperature; and *ergonomic and psychosocial factors,* such as shiftwork, time pressure, social isolation, and over- and understimulation. It also ranges over a broad array of outcomes including immunological effects, catecholamine excretion, blood pressure, risk of cardiovascular disease, and so forth (28-31). The results from these studies are the basis for much of the conventional wisdom about the "stress-health" paradigm (29-31). Yet out of this vast literature and even in critiques of its methodological weaknesses (32, 33) there is little mention of the threats to validity posed by single-sex studies. We nevertheless do suspect that the field may suffer from several methodological flaws.

Biological Plausibility

Collins, Frankenhaeuser, and their colleagues (34-39) at the University of Stockholm have performed laboratory and clinical investigations of sex differences in psychoneuroendocrine stress responses. There is rather persuasive data suggesting that women and men react differently to stress under the same experimental conditions. (Women appear to be less reactive, in terms of adrenaline excretion, in response to stress, but to interpret their performance more negatively than men.) As noted by Collins, very little is known, unfortunately, about the basic physiological relationships between reproductive cycling (e.g., menstrual phase, reproductive status) and neuro-hormonal arousal, and even less is known about how these interactions might be related to blood pressure, heart rate, and other biological pathways that lead from stress to cardiovascular disease. Because of the marked differences between men's and women's physiological systems, and the marked differences in morbidity and mortality from cardiovascular illness, there is not sufficient evidence to make the assumption that the biological pathways leading from occupational stress to heart disease are the same in both sexes.

Incomplete Theoretical Models and Generalizability

Owing to the preponderance of empirical research, not surprisingly, the major theories concerning the work, stress, and health relationship have been primarily developed and tested on males. Several different theories about stress predict reasonably well in blue-collar populations. The person-environment fit theory has provided the theoretical orientation for much of the research performed in the United States over the past several decades. More recently, the demand-control or job strain model, developed by Karasek and others (40-43), has gained increased ascendancy as the model of preference to be used in social epidemiological investigations. Although there is considerable empirical support for both of these theoretical orientations, both can be said to have undergone a similar process of evolution resulting in instruments for measuring stress that have been "calibrated" or standardized on men. This being the case, changes either in the research population to include women or in the stress measurement instrument to include issues germane to women's work may produce changes in the results obtained. For example, results in studies of occupational stress will probably shift if we change the inventory used to reflect problems that occur particularly in women's work lives (such as sexual harassment) or that are oriented toward typical women's work (such as nursing and teaching, which often involve stressful contacts with other people). Men would probably not report sexual harassment as a problem, but failure to test for harassment might mean that a major source of occupational stress has not been investigated in the total working population. The stress of responsibility for other people may not be a major stress in the lives of many men, but again, failure to consider it may pose a threat to the overall generalizability of certain studies to the entire working population. Given the status of the current research, we cannot generalize across occupations, because of the high degree of sex segregation, and we cannot generalize across individuals, because such a large proportion of the adult population has been excluded from most samples.

These problems prompt one to consider a point made by Cassel (44) many years ago: that we do not know whether particular stressors affect all people in the same manner, or whether they are idiosyncratic, affecting different people in varying ways. If one maintains the idiosyncratic point of view, then there is no cause to evaluate the systemic determinants of occupational stress.

Stress research is now impaled on the horns of this particular dilemma. The double standard is a characteristic of occupational stress research. Women workers are investigated with reference to their idiosyncracies, placed in context and understood developmentally and emotionally. Studies of male workers are performed without reference to and without a *need for reference to* leisure time activities, marital status, family structure, or emotional conflicts. For one sex, we are unconcerned with context, emotions, or developmental phases, and for the other sex, these matters are determining the research agenda. Although many of us may be personally disposed toward a research approach that includes idiosyncratic matters and reference to a developmental context, the fact remains that a foundation of basic, structurally orientated, empirically sound research on the occupational conditions of women remains to be performed.

GENDER AND WORK CONTROL

As many of the chapters in this book point out, perhaps the most critical aspect of the psychosocial work environment is control over the work process. Control is one of the most thoroughly investigated variables in the occupational stress literature. That the lack of control causes or contributes to stress is widely agreed upon by researchers who might otherwise be divided as to their theoretical emphasis on "the person" or on "the environment." There is scientific consensus that when humans or other animals are subject to lack of control, in conjunction with repeated, aversive stimuli, there will be a measurable biochemical and/or psychological response that can eventually result in mental and physical illness. The importance of the concept of work control is evident in the work of stress researchers such as Bertil Gardell (45, 46), and it is a theme that is interwoven throughout many of the chapters in this book, dedicated to his memory.

Control is also of importance because it has implications with respect to the general social efficacy of women. This is proposed because working (as a wage earner) is a major vehicle for adult socialization. Within the context of a working subculture, individuals and groups learn ways of being in the world and establish their adult identity. Thus after 10 to 20 years of working in any given occupation, individuals come to know and value themselves (and to present themselves to others) on the basis of occupational identification (I am a teacher, a computer programmer, a machinist, etc.). In examining the distribution of control in a sample of a total society, we may conjecture that there are individual, internally perceived, as well as external, structurally apparent aspects to the experience of control. Those in jobs that permit very little control cannot help but be aware that this lack of control is a reflection of social value. Certainly, jobs with the highest degree of control are nearly always those with the highest social status, and those with low control are of low social status.

We now turn to an empirical examination of the distribution of work control in various occupational groups in order to address the question of whether the experience of working life may differ as a function of sex and class.

RESEARCH METHODS

Study Sample

The conduct of our larger study on work, stress, and health has been extensively described elsewhere (43, 47–49). The data used are the Swedish Central Bureau of Statistics' (SCB) Survey of Living Conditions ("ULF" in Swedish). The ULF is the major social accounting system that is used to investigate the distribution of social resources, such as health, income, work environment, education, and housing. The ULF relies on objective data rather than subjective wishes, opinions, and attitudes. The survey data are collected in a one-hour personal interview. Our subsample of 13,203 subjects consisted of employed persons from the ages of 16 to 65; 50.6 percent were males and 49.4 percent females. This is equivalent to the rates for male/female labor participation in Sweden. The sample was further divided, based on the SCB criteria, into blue-collar (i.e., production, distribution, and service employees, 53.8 percent) and white-collar (office and professional employees, 46.2 percent).

Measurement

Work control was measured by an additive scale, consisting of a linear composite of the following items, which were scored according to whether the subject had never [1], sometimes [2], or often [3] had any of the following:

- Influence over the planning of work
- Influence over the setting of the work pace
- Influence over how time is used in work
- Influence over the selection of supervisor
- Influence over the selection of coworkers
- Influence over the planning of work breaks
- Influence over the planning of vacations
- Flexible working hours
- Varied task content
- Varied work procedures
- The possibility of learning new things
- The experience of personal fulfillment on the job

For the total study group, scores ranged from 12 to 36 with a mean of 23.73. The standard deviation was 4.78; scores were normally distributed. The Cronbach's alpha for the scale was .74.

Previous researchers using instruments similar to this one have not examined potential sex and class differences in the internal covariance structure of the scale. In order to do this, a principal component factor analysis with orthogonal rotation was performed, first for the total population, and then by subgroups for blue-collar males and females and for white-collar males and females. For the total sample and for each of the four subgroups, a similar factor structure was observed, with a nearly identical pattern of inter-item covariation. This supports the view that a common "control" domain exists, and allows for meaningful group comparisons. The subgroup Cronbach's alpha levels remained within an acceptable range, with a coefficient of .71 for blue-collar males, .65 for blue-collar females, .69 for white-collar males, and .62 for white-collar females.

Occupational categories were defined by using the three-digit Nordic Job Classification system. In order to measure sex segregation a variable was constructed by first observing the relative proportions of males and females within each of the 244 occupations represented in the study sample. Sex segregation was defined in relation to the proportion of females employed in these various occupations. The scores on the sex-segregation variable are expressed in terms of deciles, with the first decile representing occupations in which 90 to 100 percent of those employed are women, and decile 10 representing occupations in which 90 to 100 percent of the subjects are men. Intermediate levels were assigned decile scores based on the relative proportion of males and females in each. The sex-segregation variable was further simplified by constructing three categories: (a) female-segregated occupations are defined as those with 80 to 100 percent females, n = 5,284; (b) male-segregated occupations are those with 80 to 100 percent males, n = 5,394; and (c) gender-integrated occupations are those containing no more than 70 percent of either sex, n = 2,525.

The data were analyzed with the Statistical Analysis System (50); t-tests for mean differences in levels of control between various study groups were performed. One-, two-, and three-way analysis of variance using biological age as a covariate was used to examine differences in control within the sex-segregated subsample (i.e., categories a and b above, n = 10,678) across a variety of gender, class, and sex-segregation groups. The specific form of the estimable function used in the analysis adjusts for unequal cell frequencies and is not entry order dependent, resulting in a model solution where all terms are simultaneously adjusted for the effects of each other (51). Sex-class-segregation specific group means and 95 percent confidence intervals were calculated using the least-squares estimates of marginal means adjusted for unbalanced design (50, 51).

RESULTS

Occupational Sex Segregation

The distribution of the working population was examined within varying deciles of the sex-segregation variable described above. To clarify, each decile is based on the proportion of males and females within the various occupations represented in the sample. Figure 1 presents the relative proportion of individuals in the sample who are employed within each sex-segregation decile. The Swedish workforce is highly sex-segregated; nearly 30 percent of women and 30 percent of men are in occupations that are composed of 90 to 100 percent of the same sex. Moreover, over 80 percent of the workforce is employed in clearly segregated occupations, dominated by 80 percent or more of the same sex. Those working in gender-integrated occupations (30 to 70 percent of either sex) represent barely 20 percent of the total workforce.

An additional aspect of sex segregation is shown in Figure 2, presenting the number of occupations within each segregation decile. Within the male-segregated portion of the occupational structure (i.e., sex-segregation deciles 9 and 10), there is a much

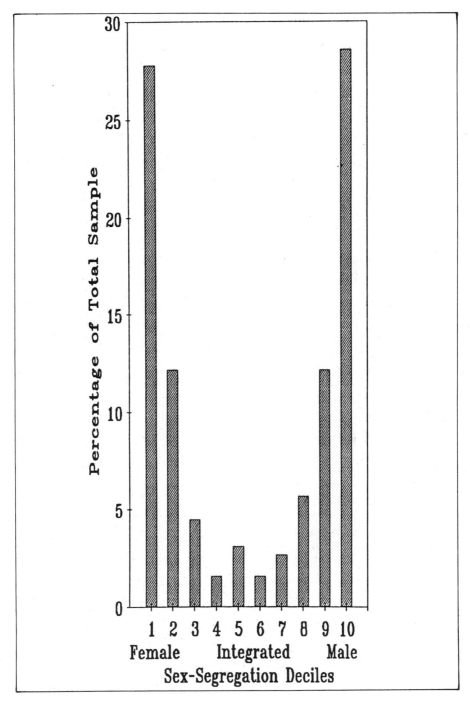

Figure 1. The percentage of the total sample of the Swedish workforce, n = 13,203, in each sex-segregation decile. Each decile represents occupations with varying levels of female subjects, i.e., decile 1 = 90–100 percent females; and by contrast, decile 10 = 90–100 percent males.

greater variety of jobs than in the female-segregated portion of the labor force (i.e., deciles 1 and 2). This would imply, for example, that a young man beginning his occupational career would be able to choose between 119 different job categories. Moreover, later in life, should he decide to change careers, he would have a much larger pool of jobs from which to choose. Conversely a young woman has only 45 occupations from which to choose, less than half of the number of jobs open to men. Although only 20 percent of the workforce is employed in gender-integrated occupations, these jobs represent approximately one third of the total number of job categories.

Thus the types of work experiences available to women appear to be distinctly different from those of men, and there is a narrower range of occupations available for women than for men. Although gender-integrated jobs potentially provide greater diversity to both sexes, they represent a rather small proportion of the labor force (20 percent). Although the finding that women and men are essentially segregated in their occupational lives will not come as a major revelation to many people, it is important with respect to the previously delineated "assumptions" concerning the entry of women into the labor market. Women do not usually enter *male* occupations, therefore we cannot assume that women who enter the workforce gain access to a set of structures, rewards, and pressures similar to those experienced by men. Rather, the above descriptive analysis indicates that women and men continue to inhabit relatively distinct occupational universes, and therefore we have reason to expect that the relationship between occupation, stress, and health status is not likely to be comparable. At a larger structural level, women as a group have less choice and control over the range of occupational possibilities. In short, they have less "life-course control."

Gender Differences in Work Control

In the bivariate analysis there was evidence of sex differences in mean levels of work control. Males were found to have a higher mean level of work control (24.35) than females (23.08), a statistically significant difference ($P < .0001$). The sex-specific levels of work control were examined for men and for women for each of the 244 occupational groups represented in the sample. We were particularly interested in the relative level of control for women in male-segregated occupations, and for men in female-segregated occupations.

The 12 largest occupational categories within female- and male-segregated and gender-integrated occupational sections are presented in Table 1. In general men have a higher level of work control than women. Of the 35 occupational contrasts displayed in Table 1, in 29 of them men have more control than women—even in occupations in which women predominate. Nearly half—13—of these mean comparisons are statistically significant at or near a .05 or borderline (.06) level of probability. In only six occupations do women have more control than men, and only one of these is statistically significant, that of cleaner. Within male-segregated occupations there is the clearest indication of lower levels of work control for women relative to men—a pattern particularly evident in the blue-collar occupations.

Gender, Class, and Work Control

As expected, white-collar workers were found to have a higher mean level of work control (26.01) than did blue-collar workers (21.76), a difference that is statistically

Table 1

Work control in Swedish females and males: Examples of the 12 largest
occupations found in each sex-segregation group

Occupation	Females		Males		P^a
	n	Mean control	n	Mean control	
Female-Segregated Occupations					
Typist	793	24.42	74	25.01	.2159
Nurse orderly	672	22.33	24	23.6	.2794
Cleaner	483	21.19	33	19.75	.0332
Shop assistant	464	22.84	75	25.70	.0000
Bookkeeper	332	24.69	62	25.17	.4029
Nurse maid	283	25.37	6	26.46	.5836
Housekeeper	265	23.71	14	26.46	.3631
Teacher	199	23.63	39	23.51	.7293
Registered nurse	185	25.10	9	26.35	.3380
Kitchen maid	161	20.66	12	19.11	.1630
Cashier	102	20.07	4	23.68	.3725
Waitress	90	20.54	14	23.56	.0641
Gender-Integrated Occupations					
Theory teacher	104	24.39	85	24.18	.5936
Social worker	93	27.3	30	28.6	.0604
Packer	80	17.21	22	19.21	.0259
Psych. attendant	78	23.05	28	25.88	.0025
Lab. technician	66	24.70	16	26.18	.2443
Music teacher	62	24.19	42	24.13	.9201
Electronic assembler	43	18.15	56	22.59	.0000
Business manager	39	28.03	102	29.49	.0121
Postal sorter	36	20.58	75	21.22	.4039
Govt. administrator	30	28.5	116	28.85	.6142
Staff officer	28	28.89	46	29.07	.8137
Physician	18	26.24	42	22.1	.2403
Male-Segregated Occupations					
Toolmaker	65	16.68	281	19.95	.0001
Traveling salesman	56	24.64	220	28.95	.0001
Machine fitter	42	17.26	399	23.15	.0000
Warehouse worker	39	19.51	164	21.56	.0027
Building caretaker	19	25.10	123	25.95	.2999
Welder	13	17.66	129	20.74	.0088
Driver	11	20.39	259	22.18	.1778
Architect	11	28.41	191	27.93	.6133
Mechanical engineer	7	27.20	248	26.7	.8579
Electrical fitter	7	17.76	187	24.65	.0000
Electrical engineer	7	26.12	151	28.02	.2801
Carpenter	0	—	156	22.64	—

[a]Probability associated with t-test for mean differences by sex within each job.

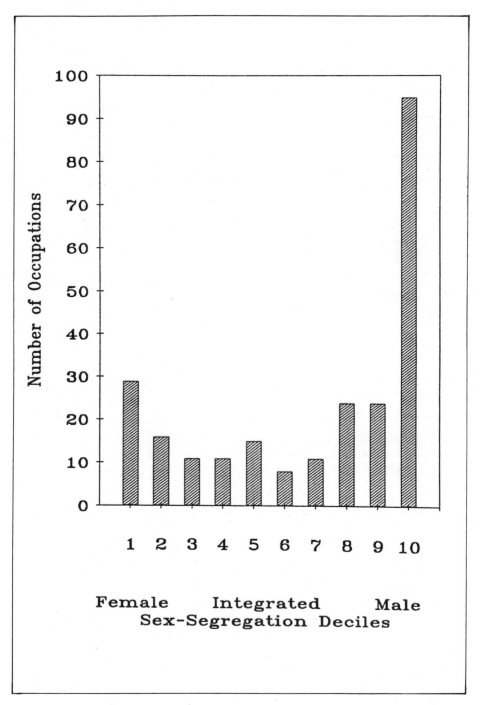

Figure 2. The number of occupational categories in Sweden, n = 244, available within each sex-segregation decile. Each decile represents occupations with varying levels of female subjects, i.e., decile 1 = 90–100 percent females; and by contrast, decile 10 = 90–100 percent males.

significant ($P < .0001$). More importantly there appears to be a substantive interaction of class with sex segregation and gender in relation to the varying levels of work control. Figure 3 presents the mean level of control observed for each combination of class, gender, and sex segregation.

White-collar workers clearly have a greater degree of work control than blue-collar workers. However, women in both white- and blue-collar work have lower levels of control than do men, *even in female-segregated occupations.* This is most notable among blue-collar men in work that is primarily female, who still report more control than do the blue-collar women. The same pattern is evident for white-collar men in female-segregated white-collar work, though the difference is less pronounced. Thus even in occupations that are traditionally "women's work," men continue to report higher levels of control, regardless of class.

The highest levels of work control are found for females in the gender-integrated and male-segregated white-collar occupations: the academic, scientific, managerial, health, and legal professions. Although women continue to have a lower mean level of control than do men in these two categories of sex segregation, it is noticeably higher than for white-collar women in female-segregated occupations. Females in male-segregated and gender-integrated occupations are relatively few in number, however.

The situation of blue-collar women in male-segregated and gender-integrated occupations is quite different from that of white-collar women, for they have the lowest mean level of control observed. Blue-collar women have the highest level of control within their own sex-segregated occupations, a pattern opposite to that found among white-collar females. These interactions of gender, class, and sex segregation clearly distinguish the most advantaged group in terms of work control—white-collar men in traditional male occupations—from the least advantaged—blue-collar females who have entered the world of blue-collar men.

In order to further examine the combined impact of gender, class, and sex segregation, an analysis of variance was performed on that proportion of the labor force employed in sex-segregated occupations. The least-square means based on an analysis of variance model are shown in Table 2. The results are similar to those displayed in Figure 3, i.e., blue-collar females in male-segregated occupations report the lowest level of work control. Moreover, in each of the class by segregation groups, men have a greater mean level of work control than do women—even in jobs that are primarily female. The 95 percent confidence intervals indicate that the mean estimates are, on the whole, significantly different from each other—except in two instances: white-collar females in male-segregated jobs do not have a statistically significant mean difference in work control compared with white-collar males in female-segregated jobs; and blue-collar females in female-segregated jobs have essentially the same amount of work control as blue-collar males in male-segregated jobs. In a t-test for least-square mean differences comparing the eight means with each other, these were the only two mean contrasts that were not found to be significantly different at a .01 probability level.

The analysis of variance model, presented in Table 3, adjusts for the effects of age and accounts for 23 percent of the total variance in the work control variable in the sex-segregated subsample. Sex and class have statistically significant main effects on

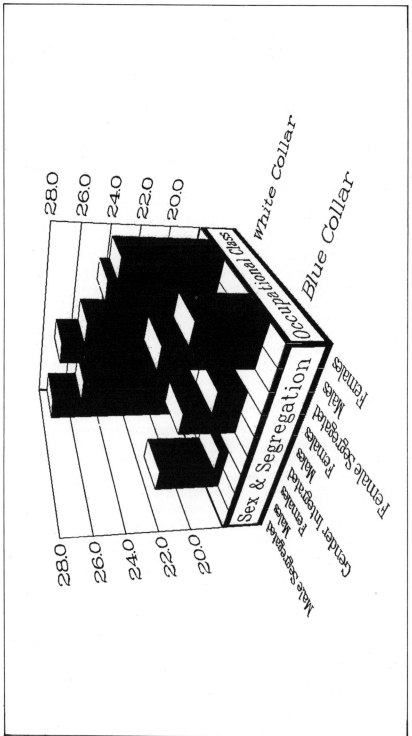

Figure 3. The observed means of work control in a random sample of the Swedish working population, n = 13,203, by sex, class, and sex-segregation group. Male-segregated jobs are those in which 80–100 percent of the subjects are male; female-segregated jobs are those in which 80–100 percent of the subjects are female; and gender-integrated jobs are the remainder.

Table 2

Work control in the sex-segregated Swedish subsample,
n = 10,688: sex-class-segregation group means and 95 percent
confidence intervals[a]

	Mean control (95% CI)[b]	
	White collar	Blue collar
Male-Segregated Jobs		
Males	27.71	22.00
	(27.52–27.90)	(21.86–22.14)
Females	25.72	18.60
	(25.07–26.37)	(18.15–19.05)
Female-Segregated Jobs		
Males	25.02	23.37
	(24.53–25.51)	(22.74–24.00)
Females	24.32	22.20
	(24.15–24.49)	(22.04–22.36)

[a]Least-squares mean estimates, adjusted for age and unequal cell size.
[b]95 percent confidence intervals shown in parentheses.

Table 3

Analysis of variance for work control in the
sex-segregated Swedish subsample, n = 10,688

	f value	P value
Main Effects		
Age (yr)	25.91	0.0001
Sex	172.39	0.0001
(0 = males;		
1 = females)		
Class	2,405.06	0.0000
(0 = white-collar;		
1 = blue-collar)		
Sex segregation	3.74	0.0533
(0 = male-segregated;		
1 = female-segregated)		
Interactions		
Sex × class	10.05	0.0015
Sex × sex segregation	36.34	0.0001
Class × sex segregation	234.33	0.0001
Model R-squared = .23		

the level of work control, and although the sex-segregation main effect variable is of borderline statistical significance ($P = .0533$), it demonstrates its effect through its presence in the significant interaction terms with both sex and class. The model reveals that the relationships between sex, class, segregation, and control are not simply additive, but rather interactive—as the three statistically significant interaction effects indicate. (The three-way analysis of variance interaction term was found not to be statistically significant and was subsequently deleted from the final model reported here.) However, bearing in mind the character of these interactions (i.e., women have the lowest control in *male*-segregated blue-collar jobs), the model indicates that both gender and the condition of sex segregation itself help explain the variance in work control, over and above the effects of age and class.

SUMMARY AND CONCLUSIONS

Before turning to my final remarks, I should mention something of the social context in which this research was performed, i.e., this study is based on a sample of *Swedish* women and men. Sweden has progressive policies on gender equality and on employment (52). Swedish law and tradition provide for full employment for women and men as well as for wage and opportunity equity. The workforce is equally divided by sex, and all workers who perform the same job, regardless of sex, age, the employer, or the location, make the same wage. This "wage solidarity" policy is roughly equivalent to unrealized U.S. proposals to guarantee equal pay for equal work. Extensive paid leave is available for maternity and paternity leave, and there is also guaranteed, paid leave to care for sick children (60 days per year, per child) (53, 54). Part-time work with full social benefits is also common in Sweden. All employed people have at least six weeks paid vacation a year. The government (at the local and the national level) provides an allowance for each child, day care, cradle-to-grave medical care, and education. Women are permitted, under the Swedish Work Environment Act, to take time off from work to breast feed. In short, the situation for women is unusually good in Sweden and the findings reported here may, to some degree, represent a "best case scenario" (52-55).

This chapter began with a critique of the scientific literature on gender and work stress. It is argued that the research to date has focused primarily on the affective and emotional aspects of working and family roles for women. By contrast, work stress researchers have concentrated on the relationship between psychosocial working conditions and the physical health status of working men. However, we continue to be comparatively ignorant about the work-related occupational stresses experienced by women. The assumption has been made, without being explicated, that the work experiences that place males at risk for ill health will function similarly for women. The use of the analogy, i.e., that by entering the labor force women are "becoming" like men, has led to the expectation that the relationship between work, stress, and health observed in men will be replicated among women.

In order to evaluate these assumptions, the present study has concentrated on one element of the psychosocial work environment considered to be crucial in the stress and illness relationship: work control. We have addressed the question of whether the experience and the distribution of work control is similar for men and women. The findings suggest that it is possible to evaluate women's working life without reference to either their marital and parental roles or to their subjective feelings. Even without investigating this socioemotional context, we still find that there are strong differences between the two sexes.

Although the experience of control does appear to be parallel in the four sex and class groups under investigation (as indicated by the results of the principal component factor analysis), there were indications of marked dissimilarities in the amount of control available in these same groups. The findings suggest that the work experience of women in Sweden is different from that of men in five important ways:

1. *Women and men are largely confined to working in jobs that are highly sex-segregated.* This finding has been reported in previous investigations; occupational segregation is common throughout the world, and throughout history as well (52, 53, 55–57). Thus, at work most people are socialized with and by members of their own sex. The topic of adult socialization at work has not been explored in the present investigation, but it may well be that the roots of sex segregation are deeper than had been previously credited.

2. *Women have fewer occupations, of a less diverse character, from which to choose than do men.* The limited career options available to Swedish women are a clear example of how "job discretion latitude" (40) can function at a structural level. We find that women are largely confined to the helping or serving professions, such as nursing, teaching, cleaning, and typing. It is conceivable that women may rotate in and out of the workforce as a way of exercising control when confronted with being structurally confined to the same type of work. There is some measure of freedom and control in being able to quit work rather than to continue reproducing the same type of experience, but at a different level or in a different context. By alternating between home life and work life perhaps some women are able to exercise more latitude with respect to the diversity of the daily life experience.

3. *Women have less control over the content and process of work than do men.* The findings of this study indicate that within both the blue- and white-collar sectors women have less work control than do men. In nearly all of the 244 specific occupations examined, men reported higher levels of control than women.

4. *Women have less work control than do men, even within female-segregated jobs.* For example, male typists, nurses, shop assistants, waiters, and others who work in predominantly female occupations have more control than do women who perform this same type of work. In only one occupation do women have significantly more control than men—cleaning. As a group, blue-collar men in work that is dominated by women report more control than blue-collar women. This is also true for white-collar men working in "women's work."

5. *The study reveals both a statistical and substantive interaction between class and gender in relation to work control.* White-collar workers of both sexes have more control than blue-collar workers. It is the handful of white-collar women in predominantly male work that indicates the possible emergence of a new pattern. The increased entry of women into scientific, managerial, health, and other professions seems to be producing increased control for this white-collar group. However, the blue-collar women in male-segregated occupations are in a markedly worse situation, with the lowest level of control observed in any group. As is evident in the inter-

actions, sex, class, and occupational segregation appear to be a powerful combination of factors that can lead either to the "high road" of white-collar males in traditional men's work or to the "low road" of blue-collar females in the world of blue-collar men.

The findings listed above are of some importance in considering the possible consequences of the entry of women into the labor market. The effects of the job socialization experiences of men cannot be generalized to women. We lack sufficient evidence from which to draw conclusions about the relationship between structural factors at work (such as occupational strain) and the health of women workers. Unfortunately, we still know comparatively little about how the experience of being occupationally channelled affects women, but this may be an excellent way to untangle the relationship that women experience to their work. As pointed out by Aneshensel and Pearlin (27) the source of women's difficulties may be a product of their position within the organization of society as a whole. If one accepts that lack of occupational control and systematic limitations with respect to job and career options might be linked to other, physiological or affective states, then the findings of the present investigation may have several substantial implications. One such ramification is that for many women working life may not necessarily represent an experience of autonomy, freedom, or an opportunity for increased participation in the economic and political life of the society. Furthermore, if larger macro-level factors are complicating or influencing the experience and/or the expression of work stress, then the type of stress that is experienced by women may not be evident when using conventional, occupationally based measures. This more global experience of lack of control may have implications—which represent major challenges in terms of measurement—for the mental and physical health of women.

I hope that the present study and discussion will serve to stimulate an interest in these issues and to encourage others in their research on women, work, and health.

Acknowledgments — I am deeply indebted to the late Professor Bertil Gardell of the University of Stockholm who initially invited me to Sweden and helped sponsor my earlier research. He is sorely missed. I would also like to thank Professors Tores Theorell and Lennart Levi of the Karolinska Institute for their continuing support of my research. Finally, I would like to thank my coworkers, Dr. Jeffrey V. Johnson and Mr. Peeter Fredlund, for their thoughtful suggestions and practical assistance in statistical and computer analysis.

REFERENCES

1. Stellman, J. *Women's Work, Women's Health: Myths and Realities.* Pantheon Books, New York, 1977.
2. Chavik, W. (ed.). *Double Exposure: Women's Health Hazards on the Job and At Home.* Monthly Review Press, New York, 1985.
3. Hricko, A., and Brunt, M. *Working for Your Life: A Woman's Guide to Job Health Hazards.* Labor Occupational Health Program and Public Citizen's Health Research Group, Washington, D.C., 1976.
4. Society for Occupational and Environmental Health. *Proceedings of Conference on Women and the Workplace.* SOEH, Washington, D.C., 1977.

5. Skrzycki, C. 'Mommy track' author answers her many critics. *Washington Post,* March 19, 1988, Section C, p. 1.
6. Passannante, M. R., and Nathanson, C. A. Women in the labor force: Are sex mortality differentials changing? *J. Occup. Med.* 29(1): 21–28, 1987.
7. Kotler, P., and Wingard, D. L. The effect of occupational, marital and parental roles on mortality: The Alameda County study. *Am. J. Public Health* 79: 607–611, 1989.
8. LaCroix, A. Z., and Haynes, S. G. Gender differences in the health effects of workplace roles. In *Gender and Stress,* edited by R. Barnett and G. Baruch, pp. 122–141. Macmillan, New York, 1987.
9. Haynes, S., and Feinleib, M. Women, work and coronary heart disease: Prospective findings from the Framingham heart study. *Am. J. Public Health* 70: 133–141, 1980.
10. Haynes, S., Feinleib, M., and Kannel, W. The relationship of psychological factors to coronary heart disease in the Framingham study (Part III). *Am. J. Epidemiol.* 111(1): 37–58, 1980.
11. LaCroix, A. Z., and Haynes, S. G. Occupational exposure to high demand/low control work and coronary heart disease incidence in the Framingham cohort. Paper presented at the Seventh Annual Meeting of the Society for Epidemiological Research, Houston. [Abstract.] *Am. J. Epidemiol.* 120: 341, 1984.
12. Hibbard, J., and Pope, C. Employment characteristics and health status among men and women. *Women and Health* 12(2): 85–102, 1987.
13. Haw, M. Women, work and stress: A review and agenda for the future. *J. Health Soc. Behav.* 23: 132–144, 1982.
14. Verbrugge, L. M. Multiple roles and physical health of women and men. *J. Health Soc. Behav.* 24: 16–30, 1983.
15. Waldron, I., and Herold, J. Employment, attitudes toward employment, and women's health. *Women and Health* 11(1): 79–98, 1986.
16. Muller, C. Health and health care of employed women and homemakers: Family factors. *Women and Health* 11(1): 7–26, 1986.
17. Barnett, R. C., and Baruch, G. K. Social roles, gender and psychological distress. In *Gender and Stress,* edited by R. Barnett and G. Baruch, pp. 122–141. Macmillan, New York, 1987.
18. Gutek, B. A., Repetti, R. L., and Silver, D. L. Non-work roles and stress at work. In *Causes, Coping and Consequences of Stress at Work,* edited by C. Cooper and R. Payne, pp. 141–175. Wiley, Chichester, 1988.
19. Warr, P., and Parry G. Paid employment and women's psychological well-being. *Psychol. Bull.* 91: 498–516, 1982.
20. Froberg, D., Gjerdingene, W., and Preston, M. Multiple roles and women's mental and physical health: What have we learned. *Women and Health* 11(2): 76–96, 1986.
21. Sekaran, U. *Dual-Career Families.* Jossey-Bass, San Francisco, 1986.
22. Staines, G. L., Pottick, K. J., and Fudge, D. A. Wives' employment attitudes and husbands' attitudes towards work and family. *J. Appl. Psychol.* 71: 118–128, 1986.
23. Osherman, S., and Dill, D. Varying work and family choices: Their impact on men's work satisfaction. *J. Marriage Fam.* 45: 339–346, 1983.
24. Pfeffer, J., and Ross, J. The effects of marriage and a working wife on occupational and wage attainment. *Admin. Sci. Q.* 27: 66–80, 1982.
25. Piotrowski, C. S. *Work and the Family System.* The Free Press, New York, 1979.
26. Hock, E. The transition to day care: Effects of maternal separation anxiety on infant adjustment. In *The Child and the Day Care Setting: Qualitative Variations and Development,* edited by R. C. Ainslie. Praeger, New York, 1985.
27. Aneshensel, C. S., and Pearlin, L. I. Structural contexts of sex differences in stress. In *Gender and Stress,* edited by R. Barnett and G. Baruch, pp. 75–96. Macmillan, New York, 1987.
28. Cannon, W. B. *The Wisdom of the Body.* W. W. Norton, New York, 1932.
29. Goldberger, L., and Breznitz, S. (eds.). *The Handbook of Stress: Theoretical and Clinical Aspects.* The Free Press, New York, 1982.
30. Selye, H. *Stress in Health and Disease.* Butterworth, London, 1976.
31. Levi, L. (ed.). *Emotions: Their Parameters and Measurement.* Raven Press, New York, 1975.
32. Kasl, S. V. Stress and disease in the workplace: A methodological commentary on the accumulated evidence. In *Health and Industry: A Behavioral Medicine Perspective,* edited by M. F. Cataldo and T. J. Coates. Wiley, New York, 1986.
33. Baker, D. The study of stress. *Annu. Rev. Public Health* 6: 367–381, 1985.
34. Collins, A. Sex Differences in Psychoneuroendocrine Stress Responses: Biological and Social Influences. Doctoral dissertation, Department of Psychology, University of Stockholm, 1985.

35. Collins, A., and Frankenhaeuser, M. Stress responses in male and female engineering students. *J. Hum. Stress* 4: 43–48, 1978.
36. Frankenhaeuser, M., et al. Sex differences in psychoneuroendocrine reactions to examination stress. *Psychosom. Med.* 40: 334–343, 1978.
37. Frankenhaeuser, M. Sex differences in reaction to psychosocial stressors and psychoactive drugs. In *Society, Stress and Disease*, Vol. 3, edited by L. Levi, pp. 135–140. Oxford University Press, Oxford, 1978.
38. Frankenhaeuser, M., and Patkai, D. Interindividual differences in catecholamine excretion during stress. *Scand. J. Psychol.* 6: 117–123, 1965.
39. Frankenhaeuser, M. Challenge-control interaction as reflected in sympathetic-adrenal and pituitary-adrenal activity: Comparisons between the sexes. *Scand J. Psychol.* Suppl. 1: 158–164, 1982.
40. Karasek, R., et al. Job decision latitude, job demands and cardiovascular disease: A prospective study of Swedish men. *Am. J. Public Health* 71: 694–705, 1981.
41. Theorell, T., et al. Changes in job strain in relation to changes in physiological state. *Scand. J. Work Environ. Health* 14: 189–196, 1988.
42. Alfredsson, L., Karasek, R., and Theorell, T. Myocardial infarction risk and psychosocial work environment characteristics: An analysis of the male Swedish work force. *Soc. Sci. Med.* 16: 463–467, 1982.
43. Johnson, J. V., and Hall, E. Job strain, work place social support and cardiovascular disease: A cross sectional study of a random sample of the Swedish working population. *Am. J. Public Health* 78: 1336–1342, 1988.
44. Cassel, J. Psychosocial processes and "stress": Theoretical formulation. *Int. J. Health Serv.* 4(3): 471–482, 1974.
45. Gardell, B. Alienation and mental health in the modern industrial environment. In *Society, Stress and Disease*, Vol. 1, edited by L. Levi, pp. 148–180. Oxford University Press, Oxford, 1971.
46. Gardell, B. Scandinavian research in stress in working life. *Int. J. Health Serv.* 12(1): 31–41, 1982.
47. Johnson, J. V. Collective control: Strategies for survival in the workplace. *Int. J. Health Serv.* 19(3): 469–480, 1989.
48. Johnson, J. V. Control, collectivity and the psychosocial work environment. In *Job Control and Worker Health*, edited by S. L. Sauter, J. J. Hurrell, and C. L. Cooper, pp. 55–74. Wiley, New York, 1989.
49. Johnson, J. V., Johansson, G., and Hall, E. M. Introduction: Work organization, democratization and health. *Int. J. Health Serv.* 18(4): 629–634, 1988.
50. SAS Institute Inc. *SAS/STAT User's Guide, Release 6.0 Edition.* SAS Institute, Cary, N.C., 1988.
51. Freund, R. J., and Littell, R. C. *SAS for Linear Models: A Guide to the ANOVA and GLM Procedures.* SAS Institute, Cary, N.C., 1981.
52. Wistrand, B. *Swedish Women on the Move.* The Swedish Institute, Stockholm, 1981.
53. Haavio-Manilla, E. (ed.). *Unfinished Democracy: Women in Nordic Politics.* Pergamon Press, Oxford, England, 1985.
54. Heclo, H., and Madsen, H. *Policy and Politics in Sweden: Principled Pragmatism.* Temple University Press, Philadelphia, 1987.
55. Levi, L., et al. The psychological, social and biochemical impacts of unemployment in Sweden: Description of a research project. *Int. J. Mental Health* 13(1–2): 18–34, 1984.
56. Roos, P. A. *Gender and Work: A Comparative Analysis of Industrial Societies.* State University of New York, Albany, 1985.
57. Alden, C. W. *Women's Ways of Earning Money.* The Woman's Home Library. A. S. Barnes and Co., New York, 1910.

PART 2

Multilevel Perspectives on Work Organization

CHAPTER 7

Dimensions of Control as Related to Work Organization, Stress, and Health

Gunnar Aronsson

To be able to control and influence one's life is a highly valued goal for the individual. Freedom and self-determination have always been central themes of literature, art, and historical studies, but also of the more "hard" sciences. Within the natural-historical tradition, control is supposed to play a fundamental role in human development and in strategies for development (1). Phylogenetically as well as ontogenetically, human beings have three principal strategies at their disposal when facing changed environmental conditions: escape, adjustment, and change. Human development is accomplished by changing external conditions, e.g., increasing individual or collective control over external conditions. Through their actions, humans gain more and more control over the living conditions that support human development.

The point of departure for this chapter is theoretical. A basic hypothesis within stress theory is that quantitative and qualitative overload as well as quantitative and qualitative underload act as stressors; these generate stress reactions and, in the long run, also may have harmful effects on an individual's physical health. A second basic hypothesis has been that the psychophysiological impact of the work environment is determined by a dynamic process of transactions in which the individual's resources are matched against job demands. To cope successfully with stressors, the individual must have possibilities and resources to exert individual and/or collective control over external events, conditions, and processes. The assumption is that opportunities for the individual to affect and control the situation will, in the long term, facilitate adaptation, although in the short term they can involve exertion and an increase in activation. An individual in a position to regulate and control the influx of impressions can maintain both physiological and psychological activation at an optimal level, which in the long run can have positive health implications (2).

The control concept is scientifically difficult and complex. "Control" signifies several different phenomena within psychology, and it is important to distinguish between the following (3, 4):

This work was supported by The Swedish Work Environment Fund.

1. Control, meaning that an individual has a determining influence on an outcome.
2. Predictability.
3. Participation: an individual has an opportunity for a meaningful role with respect to some valued outcome.
4. Control over, in contrast to control within, a situation: control to change the rules that govern a situation and/or form its structure, or to master the rules within the existing situation.

Another distinction can be made between individual and collective control. In the following sections, all these aspects of control are treated in varying degrees with reference to working life conditions.

However, before I focus on working life-related problems I would like to briefly present some evidence concerning the psychological and medical consequences of a lack of control. If the need for control is deeply anchored in the development of the species and of the individual, and is therefore of fundamental importance to the organism, there is a biological basis for questioning the physiological and pathological consequences of a lack of such control. Experimental research on control has mainly examined "the individual's obvious effect on a certain outcome" or in other words "the degree of relationship between an individual's actions and the result of those actions" (5). This research has been centered on changes in motivation, cognition, and emotion.

Motivational change means that if an individual repeatedly experiences lack of control, the readiness to act declines, mainly in similar situations but also more generally. "Helpless" persons do not expect that their actions will lead to any result and therefore make no attempt to change their situation. Cognitive effects result when the individuals, in future situations, find it difficult to see any relationship between their actions and subsequent events. Even if the actions do affect the world around them in a positive way, they do not recognize this effect, since they have the general attitude that the world around them exists quite independently of their actions. True influence is consigned to chance, fate, etc. This cognitive helplessness makes progress difficult for these individuals, at least as it relates to the knowledge of the impact of their actions. Finally, there are the emotional effects. The first reaction to noncontrol is anxiety and fear. If noncontrol exists for a long period it will give rise to depression and dejection and also to related somatic problems.

CONTROL OVER AND CONTROL WITHIN A SITUATION
(VERTICAL AND HORIZONTAL CONTROL)

Much of the experimental research concerning control has not made the distinction between control over and control within a situation. A simplified one-dimensional control concept is to be found particularly in behavioristic theories, where control is expressed in terms of mutual conditioning (6). Such theories neglect the asymmetry in situations characterized by inequality in power. In such situations the more powerful actor also controls the rules of the situation. He or she has created the structure of the situation and the rules, and also has the power to change the situation and the rules. For working life research that aims to contribute to better jobs, this distinction is necessary. Many industrial and office jobs are so one-sided and deskilled that a strategy for job changes must include changes in matters related to control over the job.

The distinction between control within and control over a situation corresponds to the distinction between horizontal and vertical job discretion in organizational theories. The horizontal/vertical work dimensions may be used when initiating or analyzing different types of work reform activities. Job rotation and job enlargement are limited to the horizontal dimension and correspond to control within. A job change that brings together qualitatively different tasks, such as the planning and the execution of tasks, is an example of a change that influences the vertical dimension, and this corresponds to control over. Later we will return to these issues with an example of new strategies used by employers in Sweden.

INDIVIDUAL AND COLLECTIVE CONTROL

In technologically advanced industrial environments (e.g., chemical plants, refineries, paper and pulp industries, and other process industries), the work process is so highly integrated that it is often difficult to distinguish the individual actor. Collectivity in highly automated work is also reflected by the fact that there is no visible product tied to an individual performance or an individual worker. In these types of work, researchers must develop a better understanding of cooperative forms, which are the material foundation for the relationship between an individual and a group. It will then be possible to judge how and to what degree collective control may reduce stress.

There is reason to be critical of the standards and ideals conventionally used for judging autonomy and control (a common definition of autonomy includes control over boundary tasks, planning, and execution). The autonomy of the craftsman is often used as a transhistorical standard, and changes are measured in deviations from this ideal. Such a point of departure only allows changes to be reflected in the degree of craft-type autonomy. In fact, such independent work is only a marginal form of activity in industrial settings. This is why real and meaningful control only exists in a collective form in this type of work. In research it is quite insufficient to study the individual job decision latitude; decision latitude must be studied at the collective level.

When focusing on the social character of the work process, the issue of individual autonomy within a collective work process becomes central, although studies linking the social character of work to stress reactions are limited. The knowledge of stress reactions and strain is limited here. In a study by Gardell and Svensson (7, 8) of a medium-sized engineering company that had gone through an advanced democratization process involving autonomy at the departmental level and codetermination at the company level, some interesting indications were found of the relation between democratization (collective and individual control) and stress. In the autonomous groups there were production undertakings that led to increased pressure. In the autonomous departments, 16 percent of the workers reported that they very often or quite often felt they had too much to do, compared with 10 percent in the nonautonomous departments. Nonetheless, the latter workers experienced higher stress levels on the job, as well as off the job. Tiredness after work was considerably more common among workers in the nonautonomous groups than in the autonomous ones.

Gardell's and Svensson's interpretation of this apparent contradiction was that through autonomy, the workers provide themselves with a means that may be used to cope with an increased workload. A heavy workload is seen as an inevitable consequence of the autonomous group system, i.e., autonomy has a price in terms of increased production responsibility (8). In studying changes in the relations between the individual worker and the collective, the study showed that autonomy was connected with:

- Increased opportunities for individual self-determination when planning one's own work and choosing work methods.
- More challenging work, with reduced feelings of understimulation and monotony.
- Greater strength and increased influence in the local union. This has made employees feel more secure with respect to uncontrolled technical development, cost reduction measures, etc.
- Less management control and supervision, because a strong union acts as a buffer between management and the individual worker.
- Cooperation and collective sharing of responsibility in the production groups, which have led to greater solidarity, which in turn affords added support to the individuals in the group.

Another example of the dynamics between individual and collective control is given in a classical Norwegian study of the "worker collective" (9). According to Lysgaard (9), the technical-economic system demands continuously increasing productivity. These demands are insatiable, one-sided, and implacable. The individual, on the other hand, is limited, many-sided, and seeks security. In such a situation it is difficult for individual workers to maintain that their demands and needs are legitimate, but these are protected by the collective as appropriate and necessary. Those who stay outside the collective can only refer to their particular limitations, needs for comfort, and anxiety in their resistance to the insatiable demands of the technical-economic system. However, the individuals have to "pay" the collective for protection and for having their needs satisfied; in some situations the individual has to put aside personal interests if these are in conflict with collective interests.

To summarize: if the work processes become more social and contain less independent, individual decision-making, it will be necessary to determine and conceptualize control, skills, and autonomy in relation to the collective autonomy. Increased collective autonomy will be a necessary, if not sufficient, condition for individual autonomy.

PRODUCTION TECHNOLOGY, CONTROL, AND STRESS:
SOME EMPIRICAL EXAMPLES

Before going into strategic questions for the future, three studies performed by the Research Group for the Social Psychology of Work, at Stockholm University, should be reported. These studies focused on the relationship between structural work characteristics (especially control) and stress and disease outcomes.

Bertill Gardell (10) performed the first broad Swedish social psychological study that analyzed consequences of mechanization and automation. One of Gardell's conclusions was that automation created conditions for increasing job discretion as well as skill level. His study showed that with automation, a number of psychologically relevant work characteristics, closely related to central psychological needs, tended to approach the qualities found in craft work. However, the requalification tendency does not include all aspects of work. One example of this is control: *"Control over work methods and control over the execution of work are still low at the same time as demands for responsibility, attention, understanding of the production etc. are high"* (10). These results served to encourage further research, and in the focus on control a theoretical bridge was established between social psychology and psychophysiological stress research.

The first of our three studies compared two groups of sawmill workers, which differed systematically in work control (11). The first group consisted of workers whose jobs were characterized by repetitiveness, physical constraint, machine-paced work, and a high demand for continuous attention (the risk group). Tasks were directly tied to the production flow. The control group consisted mainly of maintenance workers, who performed their work under less monotonous and more flexible conditions. There were clear differences in adrenaline levels between the two groups during periods of the day. The control group reached its peak adrenaline level in the morning (150 percent of baseline). This was followed by a slow decline toward the end of the work shift. The risk group started off at a level twice that of the corresponding baseline level; after a temporary decline, the excretion of adrenaline continued to increase continuously to a maximum at the end of the day. The high morning level of the risk group seems related to heavy responsibility for the production process and for their own and their workmates' level of income (i.e., piece-rate pay). Because the fairly common interruptions had an impact on productivity and income variability, the risk group workers had adopted a strategy of working hard in the early morning to compensate for inevitable interruptions later in the day. The results suggest that the work situation experienced by the risk group creates a demand for continuous mobilization of biochemical adaptation mechanisms that in the long run may prove harmful. This is supported indirectly by the fact that the risk group showed a higher frequency of psychosomatic illness than the control group.

Sawmill work is a prototype of work organized according to Tayloristic principles. It may be argued that technological development and new organizational designs may lead to abandonment of this type of work. However, from a world-wide perspective, Tayloristic organizational principles are far from out-dated. Furthermore, the introduction of computers in administrative work has transferred Tayloristic principles from the shop floor to the office, which is illustrated in the second study.

The second study was focused on stress reactions and work demands in computerized administrative work (12). It was conducted at an insurance company using video display terminals (VDTs) connected to a central computer. The group consisted of 21 women and was divided into two groups, one with extensive and the other with no or little VDT work. These groups were studied during regular work, during a day off, and during daytime and evening. In this study the adrenaline curve seems again to be related to anticipated or real interruptions. Daily, unplanned interruptions, varying from a few minutes to several hours (computer "downtime") usually occurred. The majority of the VDT operators had no other task that they could perform during these interruptions, and their own work remained undone, piling up, sometimes even until the next day. Therefore the VDT operators had adopted the same strategy as the sawmill workers, i.e., working hard in the morning to compensate for interruptions later in the day. This work strategy is reflected in the adrenaline curve of the VDT group. They started off at a fairly high level in the morning, and the curve declined over the day. The importance of computer breakdown was verified in a ministudy; a temporary four-hour unpredicted interruption caused a significant increase of diastolic blood pressure and adrenaline excretion compared with the levels occurring during regular VDT work by trained operators.

A general conclusion from these studies is that unpredictable breakdowns—in industrial as well as in computerized office work—tend to decrease experienced controllability in the work situation *even when interruptions do not occur.* Such work conditions seem to produce a special work strategy: the pace is forced early in the day to guard against any breakdown later on. The adrenaline pattern during the workday may reflect the way the employees allocated their efforts to reduce uncertainty and to increase both their feeling of and their real *control* in the situation.

The studies described above emphasize the consequences of lack of control and unpredictability in the work situation. In a third study, of local transport personnel (13), we applied the model suggested by Karasek (14) and Karasek and coworkers (15). This model combines two aspects: work demands and resources for controlling these demands. According to the model, it is the interplay of these two aspects that determines the resultant strain and any physiological and psychosomatic reactions. This model has received support in analyses of representative samples of worker populations in the United States and Scandinavia (e.g., 16–18). Thus, we expected the group with high job demands and few resources for control to be most strained, and the converse to apply to the group with many resources and low job demands.

A randomly selected group of 1,442 full-time bus/train/tram drivers and guard personnel participated in this questionnaire study. Urban public transport is characterized by the rigors of a time-table. Accordingly, the drivers work under time pressure related to traffic conditions, over which the drivers have no control. Three types of stressors were included in a summarized job demand measure, namely the frequency of

1. Stressful efforts to keep to the time-table;
2. Conflicts between ambitions to be service-oriented and tight time-tables, and conflicts between traffic safety and tight time-tables; and
3. Passenger behavior, such as complaints about conditions beyond the driver's control, conflicts, disagreements, or even threats.

Four types of resources available to the bus drivers for dealing with the demands were identified: technical resources (radio and alarm system), organizational resources (trade union support in efforts to improve work conditions), social resources (support from supervisors and fellow workers), and personal resources (personal authority in the occupational role, defined as perceived ability to handle difficult passenger contacts). It was assumed that these four resources reflect essential aspects of the individual's ability to control the work demands and were therefore important to health.

The statistical analysis showed a strong connection between resources for control, job demand, and reported ill health. Workload and resources for control were systematically related to health conditions (mental and physical exhaustion, back and joint pains, stomach trouble, difficulties in sleeping, slight mental stress, and absence due to illness). Generally speaking, all these indicators of ill health became more frequent at higher levels of job demands, but the tendency was clearly modified by the number of resources available to the driver on the job.

In addition to its scientific value—it has stimulated and vitalized research on hazardous psychosocial factors at work—this model has proved useful from strategic and pedagogical perspectives. It suggests that unwanted consequences of job stress may be avoided not merely through the elimination of psychosocial stressors, but also through the introduction of resources for control that will facilitate coping by individuals and groups.

PREPROGRAMMED WORK PROCESSES AND CONTROL

Computerization will make future production systems far more flexible than they have been up to now, with respect to both managing from above and the individual's control of the work situation. This development raises some difficult questions to be answered in the future, e.g., what choices must be made to use the flexibility of the new technology, how to prevent control from the top, and how to direct the development toward human needs and democratic work organization.

Technical-structural control, as a predecessor to the computerized production processes of today, is characterized by rigorous preplanning of work material and methods. For instance, this means that workers cannot choose their own work speed and follow their own work rhythm because pace and sequence are built in and regulated by the machinery. The study of sawmill work described above has documented the human costs of this type of organization and technique (11).

Preplanning may mean a high degree of predictability and reduction of uncertainty. In a certain sense this contributes to control for the worker, i.e., the worker knows, with a relatively high degree of probability, what will happen next. A guess is that, under some circumstances, preplanning may have a paradoxical effect; as the demands on information-processing are greatly reduced, which results in cognitive understimulation, this understimulation may balance out (compensate for) the consequences of too high sensory and motor workloads. Such a mechanism may be one of the causes of a reported lack of employee interest in work enlargement with more decision-making and responsibility. For example, during work under pressure with high demands for attention, such a change may be experienced as an increase in workload rather than a positive stimulus.

How then can work tools be formed and work processes be organized to promote control, competence development, and learning? One example of increased freedom of choice may be seen in the phenomenon called electronic integration, i.e., integration of the different steps in the production of goods or service through computerization. We may say that electronic integration is a new form of rationalization directed not toward separate tasks and functions but toward complete processes. This is possible because computer technology permits (*a*) integration of information from many sources and (*b*) distribution of information to many locations (19). Using electronics to reconnect information separated by Taylorization of work provides employees with an overview and also with varied work tasks. However, electronic reintegration does not necessarily offer a greater degree of self-determination and responsibility. Computerized work is easy to monitor, pace, register, and control. How future development will take shape—how freedom of choice will be utilized— is determined by the inner contradictions and weaknesses in the general control and work division strategies of companies, as well as by the attitudes of trade unions to the new techniques and the ideals, and qualities they want to realize in the new jobs.

STRATEGIES FOR EMPLOYER CONTROL

The marked emphasis on worker control and influence in Swedish work environment research has influenced legislation. In the Swedish Work Environment Act, control is emphasized: according to the Act, work conditions shall be arranged so that the individual can influence his or her own work situation.

One interesting question is how an employer strategy is created to cope with the increased demands for employee control and influence introduced by this legislation. Monopoly of knowledge, work division, and preprogrammed work tasks have been the employers' method for extended control of the work process. Scientific management was the embodiment of these ideas. Robotics and computers have caused rapid outdating of this type of work. In Sweden, The Confederation of Employers formulated a new philosophy of rationalization to cope with the new legislation. This project was called New Factories and was summarized as "coordinated self-determination in small groups" (20). The idea behind New Factories was to find a type of work organization that, while preserving profit, could adjust the companies to the new requirements imposed by research and work legislation. Broström (21) has analyzed the general organizational principles in the employers' counter-strategy. According to Broström, a vertical principle for work division is applied to the whole organization and not only to parts of it. Control over the conditions of production—financing, investments, planning, and development work—is centralized in management, while responsibility for execution is decentralized into what are called product shops. Product shops consist of clearly demarcated and independent units of production. The activity in these units is monitored and coordinated by a central unit, which is responsible for the function and development of the whole system. The units of production almost become companies within the company. They are responsible for whole products or families of products and their economic outcome. This means that every subsystem is nearly self-sufficient and makes finished products or finished components. The systems are stable, and buffer stocks make them resistant to stoppages. From a work environment perspective, this means that the workers are physically less constrained, and they perform production tasks and have their own resources for service and administration. This helps to give them an overview and an understanding of the work process. By means of this decentralization, the employers try to combine effectiveness with compliance with codetermination laws (21).

Development in this direction means a break with extreme Tayloristic principles, but it is hardly a break with more general principles of knowledge monopoly and management's use of this monopoly as a means for high-capacity production and exploitation. In terms of "workers' control" one could say that the top management is mainly concerned with strategic questions and with control of the total production process rather than with control of individual workers. In this type of organization, company management strengthens its vertical control while, at the same time, it gives up parts of the horizontal control to the worker or the worker collective.

REFERENCES

1. Leontjew, A. N. *Tätigkeit, Bewusstsein, Persönlichkeit.* Pahl-Rugenstein, Köln, 1982.
2. Frankenhaeuser, M. Coping with stress at work. *Int. J. Health Serv.* 11(4): 491–510, 1981.
3. Kaplan, S., and Kaplan, R. *Cognition and Environment. Functioning in an Uncertain World.* Praeger, New York, 1982.
4. Aronsson, G. *Arbetspsykologi: stress- och kvalifikationsperspektiv.* (Occupational Psychology.) Studentlitteratur, Lund, 1987.
5. Abrahamson, L. Y., Seligman, M. E. P., and Teasdale, J. D. Learned helplessness in humans: Critique and reformulation. *J. Abnorm. Psychol.* 87: 49–74, 1978.
6. Lacey, H. M. Perceived control and the methodological role of cognitive constructs. In *Choice and Perceived Control,* edited by Lawrence C. Perlmuter, and R. A. Monty. Lawrence Erlbaum Associates, New Jersey, 1979.
7. Gardell, B., and Svensson, L. *Medbestämmande och självstyre. En lokal faclig strategi för demokratisering ar arbetsplatsen.* (Co-determination and Autonomy. A Local Trade Union Strategy for Democracy at the Work Place.) Prisma, Stockholm, 1981.
8. Gardell, B. Worker participation and autonomy: A multilevel approach to democracy at the workplace. *Int. J. Health Serv.* 12(4): 527–558, 1982.
9. Lysgaard, S. *Arbejderkollektivet.* (Worker Collective.) Universitetsforlaget, Oslo, 1961.
10. Gardell, B. *Produktionsteknik och arbetsglädje.* (Technology, Alienation and Mental Health.) PA-rådet, Stockholm, 1971.
11. Johansson, G., Aronsson, G., and Lindström, B. O. Social psychological and neuroendocrine stress reactions in highly mechanized work. *Ergonomics* 21(8): 583–599, 1978.
12. Johansson, G., and Aronsson, G. Stress reactions in computerized administrative work. *J. Occup. Behav.* 5: 159–181, 1984.
13. Gardell, B., Aronsson, G., and Barklöf, K. *The Working Environment for Local Public Transport Personnel.* Report from the Swedish Work Environment Fund, Stockholm, 1982.
14. Karasek, R. A. Job demands, job decision latitude and mental strain. Implications for job redesign. *Administr. Sci. Q.* 24: 285–308, 1979.
15. Karasek, R. A., Russel, R., and Theorell, T. Physiology of stress and regeneration in job related cardiovascular illness. *J. Hum. Stress* 3(1): 29–42, 1982.
16. Alfredsson, L., Karasek, R., and Theorell, T. Myocardial infarction risk and psychosocial work environment: An analysis of the male Swedish working force. *Soc. Sci. Med.* 16: 463–467, 1982.
17. Johnson, J. V., and Hall, E. Job strain, workplace social support and cardiovascular disease: A cross-sectional study of a random sample of the Swedish working population. *Am. J. Public Health* 78: 1336–1342, 1988.
18. Karasek, R. A., Gardell, B., and Lindell, J. Work and non-work correlates of illness and behavior in male and female Swedish white-collar workers. *J. Occup. Behav.* 8: 187–207, 1987.

19. Giuliano, E. G. The mechanization of office work. *Sci. Am.* September 1982, pp. 149–154.
20. Agurén, S., and Edgren, J. *New Factories. Job Design through Factory Planning in Sweden.* Swedish Employers' Confederation, Stockholm, 1979.
21. Broström, A. *MBLs gränser. Den privata äganderätten.* (The Limits of the Co-determination Law. Private Ownership.) Arbetslivscentrum, Göteborg, 1982.

CHAPTER 8

Collective Control: Strategies for Survival in the Workplace

Jeffrey V. Johnson

Control over the work process and social support in the work setting have been identified as the two major psychosocial resources that can serve to modify the potentially stressful demands and pressures of modern production systems (1). Although these two concepts have generally been considered separately, there is considerable evidence that in the workplace itself they may function interdependently to form structures of collective control (2-5). The major work reform strategy that Scandinavians, such as Gardell, proposed and later implemented has involved the creation of collective forms of control through the development of autonomous work groups, specifically designed to address problems of work fragmentation, deskilling, and social isolation (2, 6).

Although a number of authors have referred to the concept of collective control (2, 7), it has not been systematically analyzed or presented within an occupational health context. In this book, the primary emphasis is placed on the concept of work control (8, 9). There is relatively little discussion in other chapters of either the social dimensions of control or the importance of social relations in the workplace from the point of view of stress and health. For this reason I will first present a brief discussion of social support and its relationship to work control before further examining the concept of collective control.

SOCIAL SUPPORT AND HEALTH

Over the last decade the concept of social support has emerged as one of the central research areas in the social epidemiology of chronic disease. The publication of the Alameda County study by Berkman and Syme (10) in 1979, which reported

This work was supported by the Swedish Work Environment Fund and the U.S. National Heart, Lung and Blood Institute.

meaningful associations between the degree to which individuals were involved in social interactions with others and subsequent mortality risk, has been followed by a number of increasingly sophisticated epidemiological studies (11-14). In a major recent review, House and his colleagues (15) have pointed out that the link between social support and mortality risk now has the same magnitude of scientific support as did the association between smoking and mortality in the mid-1950s.

There continues to be some debate as to precisely what is meant by the term "social support." Many authors define it in relation to its functional characteristics. Kahn and Antonucci (16) identify three key elements: affect, affirmation, and aid. Pinneau (17) puts forward a similar formulation distinguishing tangible support (assistance through intervention), appraisal support (assistance through increasing knowledge), and emotional support (communication of information related to one's socioemotional needs). Similarly, Caplan (18) suggests that social support systems serve to promote emotional mastery, offer guidance, and provide feedback. House (19, p. 22) summarizes these various formulations in a single question: "Who gives what to whom regarding which problems?"

In our own research we have suggested four routes by which social support in the workplace could affect health (4, 5, 20, 21):

1. Social support in the workplace meets basic human needs for companionship and group affiliation.
2. Work social support serves as a resource to moderate the impact of job demands.
3. Social support at work has an important influence on adult socialization through promoting active or passive patterns of behavior.
4. Social support, in combination with work control, provides a collective coping system that protects groups of workers against structural demands and pressures.

Even though the literature on social support indicates that human ties are an important factor in mental and physical health, there is still only limited information on social support in occupational settings. However, there are logical reasons why work-related social support may be important. If one considers the increasing fragmentation of older forms of social cohesion, such as the village, neighborhood, or the church, it seems possible that the interactions in the workplace are one of the few remaining sources of stable, on-going personal contact (outside the family) for many people. Work relationships may be one of the major sources of human companionship in the modern era.

Empirical research has linked inadequate social support in the workplace with a variety of illnesses in a number of research populations, including angina pectoris among male workers in Israel (22); coronary heart disease among female clerks (23); psychological problems among air traffic controllers (24); higher cholesterol values among those whose coworkers were constantly changing (25); higher levels of illness among the unemployed (26, 27); a greater physical health impact from perceived stress among male petrochemical workers (19, 28); and increased psychological strain among men in 23 occupations (17). There is also some indication that social support in the workplace may help moderate or "buffer" the impact of job stress on physical and mental health (17, 19, 29, 30).

One of the major limitations of the social support concept is the emphasis that most researchers have placed on individually based, emotional transactions. This approach reduces the primary object of research to that of the atomized individual who receives support from significant others within his or her personal social networks. The emergent properties of social groups, organizations, and collectivities continue to be ignored in the social support and health discourse. Human beings act together within and through social groups. Indeed, some paleoanthropologists suggest that group activity was arguably the most important tool permitting humans as a species to adapt to and transform their environment (31). The potential in social groups to exert control over their environment is in marked contrast to the emphasis on relatively passive emotional nurture often emphasized in research on social support. The collective control manifested in group life is of particular importance in relation to institutional structures, such as the workplace, that are relatively impervious to individual agency. Individuals can leave their specific work environment and seek out another, but rarely, unless they are in relatively privileged positions, can they personally alter the structural imperatives of the organization itself.

In much of the literature in the Nordic countries, social support is not viewed in terms of individual emotional needs. Rather, it is viewed as a structural resource for coping with the demands of the environment. Although there has been a tendency to view social relationships as a secondary factor that functions as an adjunct to individual work control, Gardell suggested the importance of uniting the two concepts as the basis for a strategy of work reform (32, p. 35):

> In Scandinavian research the concept of social support has not been used until recently. We have felt that the dimension of control was more important and could more easily be tied into trade union ideology, tradition, and policy. Today there is an increased interest in the concept, however, especially if it is at the same time linked to the concept of control. . . . By combining collective influence in management decision making with the formation of autonomous groups . . . the individual and the group will be able to achieve enlarged control over the work system and the work methods.

TOWARD AN UNDERSTANDING OF COLLECTIVE CONTROL

The concrete manifestation of control and social support is often expressed in and through informal social groups at work. Through such groups, workers devise ways of living and surviving on the job. [See Gryzb (33) for an excellent discussion of this process.] This group life constitutes a subculture in which norms, beliefs, traditions, and rituals are created. Within this culture, by discussing and interpreting the experience of work, employees come to define and make sense of their common situation and often struggle to minimize or eliminate threats to the well-being of the group. Within the context of working life, decisions, attitudes, and activities are developed and tested for their effectiveness in solving common problems (33).

The concept of the "workers' collectivity," developed by the Norwegian sociologist, Sverre Lysgaard, synthesizes the cultural and political aspects of support and control that are expressed in informal work groups (34). The workers' collectivity arises as a group level response to the demands of the production system. Because of the structural nature of these pressures, they exceed the capacity of the individual worker's ability to cope with or transform them. The collectivity serves to preserve the interests of both the individual and the group by establishing a counter-authority to that of management. Although the concrete expression of the workers' collectivity differs from place to place, Lysgaard (34) identified three conditions that contribute to its formation: (a) spacial proximity is a precondition for social interaction; (b) jointly experienced problems contribute to a common frame of reference; and (c) having equal positions encourages the formation of a collective identity. These preconditions are more likely to occur among lower level industrial and service sector employees than among administrative or professional personnel.

Even when Lysgaard's preconditions exist, collective formations do not, inevitably, arise. The concrete forms of collective control are determined by historical and technological developments that are often outside the influence of the social groups operating within the micro-environment of the workplace. Collective group formation is influenced by a number of factors, including the size of the workplace, the duration of the employment cycle, the nature of the production process, the stability of the enterprise, and the general skill level of the workforce. In some jobs, all three preconditions noted by Lysgaard are absent. For example, in machine-paced assembly-line jobs, high noise levels, a lack of physical proximity, rotating shifts, piece-rate payment systems, combined with company policies that prohibit talking, can effectively prevent the social interaction that provides the essential basis for the development of collectivity.

The existence of the conditions that naturally promote the development of active collective forms is neither random nor accidental. In fact, the elimination of workers' collectivities and collective control has been a deliberate, managerially oriented strategy since the late 19th century (33, 35-40). Frederick Winslow Taylor, the founder of "scientific management" or "Taylorism," is widely credited with initiating the decollectivization of the industrial workplace in the late 19th century (35). Taylor, the maverick scion of an upper-class family, became a machinist by serving an ordinary apprenticeship, thereby gaining entry into the workers' collectivity and knowledge of the process of collective control. On completing his apprentice training, he went to his employer and told him that if he (Taylor) was given complete power to redesign the work process, he could dramatically increase production. Over the years, one of the major targets of his scientific management approach was to be the social formations created by workers, who, as he knew from the experience of being one, exercised control over the work process through their monopoly over skill. As sociologists of the work process have documented, Taylor and those that followed him understood that job design and technology could be used as instruments of social power by management to desocialize workers, through social isolation and the disintegration of informal work groups, thereby preventing workers from exercising collective control (33, 35-40).

THE EPIDEMIOLOGY OF COLLECTIVITY, CONTROL, AND CARDIOVASCULAR DISEASE

Beginning in 1982, my colleague, Ellen M. Hall, and I entered into a series of discussions with Professor Gardell and members of his research unit at the University of Stockholm concerning the possible health effects of collective control. We suggested that by combining the concept of social support with that of work control it would be possible to begin examining the impact of collective control on work stress and cardiovascular disease risk. Later, in collaboration with Gardell and the Swedish Central Statistical Bureau, we empirically examined the combined effects of work-related social support and work control among a representative sample of 13,779 Swedish male and female workers (see 21 for a more complete discussion of methodology).

The combined impact of control and support on cardiovascular disease prevalence risk is displayed in Table 1. The Swedish working population was divided according to their joint levels of control and support, and the cardiovascular prevalence ratio was computed for each group. The most positive condition based on our theoretical predictions, the high control and high support group, was used as the reference category to which each of the combinations was compared. The highest cardiovascular disease prevalence ratio, 1.67, was found in that group with both low work control and low work social support. Moreover, there was a strong indication that a combination of both control and social support was important for cardiovascular health: when either support or control was low, cardiovascular prevalence risk was elevated. This raised the interesting possibility that workplace stress might occur without specific reference to job demands, for we found that the lack of collective control resources, or the combination of social isolation and low control, was itself a risk condition.

Table 1

The combined effects of work control and social support on age-adjusted cardiovascular disease (CVD) prevalence ratios, Sweden[a]

| Work control[b] | Work social support | | |
	High support	Medium support	Low support
Low control			
CVD prevalence ratio	1.32	1.31	1.67
95% CI	(1.02–1.71)	(0.99–1.73)	(1.31–2.19)
n	2,063	1,411	1,318
Medium control			
CVD prevalence ratio	1.23	1.48	1.41
95% CI	(0.95–1.60)	(1.13–1.94)	(1.04–1.92)
n	2,356	1,360	916
High control			
CVD prevalence ratio	1.00	1.14	1.44
95% CI	(Reference category)	(0.83–1.56)	(1.04–2.00)
n	2,471	1,180	704

[a]CVD prevalence ratios calculated using the high control, high support group as the reference category.
[b]CI, confidence interval.

In later stages of our research we developed an expanded model, illustrated in Figure 1, which added the social support dimension to the demand-control formulation developed by Karasek (41). This enlarged the earlier theoretical emphasis from the individual connection between a person and his or her job into the domain of collective relationships. The earlier demand-control formulation, for instance, was not able to recognize differences between work performed in isolation from that performed collectively, as long as levels of demand and control were similar.

We focused our attention on that set of job characteristics that we theoretically considered to be most aversive: the high strain isolated condition. Those workers exposed to this high demand, low control, and low support condition had a cardiovascular prevalence ratio of 2.17, using the low strain collective group as the reference

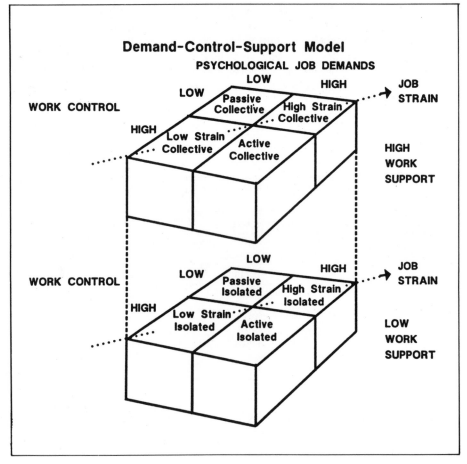

Figure 1. The demand-control-support model. Diagonal arrows represent increasing levels of job strain.

category, even after controlling for age and a number of other sociodemographic and personal lifestyle factors (21). The overall pattern of cardiovascular disease risk found in the demand-control-support model demonstrated that neither control nor support—alone—was sufficient to moderate the impact of job demands. For example, we found that the presence or absence of social support determined whether or not work control operated to reduce job strain and cardiovascular disease risk. Likewise, we observed that social support was not an effective moderator when control was low. In short, our findings suggested that a combination of *both* high support and high control was necessary to ameliorate the impact of psychological job demands on cardiovascular disease prevalence risk.

UNDERLYING MECHANISMS OF COLLECTIVE CONTROL

Although these empirical findings suggest the importance of collectivity and control in the development of chronic disease risk, they do not help us uncover the underlying social mechanisms that give rise to these observed associations. In order to do this one must consider using different sources of data. The large survey-based studies necessary for establishing basic epidemiological associations are not so useful for examining subtle social transactions occurring over time. Survey researchers construct their view of the social world from the responses of individuals to structured questionnaires. Yet if the unit of analysis is not the individual per se but the group to which the individual belongs, the processes occurring at the level of the group remain relatively invisible to the researcher. This is particularly true in social support research where we rarely, if ever, sample naturally occurring groups, but rather disparate individuals who make up relatively abstract populations. Individuals can only report, in the context of the structured interview, on their small corner of social reality. Hence the process of research is limited by both the preconceived notions of the researcher embodied in the questionnaire itself and the perceptiveness and openness of the respondent.

There are few, if any, studies of work-related social support that have used more qualitative methods of data collection involving participant-observation techniques. This type of research has been extremely valuable in the sociology of work field, where much recent debate concerning the nature and meaning of informal social activity in the workplace has been stimulated by the participant-observation work of Burawoy (42) and others (e.g., 33). Likewise in the field of social network research, Carol Stack's (43) anthropological field work in an urban black community has been very valuable in suggesting the mechanisms by which social networks are created and maintained.

For this reason, I would like to refer to my own experience as a printing pressman to help provide more concrete examples to illustrate the mechanisms by which collective control can affect health. My major work experience was in the pressroom of a midwestern newspaper with a daily circulation of approximately 400,000. The workforce consisted of 2,000 employees, most of whom were organized into trade unions. The pressroom was a football field in length with six, nine-unit presses, three stories high, running along each side. Production of the newspaper was characterized by extreme time pressure, intense noise levels, and constant exposure to ink mist and paper dust. Each press was manned by rotating crews of up to 25 journeymen and apprentices. The size and the complexity of this production process provided the technological context for the formation of cooperative social relationships: learning to work together was necessary for survival in this job setting. The power of the union and the strong traditions of the craft established the social context for the formation of collectivity. New workers were chosen by an "apprentice selection committee" made up of union members. These new employees learned the skills and traditions of the craft during the four-year apprenticeship, a socialization experience also controlled formally and informally by the workers.

Collective control was expressed in a variety of ways, ranging from individual exchange to cultural innovation and political activity. The following types of collective activities, though not consciously devised to be protective, nevertheless functioned as psychosocial resources, helping to alter or alleviate stressors encountered on the job:

1. Exposure modification through task reorganization: Workers devised a "relief system" that reallocated duties, thereby allowing for reduced time of physical exposure for any individual in the most arduous production areas.
2. Protection of the vulnerable: The work group gave older workers less physically demanding tasks, and young, inexperienced workers were assigned duties within their skill range.
3. Regulation of effort: Union rules and informal traditions established realistic guidelines as to when and how work was to be performed, therefore discouraging an overexertion of effort on the part of any individual.
4. Transforming the arduous through cultural creation: The boredom and monotony of the job were counteracted by jokes, rituals, and elaborate games.
5. The provision of emotional sustenance: Long-term friendships, extending from work into free time, provided emotional and instrumental social support.
6. The transmission of information and knowledge: Workers transmitted skills to each other, thereby alleviating the anxiety associated with lack of experience or knowledge. This learning from others continued well past the apprenticeship period.
7. Provision of an alternative system of accomplishment: Participation in collective life provided individuals with the emotional rewards of pride and accomplishment, both through the exercise of acknowledged skill and through formal or informal leadership in union or shop floor activities.
8. Dealing with authoritarian supervision: The behavior of foremen and supervisors was controlled through the counter-authority of the union and production team organizations. If a supervisor "attacked" or humiliated an individual, direct action would be taken against him by the collectivity, which would serve to make him look bad in the eyes of higher management.
9. Work actions: Job actions such as slow-down strikes would be organized to register disagreement in the case of serious disputes with supervisors or management.
10. Organizational influence through collective bargaining: Through the formal agency of the union, work rules and procedures considered to be important by the collective would be defended or expanded during contract negotiations.

These social actions are not presented as general principles but as examples of occupationally and historically specific collective control mechanisms devised by a particular group. Other occupational groups, facing a different set of survival requirements and demands, will necessarily create their own distinctive strategies. Workers' collectivities are historical occurrences, and like living systems, they come into being and pass away. Unlike formal institutions, they must be constantly renewed through the daily actions and feelings of their members. Herein lies both their strength and vulnerability. On the one hand, collective control mechanisms are immediate, locally based expressions of the desire for democratic control over the work process. On the other hand, their influence and continued existence is determined by technological and historical imperatives that often lie outside the boundaries of an actual workplace. For example, with the advent of computerization and the subsequent changes in the balance of power between the newspaper publishers and the printing trade unions, many workers in this industry were eventually to become decollectivized over the course of the last two decades (44). This did not happen overnight, and certainly not without considerable struggle, but as an example it serves to emphasize the insights of Gardell, Gustavsen, and others, who have noted that work environment reform (and perhaps one should add, in some cases, preservation) must necessarily be based on a multilevel strategy (2). That is, ultimately it is not sufficient to intervene only at the level of the specific worksite, because in order for any positive change to be achieved, questions of power at the organizational and societal level must be resolved as well (2, 45).

COLLECTIVE CONTROL AND PSYCHOSOCIAL INTERVENTION

It is an historical irony, perhaps, that the rationale given for both decollectivization and recollectivization is often the same: the need to redesign the job in order to enhance productivity. Today it has become commonplace within management circles to talk about restructuring work along the lines of the "Japanese model" by introducing team work, quality circles, and various forms of "participatory management." Similar job design procedures in western Europe, referred to as "autonomous work groups," have also attempted to reconstruct collective forms, often within highly mechanized, machine-paced industries. The basic principles underlying these developments are often drawn from sociotechnical design theory, which emphasizes that work should be organized in groups that have control over decision-making and are responsible for a complete production or activity cycle (6, 46, 47). The insights of sociotechnical theory grew out of the historical events following the mechanization of the Durham coal fields in England, shortly after World War II. Researchers from the Tavistock Institute were called in to investigate an epidemic of psychosomatic disorders among coal miners who had recently undergone a work restructuring that effectively prevented them from working collectively as they had done in the past. Through what was perhaps one of the first "action research projects," the Tavistock researchers learned about the old collective work traditions from the miners, and eventually were to reconstitute similar social forms designed to meet the new technical production requirements. It is important to emphasize that it was the miners who taught the principles of collective control to the Tavistock researchers, who went on to develop sociotechnical and autonomous work group theory as a way of explaining what they had learned.

Now, almost four decades later, hundreds of experiments using these principles have taken place in England, Ireland, Norway, and Sweden and are beginning to defuse to the United States as well (6). It usually comes as a considerable surprise to researchers or managers when work group experiments encounter strong resistance from workers who do not want either their jobs or their own social configurations "reconstructed" under (even a well-intentioned) outside authority. There have been recent examples in the United States and Britain in which efforts to introduce changes based on some variation of the autonomous work group model have been strongly resisted. Although the promise of a more humane work environment is often the expressed rationale for such efforts, many workers, with considerable justification, believe that productivity concerns (and not worker well-being), as well as an effort to erode existing work rules and union authority, are the genuine, underlying motivations for the institution of these new job designs.

For health professionals concerned with developing intervention strategies for ameliorating work-related stress and promoting occupational health, a critical distinction must be made between the genuine workers' collectivity that grows out of the needs and aspirations of the workforce, and the artificially constructed collectivity that quite often embodies the interests of management. Parker and Slaughter (48) two former auto workers, report that the group or team approach presently being used by General Motors–Toyota, can actually turn into a form of "management by stress" (48). Rather than doing away with scientific management forms of production, "management by stress," according to Parker and Slaughter, represents an intensification of Taylorism (48):

> Taylor believed that management's engineers and time-study men could capture workers' knowledge of the production process all at once, after which workers would revert to being nothing but hired hands. Management-by-stress managers understand that workers continue to know more about the actual performance of their jobs than higher management does, and so make the process of appropriating that knowledge a never-ending one.

Although most interventions that use the autonomous work group model achieve results markedly more humane than these, Parker's and Slaughter's comments serve as a valuable warning concerning the limitation of an uncritical advocacy of a simple "group" approach. Moreover, an important limitation of many reform efforts continues to be a lack of understanding of the complexity of workplace social formations. Given that informal as well as formal power struggles are a nearly universal component of working life, workers can be expected to have developed collective forms of empowerment and control that may not be visible to the outside observer. The most successful intervention efforts will be those that are based on an awareness of these forms and that attempt to provide an improved environmental context for their expression.

REFERENCES

1. Marmot, M., and Theorell, T. Social class and cardiovascular disease: The contribution of work. *Int. J. Health Serv.* 18(4): 659–673, 1988.
2. Gardell, B. Work participation and autonomy: A multilevel approach to democracy at the workplace. *Int. J. Health Serv.* 12(4): 527–558, 1982.
3. Aronsson, G. Work Content, Autonomy, Stress Reactions. Ph.D. dissertation, Department of Psychology, University of Stockholm, 1985.
4. Johnson, J. V. The impact of workplace social support, job demands and work control upon cardiovascular disease in Sweden. *Environmental and Organizational Psychology Research Monographs* (University of Stockholm) 1: 1–240, 1986.
5. Johnson, J. V. Control, collectivity and the psychosocial work environment. In *Job Control and Worker Health*, edited by S. Sauter, J. Hurrell, and C. Cooper. John Wiley, London, 1989.
6. Sandberg, T. *Work Organization and Autonomous Groups.* CWK Gleerup, Lund, Sweden, 1982.
7. Aronsson, G. Dimensions of control as related to work organization, stress and health. *Int. J. Health Serv.* 19(3): 459–468, 1989.
8. Johnson, J. V., Johansson, G., and Hall, E. M. Introduction: Work organization, democratization, and health. *Int. J. Health Serv.* 18(4): 629–634, 1988.
9. Johnson, J. V. Introduction: Structural barriers to change in the workplace. *Int. J. Health Serv.* 19(1): 117–119, 1989.
10. Berkman, L., and Syme, S. L. Social networks, host resistance and mortality: A nine year study of Alameda county residents. *Am. J. Epidemiol.* 109: 186–204, 1979.
11. House, J., Robbins, C., and Metzner, H. The association of social relationships and activities with mortality: Prospective evidence from Tecumseh community health study. *Am. J. Epidemiol.* 166: 123–140, 1982.
12. Blazer, D. Social support and mortality in an elderly community population. *Am. J. Epidemiol.* 115: 684–694, 1982.
13. Schoenbach, V., et al. Social ties and mortality in Evans County, Georgia. *Am. J. Epidemiol.* 123: 577–591, 1986.
14. Orth-Gomer, K., and Johnson, J. V. Social network interaction and mortality: A six year follow-up of a random sample of the Swedish Population. *J. Chron. Dis.* 40: 949–957, 1987.
15. House, J., Landis, K., and Umberson, D. Social relationships and health. *Science* 241: 540–545, 1988.
16. Kahn, R. L., and Antonucci, T. Convoys over the life course: Attachment, roles and social support. In *Life Span Development and Behavior*, edited by P. B. Baltes and O. Brim, Vol. 3. Lexington Press, Boston, 1980.
17. Pinneau, S. Effects of Social Support on Psychological and Physiological Strain. Doctoral dissertation, University of Michigan, Ann Arbor, 1975.
18. Caplan, G. Mastery of stress: Psychosocial aspects. *Am. J. Psychiatry* 138: 413–419, 1981.
19. House, J. *Work Stress and Social Support.* Addison-Wesley, Reading, Mass., 1981.
20. Johnson, J. V., and Hall, E. M. Social support in the work environment and cardiovascular disease. In *Social Support and Cardiovascular Disease*, edited by S. Shumaker and S. Czajkowski. Plenum Press, New York, 1989.
21. Johnson, J. V., and Hall, E. M. Job strain, work place social support and cardiovascular disease: A cross sectional study of a random sample of the Swedish working population. *Am. J. Public Health* 78: 1336–1342, 1988.
22. Medalie, J., et al. Five year myocardial infarction incidence, 2: Association of single variables to age and birthplace. *J. Chron. Dis.* 26: 329–349, 1973.
23. Haynes, S., and Feinleib, M. Women, work and coronary heart disease: Prospective findings from the Framingham heart study. *Am. J. Public Health* 70: 133–141, 1980.
24. Rose, R., Hurst, M., and Herd, A. Cardiovascular and endocrine responses to work and the risk of psychiatric symptoms among air traffic controllers. In *Stress and Mental Disorder*, edited by J. Barrett. Raven Press, New York, 1979.
25. Cassel, J. The use of medical records: Opportunities for epidemiological studies. *J. Occup. Med.* 5: 185–190, 1963.
26. Cobb, S., and Kasl, S. *Termination: The consequences of job loss.* NIOSH Publication No. 77-224. National Institute for Occupational Safety and Health, Cincinnati, 1977.

27. Jahoda, M. *Employment and Unemployment: A Socio-Psychological Analysis*. Cambridge University Press, Cambridge, England, 1982.
28. House, J., et al. Occupational stress and health among factory workers. *J. Health Soc. Behav.* 20: 139–160, 1979.
29. LaRocco, J., House, J., and French, J. Social support, occupational stress and health. *J. Health Soc. Behav.* 21: 202–218, 1980.
30. Karasek, R., Triantis, K., and Chaudhry, S. Co-worker and supervisor support as moderators of associations between task characteristics and mental strain. *J. Occup. Behav.* 3: 147–160, 1982.
31. Leakey, R. E. *Origins*. E. P. Dutton, New York, 1977.
32. Gardell, B. Scandinavian research in stress in working life. *Int. J. Health Serv.* 12(1): 31–41, 1982.
33. Gryzb, G. J. Decollectivization and recollectivization in the workplace: The impact on informal work groups and work culture. *Economic and Industrial Democracy* 2: 455–482, 1981.
34. Lysgaard, S. *Arbeiderkollectivet*. (Workers' collectivity.) Universitets forlaget, Oslo, 1961.
35. Braverman, H. *Labor and Monopoly Capital*. Monthly Review Press, New York, 1974.
36. Zimbalist, A. *Case Studies on the Labor Process*. Monthly Review Press, New York, 1979.
37. Montgomery, D. *Workers' Control in America*. Cambridge University Press, Cambridge, England, 1979.
38. Thompson, P. *The Nature of Work: An Introduction to Debates on the Labour Process*. Macmillan Press, London, 1983.
39. Noble, D. *Forces of Production: A Social History of Industrial Automation*. Alfred A. Knopf, New York, 1984.
40. Edwards, R. *Contested Terrain: The Transformation of the Workplace in the Twentieth Century*. Heinemann, London, 1979.
41. Karasek, R., et al. Job decision latitude, job demands, and cardiovascular disease: A prospective study of Swedish men. *Am. J. Public Health* 71: 694–705, 1981.
42. Burawoy, M. *Manufacturing Consent*. The University of Chicago Press, Chicago, 1979.
43. Stack, C. *All Our Kin*. Harper & Row, New York, 1974.
44. Zimbalist, A. Technology and the labor process in the printing industry. In *Case Studies on the Labor Process*, edited by A. Zimbalist. Monthly Review Press, New York, 1979.
45. Gardell, B., and Gustavsen, B. Work environment research and social change: Current developments in Scandinavia. *J. Occup. Behav.* 1: 3–17, 1980.
46. Herbst, P. *Sociotechnical Design*. Tavistock, London, 1974.
47. Herbst, P. *Autonomous Group Functioning*. Tavistock, London, 1962.
48. Parker, M., and Slaughter, J. Management by stress. *The New York Times*, December 4, 1988.

CHAPTER 9

Organizational Change and Health at Work

Gunnela Westlander

ORGANIZATIONAL CHANGE: A PSYCHOLOGICAL PERSPECTIVE

"Change is good for people; you can even say that any change is better than none at all." This is not an unusual statement. It is often made by top management, and reflects the quite natural fear of stagnation in business. To survive as an organization, management must constantly pay attention to what is going on in the world outside, and must be constantly ready for change. Sudden changes forced by outside influences—such as a loss of interest by a major customer, changes in demand, sudden appearance of new competitors, demands for information from government authorities, or Acts of Parliament restructuring the public sector—must produce immediate, but at the same time, sensible reactions from management. The reaction is often to reorganize part or all of the business activity, rather like regrouping troops to form an effective defense. The situation is hardly one that puts the needs or health of the individual in the foreground, or provides the time required for long-drawn-out participation negotiations. Even if, in the long run, such negotiations would be constructive, the fact is that management usually places its hope in the obedience and trust of the employees. Those who want to remain employed must accept the situation. Reorganization as defensive action has differing psychological characteristics for various staff categories.

The prerequisites for gaining a true picture of how well or badly the ship is being navigated are completely different at the management and employee levels. At the risk of oversimplifying the situation somewhat, we can speak of two types of "uncertainty feelings":

1. Knowing about the uncertainty of the organization's continued existence or success.

133

2. Not knowing about the uncertainty of the organization's continued existence or success.

The first type of uncertainty feeling will be found in decision makers, and the second in employees in non–decision-making posts. Related to these two types of feelings is the opportunity to deal actively or passively with the situation. "Knowing about the uncertainty" means that the person in question can make an evaluation of the varying advantages and disadvantages in coping with the uncertain situation (can obtain more information, try to influence people, etc., or–in a negative response– avoid the situation in various ways). "Not knowing about the uncertainty" means that the individual has difficulty in making such a judgment (taking a wait-and-see approach, in an unsettled and diffuse state, letting others take action).

Psychologically, especially in preventive environment work, these differing feelings of uncertainty are very important. We must clearly note the difference between the two. One side will feel alienated toward the subjective reality of the other side. The initiative for a change in organization usually comes from high up in the hierarchy and the primary aim is increased efficiency. Work on organizational changes vitalizes managers' work content; new conditions must be dealt with. This becomes a positive challenge, often a stimulation. Among nonmanagement employees, a reorganization has a more conditional function: it is a good thing only to the extent that it improves, or leaves unaltered, the employees' current and future work situation. People in specialist administrative positions or organizational experts show a third reaction pattern: the reorganization is interesting, whatever the result. It can be looked on as an experiment showing how the employees and business are affected–knowledge that will be of value in the future to an administrator or organizational expert in the same or another company.

In other words, changes in organization are complicated actions not only because of the practical changes that must be introduced, but also because they often have psychological consequences. The result is that the atmosphere at work reflects differing interests in the proposed changes and various types of psychic stresses. This complex social reality is difficult to study in a systematic way.

What do we know about the link between organizational change and individual working conditions that will be of value in preventive work? Business economists, sociologists, and psychologists are interested in the phenomenon of organizational change, but from different points of view. In research on the psychology of work and organization, attention is directed to the employees and their conditions. An effort is made to obtain systematized knowledge about the effects of organizational change on individual health and work opportunities. It is this approach that gives us information on the mental health consequences. This perspective is interesting and important because it provides necessary insight about people that supplements the view of company management. All those working in preventive fields need such knowledge. The theme of this chapter is the link between organizational change and the mental health and working conditions of the individual.

The concept of organizational change is complex. It covers everything from a change in the total macrostructure of a company to alterations in work allocation–

coordination of activity in precisely defined smaller units; it may involve changes in administration or in production. This chapter includes a number of examples of organizational changes initiated on various levels. Analyses are intended to demonstrate the character of the changes and the way in which they are related to the objective and subjective working conditions of the employees, who must operate and fulfill their jobs according to the new principles of the initiators.

Since organizational changes in one way or another rearrange the work-based relations between employees, the most easily observed dimensions of health are those included in the psychosocial domain (1). The core dimensions are the more enduring attitudes to job quality and the feedback one gets in the form of one's own competence and personal development; the social satisfactions (of contacts, collaboration, belongingness, team spirit, cohesiveness); and finally the emotions (security, anxiety, stress and strain) deriving from these conditions. Mental health is used in the text as a general term for these dimensions.

MATERIALS AND METHODS

What has struck me during my field investigations is the variety of interest shown in the health of employees, especially their mental health, when organizational changes are taking place. In some cases the matter is left totally to chance; there is a complete lack of interest or consideration by top management and among the members of the safety and health committees. Nobody sees it as his or her responsibility. In other cases there may be an interest, but no experience to base it on—especially when testing new technology. On the other hand, in some cases one can glimpse a combination of efficiency and health reasons as the motivation for organizational change. The case in which the *main* objective is to improve employee mental health is a rarity. (Here I exclude such changes that are made for research purposes.)

This spectrum of cases is the main subject of this chapter. The material on organizational change has been taken from some ten years of my own research. In the various projects there have been case studies with a more penetrating approach. Some of these have been processed in cross-study analysis form (2, 3), others have been reported as unique cases. They illustrate natural contexts, local development attempts within the framework of more or less meager economic conditions. As a research worker in the role of passive observer I have been able to follow and to learn from these case studies. Most examples deal with administrative work, which is due to the more recent line of research I have undertaken in office technology and working environments rather than to any preference for these types of occupations.

I will start by addressing the problem of causality. It may be important to demonstrate how differently measures of organizational change can be related to the employees' job situation. After this short exposé a number of cases will be presented as empirical findings of three categories of organizational changes: first, some cases in which health aspects were left to chance; second, some examples in which some consideration was shown for the personnel's health at work; and third, a case that started out with the main objective of improving employee mental health and attained the goal by an organizational change.

THE LINK BETWEEN ORGANIZATIONAL CHANGE AND INDIVIDUAL WORKING CONDITIONS

One question that arises in situations where wide-ranging structural changes have been carried out is if, and how, these changes have affected individual job satisfaction. This question often comes up in retrospect, asked by some thoughtful person who suddenly sees the importance of the effect on the staff. In fact, the question is not easy to answer. It requires a penetrating analysis in which the changes themselves must be kept apart from the employees' work tasks.

This situation can be illustrated by three examples (discussed in more detail later)— three departments (here called E-TOWN, SECUR, and P-BOARD) from different companies, municipal authorities, and state utilities, which have been studied for a period of time (4). The changes that took place were decided on at top management level and involved transformation of the total structure of the organizations. Table 1 gives a summary description of the three cases in a two-year time perspective. As can be seen, the three departments are the result of different types of structural change. In E-TOWN and SECUR, two departments were combined but with differing intentions. In E-TOWN, management intentions were to combine several specialist areas in order to broaden competence for the assignments that were to be carried out. In SECUR it was a purely administrative coordination under one manager. Most of the staff in both cases were satisfied with the changes, but for completely different reasons. In E-TOWN it was said that the new arrangements had brought about greater job enhancement (the change had a direct effect on the work of the employees). In SECUR, the merger did not in general affect the work of the individual employee, nor the long-established work and cooperation methods. Except for the departmental manager, all personnel could continue as before with their work, something that was felt to be very satisfactory.

In the utility that included P-BOARD, the structural change was aimed at an increased level of specialization and hierarchy, and for P-BOARD this meant intervention in a cooperation pattern that had been operating satisfactorily for many years. The intervention was regarded with dislike, as a threat to the well-established feeling of community.

If we compare the structural changes in terms of psychological consequences for the employees' work we can create the following ranking:

E-TOWN: The structural change resulted in a positive effect on the individual (the majority) and thus gained acceptance.

SECUR: The structural change was accepted but left the working conditions of individuals fairly undisturbed, which was the intention.

P-BOARD: The structural change had a negative effect at the individual level; it caused irritation and anxiety, was thwarted, and so had no immediate break-through.

HEALTH ASPECTS LEFT TO CHANCE

We shall first look at the situation in which organizational change originated from a top management decision. No thought was given to the employee's health at work or to how employees in the lower ranks of the organizational hierarchy were to tackle the situation.

Table 1

Office units in a time context—from one form of organization to another

	E-TOWN	SECUR	P-BOARD
Previous form of organization	In central local government there was a department dealing with organizational matters and a planning group for statistics and premises planning.	Training and information were the responsibility of two departments within the same company.	Information was the responsibility of one department (the same as after the reorganization).
Changes that were made	When local government was reorganized these two units were combined to form what was called a development department. The planning group's chief statistician was appointed manager. The former head of the organization department worked part-time in the new unit. The change led to the integration of electronic data processing and organizational duties. The change went smoothly.	When an incorporated company was formed, the organization was broken up to form 13 subsidiary companies and a holding company. Training and information were coordinated under one executive.	To solve the problem of an unusually high average age among the staff of the utility, a firm of consultants was engaged to find ways of attracting younger people to apply for vacant posts. The solution proposed a new form of organization with the creation of jobs that would increase promotion prospects. All departments were reorganized. P-BOARD relinquished centralized management combined with multifaceted job positions in favor of a decentralized management form based on functional organization. One intended consequence was a certain growth in specialization and the establishing of middle management posts with functional responsibility.
Time when the investigation started.	The reorganization had been tested for a year and, during this period, had become stable. All staff members with the exception of one office clerk expressed satisfaction with the new organization.	The new organization had been in force for a year. All staff members expressed satisfaction with the reorganization.	The reorganization had been tested for some 6 months. It had resulted in more specialized work for everyone, changes in cooperation patterns with more limited contact areas, and less chance of "going over to each others' job" when necessary. It was difficult to link functional responsibility to the role of manager since people previously cooperated at the same level. The manager was anxious to have the new form of organization accepted and realized in full. Others, with a couple or so exceptions, expressed doubt. The division of responsibility was thought to be too restrictive.

137

Five Cases of Office Rationalization

The following examples come from a study carried out in 1983 (5-7). The five cases described in Table 2 show how word processing technology was adopted as a solution to a need for rationalization expressed at the top level. In the five companies there was no experience or philosophy to handle the human consequences of such a technology. The effects of the introduction of this technology were examined retrospectively two years after the introduction of the word processing and text editing system. In these five cases, office staff can be seen as the final link in a chain of demands: external factors force the company to adapt; this in turn affects the office functions, which finally decide what demands are placed on office staff. From a health standpoint, the question ultimately is how can office work be organized to give the employees a chance to overcome the demands for rationalization coming from above?

In the first example, the secretaries were reorganized and given new word processing and text editing technology without being asked to participate in the preparatory work. Management demands for increased efficiency were directed at the secretaries as an isolated group. Most of them suffered a deterioration in working conditions. Psychic stress and unhappiness with the conditions were common, even after two years.

The third example resembles the first in the way the demands for rationalization came from the top down. Here external specialists also participated and led the reorganization. Both secretaries and insurance workers had to radically change their working routines. It was the claims adjusters who came off worst.

The other cases resemble the above in that the directive was a general tightening-up. But the common factor for the third, fourth, and fifth examples was that the changes, which had been decided on in advance, were not forced on the employees. Instead, the employees were highly involved in deciding how rationalization should take place and what the concrete efficiency targets should be. This strengthened the feeling of solidarity between the employees, and it proved possible to deal gradually and jointly with situations of stress.

The five cases show a spectrum of health-relevant reactions ranging from increased interest in work and a feeling of unity, through minor disappointments, to an obvious deterioration in work satisfaction (due to monotony and isolation). Some people felt extreme dissatisfaction, but could choose to change jobs at an early stage and so were not available for the retrospective investigation.

A Problem of Organization Converted into an Individual Health Problem

When the consequences of an organizational change result in a markedly reduced level of mental health in someone involved, it is not unusual for the organizational circumstances to become overshadowed and concealed while attention is focused on the suffering individual and his or her personal qualities. The working atmosphere can become so emotionally charged that it takes an outsider to reveal the distortions in interpretation that have taken place in the company to give rise to the deteriorating situation. The following authentic case illustrates a structural change in a company making efforts to expand its business.

The Grand, the principal hotel in the small town of Pinemarket (10,000 inhabitants), had just been renovated. The dining room was now supplemented by an evening

Table 2

Organizational factors behind transition to word processing (WP) technology in five companies

I. A department of central administration (engineering company)	II. A head office (shipping company)	III. A department of claim damages (insurance company)	IV. An engineering department (public defense service)	V. A section of administration service (engineering company)
A successful engineering concern is put into an unexpected competitive situation.	A well-known transport industry is surrounded by growing competitive pressure.	A big insurance company is constantly in search of policy-holders.	A public defense utility service is exposed to (a) changed directives from the government and parliament, (b) instructions to reduce its staff, and (c) expectations that it will make investments at a good price for the national defense.	A big engineering industry takes a long view to practice a more strict economy by decentralizing budget responsibility to the department level.
The executives expect declining profits. They order the administrative functions to practice strict economy.	Management plans to meet this pressure by strengthening company effectiveness. Order is given that new technology communication systems be introduced so that customers will be reached within a shorter time.	New types of insurance are often created. The number of insured increases, which means higher demands on productivity.	The executives must follow the instructions but also do good business on behalf of the government. The lack of uniformity in office activities is a big problem.	The administrative section is suddenly put into a state of insecurity and uncertainty over whether their services are needed by other departments.
The management of the administration reacts by planning to cut the salary cost of the central department.	The manager in charge of administration decides to use the main computer of the company for all information technology needed by the head office. Courses are organized for the administrative staff.	The insurance company has at its disposal a staff of rationalization specialists who are expected to give support to the operative department by introducing new efficient work routines.	In one engineering department difficulties with the immense typing load are resolved by introducing computer technology.	The administrative section decides to make a large-scale effort in administrative support systems to support the manufacturing parts of the company.
Secretarial work is reorganized, typing pools are arranged, WP systems are introduced, and part-time work is offered.	All secretaries are requested to be highly efficient and to work fast in order to provide their superiors with better written information for decision-making.	WP equipment is installed and typing pools are organized in one of the claim damage departments.	The employees at various positions get together to find a suitable way to handle the WP procedure. They manage to reach a more even work flow. The tasks of the secretaries stay the same, but some technical knowledge expands their professional competence.	A multifunctional system is bought with programs of word processing, statistics, mathematics, registration, and so on, which should be able to create the administrative support. All members of the staff take the courses necessary to manage the computer.
A spontaneous turnover is the consequence of many negative attitudes among the office workers. The remainder of the secretarial staff has an isolated and monotonous job situation. Their superiors stay intact of the reorganization.	The consequence is spontaneous endorsement by the secretaries, and a more stimulating job atmosphere, whereas the content of job remains the same.	To manage the growing number of policy-holders with the same personnel, all written communications are transformed into standardized wordings.		Superiors and clerks of the section participate in intensive teamwork in order to prove their vital importance to the other departments of the company.
		Claims adjusters as well as secretaries have to change work routines radically. The secretaries (most of them previous key punch operators) experience upgrading in their jobs, whereas the claims adjusters find their jobs downgraded.		

restaurant, a discotheque, and "The Grill," a breakfast restaurant and coffee house. The restaurant owner hoped that The Grill would attract passing trade, young people and customers who wanted to eat at a reasonable price. Eight staff members were needed to run The Grill—serving staff and kitchen helpers. Six women and two men about 20 years old were asked if they wanted to leave their present jobs (washing-up, cleaning, and laundry work) and move over to The Grill. They all accepted. One of the oldest waitresses from the dining room was asked to take charge; she was in her fifties and one of the old school: smart and neat when waiting at table—the diner was always right. Things went wrong right from the start. There was a clash between the supervisor's demands for discipline and order and the youngsters' lack of interest in exaggerated smartness. But, because the youngsters had no respect at all for their supervisor, she could make no progress. She asked to be relocated.

A male cook, 25 years old, took over. He believed an impersonal, hard attitude toward the staff was the best way to improve standards at The Grill. There was no success this time either. Things became so bad that he also asked for a new assignment.

Management (two senior staff and the owner) now had the problem of finding someone they could ask to take over the somewhat hazardous position of supervisor of The Grill. Their choice fell on Eve, generally recognized as one of the most effective waitresses at the hotel. She was 28, small and frail but tough, with quick reactions and very good at her job. Eve accepted the job of supervisor at The Grill, partly because it was a promotion and partly because the new working hours suited her better for family reasons. Naturally, Eve had a different way of approaching the young staff. First of all she wanted to create a feeling of trust. By taking an intensive part in the practical work she managed to win the sympathy and confidence of the staff. She started a carefully planned course of training and hoped that management would soon see a change in their working attitudes and stop regarding them with mistrust. This did not happen. Management continued to show disapproval of the youngsters, and this created anger and aggression at The Grill. Eve had a difficult job in persuading management that things were going the right way at last.

Eve's relationship with her superiors became more and more complicated. They were doubtful about her way of management; they were impatient that it took such a long time to improve things at The Grill. Eve became bitter because she was not appreciated for all the work and effort she had devoted to her job as supervisor. She started to experience palpitations of the heart on her way to work, a slow spread of dissatisfaction came over her, and she often lay awake at night worrying about the day ahead at work. After six months Eve felt the signs of an unexplained poor physical condition. She experienced long periods of listlessness and, what was worse, a sort of pounding of the heart that came when she least expected it. She visited her doctor. She was put on sick leave for a month, and there was a discussion about the difficult position at work. Eve was told, in a friendly but firm way to "do something about it."

Eve returned to work, rested of course, but without any hope of being able to change anything. Management did not dare to criticize her openly for her all too flexible attitude toward the staff, but the way they looked at her told all. The atmosphere became increasingly tense. The reputation of The Grill had gone downhill. The number of customers fell, the business went from bad to worse. The year-end balancing of the books showed an unfavorable result for The Grill. Management called Eve up to the office, and talks started, on a careful note, about the critical situation. However, things soon became disagreeable when Eve realized that she was regarded as an accessory factor to the loss-making situation.

Eve reacted with a nervous breakdown. She had been given a thankless task. She could neither defend herself nor produce arguments to back up her way of working, despite the fact that she was convinced that she was right in her approach to the problem. So it went on for another six months without any improvement. The Grill closed down and Eve left the company.

An outside observer can see that the problem grew out of a good idea, an expansion of the business; however this was carried out in a clumsy fashion. It is true that the material framework was drawn up with skill, aiming to attract new types of customers. But the other important factor necessary to success of the project—staff development— was forgotten in the belief that it would be sufficient to demand trust and loyalty from the staff. There was no management training for the new duties, and no preliminary vocational training for the staff sent from washing-up, cleaning, and laundry jobs to serving customers. The staff was omitted from management's new business ideas and so could not contribute to making them a success. Eve, with her intense vocational ambition, had to suffer the most.

The shortcomings in the plan for organizational change had been redefined by management and many employees to be a personal problem deeply rooted in Eve. A critical analysis of the course of events would lead us to characterize Eve as the bearer of the problem, not the problem itself. A clinical psychological evaluation, aimed at helping Eve should—but very seldom does—have this overall view as a basis. The problem, then, is made to circle around the difficulty of one individual to adapt. And what is worse, the shortcomings in the company's procedures to reach its new objectives will not be eliminated.

HEALTH AT WORK TAKEN INTO CONSIDERATION

We will now deal with the type of situations in which organizational change is motivated by mixed reasons including aspects of efficiency as well as employees' well-being and health at work. We take the examples from the three departments (E-TOWN, SECUR, and P-BOARD) mentioned earlier (Table 1). The organizational change under study was linked to a technological innovation. This consisted of producing written information with the help of word processing and text editing systems. The secretarial staff's electronic typewriters were replaced by a multistation, shared logic system (4). A new tool was introduced, and in this context the utilization of this became an organizational problem for the employees. Will an organizational change be required at the same time or can the old arrangement be kept? And what does the selection of an organizational solution mean to the health and well-being of the staff?

In order to understand the staff's opportunities for creating a good working atmosphere, researchers examined the following questions. Where in the organization did the initiative come from? How was procurement of the system prepared? What opportunities were offered by management and specialists to the employees in the departments in question?

Interest and involvement from top management and from specialists of automatic data processing, rationalization, and purchasing varied greatly for each department.

E-TOWN: The initiative for acquisition of the word processing system came from within the office unit (from the manager, persuaded by the secretarial staff). The need was generally and specifically acknowledged by all staff, and was also recognized outside the office unit by the top management and employees and in the purchasing department. The manager also carried out rationalization and automatic data processing functions, which probably helped to strengthen the internal demand. From the point of view of the department this can be characterized as an *immanent change (i.e., from within) with full support from management and specialist functions and the employees in the office units.*

SECUR: The initiative arose from outside the office unit, the idea was supported by the rationalization specialist, and the proposal was acknowledged to be useful by all those in the office unit. Outside the unit there was both approval (from purchasing) and opposition (from top management). This situation can be described as *a change imposed externally with support from inside the unit but with a certain degree of opposition from outside.*

P-BOARD: The initiative came from an external source; the rationalization department wanted to test office automation in the company. The need for change appeared in a diffuse way both from the initiator and within the office unit. Top management and other involved functions supported the test method. This was *a change imposed externally with vague support internally and also with vague objectives dictated from outside.* The manager and his department were forced into various forms of dependence on the rest of the company.

In this situation, how did managers deal with their respective departments? They reacted in different ways. Some actively participated and put themselves at the head of their staff (SECUR); some were passive and delegated preparations to their staff (P-BOARD); some tried to cooperate actively with their staff (E-TOWN). But regardless of how they saw their own practical efforts toward their staff, all managers, right from the start, had an idea of how work would be organized when the new equipment was installed.

The P-BOARD was a case of full consensus. All employees were in agreement, and all staff were considered to be involved in the plans. SECUR was a case of partial consensus. The manager and secretarial staff were in agreement but other employees were excluded. E-TOWN had no consensus. The manager and secretarial staff were not in agreement and other employees were excluded, at the request of the secretaries.

After a year, the employees were asked about how they thought the work should be distributed around the word processing and text editing equipment. The lack of agreement continued at E-TOWN and SECUR, while there was general agreement at P-BOARD. A comparison of the problems that arose in the three office units reveals that they primarily involved the same things: defects in the equipment, lack of operational knowledge, and related stress. Thereafter the main problems varied greatly depending on how the written work was organized when the word processing equipment was adopted.

Health Consequences

The workload from written work changed during the year. In the case of E-TOWN the staff seemed to be given more work. At P-BOARD the workload increased in the form of greater time pressures and more problems in cooperation between the secretaries and other staff. In SECUR work was judged to be lighter in some cases: less time pressure, easier planning; in other respects changes were only minor.

When faced with the introduction of office automation relatively few people felt lasting anxiety, perhaps three or less in each office unit—mainly secretaries. Instead, more felt an increase in security in their own work situation. After installation of the system quite a number of strains and stresses arose during its implementation. SECUR had the additional problem of the company being restructured at the same time, with the future being uncertain for the individual employees. Some staff members were affected more than others. In some cases we can speak of a drastically unhealthy effect, the reasons for which varied, as did the symptoms of mental discomfort. Were there elements of organizational factors, or factors arising from the introduction of word processing equipment, or perhaps both?

Because these three studies were prospective, it was possible to obtain a detailed picture of the course of events. The common denominator for these three places of work was office computerization, although the organizational changes were different in nature. It is interesting to note that some staff members are resistant to any change in existing work routines, whereas their departmental managers are keen for such change.

When comparing the initiative-takers' interest in employee health, SECUR seems to stand out as the employer most steered by a predominant aim of increased efficiency, whereas the other two had clear traces of health objectives, especially P-BOARD. The departmental managers emphasized the value of job development, job status, and lower work loads. But this had no unambiguously positive effects, and some employees suffered from the situation.

HEALTH AT WORK AS THE MAIN GOAL—ORGANIZATIONAL CHANGE AS THE METHOD

Of great interest are organizational changes that have, as it were, grown organically from inside a company, but there are few documented examples. The following organizational change was studied in one of the major Swedish engineering companies. Here we find a good example of changes in which the main objective was to improve the level of health at work. This is the single such case in the range of cases discussed in this chapter. In order to leave the reader in a more optimistic frame of mind, I will let this case stand as the last example.

The locality is a large industry in a rural area where it is not easy for trained secretaries to find other jobs. In practice, staff members are forced to accept what this employer can offer if they want to carry on using their special working skills. At the time of the study some 50 women worked as secretaries. Most of them were married to men also employed by the company and so were doubly bound to whatever work the area could offer. The common problems for the secretaries were related to duties and salary scales. The company offered no opportunities for job development, training, or promotion, and the work of the secretaries mainly consisted of simple routine duties; thus some of the secretaries were regarded as surplus to requirements. Management saw secretarial positions as "the end of the line," a staff policy that created great irritation among the secretaries. The work changes that arose out of this discontent went on for four years (8).

The intention was to obtain professional vocational development within the framework of secretarial employment; the problem was that there was no demand for this either from management or from other staff categories. So the 50 secretaries had to carry through their objectives in the face of strong opposition. Here is a summary of how their efforts to bring about change progressed step by step.

The problem was first raised at a local meeting of the white-collar union. One of the secretaries was present. She pointed out that most of her colleagues did work that seemed to fall into other occupational classifications. The matter was noted but no action was taken. Some secretaries then approached the union's local committee and asked the chairperson to arrange a meeting with a number of the company's executives. This was done. Salary scales and vocational development for the secretaries were discussed, but interest declined after the meeting.

An internal consultant took over the problem and tried, in vain, to make the union take responsibility for some follow-up. A second internal consultant, an expert in job evaluation, became involved. Together with a firm of consultants, a survey was carried out among the secretaries. The result showed widespread dissatisfaction.

At the request of the union and management, the consultants arranged a number of conferences for the secretaries and their immediate superiors. The intention was to clarify for management the secretaries' working conditions and, in more explicit form, their wishes for vocational development, all within the framework of their secretarial duties. A great deal of hard work was done at these conferences. Prejudices and oppositional attitudes were ventilated. A list of problems was drawn up. A total of 45 managers and 53 secretaries participated.

After this problem analysis stage was completed, the consultants made it clear that their contribution was over. The secretaries now decided to take on the job themselves. Among possible solutions, they selected a business-economic strategy, with the surmise that it would increase managerial interest in the matter. They divided themselves into small, specialist working groups (technology, ergonomy, purchasing, etc.). Each group took it upon itself to produce proposals for improving secretarial work. They also worked out a cost calculation for each proposal.

During the next few years 22 working groups were formed to solve varied problems. Six working groups were in operation four years after the start. From the names of these groups we can see where their interests lay: technology in the future, office materials, travel service, copy-saving measures, training, sensitivity training. The groups were more and more successful in gaining attention for their proposals, many of which were carried through.

A number of rationalization measures arose from the studies made by the groups: now nobody does any unnecessary work; manuscripts are accepted as working material; secretaries only perform copy typing when necessary. An office computer system has been procured. The secretarial group lost ten staff members by natural wastage (usually moves to another part of the country.) The secretaries were now consulted by the company's recruitment department when a vacant secretarial post was to be filled. They were asked to propose reorganizations so that new staff would not be needed. Up to now, 19 secretaries have been promoted to a higher job classification with higher salaries as their work became more skilled. Management is satisfied with the organizational changes that have taken place.

The original idea of the project was to cut out unnecessary and low-skill duties from secretarial work and to add more high-skill duties. This succeeded; at the same time a great deal of expensive duplication of work and long-winded working routines was discovered. After a while, the project continued in other forms. It was integrated into the work of the staff department under the name RGSD (Reference Group for Secretarial Development).

For some while, this organizational change became known all over the country. A number of group members were invited to committees and conferences around the country to describe the project.

Health Consequences

These work changes were of immense personal importance to the secretaries. For most, it meant a greater consciousness of their vocational role and of the opportunities for improving the secretarial function in the company. A team spirit arose from looking at problems common to them all. As a job collective they saw, step by step, the result of their tenacious work. The improved vocational opportunities came from their own efforts.

The only doubt remaining to an outside observer wanting to evaluate the success of this organizational change is: did the improvements in job quality occur because the ten secretarial jobs, lost through natural wastage, were not replaced? This must have been a contributory factor. The municipality lost a few job vacancies, but at that time there was plenty of work available in that region of the country.

POSTSCRIPT

This last case has some unusual features in addition to the emphasis on vocational development. The initiative came mainly from a low level in the hierarchy. The contribution from management was almost a passive participation; managers took part to allow themselves to be influenced; the internal consultants participated to create the opportunities needed to bring about the changes. Management also saw the whole thing as an exciting experiment, which in this case had a vitalizing effect on the secretaries, who felt that responsibility, in the last resort, rested on their shoulders.

The chosen solution was extremely "system-friendly"; that is, the secretaries used business-economical considerations as a framework for their improvement proposals. They consciously used rationalization of administrative work in the company as a means to achieve their own objectives—higher qualification levels in their own work. By acting in this way the secretaries skillfully blocked the fateful process (described earlier in this chapter) in which an organizational problem mutates into individual deadlocked states of discontent.

So in this last case, we find a number of ingredients that made organizational change a success both for mental health and for efficiency. Expressed more generally, it is a matter of the following:

- The initiative came from and was forced through by those directly affected.
- Support, especially instrumental support, was offered by specialists in personal development.
- Room to work for the change was given by management.
- Among those directly affected there was a consciousness of the business-economical side of the matter.
- There was familiarity with the organization in general and with its structure.

In the other examples of organizational change dealt with in this chapter, isolated fragments of this can be found, with the one exception that the change was more or less forced on people from above. Those finally affected were the "object of" the change rather than the agents of change. In such a situation the only thing for the employees to do is to try to tackle the demands in the best manner possible. The various cases show the range in such interplay in situations where there is no room for maneuver. The question that must be asked is, could one have intervened to prevent the negative consequences that obviously occurred? One frequent answer is that no one could foresee how things would develop, and so it would be difficult to know what preventive action might have been taken. This rather resigned attitude is widespread.

Research workers who carry out prospective studies are constantly being reminded of the unpredictable: quite simply, the original hypotheses do not prove correct.

A great deal happens in interpersonal relationships at a very early stage after change is initiated. In contrast to laboratory experiments or in meetings where group questionnaires can be taken, the situation (i.e., the process of change) is not under control. Researchers who study organizational change should find this unpredictable process fascinating and not irritating. Industrial sociologists ought to have the same feeling. The idea of evaluating final effects should be abandoned. We must realize that preventive work consists of being at hand the whole time and providing adequate support. One should be especially careful with formal superior-subordinate (employee) situations. During organizational change, relationships should be marked by a feeling of cooperation, at least at the informal level. Resources for all these activities are available in most present-day Swedish companies, with their personnel functions, organization department, company-run health departments, and interested union representatives. It is just a matter of using them.

Finally, we can categorically state that organizational change is very demanding. It often leads to periods of lassitude, tiredness, and irritation. The important thing is to prevent these feelings of lassitude from becoming permanent and to turn them into something positive. That extra individual effort that we all must make should help us to learn something new, valuable, and enriching for the future.

REFERENCES

1. Work Environment Fund. *Human Work Environment. Important Behavioural Work Environment Research*, Report 1984: 4. Stockholm, 1984.
2. Yin, R. K. *Case Study Research, Design and Methods*, Applied Social Research Methods Series, Vol. 5. Sage Publications, London, 1984.
3. Westlander, G. *On Context-oriented Approaches: A Discussion of Methodics Related to Research into the Psychology of Organization*, Report 1985:8. The National Swedish Board of Occupational Safety and Health, Stockholm, 1985.
4. Westlander, G. *Office Automation as a Driving Force, How People Act and Work Changes: A Cross Case Analysis of Office Workplaces*. Studentlitteratur, Lund, 1986.
5. Westlander, G. *Office Automation, Organizational Factors and Psycho-social Aspects with Special Reference to Word Processing*. Reports from the Department of Psychology, University of Stockholm, Suppl. 61, November 1984.
6. Söderberg, I. Office work and office automation, influence over working environments and work organization. *Nordic Ergonomics–Research and Practice*. 2: 4–14, 1984.
7. Westlander, G., and Söderman, E. *Office Work in Transition, Empirical Studies of the Introduction of New Technology in Word Processing and Text Production*, Report 1985:7. The National Swedish Board of Occupational Health and Safety, Stockholm, 1985.
8. Westlander, G. *Woman and Working Life*. Natur och Kultur, Stockholm, 1981.

CHAPTER 10

Origins of Authority: The Organization of Medical Care in Sweden

Rolf Å. Gustafsson

The Swedish health care system is mainly hospital-based, highly specialized, and nonprivate (1). It is also characterized by severe manpower problems, most notable of which are an extremely high rate of labor turnover among auxiliaries and work alienation. These features have remained almost constant throughout the whole postwar development of the welfare state, though different aspects have been emphasized at different times. For example, there are now reports of severe difficulties in recruiting students into courses to qualify as nursing aides (2, pp. 179-180). In the 1950s and 1960s Sweden experienced the classic problem of nursing shortage. In the 1970s attention was directed at the quality of care. It is no coincidence that in 1978 one of Sweden's most distinguished writers published a celebrated novel (later to be filmed) of life in a large-scale general hospital, presenting a vivid picture of dehumanized care (3).

This forms the general background to a request directed to Bertil Gardell in the mid-1970s to undertake a research project dealing with the psychosocial work environment at general hospitals. The initiative was originally taken by the Swedish Federation of Municipal Workers, which organizes almost all health care personnel in Sweden with the exception of registered nurses and physicians. Nursing aides constitute roughly 50 percent of all health care personnel in Sweden (2, pp. 179-180). In the mid-1970s there was a growing concern for psychosocial work environment issues in the Swedish labor movement (4). In order to avoid the risk of being perceived as the advocates of a partial view, Bertil Gardell and I, when setting up the infrastructure of the program, included on the advisory committee related to the project all the labor unions involved in the health care sector. The result was a study reported in 1979 (5) using the conceptual framework, and within the political context, described in other chapters of

This work was supported by the Swedish Work Environment Fund.

149

this book. Taking our earlier research on hospital organization as a point of departure, in this chapter I describe some of the main results of a newly published historical-sociological study, in which the original work environment approach has been developed into a research framework that covers the health care sector as a whole and its relation to society (6).

In 1979 we came to the conclusion that there is a general discrepancy between perceived needs and organizational structure in Swedish somatic hospitals; the work organization is constructed *as if* cure and medical treatment were the specific and all-important goals of almost all kinds of health care work. In the hospitals, ward staff are forced to ignore a wide spectrum of psychosomatic illnesses and complaints, information-emotive tasks, and preventive measures, though a constant awareness of such factors is crucial in their daily work. Basic work-related problems could be interpreted as responses to this discrepancy. The standard organizational model for general hospitals—for which we formulated the concept of *"the acute care model"*—involves a merger of medical and administrative hierarchies. Both hierarchies are characterized by a high degree of horizontal and vertical fragmentation of the work process. The medical hierarchy is imbued with a professional science-based ideology. The administrative hierarchy channels Taylorism into the health care sector. This structure forces large segments of the hospital staff to accept a work content that is not appropriate for the needs of patients; neither does it develop the capacities of the personnel or provide work satisfaction.

Such a structural interpretation of the built-in contradictions in the work environment poses wider questions concerning the role of the welfare state and the professionals within it. Diderichsen divides the state of crisis in the Swedish health care system into the following different problem areas (1, p. 196):

> 1. The reproduction of the physical and psychological quality of the labor force is not improving in any relation to the increasing costs of the system.
> 2. Because of the economic crisis of the society as a whole, the idea that more experts can solve health problems cannot be reproduced either, because there is no money for more experts.
> 3. The economic restrictions also mean that the health sector cannot supply enough jobs to compensate for the job rationalizations within industry.
> 4. It also means that the health sector is no longer the expanding market for drugs and technology for Swedish industry that it once was.

Points 1 and 2 indicate that work environment problems in the health care sector are related to both sides of the cost-effectiveness crisis. The alienation of hospital staff and the health hazards they face at work are not only counterproductive in terms of their contribution to the general output of work-related illness. A dissatisfied labor force in the health care sector, with high rates of labor turnover, and a work structure dominated by technological rationality, will continuously press for an enlarged budget while working as inefficiently as before in terms of the quality of care or the promotion of preventive measures. A purely quantitative solution therefore seems impossible. It is true that a better and more stably staffed hospital organization, based on the acute care model, probably means a less dissatisfied, a less unhealthy, and a less underpaid labor force, but its work would still be fundamentally misdirected. This leads to the conclusion that work environment research in the field involves more than the study of work-related problems such as stress, lack of social support, ill health, etc., among health care personnel.

Given that in round figures 70 percent (1985) of all nonprivate health care personnel in Sweden work within hospital-based somatic care [only 7 percent of all health care personnel are privately employed (2, p. 178)], and given the centralized planning structure, there are good reasons to analyze the acute care model. Our historical-sociological approach is further justified by the fact that no attempts have been made so far to trace the historical roots of the basic dilemmas facing the contemporary Swedish health care sector.

LOOKING FOR HISTORICAL ROOTS TO STRUCTURAL PROBLEMS

When we approached this new field of research, an exploratory design was considered most appropriate. The study was based on a broad inventory of Swedish secondary literature (published between 1866 and 1985) in the field of medical history with special reference to administrative, political, and legislative development. In order to make this vast amount of material manageable, the comparative aspect of the study was kept to a minimum. The research design has the form of *a historical case study in which the structural antecedents of the acute care model are looked for.* This means that no causal conclusions can be inferred from the results at this stage (7); this is an important task for further research in which we hope our case study will be of benefit. Sweden is a comparatively homogeneous country which has experienced few violent and drastic political changes. Historically, it has been on the periphery of cultural currents. This probably explains some of the continuity revealed by the case study.

The works of Philip Abrams (8) and Theda Skocpol (9) are taken as starting points in formulating the theoretical perspective of the study. Skocpol, although advocating the use of a more causal/analytical framework, gives an adequate account of this general approach (9, p. 368):

> Interpretative historical sociologists . . . are skeptical of the usefulness of either applying theoretical models to history or using a hypothesis-testing approach to establish causal generalizations about large-scale structures and patterns of change. Instead, these scholars seek meaningful interpretations of history, in two intertwined senses of the word meaningful. First, careful attention is paid to the culturally embedded intentions of individual or group actors in the given historical settings under investigation. Second, both the topic chosen for the historical study and the kinds of arguments developed about it should be culturally or politically "significant" in the present: That is, significant to the audiences, always larger than specialized academic audiences, addressed by the published works of interpretive historical sociologist.

What Skocpol describes as trans-historical concepts are avoided, as well as any form of evolutionism. A Marxian conceptualization is not abandoned, but there is no attempt to test or apply a specific theory. The lack of a sociological overview of the Swedish health care system calls for an exploratory design. With reference to organization theory, two "open concepts" are formulated. These provide important structuring themes for the historical investigation:

- *Activity demarcation*: Which motives and factors helped to make individual cure the main goal, out of a diffuse context in which social control, custody, philanthropy, and prevention were living alternatives?
- *Control*: Which motives and factors structured the hierarchy of the Swedish medical administration (control over the agenda) and the internal structure of the somatic general hospitals (control within the acute care model)?

SOME BASIC ORGANIZATIONAL PATTERNS

Figure 1 summarizes some of the organizational patterns that should be interpreted as the effects of an ongoing organization process that has been sustained over a period of 400 years. The five key organizational traditions that were most important in the shaping of the acute care model are represented by the five numbered lines. The figure does not deal with quantitative aspects. It focuses on these important traditions with reference to their interorganizational activity demarcation and control structure. Our aim is to illustrate "turning points" in the overall organization process. When, where, and why were the different traditions *established and consolidated in the form of specific formal organizations*? The heavy line in the center of the Figure marks the ancient division between surgery and medicine. This division is interpreted as forming two arenas: the one comprises needs of an intangible character, which often require care on a long-term basis, and which are difficult to interpret and evaluate; the other arena is characterized by needs that are comparatively easy to detect and evaluate and for which short-term treatment is possible.

Our purpose here is more to illustrate the line of reasoning than to provide a fully fledged analysis. *We focus on four important and clearly identifiable events (E1, E2, E3, and E4 in Figure 1) which consolidated the organizational traditions that culminated in the creation of the acute care model.*

The different organizational traditions depicted in the figure have been intensively studied over a period extending from the late 15th century to the late 19th century. In the 1870s and 1880s a new medical paradigm (the germ theory of disease) was formed, thus making a break with established humoral pathology (10). This launched modern medical theory. Organizational initiatives (state commissions, legislation, policy documents, etc.) referring to medical theories and ideologies before the 1870s are therefore described as *premedical* in this context. *Extramedical* factors refer to societal influences of different kinds (political and economic changes as well as changes in social structure and related public health problems).

Solid historical evidence indicates that the basic features of the acute care model were, formally and practically, constituted 10 to 20 years before the advent of modern medicine. *This means that premedical and especially extramedical factors can be shown to be important in shaping the Swedish health care system.* The system is therefore only partially a product of modern medicine; the traditional heritage (social control, military needs, social position of the physicians, mercantilism, etc.) is more important and pervasive than has generally been thought. This is the "yoke of tradition" in Swedish health care, a yoke that has fostered the structural inertia now faced by the government in making health policy proposals; since the 1930s the

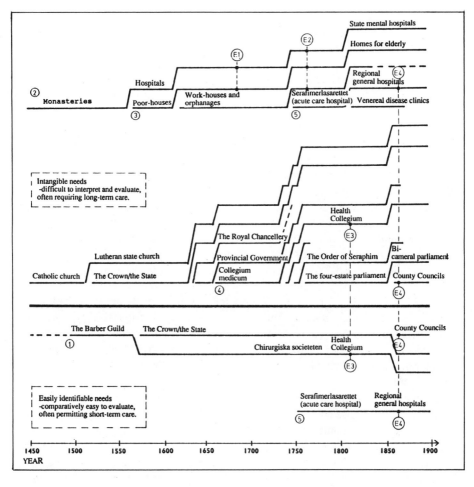

Figure 1. Some of the basic organizational traditions of health care, welfare, support, and social administration in Sweden over 400 years.

government has advocated a build-up of primary care, and since the 1970s it has been in favor of preventive measures (11, 12). Let us now take a closer look at the empirical material in order to get to grips with the historical roots of the contemporary health care sector.

AN OUTLINE OF SWEDISH CARE IN THE MIDDLE AGES

In 1349 Sweden was struck by the international plague epidemic. It was imported through a Hanseatic commercial vessel in Bergen (Norway). Present historians estimate the death rate to have been one in three of the Swedish population, but no decisive effects on organizational structure can be related to this event. This is an early example of the relative autonomy of the "health care system." The same phenomenon is evident and more reliably documented in later phases of its development: basic threats to public health seldom lead to a restructuring of "the health care system."

By the end of the 15th century there were three embryonic elements to the system under study:

1. *Barber surgeons* (line 1 in Figure 1): This group was formed into a craft guild with formal privileges as burghers and corresponding responsibilities to the crown (Stockholm 1496 and 1571). In the case of war the Barber Guild was obliged to provide the army and fleet with war surgeons.

2. *Hospitals* (line 2 in Figure 1): The nucleus of this institutional branch is to be found in the monasteries, in infirmaries for sick and old monks, and in wayside lodgings (hospices). These institutions could be described as asylums for a broad spectrum of "inmates." Later, they became leper asylums. The Swedish word for leper (spetälska) is derived from the word hospital (spetal). Important factors in the activity demarcation of the institutions in this early phase were the Catholic commandment (1215) forbidding monks from engaging in surgery and blood letting, and the Platonic university tradition, which had a derogatory view of manual labor. The latter influence was indirect, as the first Swedish university (in Uppsala) was not founded until 1477. Formal domestic medical education came into being at the end of the 17th century (13).

3. *The parish* (line 3 in Figure 1): Ancient Swedish local laws (landskapslagarna 1250) laid down some responsibilities on the parishes to support the poor, which were carried out in the context of and partly financed by the tithe system. This triggered off local developments in which poor-relief was given under the authority of the master, a system that slowly changed into disparate attempts to lodge the needy in poor-houses.

Decisive to this early organization process were extramedical factors, in particular proximity to the growing center of power, which strengthened these embryonic formal branches. Ethnomedicine lacked such a relationship with the center, which probably was an important factor in impairing its chances of gaining recognition. It was these sociological factors, rather than their efficiency in terms of healing or support, that led to the step-by-step consolidation of the formal system in terms of resources, stability, and social legitimation.

ORGANIZATIONAL SECULARIZATION AND CONSOLIDATED HIERARCHICAL CONTROL

Gustav Vasa (king of Sweden, 1523-1560) strengthened the Swedish national state. The Lutheran reformation is generally seen against this background. The succeeding period in the history of Sweden was characterized by the strength of the nobility. During the 17th century, in cooperation with the crown, serious attempts were made to install a Swedish Great Power in the Baltic. The death of Karl XII (1718) put an end to this epoch.

Certain important steps in the shaping of the "health care system" can be related to the underlying societal development that took place during this period. Organizational secularization was the most prominent factor, not in the parishes but in the *central* institutions of the former Catholic Church, i.e., the monasteries and the hospitals related to them. This can be related to the fact that Gustav Vasa established a state-controlled church which, while allowing the crown to consolidate its own political and economic power, also involved the inheritance of important administrative tasks within the hospital system. The growing importance of the burghers in local town administration furthered this partial secularization of the hospitals, but changed little in terms of activity demarcation. This development was codified in the church law of 1571, which set the guidelines for hospital and poor-house administration (though poor-houses were built in fewer numbers). It is worth stressing that these crown responsibilities were an unwanted part of the development toward a state-controlled church, which had been formed for political reasons. It is therefore logical that no new ideas were brought into the system at this stage; nor were any attempts made to transcend established activity demarcations. The prevailing ideology was still that of traditional Christian philanthropy.

A milestone in the consolidation of this phase of the organization process was reached in 1642 (E1 in Figure 1). Queen Christina issued a royal decree that applied to beggars and the poor. This was a reaction to great domestic problems, especially the growing impoverishment of the peasantry resulting from the hardships that followed the era of Great Power politics. Christian motives still played a legitimizing role, but a harsher attitude toward the poor can be detected in this decree. This can be interpreted as a consolidation of the organizational structure along traditional lines which took place against the background of a tightening social situation, itself generated by the pressure of the impoverished peasantry. At the same time, the central power consolidated the responsibility of the *parishes* to care for "their own poor." In the same decree an attempt was made to further solidify the activity demarcation implicit in the foregoing development; the sick, the contagious, and those who lacked the capability of taking care of themselves should be placed in the custody of the *crown-hospitals*. This meant, in fact, the beginnings of the compartmentalization of social and medical problems. This division remained formally intact in organizational terms in Sweden right up to the 1960s; mental hospitals were state-owned while social work came under the head of the commune/municipality (mental hospitals are now run by the county like somatic hospitals, but the parish/commune tradition is still unbroken).

In 1663 a royal decree entrusted a group of eight medical doctors with the duty and privilege of keeping a strict watch on "charlatans in medicine" and of conferring official approval upon medical doctors who intended to practice medicine in Sweden. They were also charged with the task of supervising the drug trade and the women who assisted at childbirth. This led to the formation of the *Collegium medicum*, and here we find the embryo of the central medical administration (line 4 in Figure 1). This was a first step in the professionalization process, which at this time can be considered an integrated part of the ongoing strengthening of the state apparatus. The forming of Collegium medicum led to an intense struggle between the leading interest groups in this arena, i.e., the Barber Guild and Collegium medicum itself. This was settled in the 1680s when the Barber Guild, under protest, gave in to Collegium medicii demands to examine and supervise barbers. The barbers were also forbidden to prescribe certain drugs and to handle medical matters provided there was a doctor medicus available within reasonable distance. It is important to note that the controversies between medical doctors and barber surgeons did not have any direct or explicit bearing on institutional care at this stage. These matters were not taken account of in the interprofessional struggle, which focused on *the conflict between theoretical wisdom and manual labor as well as commercial competition and social status in general.* This is well documented in the Swedish case.

In this context it is interesting to take a closer look at an argument of Ehrenreich and English (14). From their line of reasoning the prosecutions of witches in Europe can be interpreted as the result of a struggle between male (theoretical/professional) medicine on the one hand and female ethnomedicine on the other. Sweden witnessed its most intensive period of prosecutions between 1668 and 1677; 240 people, mainly women, were sentenced to death (15). This could be seen as an act of patriarchalism intertwined with strivings for professional dominance, but the most reliable information available indicates that neither Collegium medicum nor the Barber Guild took an active part in the prosecutions. The president of Collegium medicum, Urban Hjärne, on the contrary, helped to put an end to the prosecutions. Our wider perspective on the organization process indicates that female ethnomedicine did not threaten the vital interests of the Collegium medicum or other formal organizations in the field.

THE FOUNDING OF SWEDISH GENERAL HOSPITALS FOR ACUTE CARE

This epoch in Swedish history is commonly described as "the age of liberty" (1719-1771), which meant, in short, a strong position for the four estates of parliament and a weak monarchy. Central power was in the hands of the nobility, the burghers, and the clergy, but the position of the peasantry was also strong in comparison with other countries in contemporary Europe. Great Power politics were in decline and a period of domestic reconstruction began.

The role of the prosperous parts of the growing middle class is of great importance here. The members of Collegium medicum belonged to this social category; not being members of the nobility or the established estate of burghers (ofrälse ståndspersoner), they had no direct access to parliament, but they had, nevertheless, increasing influence on the central administration. The first known use of the term "middle class" in Sweden dates from 1793 and can be attributed to the son of the world famous pediatrician, Nils Rosén von Rosenstein. It can be shown that these extramedical forces played an important role in strengthening the position of Collegium medicum within the central administration (6, pp. 215-220).

Mercantilist ideas and policy had a strong hold on the parliament. This was of decisive importance. A unique era in Swedish medical politics opened up, which meant the breakthrough of ideological secularization. The qualitatively new interest in the reproductive sector was clearly based largely on economic considerations. *Population growth was on the agenda.* The unique availability of population statistics in Sweden is a heritage of this period. This was a result of the effect of mercantilist doctrines on a large labor force and low wages and associated attempts to strengthen the economic power of the state. Plans for improving public health were put forward and partly activated, but these initiatives declined in parallel with the diminishing interest in mercantilism at the end of the 18th century.

The first Swedish hospital for acute care (Serafimerlasarettet 1752) should be seen in connection with this heightened interest in medical issues (line 5 in Figure 1). The planning and introduction of this new kind of institution were based on a broad spectrum of motives: the need to control the epidemics, the interest in population growth, the advocation of a scientific medicine channeled through Collegium medicum, and a need to train war surgeons. When consulted on the planning of the new institution, Collegium medicum stressed the need for clinical studies and advocated the implementation of a rule that only "curable" patients should be admitted.

A royal decree of 1763 (renewed and slightly changed in 1766) on the administration of hospitals and orphanages had a number of direct and indirect effects in terms of activity demarcation (E2 in Figure 1):

- *State hospitals* were now formally reserved for the "dangerous and dreadful," i.e., the contagious and mentally ill. People in these categories were considered incurable and to belong in custody.
- *The parishes* were once again supposed to set up poor-houses for the old, the poor, and those who were incapable of taking care of themselves, but still not totally helpless or dangerous.
- The role of the *Serafimerlasarettet* as a prototype institution reserved for "the curable" was confirmed. From 1765 it was also permitted to use regional resources for the setting up of regional hospitals for acute care (länslasarett).

The decree of 1763 was clearly in line with the foregoing development, though it meant a consolidation and rationalization of the organizational heritage. Collegium medicum was only peripherally involved in this important process of activity demarcation, which was largely governed by mercantilist ideas. *Resources were expected to be saved in order to be reallocated to orphanages, with the explicit purpose of encouraging the growth of "a larger and better labor force."* The explicit principle of sorting people according to their "repairability" provided the basis for organizational structures that still operate in Sweden.

Serafimerlasarettet–the prototype Swedish general somatic hospital–was named after the Order of Seraphim (Serafimerorden 1748), which consisted of honored members of the nobility. The administration of institutional care was placed in the hands of this political and social elite, ostensibly for philanthropic reasons, but other motives included a wish to secure close contact with the crown and a desire to make the administration more efficient. The Order of Seraphim's administrative tasks could be described as follows: it provided members for the board of Serafimerlasarettet (1751-1787), and it administered and controlled state hospitals and orphanages (1773-1877) as well as regional hospitals for acute care (wholly, 1776-1817; partly until 1859). Medical doctors and surgeons had little interest in this new kind of institution, except for the opportunities it provided for clinical studies. In practice, Serafimerlasarettet still had the character of a philanthropic institution. Activities in this field were alien to theoretical medicine as well as to surgery.

CONSOLIDATION OF THE POSITION OF PHYSICIANS IN THE CENTRAL MEDICAL ADMINISTRATION

During the Gustavian era, as it is traditionally described in Swedish history (1772-1809), the crown regained its leading political role. The influence of mercantilism declined, which led to a void in medical policy. The influence of the French enlightenment was generally weak in Sweden and left almost no discernible trace in debate or activity in the medical-administrative field. In this period, however, a number of initiatives from the earlier period were completed; but the core of mercantilist medical politics (population growth and public health) was marginalized in the organization process.

The old struggle between Collegium medicum and the Barber Surgeon Guild was brought to an end. The temperature of this struggle had risen around 1750 when the mercantilist era had provided Collegium medicum with an opportunity to put forward its demands. The failure of the Barber Surgeon Guild to provide the armed forces with trained surgeons proved to be of great importance. In the wars between Sweden and Russia in 1788 and 1809, large sections of the Swedish forces were killed by epidemics rather than in combat. This catastrophy in military medicine was widely discussed. The setting up of a key committee on medical administration (1810-års allmänna medicinalkommitté) should be seen against this background. The regent took an active part in setting the agenda. These events are important examples of the central role of military needs in the formation of the Swedish health care system.

The Barber Surgeon Guild (now named Chirurgiska Societeten) was dissolved by a Royal decree in 1797, and Collegium medicum now established hegemony over the medical administration (surgeons were invited to participate in the strengthened Collegium medicum). Growing criticism of the guild system played a role in this development. The fact that medical doctors belonged to the upper segments of the growing middle class was of some importance, but military needs were probably central. This line of development was completed by the formation of the Health Collegium in 1813 (E3 in Figure 1), which meant that the central medical administration acquired the status of a full civil service department on a level with other departments. This had long been on the agenda of Collegium medicum. (The Health Collegium was reorganized in 1877 and renamed the National Board of Health; from 1967, the National Board of Health and Social Welfare.)

The discussions that followed the collapse of military medicine gave rise to the advocation of *the provision of limited medical education for priests* as well as suggestions for a new kind of war surgeon (routinier). This led to an intensive public debate. The main result was the founding of Karolinska Institutet in the 1810s. Originally directed toward training in surgery (especially war surgery), it soon became a leading medical school and famous research institute (initially covering medicine and surgery, later the whole field of medical science). The so-called "priest medicine" (medicinae pastorales)—which was an attempt to install a kind of "bare-foot" medicine against a background of declining mercantilist medical politics—never became widely established. In 1841 the limited efforts made to promote it came to an end. This process gives support to the interpretation that military needs were, in fact, of central importance.

CONSOLIDATION OF THE ECONOMIC AND ADMINISTRATIVE RESOURCES OF THE GENERAL HOSPITAL

In 1864 a regulation of the hospital boards was issued. This meant the definite consolidation of the two hierarchies (medical and administrative) within the work organization of the somatic general hospitals, i.e., the formation of the acute care model (E4 in Figure 1). The existence of county councils (landsting) as an economic base and as a locus of regional self-government was a necessary condition of the implementation of the regulation of 1864. The motives underlying the creation of county councils in 1862 (1862-års kommunal och landstingsförordningar) are therefore interesting in this context. It can be shown that liberal ideas on parliamentary democracy and local self-government were driving forces (16). Generally, there was little medical-political discussion in the middle of the 19th century, and almost none in connection with the planning of the counties. This indicates that the government and parliament pursued pragmatic medical policies in this important phase of development.

Moreover, while the 1864 regulation helped to stabilize the general hospitals (lasarett), it was mainly the result of a compromise between the Health Collegium and the old hospital boards, who were in conflict over the role and composition of the boards. Health Collegium, now interested in institutional care, wanted to strengthen the position of the physicians. The chairpersons of hospital boards, who had administrative control and economic influence, opposed this. The internal division of the hospital structure into two hierarchies was the solution: *the medical hierarchy* with physicians at the top, and the Health Collegium as an external authority, controlled professional medical standards; *the administrative hierarchy*, with laymen at the top, took charge of "purely" managerial tasks with the county councils as their main sponsors.

It seems reasonable to interpret the consolidation of the acute care model as a result of the combined effects of petrified organizational traditions, political compromises, and extramedical societal development.

The intensified proletarianization of the peasantry during the same period was of great importance to the stabilization of the responsibilities of the parish/commune to provide poor-relief. In spite of a long ideological debate over the issue, the 1847 decree on poor-relief (1847-års fattigvårdsförordning) basically consolidated the old structure, though taking into account the need for a more mobile labor force and less paternalistic attitudes. Discussions on these issues took place in isolation from the parallel debate on the internal structure of the general hospitals and their role in the health care sector. Today the commune still organizes and administers poor-relief, though using the concepts of social work and social services.

CONCLUSIONS

This brief description of milestones in Swedish health legislation up to the 1860s reveals a considerable degree of continuity. There are no theoretical reasons to have expected serious attempts to reform this organizational paradigm during the period that followed, characterized as it was by the dominance of technical-medical rationality fostered by the germ theory of disease. On the contrary, scientific medicine benefited greatly from the foundations laid earlier. This led to the petrification of the acute care model. Rosen (17) and Perrow (18) give a similar picture of international and American developments, though their analyses present a less centralized and less homogeneous picture. From our analysis it is clear that Swedish welfare state policy, which has made some important progress in terms of equality, still has taken the general hospital and its acute care model for granted as a building block in the construction of the welfare state.

The conclusions on work environment issues that can be drawn from this study should be seen in the context of the pervasive efforts to rationalize and Taylorize Swedish general hospitals during the 1950s and 1960s. These efforts were supported by a series of government reports in which experts trained in scientific management reported the results of the studies they had carried out in hospital wards. The movement toward economic rationalization was further encouraged by the setting up of publicly financed planning and management authorities. This primarily hit auxiliaries, but also aggravated work environment problems for nurses and led to the dehumanization of care. Being a large-scale organization with clear chains of command, solidly founded on a long tradition of activity demarcation, the general hospital was an almost ideal location for the implementation of a control structure dominated by economic and medical rationality. The acute care model easily became a victim of this desire to further fragment the work process.

In this context, a critical assessment of Anglo-Saxon nursing research is called for in order to balance the views that have been a product of the growing Swedish interest in this field since the late 1960s. *It is clear that professionalized nursing necessarily involves the petrification of the position of auxiliaries within the acute care model* (19). Represented by three different labor unions and professional societies, physicians, nurses, and auxiliaries run the risk of being trapped within the traditional structures. Being professionals and semiprofessionals, integrated in an old organizational structure based on petrified activity demarcations and control structures, health care personnel easily lose sight of the alternatives available and beg for more financial resources, more "science," and more experts. At the same time it seems reasonable to assume that the room for financial expansion is diminishing, at least as long as the structure blocks new health policies as well as fundamental changes in work organization. Any initiative that breaks with contemporary rigid medical-technical rationality inevitably faces the "yoke of tradition" in the Swedish health care sector.

In order to avoid trench warfare within the terms of the out-dated acute care model, there are good reasons to develop a critical historical understanding of the contemporary health care system. The realization that the acute care model is basically shaped by extramedical and premedical factors will provide health care personnel with a strong weapon in the ideological struggle for a renewed work organization.

Acknowledgment — The author thanks Dr. Jon Kimber for help in checking the English text.

REFERENCES

1. Diderichsen, F. Ideologies in the Swedish health sector today: The crisis of the social democracy. *Int. J. Health Serv.* 12(2): 191–200, 1982.
2. National Board of Health and Welfare. Folkhälsorapport 1987 (Report on Public Health 1987). *Socialstyrelsen redovisar 1987:15.* Socialstyrelsen, Stockholm, 1987.
3. Jersild, P. C. *Babels hus.* Bonniers, Stockholm, 1978.

4. Gustafsson, R. A., and Kjellberg, A. *Behavioral Scientists and Workers—A Brief History of Swedish Work Environment Research.* The Swedish Work Environment Fund, Stockholm, 1987.
5. Gardell, B., and Gustafsson, R. A. *Sjukvård på löpande band.* Prisma, Stockholm, 1979.
6. Gustafsson, R. A. *Traditionernas ok—Den svenska hälso-och sjukvårdens organisering i historie-sociologiskt perspektiv* (The Yoke of Tradition—The Swedish Health Care System in a Historical-Sociological Perspective. With a summary in English). Esselte-Studium AB, Stockholm, 1987.
7. Skocpol, T., and Somers, M. The uses of comparative history. *Comparative Studies in Society and History* 22(2): 174–197.
8. Abrams, P. *Historical Sociology.* Open Books Publishing Ltd., Somerset, 1982.
9. Skocpol, T. (ed.). *Vision and Method in Historical Sociology,* Chapters 1 and 11. Cambridge University Press, Cambridge, England, 1984.
10. McGrew, R. E. *Encyclopedia of Medical History,* pp. 25–30. Macmillan Reference Books, London, 1985.
11. Statens offentliga utredningar. *1984:39. Hälso-och sjukvård inför 90–talet.* SOU, Stockholm, 1984.
12. Serner, U. Swedish health legislation: Milestones in reorganisation since 1945. In *The Shaping of the Swedish Health System,* edited by J. Heidenheimer and N. Elvander, pp. 99–116. Croom Helm, London, 1980.
13. Kock, W. Medical education in Scandinavia since 1600. In *The History of Medical Education,* edited by D. O. O'Malley. UCLA Forum of Medical Sciences, No. 12. University of California Press, Los Angeles, 1970.
14. Ehrenreich, B., and English, D. *Witches, Midwives, and Nurses. A History of Women Healers.* The Feminist Press, New York, 1973.
15. Ankarloo, B. *Trolldomsprocesserna i Sverige* (The Swedish Witchcraft Trials. With a summary in English). Rättshistoriskt bibliotek, band 36, andra upplagan, Nordiska bokhandeln, Stockholm, 1984.
16. Nilsson, G. B. Förberedelse för en representationsreform. Landstingsfrågans slutskede 1860–1862. (With a summary in English.) *Historisk Tidskrift* 2: 285–343, 1969.
17. Rosen, G. Historical sociology of a community institution. In *The Hospital in Modern Society,* edited by E. Freidson, pp. 1–36. The Free Press, New York, 1963.
18. Perrow, P. Goals and power structures: A historical case study. In *The Hospital in Modern Society,* edited by E. Freidson, pp. 112–146. The Free Press, New York, 1963.
19. Johnson, M. Big fleas have little fleas—Nurse professionalisation and nursing auxiliaries. In *Nursing Auxiliaries in Health Care,* edited by M. Hardie and L. Hockey, pp. 103–117. Croom Helm, London, 1978.

CHAPTER 11

The Political Implications of Psychosocial Work Redesign: A Model of the Psychosocial Class Structure

Robert Karasek

Over the past three decades, in fact since 1859, a range of scholars in various fields have built scientifically convincing and morally compelling arguments that work tasks in industrial societies should be restructured—to improve their *"psychosocial"* aspects such as increased self-determination, reduced social alienation, and reduced risk of illness. However, there has been little marked progress toward these goals, during a time when material well-being has improved substantially and when the physical hazards of work have been much diminished. I feel that we have made little political progress in a psychosocial direction because psychosocial contributions have not yet been woven into a framework as integrated, comprehensive, and therefore as politically usable as the existing political economic synthesis.

The "existing political economic synthesis" is not just American free market capitalism, but is represented by seemingly diverse environments that are all fairly uniform in their hostility to psychosocial job change. These include organizational structures and their imbedding national contexts as disparate as Western multinational corporations; Eastern-bloc state bureaucracies; and even public sector bureaucracies in "third-way" social democratic countries (such as Sweden).[1] Many readers will find it questionable to amalgamate such apparently diverse examples.[2] But in spite of their substantial diversity in distribution of the economic rewards, all three of these examples have many fundamental elements in common. They all use a market-based measure of value from production (exchange value, of the neo-classical economic form, based on markets of strangers and real-number system quantification of output).

---

[1] The national health plan for the 1990s in Sweden, and several analogous initiatives from Swedish industry and unions, are recent exceptions.

[2] Numerous "smaller" differences exist that cannot be discussed within this limited space. The author acknowledges their existence, but wants nonetheless to illuminate high-level similarities.

They all use Weberian justifications of hierarchical organizational efficiency. They all use Adam Smith–based justifications of the efficiency of large-scale production. They all rely on social welfare maximization through enterprise productivity maximization. Finally, they all have used Frederick Taylor–based justifications of micro-control of worker tasks, skills, and social relationships. The chief difference among these examples is different distribution systems for production surplus (and, now disappearing, differences in firm profit motivations). Since these examples comprise what is usually called the "full political spectrum," we must have an incomplete representation of the true political spectum. Fundamentally new alternative political conceptions must be found.

I refer to the congruent elements of the above examples, hereafter, as the single "conventional model" [others refer to it as "economism"; Melman (1) refers to it as "managerialism"]. Psychosocial research and practice have provided what now seems like an endless set of counter-examples—illustrating undesirable features of the conventional model for many increasingly important groups in society. But for psychosocial issues to serve as a basis for alternative political dialogues, psychosocial issues must be integrated into an alternative model as comprehensive as this "conventional model." A new synthesis is required that starts with a new definition of production output "value" from the firm—relevant to psychosocial well-being in a national economic context. This new output value definition could, in turn, legitimate alternative models of work's social organization and illuminate new political strategies. It should be noted that the use of the term "value" in this chapter refers to a measure of a firm's production output—an economist's definition of value. The usage is thus *entirely different* from the concept of "value systems," understood as religious or cultural belief systems.

Of course, such new measures of a firm's production output can hardly entirely replace the existing measures of conventional materialistic economic output; they will supplement it. But my view is that without such basic new measures, there is little hope for more widespread psychosocial change of work environments. Our old organizational structures and political dialogues are too tightly linked to the conventional output value definitions themselves. These conventional measures are a quite limited reflection of the true and potential output from even our current economic structures, and a major damper on more creative output.

Development of a model of "psychosocial class" based on a new definition of output, and discussion of some of its basic political implications, are the specific focus of this chapter. A comprehensive alternative to the conventional model must include a new definition of psychosocial class to describe the "haves" and "have-nots" in the alternative production output ("value") system. The first step will be a brief review of literature to indicate failures of the conventional model to predict many important psychosocial outcomes. A new production value system measure (New Value) related to work's psychosocial costs and benefits is then defined, and its production organizations are briefly discussed. To empirically illuminate the psychosocial class structure, a set of three two-dimensional "maps" of current occupations in the U.S. work force is used. Finally, political implications of psychosocial job change are deduced by examining relationships and conflicts between newly identified occupational groups.

SHORTCOMINGS OF THE CONVENTIONAL MODEL FOR
PREDICTING PSYCHOSOCIAL OUTCOMES

The primary rationale for a new output value system for production organization is the fact that a new set of psychosocial conceptions of production output is needed to effectively predict the costs and benefits of present-day work organization. Below I briefly review the shortcomings of the conventional model from the perspectives of the social and medical sciences, economics, and management theory. A goal of this review process will be to identify the new set of dimensions of the psychosocial work environment. I am also arguing that unidimensional measures of production outputs and reward must be replaced by multidimensional psychosocial conceptions.

Conventional social class models are based on the distribution of the economic output value of the firm into worker's wages or owner's profits, discussed most comprehensively by Marx (2). Current scales of "conventional" social class are now based on average incomes of occupations, or the education levels presumed to ensure access to those incomes—such as the Duncan Socioeconomic Index (3) discussed below. However, the focus of the discussion will be a *very different* set of psychosocial measures, more strongly associated with Marx's earlier (and distinct) concept of alienation (4). Those concepts will be redefined to more narrowly fit recent research issues: development of stress-related disturbances and illness, a passive orientation toward production and society, and fragmentation of social collectives. Discussion will be focused around the individual-level costs in terms of illness and adverse behavior change, which can also be shown to be linked to specific psychosocial job dimensions (decision authority, skill use, job demands, job security) relevant to conventional management practice. To prove the point it must be shown that the costs and benefits predicted by psychosocial approaches are *independent* of the conventional model.

*A Social and Medical Science Critique: The Conventional Model's
Inability to Predict Health and Well-Being*

Decision Authority, Skill Use, and Health.   One of the broadest findings by Kohn and Schooler (5, 6) is that "occupational self-direction" (substantive complexity and intellectual flexibility) affects a variety of measures of psychological functioning, irrespective of "conventional" social class.[3] In the area of psychological health, low decision authority and skill requirements are associated with a variety of psychological strain measures controlling for social class (8) for machine-paced auto workers (9), for lumber mill employees (10), separately for 23 occupations (11), and for white-collar occupations (12). Associations between low decision latitude and coronary heart disease, controlling for social class, are demonstrated in longitudinal and prevalence studies of Swedish workers (13, 14) and in a prevalence study of U.S. workers (15).

Decision Latitude and Socialization of Behavior.   Mortimer and Lorence (16), in a longitudinal study, found that work autonomy also influences value systems, with

---

[3] Elsewhere Kohn (7) discussed how psychosocial characteristics of work can be the mechanism of transmission for broad social class values (including the new definition in this chapter).

conventional class held constant. Job decision authority and skill level are associated with political participation, controlling for social status (17-19), with evidence of "socialization" in longitudinal studies (19). Similar job characteristics show association with leisure behavior (8, 20, 21) also in longitudinal studies (21), even when social class is held relatively constant. In a nationally representative study of the Swedish population (8), the variance could be apportioned between psychosocial measures and conventional social class measures: 76 percent of the variance in leisure and political participation measures was explained by psychosocial measures. Psychosocial leisure and political covariation with "active-passive" work was observed while conventional status measures were held constant (within the 60 percent of Swedish population with statutory minimum education).

Social Support, Health, and Behavior. Studies also document the association between social support and psychological strain (12, 22), controlling for social class, and demonstrate associations between individuals' social networks and the incidence of coronary heart disease, controlling for social class (23, 24). The impact of social integration in an occupationally homogeneous community structure for leisure behavior patterns and political participation has also been demonstrated (25, 26).

Job Insecurity, Physical Demands, and Health. Although job insecurity is significantly associated with class, field studies have tended to hold class constant and still confirm associations with psychological health (27-29). The destructive longitudinal impact of unemployment on leisure and community social activities has also been well-documented (30, 31) with class held roughly constant. Although physical exertion and social class are significantly correlated, negative associations between physical exertion and heart disease are found in field studies, where class is rigorously controlled (32) for longshoremen (33), and with opposite, but still class-independent, findings (14) for concrete workers. Of course, physical stressors in the form of toxic exposures are much more common in "conventional" lower-class jobs: coke oven cleaners, vinyl chloride chemical process workers, pesticide mixers, and asbestos workers.

Can psychosocial measures of the job predict psychological strain outcomes better than a conventional status scale, such as the Duncan Socioeconomic Index? Using a composite measure of psychological strain in the U.S. Quality of Employment Surveys and using occupation level decision latitude, psychological workload and physical exertion we predict occupational level psychological strain with an R^2 of 33 percent versus 7 percent for the conventional Duncan occupational status scale (34). Overall, these psychosocial measures of increased risk of psychological strain define a strain-risk dimension that is almost orthogonal to conventional social class measures (see p. 181). This is certainly a major reason why conventional "social class" measures could fail to find associations.[4] Of course, conventional white/blue-collar distinctions still capture many important life phenomena—particularly with respect to material

---

[4]Many psychosocial researchers have demonstrated weak findings with conventional measures in firm-level and task-level studies. For a discussion of the poor performance of social class to predict psychoactive impairment see reference 35.

well-being and physical hazard exposure. However, the fact that so many contemporary behavioral health and well-being phenomena are not captured by conventional social class models makes a strong case for new conceptions.

The Impact of Scientific Management

We can see how the conventional management goal of maximization of the economic output of work could fail to effectively address its psychosocial outputs through a closer examination of one of these conventional job design philosophies—Taylor's scientific management. Other chapters of this book as well as my own research (36) have identified the psychologically stressful job as one that is low in task decision freedom and skill level, high in psychological demands, low in physical exertion (see the later section, "The Psychosocial Class Structure and Its Distributional Consequences"), and socially isolated from workmates (37). It is noteworthy that a "stressful" job could be an embarrassingly direct result of the specific job design recommendations of Frederick Taylor's *Principles of Scientific Management* (38), which were nominally intended to increase productivity (and wages). Under scientific management the worker was left with little possibility for psychological relaxation. Increased productivity was to come from an increase in work pace from elimination of "wasted motions" in craftworker's jobs. Many of these apparently "wasted" motions were actually the workers only "rhythmic respites" from *psychological pressures* of production. Also, the worker was restricted from making decisions about how to perform a job. This reduction in decision latitude was seen as a *loss of control*, not as a desirable "lifted burden" by workers. The transformation was so thorough as to deprive workers of possibilities for self-pacing, and self-initiated improvements to the work process. To craftsmen the ultimate loss was the loss of mastery of a "trade" capable of rendering a complete service to a customer. The "divide and conquer" aspects of job fragmentation placed workers at the mercy of the new market middlemen (39) and of engineers' and managers' planning requirements.

This lack of decision latitude under conditions of *low* psychological demands leads to "passivity" instead of stress, a problem at least as damaging from a societal perspective. Passivity could be further induced by Taylor's final principle, a rigorously enforced *social isolation* of workers, isolation of their task elements, and isolation of their wage rewards. Group work, with its Taylor-exaggerated dangers of lost productivity through loafing and feather bedding ("soldiering") and its power to resist imposition of management-conceived work structures, was to be eliminated. This elimination of work groups and threats against unions undercut both the social support of the work group and the possibility of easy cross-training of skills. It ultimately undercut the flexibility necessary for restructuring work processes to meet constantly changing market and technological demands.

An Economist's Critique: The Conventional Model's Inability
to Describe Current Productivity

The conventional model now fails to predict production output adequately, even in a technical sense. This is because production has undergone a new set of changes, fully as dramatic as those of the Industrial Revolution, since Smith, Marx, and later, Taylor outlined their principles of production and distribution. These changes have undermined the technical utility of "conventional" production principles and reinforce the need for new measures of output value for society's production structures.

1. The true nature of output in the service industries is "unknown" at present, and is beyond the analytical capabilities of conventional economic and productivity analysis to even describe. Service industries now employ over double the number of workers as manufacturing. The difference between service outputs and conventional goods output (exchange value) is fundamental. I would define "service" as adding value to a person (or growth-capable-entity), as opposed to adding value to an object (i.e., machining cast iron), which occurs in "goods" production.

2. The previously "hungry-for-products" mass consumers in the industrialized world have now been replaced by populations that often need to be persuaded to buy something (with advertising expenditures that exceed production costs for many popular products) and taught how to "need" the products that technology can make available (home computers). "Biological" needs alone will no longer generate sufficient demand for employment to keep these populations constructively employed (given present income distributions). Desirable new products are those that stimulate demand (in a constructive way) not satiate it. This truly necessitates a new definition of output and productivity, since our previous models are based on satiation of "fixed" (i.e., biologically guaranteed) needs by "scarce" products (40).

3. Education levels and skill resources of populations are increasing while the physical resources that formed the basis of "conventional production" are declining or are fragile (natural resources, land, pollution risks from overutilization). The work forces in industrialized countries have dramatically higher levels of educational training and more experience in democratic participation than the rural, immigrant laborers discussed by "old" production theorists. A surplus of skills combined with rigidly hierarchical organizational systems lead to dissatisfaction, boredom, or disengagement from work. Products that need no skills in their production become inconsistent with major quality-of-life (working life) desires of workers. Mass-produced products, although cheap in one sense, create social costs in terms of underutilized skills.

At the other end of the bifurcated skill spectrum, the present base of installed capital equipment now cries out for workers skilled enough to make expensive capital pay off. Capital's productivity in the United States has not increased for decades (41). Most of automation's effects in the United States have been merely to replace expensive labor with expensive capital.

4. Management literature has recently critiqued the myopic concern for short-term cost reductions (42). They have shown that it can lead to long-term disastrous failures to invest adequately in new capital equipment or human capital. The "short-term" focus also undermines "innovation," management theorist's current number one priority, since innovation yields uncertain future benefits.

5. The newest technologies (software, computer chips, sensor systems, etc.) often imply the possibility of production smaller in scale and often do not technically require the vast organization or expenditures for direct production that steel mills, railroads, or shipyards of the past required.

*An Organizational Theorist's Critique: The Conventional Model's
Inability to Facilitate Innovation and Creativity*

Generations of modern management theorists have also documented the need to go beyond our present conventional (i.e., hierarchical) organizational models in order to understand actual productivity. Already in the late 1920s, the human relations approach illustrated the importance of social interaction patterns, not just economic rewards or skill specialization, in determining work's actual productivity. Organization theorists from Merton (43) to Melman (1) criticized Weber's (44) hierarchical bureaucracy as dysfunctionally rigid, and easily co-opted by existing power structures to serve ends differing dramatically from simple economic efficiency. The issue is further focused by the most recent generation of critics such as Peters and Waterman [*In Search of Excellence* (42)] and Swedish industrialists, Carlson and Gyllenhammar. These writers highlight the fact that simple short-term economic criteria used to justify the hierarchical model in its original form could no longer be the sole validation of an organization's performance.

But if simple short-term profitability was not sufficient, what should be the measure of output? One of the ever-present themes of these critiques has been under-utilization of creative resources at all levels: workers skills unutilized or insufficiently developed, and organizations that rigidly lock up rather than facilitate creative adaptions to their environments. This is reflected in a new pressure, visible in many management- and business-oriented journals, to develop new management strategies for innovation, research and development, and other "growth-oriented" productive activities. These developments are another justification for a new definition of value from production.

NEW VALUE: A NEW DEFINITION OF VALUE FROM PRODUCTION OUTPUT

Thus, the need to formulate new production output measures that reflect the "creative" capabilities of individuals and organizations comes from many directions—sociologists, epidemiologists, psychologists, economists, and management theorists. To satisfy the critiques above, a value system is needed that reflects the creative growth of individuals and productive innovation of enterprises, that is also adapted to (a) services to people, (b) the need to develop and use skills, and (c) the need to stimulate socially sanctioned and constructive challenges, and that (d) goes beyond object-based value (materialism). In more methodologically specific terms, this measure should also be affected by psychosocial job characteristics such as skill development and use, autonomy, psychological stimulation and overload, physical demands, and creative and supportive social interactions.

The output value of the firm in conventional terms is, of course, now measured in monetary form. However, modern economic structures in reality permit a much broader-definition of output value than this, as Marx claimed over a century ago (2, 4). Dollars, marks, yen, etc. are the metric of only the *marketplace*-determined value of production output. Here, "value" is measured by the price someone will pay for that output in an auction—among strangers—which is presumed to be a reflection of the production output's "true utility" for the customer. This form of output value usually lies in physical objects (or in service "deliverables")—some *thing* with clear boundaries that can be physically "packaged" and transferred from the producer to the consumer. Marx called this "alienable" or "exchange" value, and called the resulting economic system "materialism" because it commonly dealt with value in the form of material objects. Marx differentiated "exchange value," which can be so easily removed from the laborer, from other output value that occurred in more natural (precapitalistic) production: "use value." He claimed that "use value" was overlooked by the conventional economic system. The new definition of output value given below is one subcategory of "use value"—one that I think is particularly suited to developments in our emerging economy.

In order to serve as a basis for a modern economy, a type of production output value must fulfill a few simple conditions: it must be produced by one party, and needed by another. There must also be something very "desirable" about the value that will ensure many cycles of trade, to ensure robustness of commerce and perfection of production capabilities. "Skills" can fulfill such conditions. Indeed, commerce in skills is an important part of modern economics: both in the cooperative movement, on the one hand, and in high-technology transfers, on the other (45). When "skills" are used as a measure of production output, however, a very different set of production and trade structures follows. Active learning becomes a fundamental aspect of productivity. We will now define a new form of output value related to skill development.

In the New Value production situation *the producer provides the kind of output that can facilitate the development of new skills or capabilities in the user* (a consumer of sorts). Since the new skills are associated with growth of capabilities by the user, these will usually lead to a *new set of needs* by the user ("stimulation") to use even more sophisticated, tool-like (*conducive*) goods and services in the future—to build still further skills and to stimulate more sophisticated demand of the output [see discussion in Karasek and Theorell (46)].

For example, the user's carpentry skills are enhanced (i.e., New Value is produced) through the use of a good hammer (the hammer is in this case "conducive" to New Value development). These new skills lead to the further desire and the possibility by the user to do more things with the hammer, and indeed to require different forms of hammers to get new carpentry jobs done in the most effective way. It is also the same with education, where provision of the "service" of education enhances the capabilities of the user, and stimulates him or her to seek further education and still further development of capabilities. Indeed, many of the most common forms of New Value facilitating (conducive) outputs in the contemporary economy are in the service sector (where conventional economics is very analytically unsuccessful: education, research and development, health promotion). Computer software is another example of a New Value facilitating product—which illustrates the utility of this value framework to address modern production reality. If a piece of software is good, of course, it will increase the user's capabilities for getting the originally specified job done. Good software has a quality that is characteristic of good "tools": they are *conducive* to learning through *their use*. Additionally, as it is used, it may allow the user to "master it," and this mastery may stimulate the user to request an updated version of the software that provides him or her with an expanded set of capabilities. This new demand goes beyond original needs. Of course, bad software may be low in New Value: time spent in mastery may be impossible to apply elsewhere or to expand. Poor instructions or faulty operation may make "learning" a frustrating experience.

The process of stimulating new needs in the consumer is part of a desirable process of creative capability growth. We take this as sufficient evidence that New Value fulfills the desirability condition noted above (it is a basic human form of motivation) (47). In the case of conventional, material output value, unmet needs are often undesirable: the planned obsolescent car. By contrast, the "desirability" cornerstone of the conventional economic output value is the tension reduction associated with satiation of biologically driven needs (40). I will now summarize several characteristics of New Value that differentiate it from the conventional economic value output of production processes.

1. *New Value is not "zero-sum."* Conventional (neo-classical) economics deals with desirable goods that are scarce—what one person gets, the other cannot have. This conception is certainly appropriate for the most basic necessities of life such as food and shelter, and mass-produced objects of all kinds. However, the value of education cannot be described in this way. Lessons may be taught over and over to many individuals, never diminishing in utility for any one of them. Also, a little education, rather than satiating desire to learn about a topic, may whet appetites to learn more—and lead to further growth of capabilities. It is interesting to contrast the value of the skill of "cake-baking," which a teacher could transfer to many pupils, to the value in the "cake" itself. The cake itself has zero-sum value as reflected in the well-known adage "you can't have your cake and eat it too." But you *can* teach cake-baking, and not lose your own cake-baking skill in the process (indeed, your skill might be enhanced). The value of the skill is not "alienated" from its producer during exchange.

2. *New Value is process oriented.* It is created during an appropriate collaborative *social process* occurring between user and producers. These processes are not evaluated in conventional economic perspectives. Many of the products or services may not be for direct commercial sale, but will be produced for one company for incorporation into the production process of other companies—a *chain* of leveraged production. In such production chains each capability received from the previous producer enhances the next producer's capability to produce more effective products. In this manner the user is often a producer as well.

3. *New Value reflects long-term value.* New Value production is inseparably linked to growth of capabilities or skills—of workers, of engineers, of companies, and fundamentally, of the customers who use New Value goods or services. Since capabilities develop over time, this analytical framework has a "long-term" focus as opposed to the short-term, instantaneous market assessment evaluations of the conventional economic model.

4. *New Value resides in the person not the object.* This New Value must ultimately reside, not in physical objects, but within beings or other *growth-capable* entities, such as organizations, because a skill has no value without a user. The user's capabilities determine the ultimate effectiveness of the tool—they are "cofactors" in

production. The value to each user is unique in a more fundamental way than (universal) human biological needs for food or shelter. The New Value resides in the user, and has not really been "alienated" from the producer (see point 1 above). Although it is nonphysical in nature, it may be facilitated in its production by physical goods (conducive tools).

The kinds of value discussed above are very poorly measured by short-term economic calculations because of the future orientation, and the uniqueness of the product's fit to each customer. This chapter does not allow for full discussion of the New Value system, or equally important, the relationship between it and conventional exchange value (regular economics) system. An excellent discussion of the shortcomings of conventional economic models, in a theoretically consistent manner, is provided by Lundvall (48). For other discussions of New Value see Karasek and Theorell (46) and Karasek (49). A brief comparison would show that the New Value system would always be "secondary" to conventional economic value, since it is always made second priority in times of true adversity by biologically driven scarce value needs (these are well handled by existing modes of economic analysis). On the other hand, New Value's valuation of socially creative productive relations, and the fact that it subsumes material value into the subsidiary category of "tools" (evaluated as skill facilitators), make it the logically more general value system, and thus a more "primary" framework than conventional materialism under the conditions of an increasingly populated and educated world.

How well does the definition of New Value capture the concerns of psychosocial work environment researchers? I feel that it directly addresses the need for "active" participation, self-determination, and growth of skills. At its core, New Value is a rejection of the concept of "alienation," since New Value accrues within individuals and social groups learning new skills, not in material objects. The new customer/producer linkages can arguably be considered a platform for development of a positive sense of self-esteem (social identity). Also, community social networks would be stabilized through the reciprocal connections involved in New Value development, by comparison to free market conditions. Psychological demands, however, may be only moderately diminished (to the "active" job level—roughly average risks). This could be a major improvement over existing Taylorized jobs, but may not yield the kind of work conditions that would be considered "relaxed." Chronic illness risks, associated with work stress, could be substantially reduced since U.S. and Swedish research findings that associate heart disease risk with low decision latitude have "learning" new things (Sweden) and "creative work" as central questions in the decision latitude measure. Other researchers have speculated that "passive withdrawal" is associated with reduced immune system effectiveness. Such a mechanism would imply significant health benefits from the "active" work producing New Value. The fact that there appear to be close linkages between psychosocial job characteristics and New Value will allow use of job characteristic distributions in the national populations as a device for understanding the distribution of New Value in society.

Organizational Forms

What organizational forms are consistent with the New Value system outlined above? Production organized on the basis of relatively autonomous work groups (as opposed to isolated workers with specialized skills) is consistent with New Value production. Such work groups have been a common theme in the last decade of Industrial Democracy and Quality of Worklife experiments [see, for example, Trist (50)]. In addition, close, and dynamic customer/producer linkages (51, 52) will be necessary to sustain New Value production. "Customer-driven production," which has become a topic of current discussion among production organization theorists (53, 54), implies major departures from conventional hierarchical organizational structures. To be effective such new production methods should involve much more direct communication between population worker, designer, and consumer to allow the custom product changes to be specified, checked, and updated.

These new communications structures provide the feedback channels that allow the worker to fully utilize and then increase his or her skills by satisfying the dynamically developing needs of the customer (New Value development for the producer). These feedback channels provide the customer with the possibility of creative growth in his or her own capabilities, based on creatively evolving products that encourage their own further uses (New Value development for the user). These customer/producer dialogues result in constantly updated product designs, and also necessitate flexibility to redesign the organizational structure itself. The duality of these productivity-related benefits underscores the importance of symmetrical analysis of both the producers' and the customers' actions. These communication requirements imply "smart customers" as well as smart producers (52). It obviously changes relationships with the customer, but internal production structures must also change. These new, relatively horizontal communication linkages between direct producer and consumer and within the company are hypothesized to be the key to significant improvement in creative opportunities in the job structures of both producers and consumers—with improved health status for both also following as a consequence.

We can see not only more responsible roles within companies for workers engaged in such production, but also more responsible roles outside, toward the community and other consumers. Small-scale, decentralized production entities with fewer intermediating distributors, and fewer world-scale marketing approaches, are implied by the close consumer/producer linkages. These suggest a more community-based economic system. Such notions are hardly new; they have grown apace with the development of the Industrial Revolution itself, from Proudhon (55) to Schumacher (56) and Piore and Sable (54).

THE PSYCHOSOCIAL CLASS STRUCTURE AND ITS DISTRIBUTIONAL CONSEQUENCES

Methodology

In this section I will attempt to outline empirically the implications of this New Value structure (and its organizational forms) in terms of a new "class structure" of occupational groups. The attempt will be limited from the outset since it will examine only the "inputs"—psychosocial job dimensions—and not the "outputs"—either New Value or economic value. I hope that understanding of the output "distribution benefits" from this class structure model will come from the inferences that the reader can draw directly from the occupational titles (manager, teacher, janitor, waiter, and machinist) in the occupational plots. We are empirically restricted from utilizing New Value *outputs* as an empirical measure, since little measurement progress in this direction has been made. Of course, I have claimed in the previous sections that the *inputs* of psychosocial work experience (below) are relevant for development of illness risk, active learning orientation, and social affiliation at work. However, New Value productivity has been tested neither at the firm nor the individual level.

The "new" occupational class system is based on definition of nine basic occupational subgroups (Table 1). The nine groups represent differentiation of "haves" and "have nots" on two parallel value systems. First is, of course, the conventional economic value system (A-system), which could hardly be overlooked, with owners and managers at the highest status levels, and physical laborers at the lowest status. Second is the New Value status system (B-system) based on the "possession" of jobs that yield chances for New Value development for the worker: personal growth, active social participation, positive social identity, and freedom from stress-related illness. At the top of the New Value status system are professional jobs. At the opposite end of the New Value status scale are not only the routinized assembly-line jobs where skills may be lost (instead of gained), but groups of occupations where the workers are forced into personally demeaning roles in customer contacts. Three status levels (I, II, III) are differentiated within each system, but several subgroupings will also be needed to capture important diversity of experience. A fourth, low status level (IV) is needed to represent occupations that are marginal to the production of either type of value. The nine groups are presented with 38 illustrative occupations, which are empirically located on plots of decision latitude and psychological demands, decision latitude and physical demands, and decision latitude and social support. (See Figures 1 through 4.)

Data come from the U.S. Quality of Employment Surveys, three nationally representative samples of U.S. male and female workers (working over 20 hours a week) commissioned by the U.S. Department of Labor and undertaken by the University of Michigan's Survey Research Center in 1969, 1972, and 1977 (n = 4,495) (34, 46, 57). The 38 occupations were selected to be illustrative of the full range of occupations in the U.S. Census 1970 occupation classification system, which has over 200 occupational categories with a sufficient number of respondents for scoring (34, 36). Of these, approximately 130 are plotted for males only in Figure 1 to show the actual distribution of individuals on the two axes (dot size is proportional to sample numbers). [Label space did not permit all labels to be printed. The reader can compare selected occupations to the full range of occupations shown in reference 15, Figure 1, p. 912.] Some of our 38 occupations are female-dominated so the overall distribution is not identical (46).

The plots are based on four psychosocial job characteristics (see reference 46 for discussion of their selection). The decision latitude scale is an equally weighted combination of two correlated scales: decision authority (autonomy) and skill discretion (decisions with respect to skill use). The psychological demands scale emphasizes mental workloads of the task, but includes other psychological burdens of work as well. The social support scale contains both coworker and supervisor contributions, as well as both instrumental and socioemotional components. All scales are highly

Table 1

The psychosocial class structure: Nine psychosocial status occupational groups
identified in the U.S. Quality of Employment Surveys 1969, 1972, 1977
(n = 4,495 males and females)

IA. High economic value status occupations: managers of economic value
production, and distribution
1. Managers—trade
2. Public officials
3. Bank officers

IB. High New Value status occupations: professionals and sophisticated knowledge
workers
1. Architect
2. Physician
3. Engineer—electrical
4. Teacher—high school
5. Natural scientist

IIA. Mid economic value status occupations: craftsmen and independent workers in
economic value production
1. Carpenter
2. Farmer
3. Machinist
4. Lineman
5. Repairman

IIB. Mid New Value status occupations: midlevel professionals and administrators
1. Clerk supervisor
2. Nurse
3. Foreman
4. Programmer
5. Health technician
6. Stationary engineer (future process operator)

IIIA. Low economic value status occupations: physical laborers in economic value
production
1. Miner
2. Construction laborer
3. Freight handler

IIIB1. Low New Value status occupations: bureaucratized, impersonal service
production without direct client contact
1. Dispatcher
2. Deliveryman
3. Fireman

IIIB2. Low New Value status occupations: commercialized, service
delivery (exchange value distortion of "service" delivery)
1. Sales clerk
2. Nurses aid
3. Waiter

Table 1 (Cont'd)

IIIB3. Low New Value status occupations: routinized machine-paced jobs without customer contact (exchange value distortion of primarily nonphysical labor)
  1. Assembler–electric/transport industry
  2. Cutting operative
  3. Garment stitcher
  4. Billing clerk
  5. Keypuncher
  6. Telephone operator (future low-status information operative)
  7. Office computer operator

  IV. Lowest status New Value and economic value occupations: marginalized, ancillary, and temporary workers ("secondary" labor market jobs)
  1. Janitor
  2. Watchman
  3. Gas station attendant
  4. Temporary worker (not assessable in Q.E.S. data base)

---

reproducible across national surveys, and have acceptable internal scale reliabilities. However, although decision latitude and physical exertion discriminate between occupations very well (better than income from the job), psychological demands and social support do not discriminate very well. Thus, these latter two scales may contain a larger element of subjective information (of course, only "group-validated" job appraisals are reflected in the job scores plotted in Figures 1 through 4). The scale construction information for the job characteristics scales is further discussed elsewhere (34, 57).

Three Views of the Psychosocial Class Structure

Before a detailed discussion of the work situations of these groups is presented, I will discuss several themes relevant to the political implications of the psychosocial class structure that can be illustrated by inspection of the set of three plots. (See discussion in reference 46.)

Locus of Conventional Social Class Conflict (Figure 3). Conventional social class status is most clearly depicted on Figure 3: the decision latitude (i.e., "control") and physical exertion plot. Here we see "capitalists" (bank officers) and managers (group IA upper left) clearly differentiated from the manual laborers in the lower right (group IIIA). This difference, spanning the whole of Figure 3, was the basis of Marx's class conflict: control over the means of physical production (i.e., exchange value). It is interesting that the independent farmer in the upper right of the figure, the model citizen for the framers of the U.S. constitution, is independent of this main class conflict axis. Perhaps this divergence of everyday work experience is the reason why there has traditionally been such difficulty in instilling small-scale farmers with a sense of "oppressed proletarian class" consciousness, regardless of their apparent helplessness at the hands of large economic concentrations.

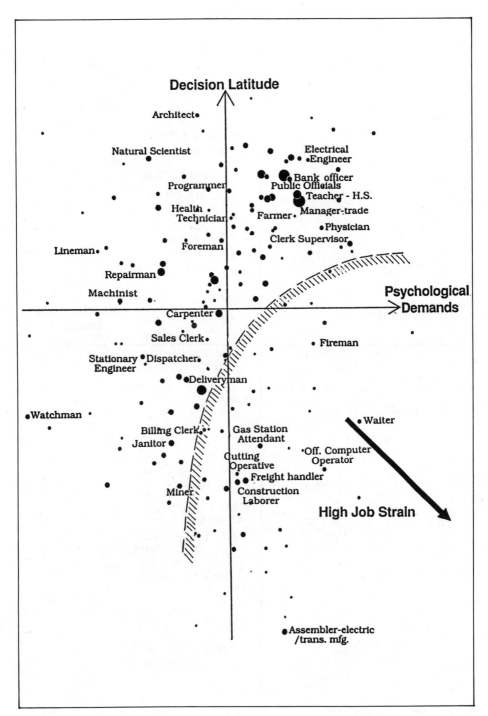

Figure 1. The occupational distribution of decision latitude and psychological demands among men (n = 2,897) based on U.S. Quality of Employment Surveys 1969, 1972, 1977.

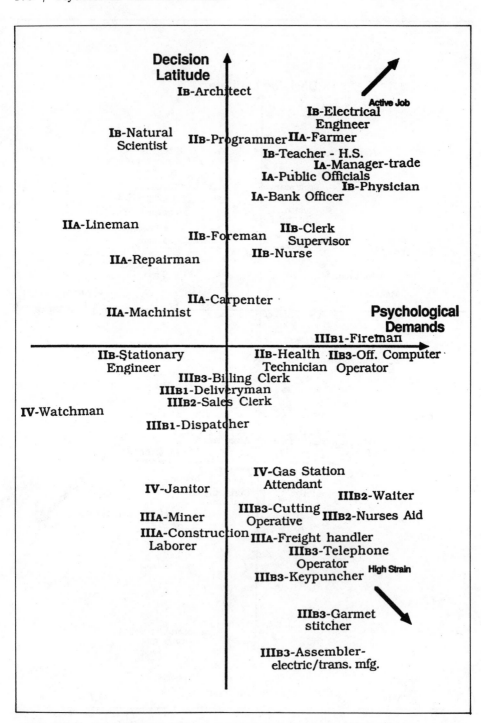

Figure 2. The occupational distribution of decision latitude and psychological demands among men and women (n = 4,495) based on U.S. Quality of Employment Surveys 1969, 1972, 1977.

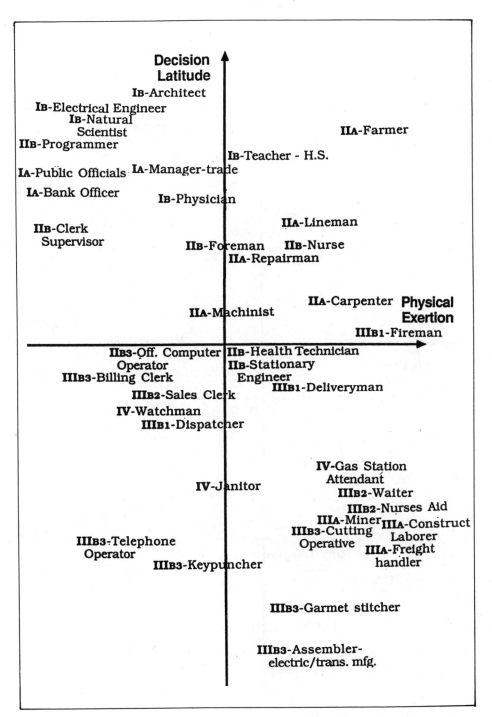

Figure 3. The occupational distribution of decision latitude and physical exertion among men and women (n = 4,495) based on U.S. Quality of Employment Surveys 1969, 1972, 1977.

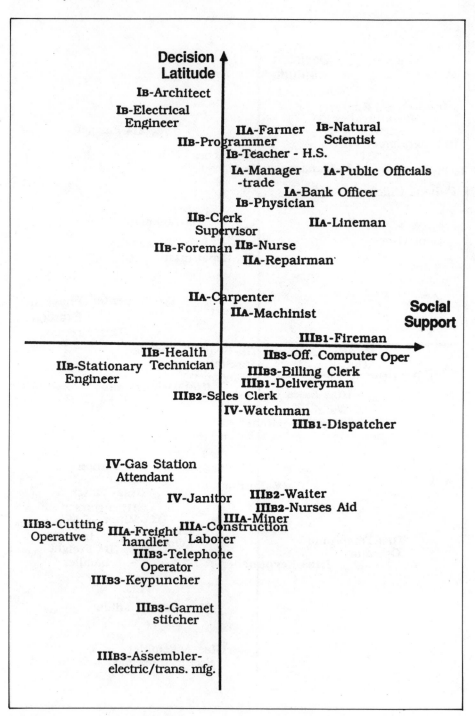

Figure 4. The occupational distribution of decision latitude and social support among men and women (n = 4,495) based on U.S. Quality of Employment Surveys 1969, 1972, 1977.

New Value Social Class Conflicts (Figure 2). The next important theme is best illustrated on Figure 2, which plots occupations on decision latitude and psychological demands. The most negative psychosocial condition, exposure to long-term stress, is most salient in the lower righthand corner. Here we see many machine-paced jobs and low-status "commercialized" service jobs (groups IIIB2 and IIIB3). In the opposite (upper left) corner are "low-strain" jobs: forester (too small to be labeled–see Figure 1), linemen, and natural scientists (groups IIA and IB). This diagonal job strain axis, however, is almost orthogonal to the locus of increasing "conventional" economic status as it would appear on Figure 2. Conventional status is highest in the upper right with professional and managerial jobs, but low economic status jobs are actually spread over all the other three quadrants of Figure 2. Thus "psychosocial class status" is almost orthogonal to "conventional class status" when viewed on this plot, which predicts two of the most important psychosocial outcomes: stress risk and active versus passive behavior patterns. It is this plot, then, that confirms most clearly the need for a second value system/political synthesis.

Figure 2 illustrates several relationships discussed in detail elsewhere (36, 46). Managers are not the group most at risk for stress-related illness, since managers and professionals have "active" jobs in the upper right of Figure 1 (groups IA and IB). These jobs are medium in stress-related risk, but highest in New Value. Also, many more female-dominated occupations exist in the lower right of Figure 2 (compare Figure 2, males and females, with male occupations plotted on Figure 1), and many of these are the newly created "office work" (pink-collar) occupations that are now affected by office automation (group IIB3). While many male-dominated jobs have high decision latitude to accompany high psychological job demands, for females these high demands usually appear in combination with *low* decision latitude.

It is interesting to note that many small occupations in the upper lefthand corner of Figure 2–foresters, millwrights, peddlers, blacksmiths [labeled only in Figure 1 (34)] – were often craft occupations (group IIA), which now seem like relics of Chaucer's middle ages. These are working-class jobs *low* in psychological strain, albeit high in physical demands. The "new" working-class jobs created for mass production industries by Taylor's scientific management philosophies are in the lower right corner of Figure 2, at the top of the psychological strain risk scale (for example assemblers in group IIIB3). Although these cross-sectional data do not provide any legitimate basis for testing longitudinal changes, this pattern of occupations suggests that jobs since the Industrial Revolution may have traded physical demands for psychological demands, and lost autonomy at the same time.

Social Support and the Occupational Structure (Figure 4). Figure 4 plots occupations on decision latitude and social support and illustrates the fact that many of the "Taylorized" mass-production jobs in the high-strain quadrant of Figure 2 (group IIIB3) are also low in social support–a triple penalty (there is a positive correlation between these two dimensions). By contrast many of the desirable "active" professions in the upper right of Figure 2 are also *high* in social support as well–a triple reward (group IB). It also illustrates one occupational group that is often otherwise forgotten: low decision latitude jobs with high social support. These workers, often unionized members of public service bureaucracies, work "behind the scenes" to keep society in operation. Their service, however, is impersonal (group IIIB1) in comparison to higher status service professionals.

JOB REDESIGN STRATEGIES FOR THE NEW VALUE IMPOVERISHED: "ROUTINIZED," "BUREAUCRATIZED," AND "COMMERCIALIZED" WORKERS

We can identify five of the nine occupational groups with obviously oppressive, problematic job situations. Two of the groups have problems that have been clearly identified since Marx's time. Physically oppressive jobs (group IIIA) need protections from physical health risks (as well as needing higher wages), and the lowest status category (group IV) is marginal primarily because of continued economic deprivations. These often occur within population groups, such as minorities, that cannot acquire the initial skill (New Value capital) to acquire other jobs. The conventional exploited, low-status, poorly paid physical laborers (group IIIA at the lower right of Figure 3) may be partially included in the New Value exploited (Figure 2, lower right), in that some low-wage physical laborers also have high-strain, socially isolating jobs (some also have "passive" jobs—low in psychological demands), but these occupational groups are decreasing in the U.S. work force. Also admittedly, the beneficiaries of the conventional production structure (owners and managers, group IA at the upper left of Figure 3) may not differ dramatically from the beneficiaries of "New Value" (professionals, group IB at the upper right of Figure 2), when many professionals are highly paid (e.g., doctors, lawyers in the United States).

However, three of the nine occupational subgroups have deprivations that are more clearly understood in terms of their lack of "New Value": workers with "routinized," "bureaucratized," and "commercialized" jobs (groups IIIB1, IIIB2, and IIIB3). New solution strategies—beyond economic compensation or physical health hazard prevention—will have to be developed to remedy the problems of these groups (see discussion in reference 46). The first group (IIIB3—assemblers and other routinized jobs) includes victims of restricted learning opportunities, social isolation, and restricted possibilities for development of a positive social identity because their work is so fragmented and distant from customer feedback. Solutions for these problems have been illustrated in several decades of Scandinavian (and to a lesser extent, U.S.) Industrial Democracy and Quality of Worklife projects: enriched and enlarged jobs can often provide greater skill variety and autonomy. Autonomous work groups can provide these, as well as social contact and product quality feedback.

Sharing of decision-making opportunities that are presently "hoarded" (as a zero-sum economic commodity) by high-status managers and professionals in groups IA and IB could provide more New Value in jobs. For example, although we find that increasing decision-making opportunities for almost all occupations appears to be associated with reduced stress, for high-level managers fewer decisions appear to be associated with less stress (36). In such jobs decision-making is the primary demand. By sharing these decisions, the high-level managers and their lower-level associates might both become better off. Such job redesign policies obviously have broad distributive political implications, which are discussed in greater detail elsewhere (46, chapter 9).

A New Value perspective can offer further insights for routinized workers. Changes in customer relations involving redesign of the service or product have less often been part of the above "job redesign" solutions. This has placed an effective upper limit on the New Value growth capabilities in these jobs. However, with new market structures linking consumer and producer in a series of interactive product or service "customizations," further New Value increases should be possible. Such linkages have been observed even in previously mass-produced goods (for example, trucks): when customers have been brought into direct contact with workers (see discussion, reference 46, chapter 7), they generate demand for more customized products. Workers' skills then return to craft-like skill and responsibility levels (group IIA)—a major improvement. This is not a "return to the past" because the economic feasibility of such customized production is often the result of new computer-based, flexible technologies. Of course, the new production technology to make such outputs economically affordable (a "conventional," but still necessary criterion) can be expensive, but these costs have recently been borne by networks of small firms (54).

Two other disadvantaged groups (IIIB1 and IIIB2) have jobs in which the New Value output that is usually otherwise present in service jobs is *distorted* by transformation into an economic commodity. It is ironic that production and management policies that are a holdover from "old" economic value production policies could be used to destroy the New Value production capability of these jobs. One relevant discussion is Gardell's and Gustafsson's *Health Care by Assembly Line* (58), which shows the negative consequences for both workers and patients that result from misapplying conventional production rules in a sphere of activity where New Value production could easily occur.

These latter two subgroups differ in the degree to which they have direct public contact (46). Group IIIB1 involves "impersonal" service workers such as deliverymen and dispatchers who have less direct customer contact than IIIB2—waiters and sales clerks. Group IIIB1 has the additional problem of low decision latitude because of large bureaucratic work organizations. Group IIIB2 has more personal freedom but is beset by a "commercial" denigration of the service function in the impersonal market place that transforms it into an impersonal commodity. This is unfortunate, since such jobs might otherwise bring significant respect: food delivery and preparation, and health care with its requirement of constant, skilled, direct attention. The low status and commercialization often lead to disrespectful treatment of workers by customers, as well as by higher-status coworkers. Social support is often lower than for group IIIB1 also. It is interesting to note that IIIB1 occupations are often male dominated and IIIB2 occupations often female dominated. [An analogous sex difference is observable between IIA (craftsmen) and IIB (midlevel professionals and administrators) who are more often female.]

I feel that for both of these groups, customer contacts in which specially tailored services were delivered to "responsive" customers who saw the new service workers as highly skilled "equals" would increase New Value. In several cases, New Value–oriented strategies that provided the patients of health care institutions with skills to take care of their own lives led not only to more active patients (who were also healthier), but also to more satisfied and creatively stimulated workers in the health care institutions (46, 59, 60). This increase in customer satisfaction, and in positive social identity for workers, stands in stark contrast to the "over-bureaucratization" and "commercialization" of the "assembly-line" health care production structures noted above.

DISCUSSION OF POLITICAL AND ECONOMIC IMPLICATIONS

The Political Implications of Overlooking the "New Value Impoverished"

The discrepancy between Figure 2 and Figure 3, in which occupations are plotted against decision latitude and psychological and physical work demands, respectively, provides insight into why conventional "left/right" or capitalist/socialist political dialogues fail to capture many important well-being distribution issues for increasingly large population groups. There are very large differences in the "exploited" in these two value frameworks. Three major occupational groups that have grown dramatically since Marx's time are omitted in "conventional" political analysis. These "New Value impoverished" constituencies often have low wages, but they are most clearly deprived in terms of New Value benefits: "routinized" white- and blue-collar jobs, "bureaucratized" service professionals, and "commercialized" service professionals. These groups have been overlooked until recently even by labor unions in the United States (most such workers are still unorganized), and no political parties in any Western industrial democracy (or in socialist countries) have made their working conditions a political issue in any significant way. The freedom to use and develop skill, the freedom from unnecessary work method regulation, and the need for job structures that lead to a customer's respect and reward, have yet to appear on political party platforms. I believe the result is that many voters feel that politicians have failed to address many of their major needs. These are large occupational groups, and among women, probably represent a majority of workers. Addressing their needs constructively could have significant political implications.

A New Economic Landscape: Diseconomies of Scale and Passivity-Induced Economic Depression

Recently we [Sioukas and Karasek (61)] have found evidence confirming Adam Smith's, dictum (hardly surprising, but rarely empirically tested) that as markets grow larger, increased specialization of labor and thus reduced decision latitude occurs. Thus, the conventionally touted economies of scale could often be offset by New Value *diseconomies* of scale linked to this loss of decision latitude. The New Value penalties of expanded (world) markets could be very large: reduced productive innovation and human capital development for firms as well as increased illness risk, passivity, and damaged social identity for individuals. These "costs" have heretofore been almost entirely overlooked by conventional economists and company financial officers who make our major economic decisions. This inclusion would often tip the scales away from the decision to expand companies, market scales, and control systems.

Also, as I observed earlier (8, 19), the maintenance of stable economies and economic growth probably requires consumers with "active," as opposed to "passive," jobs. Although advertising can create great demands for "conventional" production, most economic growth has been created in service sectors where New Value is an important (if previously undiscussed) component of output. A number of researchers

(8, 18–20) have presented evidence that active jobs lead to active participation outside work in both leisure and political activities. These active lifestyles create demands for other people's services. Travel, sports, arts, political activism, hobbies are all more often pursued by active job holders. Only "low-activity" mass cultural leisure [television watching is presumed to fit, but was not explicitly measured (8, 19)] is more common among passive job holders. Thus "passive" lifestyles might, for example, create demand for video cassettes. *Worldwide* production and distribution of the cassettes, however, creates demand for fewer additional jobs than the "service intensive" active leisure pursuits noted above. The implication is that New Value is a vital ingredient to maintenance of employment demand in advanced economies where fulfillment of biological needs alone no longer provides sufficient demand to provide jobs for the majority of the population.

As an extreme example, consider what happens when vocal music, a New Value stimulating output, is produced and distributed as a conventional economic commodity instead. With present duplication and distribution facilities, a single singer with excellent voice can "efficiently" fulfill the world's demands to hear music (consider the scale of distribution of a few pop super-stars). This singer will make enormous amounts of money, but his or her accompanying expenditures will certainly not stimulate whole economies. Mainly, this music preempts the possibilities of active vocal creation by local artists. Those artists' creations could keep "alive" the demand for the goods and services of their countrymen in performance contexts that are very socially involving (and stimulate more singing), and also provide for the artist's own individual satisfaction. Although cassette music "costs" less than live music, it creates a set of New Value losses that may not make it worth the price. Products that decrease skills through their use, rather than increasing them (nonconducive, "stupidifying" products) may carry *long-term risks* for the society. Thus, New Value production theories would contend that the most dynamic vocal music economy would involve many, independent, creatively active singers—not a single world producer.

Keynesian economists analyzing national depressions of insufficient demand [and world-Keynesians (62)] emphasize the need for sufficient equality of income distribution to ensure that wage earners can buy products of an economy's industries to keep the economy running. There are clearly New Value distribution requirements at the macro-level as well: it is not consistent with a stable "total" economy to have all New Value opportunities concentrated among a new elite, with all the rest of society in passive jobs—even if all members of society are satiated with material wealth. Also, economic growth and stable employment in the context of increasingly efficient production technologies require product innovation that can be more easily discussed in New Value terminology than in the neo-classical economic framework.

The political implications of passive withdrawal from political participation raise an even bigger problem for passive jobs, low in New Value—dropout from the democratic process: low voter turnouts (now 49 percent for presidential elections in the United States) and trivialization of political debates. For workers with statutory minimum education levels [60 percent of the Swedish population in 1968 (8)], the job psychosocial character had stronger associations with political participation than did formal education: passive jobs, low political participation. The workplace was the classroom for many members of industrial society: behavior patterns are learned there, as Kohn and Schooler (5) have indicated. Bureaucratized, commercialized, routinized jobs may not generate the active participation that the drafters of the U.S. constitution (often independent farmers, with physically active jobs in Figure 3) deemed essential for democracy's survival.

Conflicts Between Conventional Economic and New Value Systems

There is a need to develop some equitable means for balancing New Value and economic value rewards. How many dollars of salary should be given up for additional "creative opportunities"? Note that the answer is not just a personal choice but also must be decided on the basis of maintaining societal economic growth. Some insight into resolving this problem may be obtained from examination of recent "pay-for-learning" wage compensation programs in which employees are paid for acquisition of knowledge that also increases their productivity. Here New Value and economic value to employees accrue in parallel (63). More problematic and probably more common is the situation in which an employee has been paid a small amount of money for an "enjoyable" creative experience, and is then fired and has no entitlements in our present legal system to the future economic value rewards from his or her production. Of course, writers' unions in the United States do bargain over future royalty provisions for their creative works, and copyrights also address such issues. Perhaps the most problematic recent development is in the artificial intelligence field where the company's explicit goal is to "get the knowledge out of the employee's heads" and into its computer systems (the so-called "expert system"), so that it may be possessed and controlled like any other item of conventional economic capital for the company. An alternative solution would be to develop the expert system for use and control by the original expert to enhance his or her capabilities (like the machinist's tool box).

In general there are deep theoretical conflicts between value systems: the social optimum distribution for a New Value facilitating product is to give the "skill" to everyone—no one's skill will be worse off as a result. However, conventional economic resources are scarce by definition, and they must be distributed only to the most profitable users. Also, New Value benefits may take much energy to produce but the benefits are not as easily "captured" as for material objects (a "public good" to economists; the benefits cannot be easily isolated to a single group willing to pay). Such problems are often faced by private companies that have made a New Value investment in research, and want to be certain that it is their company, and not a competitor company, that reaps the economic benefits from that investment.

In contrast to this "old value" perspective on firm competition, some of Western Europe's most economically dynamic regional economies (54) have been based on networks of small creative companies that profit by mutually sharing stimulating New Value investments with each other (a combination of competition and cooperation). Here a basis of social and community cohesion seems to supply the prerequisite trust to ensure equitable economic value distribution. New Value investments pay off in the long term, but development of new, community-based institutional frameworks to deal with distributional conflicts are needed for long-term decision-making. The local focus of institutions needed to capture New Value benefits (and their potential social stability) contrasts with the unlimited scale of economic market transactions, and their unfettered freedom of action.

Macro-Level Conflicts. The initial definitions of New Value production noted that it requires a platform of satisfaction of basic biological needs. This implies that bad times, in conventional economic terms, can lead to a "scarcity" mentality that will very likely find New Value superficial and irrelevant. Thus, New Value political foci can always be undermined through malicious inefficiency.[5] It is ironic that in times of conventional economic downturn, "innovation" is most needed to avert further decline, and yet it is at just such times that New Value issues are most easily threatened, often by irresistible calls from *both* the old right and the old left for a return to the conventional "basics." Obviously such vulnerabilities would mean that New Value advocates must take great precautions to avoid such economic downturns.

Changes in the level of New Value production could also reinforce or dampen economic growth tendencies. One important implication of this is that economic "upturns" might be generated by New Value investments as well as or better than by conventional economic investment in capital-intensive manufacturing industries. The Danish community of Holstebro demonstrated this in the 1960s. On the verge of economic collapse after decades of population and basic industry loss, this city decided to "invest" in education, youth, and the creative arts. Its success over the next two decades provided a catalyst for economic development of an entire region of rural Denmark (64). Similar revitalizations of dying inner cities in the United States have been started by artists, whose New Value-rich transformations have stimulated other members of their communities to rejuvenate. These actions have boosted the desirability of these areas to the point that the artists themselves have been forced to leave because of their own lack of personal (conventional) economic resources to pay the rent (!)—an irony that must certainly be redressed as we begin to examine more fully the joint distribution of New Value and economic value inputs and outputs in modern society.

CONCLUSIONS

In many ways this chapter presents only a first step—an initial attempt to define a new measure of psychosocial output, an attempt to identify a new class structure to go with it, and speculations on the resulting political consequences. Many of the arguments here fall woefully short of the comprehensive literature reviews needed in the many topic areas addressed. We must hope that future attempts will offer more elaborated definitions of production output value and organizational forms, both tested with empirical studies. Even more important, future research may make progress measuring and analyzing a broader range of "New Value" outputs, instead of the input job characteristics that are measured here. Only in this manner can the true political consequences of psychosocial job change be assessed. In any case, future research in this direction will require integrative thinking combining social research and its political implications—the legacy of Bertil Gardell's work.

---

[5] There is at least the theoretical possibility that individuals who have reaped great benefits in the conventional economic system could run a New Value–oriented economy so poorly that scarcity of basic necessities returns the emphasis to conventional values—and returns them to power.

REFERENCES

1. Melman, S. *Profits without Production*. Alfred A. Knopf, New York, 1983.
2. Marx, K. *Capital: A Critique of Political Econony*. International Publishers, New York, 1967 (1867).
3. Duncan, O. D. A socioeconomic index for all occupations. In *Occupations and Social Status*, edited by A. J. Reiss et al. Free Press, New York, 1961.
4. Marx, K. *Grundrisse der Kritik der Politischen Oekonomie*. Berlin, 1953 (1859).
5. Kohn, M., and Schooler, C. Occupational experience and psychological functioning—an assessment of reciprocal effects. *Am. Sociol. Rev.* 38: 97–118, 1973.
6. Kohn, M., and Schooler, C. The reciprocal effects of substantive complexity of work and intellectual flexibility: A longitudinal assessment. *Am. J. Sociol.* 84: 24–52, 1978.
7. Kohn, M. *Class and Conformity: A Study in Values*. Dorsey Press, Homewood, Ill., 1969.
8. Karasek, R. The Impact of the Work Environment on Life Outside the Job. Doctoral dissertation, Massachusetts Institute of Technology, 1976. (Distributed by NTIS, U.S. Dept. of Commerce, Springfield, Va., 22161. Thesis order #PB 263-073.)
9. Kornhauser, A. *The Mental Health of the Industrial Worker*. Wiley, New York, 1965.
10. Gardell, B. *Produktionsteknick och Arbetsgladje*. Personaladministrativa Radet, Stockholm, Sweden, 1971.
11. Caplan, R. D., et al. *Job Demands and Worker Health*. NIOSH Publication No. 75-160. U.S. Government Printing Office, Washington, D.C., 1975.
12. Karasek, R., Gardell, B., and Lindell, J. Work and non-work correlates of illness and behavior for male and female Swedish white-collar workers. *J. Occup. Behav.* 8: 187–207, 1987.
13. Karasek, R., et al. Job decision latitude, job demands, and cardiovascular disease: A prospective study of Swedish men. *Am. J. Public Health* 71: 694–705, 1981.
14. Theorell, T., and Floderus-Myrhed, B. Work load and myocardial infarction: A prospective psychological analysis. *Int. J. Epidemiol.* 6: 17–21, 1977.
15. Karasek, R., et al. Job characteristics in relation to the prevalence of myocardial infarction in the U.S. HES and HANES. *Am. J. Public Health* 78: 910–918, 1988.
16. Mortimer, J., and Lorence, J. Work experience and occupational value socialization: A longitudinal study. *Am. J. Sociol.* 84: 1361–1385, 1979.
17. Karasek, R. Job Socialization, a Longitudinal Study of Work, Political and Leisure Activity in Sweden. Paper presented at IX World Congress of Sociology (RC30), Uppsala, Sweden, August 15, 1978. Swedish Institute for Social Research, Stockholm University.
18. Elden, M. Political efficacy at work: The connection between more autonomous forms of workplace organization and a more participatory politics. *Am. Pol. Sci. Rev.* 75: 43–58, 1981.
19. Karasek, R. Job socialization and job strain: The implications of two related psychosocial mechanisms for job design. In *Man and Working Life, Social Science Contributions to Work Reform*, edited by B. Gardell and G. Johannson. Wiley, London, 1981.
20. Meissner, M. The long arm of the job: A study of work and leisure. *Indust. Relations* 10: 239–260, 1971.
21. Goiten, B., and Seashore, S. *Worker Participation: A National Survey Report*. Survey Research Center, University of Michigan, Ann Arbor, Mich., 1980.
22. LaRocco, J. M., House, J. S., and French, J. R. P. Social support, occupational stress, and health. *J. Health Soc. Behav.* 21: 202–216, 1980.
23. Berkman, L. F., and Syme, S. L. Social networks, host resistance, and mortality: A nine-year follow-up study of Alameda County residents. *Am. J. Epidemiol.* 109: 186–204, 1979.
24. Marmot, M. G. Socio-economic and cultural factors in ischaemic heart disease. *Adv. Cardiol.* 29: 68–76, 1981.
25. Brown, R., et al. Leisure in work: The "occupational culture" of shipbuilding workers. In *Leisure and Society in Britain*, edited by M. Smith, S. Parker, and C. Smith. Allen Lane, London, 1973.
26. Young, M., and Willmott, P. *Family and Kinship in East London*. Routledge & Kegan Paul, London, 1957.
27. Kerckhoff, A., and Back, K. *The June Bug*. Appleton-Century-Croft, New York, 1968.
28. Kasl, S. V., Gore, S., and Cobb, S. The experience of losing a job: Reported changes in health, symptoms, and illness behavior. *Psychosom. Med.* 37: 106–122, 1975.
29. Cobb, S., and Kasl, S. *Termination: The Consequences of Job Loss*. U.S. Department of Health, Education and Welfare, (NIOSH) Pub. No. 77-224. U.S. Government Printing Office, Washington, D.C., 1977.
30. Liebow, E. *Tally's Corner*. Little, Brown & Co., Boston, 1967.

31. Jahoda, M., Lazarsfeld, P., and Zeisel, U. *Die Arbeitslosen von Marienthal*. Verlag fur Demoskopie, Allensbach and Bonn, 1960.
32. Milvy, P., Forbes, W., and Brown, K. A critical review of epidemiological studies of physical activity. *Ann. N.Y. Acad. Sci.* 301: 519–549, 1977.
33. Paffenbarger, R. S., and Hale, W. C. Work activity and coronary heart mortality. *N. Engl. J. Med.* 92: 545–550, 1975.
34. Karasek, R., Schwartz, J., and Theorell, T. Job Characteristics, Occupation, and Coronary Heart Disease: Final Report to NIOSH Stage 1, pp. 1–179. Mimeo, Department of Industrial Engineering and Operations Research, Columbia University, October 1982.
35. Dohrenwend, B. S., and Dohrenwend, B. P. (eds.). *Stressful Life Events: Their Nature and Effects*. Wiley, New York, 1974.
36. Karasek, R. Job demands, job decision latitude, and mental strain: Implications for job redesign. *Admin. Sci. Q.* 24: 285–307, 1979.
37. Johnson, J. The Impact of Workplace Social Support, Job Demands, and Job Control upon Cardiovascular Disease in Sweden. Doctoral dissertation, Department of Psychology, University of Stockholm, Report #1, 1986.
38. Taylor, F. *Principles of Scientific Management*. Harper Brothers, New York, 1947.
39. Thompson, E. P. *The Making of the English Working Class*. Vintage, New York, 1963.
40. Scitovsky, T. *The Joyless Economy*. Oxford University Press, Oxford/New York, 1976.
41. U.S. Congress, Office of Technology Assessment. *Technology and Structural Unemployment: Reemploying Displaced Adults*. OTA-ITE-250. U.S. Government Printing Office, Washington, D.C., February 1986.
42. Peters, T., and Waterman, R. H. *In Search of Excellence*. Alfred A. Knopf, New York, 1981.
43. Merton, R. Bureaucratic structure and personality. *Social Forces* 18: 560–568, 1940.
44. Weber, M. *The Theory of Social and Economic Organization*. Free Press, New York, 1947.
45. Killing, P. Technology acquisition: License agreement or joint venture. *Columbia J. World Bus.*, Fall 1980, pp. 38–46.
46. Karasek, R., and Theorell, T. *Healthy Work: Job Stress, Productivity, and the Reconstruction of Working Life*. Basic Books, New York, 1989.
47. White, R. Motivation reconsidered: The concept of competence. *Psychol. Rev.* 66: 297–333, 1959.
48. Lundvall, B. A. *Product Innovation and User-Producer Interaction*. Industrial Development Research Series No. 31, Aalborg University Press, Aalborg, Denmark, 1985.
49. Karasek, R. A. New Value, pp. 1–48. Mimeo, Department of Industrial Engineering and Operations Research, Columbia University, New York, 1981.
50. Trist, E. *The Evolution of Socio-Technical Systems*, No. 2. Ontario Quality of Working Life Center, Ont., June 1981.
51. Karasek, R., and Chignell, M. The function/structure approach to design for computer-integrated manufacturing. *Society of Manufacturing Engineers Technical Paper*, MS86-973. Long Beach, Cal., 1986.
52. Karasek, R. Making customer-initiated variety feasible for CIM: Customer-oriented product design software. In *Social, Ergonomic and Stress Aspects of Work with Computers*, edited by G. Salvendy, S. Sauter, and J. Hurrell. Elsevier Science Publishers, Amsterdam, 1987.
53. Bosrup, L., and Sandell, P. *Coordinated Customer Directed Manufacturing*. Sveriges Mekanforbund, Prodevent Project IVF No. 76604. Stockholm, Sweden, 1976.
54. Piore, M. J., and Sable, C. F. *The Second Industrial Divide: Possibilities for Prosperity*. Basic Books, New York, 1984.
55. Proudhon, P. J. *Systeme des contradictions economiques, ou philosophie da la misere*. Two volumes, edited by Roger Picard. Marcel Rivere, Paris, 1923.
56. Schumacher, E. F. *Small is Beautiful: Economics as if People Mattered*. Harper & Row, New York, 1973.
57. Schwartz, J., Pieper, C., and Karasek, R. A procedure for linking job characteristics to health surveys. *Am. J. Public Health* 78: 904–909, 1988.
58. Gardell, B., and Gustafsson, R. A. *Sjukvand pa Lopandeband*. Prisma, Stockholm, 1979.
59. Arnetz, B., Eyre, M., and Theorell, T. Social activation of the elderly, a social experiment. *Soc. Sci. Med.* 16: 1685–1690, 1983.
60. Svensson, L. *Grupper och Kollectiv: en Undersokning av Hemtjanstens Organization i Tva Kommuner*. Arbetslivscentrum, Stockholm, 1985.
61. Sioukas, A., and Karasek, R. Market Scale and Specialization of Labor in U.S. Manufacturing Industries: An Empirical Test and Job Design Implications. Department of Industrial and Systems Engineering, University of Southern California, Los Angeles, 1989.

62. Meade, W. J. *Mortal Splender, The American Empire in Transition*. Houghton Mifflin, New York, 1987.
63. Jenkins, G. D., and Gupta, N. The payoff of paying for knowledge. *Natl. Productivity Rev.* 14: 121–136, Spring 1985.
64. Holm, I., Hagnell, V., and Rasch, J. *A Model for Culture: Holstebro*. Almqvist and Wiksell International, Stockholm, 1985.

PART 3

Workplace Democratization: Action Research

Worker Participation and Autonomy: A Multilevel Approach to Democracy at the Workplace

Bertil Gardell

INTRODUCTION

A 50-Year Perspective on Productivity and
Worker Participation in Sweden

The ideas of scientific management, the human relations movement, and the welfare state came to influence Scandinavian working life very much at the same time—after World War II. The ultimate goal accepted by politicians, management, and the unions was to raise the material standard of living and create resources for social reforms in society at large. Practically all means that increased productivity were accepted as long as they did not immediately threaten the physical health of workers. Social and psychological costs for the workers were neglected or simply not understood; in any case, increased wages and shorter hours of work were regarded as compensation enough for whatever constraint on the worker more rational production methods might imply. For the few who could not adapt readily to new demands "the good society" provided new opportunities in the form of retraining and relocation or, as a last resort, shelter and the means for a decent life outside the labor market.

The systems of ideas behind time and motion studies, "scientific" wage systems, theories of administration, and so on, on the one hand, and human relations on the other, are in themselves relatively separate. Human relations did not deal to any great extent with issues of technology and formal organization, just as scientific management generally neglected social and human issues. The two systems of ideas existed in a nonmediated relationship. For those who wanted to draw upon both sets of ideas in their practical work—as many managers did—this lack of a mediated relationship on the

This report is based on a comprehensive case study performed through the Department of Psychology, University of Stockholm, and financed by the Swedish Center for Working Life.
Editors' note. This chapter was originally published in 1982 in the *International Journal of Health Services*.

theoretical level led to one of two conclusions: that the ideas were compatible and could supplement each other, or that they were antagonistic. The first belief seems to have prevailed among Scandinavian managers in the 1940s, 50s, and early 60s. In practice, it often led to calling in human relations specialists to clear away or smoothen the social and human problems created by scientific management approaches to rationalization and work organization.

In Scandinavian research, the view that scientific management and human relations were antagonistic sets of ideas emerged around 1960. In the 1950s, a number of researchers had raised the question: Is it really possible that functional specialization, technical control, and so forth can be increased more and more without harmful social and human consequences? In Norway, one answer to this problem was given by Lysgaard (1) in his study of the "workers' collectivity." Starting from the informal relationships between workers that were demonstrated in the Hawthorne studies (2), Lysgaard elaborated these and pointed to the existence of a broader, more "political" workers' collectivity at the workplace. This collectivity emerges from the workers' need for protection against the demands and pressures of the technical and economic system. The collectivity develops joint norms, drawing not only upon concrete experiences in the workplace but also upon general political ideas, such as those found in socialism.

The 1960s also saw the emergence of a strong empirical tradition in Scandinavian work research, particularly in Sweden, starting from conceivable conflicts between the two systems of ideas (3, 4). This research established that the following conditions have negative effects on workers (5): machine pacing of work rhythm and technical control of work methods; monotonous, repetitive work activating only a limited part of total human capabilities; lack of possibilities for contact with other people as part of the ongoing work; piece-rate and related payment systems, which besides contributing to employee wear and tear, are often detrimental to the observance of safety requirements; and authoritarian and detailed control of the individual, be it through foremen or impersonal systems, e.g., computer-based planning systems.

The less content the work has—objectively—and the less the worker has control over planning and working methods, the less rewarding is the work situation and the more work is experienced as constrained and meaningless. This situation is bad in itself, because it means a lower quality of life. The effects are accelerated by the fact that dissatisfaction and strain may lead to impaired physical and mental health. People with narrow and constrained jobs also seem to take less part in political, social, and cultural activities outside the job. We know, furthermore, that the risk of being expelled (shut off) from working life is highest among people whose jobs are most difficult in terms such as those outlined above (6).

A system of nationwide collective agreements which regulated development in economic life emerged as early as the 1930s. After World War II, national collective agreements also included a system for joint consultation through Work Councils. Neither of these agreements foresaw a rising conflict between productivity goals and work environment. Workers' access to information and their consultative role in management decisions were not effective enough instruments for the workers to be able to counteract fragmentation of jobs and stress and alienation in the workplace. The workers' representatives in the Work Councils also had difficulties in informing the rank and file of what was going on in the meetings. The ordinary workers by and large felt that they were rather powerless and had no say in their day-to-day activities. The emerging work research also demonstrated the powerlessness of the Work Councils and emphasized instead the importance of worker say on the shop floor for job satisfaction and well-being. In various research reports, claims were voiced on changes in job design to meet human needs and on a work organization based on autonomous groups.

Today the main problem is not to state the requirements of a more humane work organization—these have been put forward in much the same terms by many—but to develop strategies for bringing about such a work organization as a living and growing reality. In this respect, Scandinavia provides a fund of experience on which to draw. We can, for example, look back on comprehensive series of field research into new forms of work organization that are still unparalleled in other parts of the industrialized world. In recent years we have also seen the emergence of more total strategies on the level of society, founded on legislation and the commitment of public resources as well as on national trade union policies. To what extent have these various strategies been able to solve some of the problems involved? Let us take a look at the experience gained during the last 10 to 15 years with the various strategies that were applied during that period.

Recent Efforts at Industrial Democracy in Scandinavia

Field experiments with autonomous work groups and related forms of work organization emerged in the Scandinavian countries in the early 1960s. The development started with the Industrial Democracy Program in Norway (7–9). This program emerged as a collaborative scheme; the two main organizations in working life—the Employers Confederation and the Federation of Trade Unions—engaged in a practical effort together with researchers. The program was drawn up in terms of phases, the first dedicated to testing forms of work organization at specially selected work sites and the second to diffusion of the experience gained in this way. In the diffusion process, the employee and employer organizations were to play a dominant role, while the experimental phase would naturally be characterized by the researchers taking more of the initiative and generally showing a "high profile." A similar program emerged in Sweden, perhaps with somewhat weaker participation by the main labor market organizations.

These experiments and other efforts demonstrated the feasibility of autonomous work groups under varying technological conditions. They showed clearly that a change in people's immediate work situation is a necessary element in reforms concerning social and human problems in working life.

On the basis of these experiences, one can set forth the following proposals concerning autonomous groups: Work should be based on groups and not on individuals. The group should be given the responsibility for planning and performing work within a given area. The current division between planning and control on the one hand and execution on the other should be brought to an end, with planning and control restored to the primary work group. Foremen and technical experts should be geared to the needs and demands of the production groups—as resources for these groups— and not to functional requirements specified by higher organizational levels. A work organization that has such production groups as its primary building blocks seems to have the potential for counteracting problems of fragmentation and coercion, among other things owing to the following properties of the groups: (*a*) in a group context, the individual can expand his or her possibilities for attaining some degree of freedom and competence through work; (*b*) opportunities for learning and for variation in work are improved; (*c*) the individual and the group can achieve improved control over the rhythm and methods of work; and (*d*) opportunities for contact, support, and solidarity among people are improved.

In addition to showing that this form of organization is a building block in the network of solutions involved in a reform of working life based on human and social values, the early experiments established that autonomous groups may be superior even from traditional economic and technological points of view. The demonstrative value of these experiments was, in other words, quite high. In spite of this, diffusion proved to be problematic. There are many reasons for this, though even those who are heavily involved in the work have not reached general agreement on the explanations. One set of reasons relates to conservatism and protection of established positions of power and control. Another important reason is that these experiments were based to a large extent on individual companies as the unit of change. This meant that nothing could be achieved that was not accepted by local management. Furthermore, it meant that the experiments were designed to achieve a growth process within the hierarchical boundaries of the local plant, with more limited emphasis being placed on learning and development among groups and collectivities of people encompassing several workplaces in different companies. This was especially significant for workers and the trade unions. A third reason for the lack of diffusion from the early work experiments is that it was not possible to generate a fruitful relationship between traditional characteristics of trade union work and organization on the one hand and what happened in the field experiments on the other. This was reflected—in Sweden as well as in Norway—in the difficulties the trade unions have had in relating to these projects. They have tended to sit on the fence with neither all-out commitment nor absolute rejection.

In Sweden, shop floor experiments under joint bodies from the central organization in the labor market (SAF-LO-TCO) soon showed the trade unions that this was not a way to reach their goal of "worker influence on all levels in the company." On the contrary, it became evident that development was confined to worker influence on the immediate job and that local management had no interest in furthering worker participation in more strategic management decisions. The shop floor experiments under the supervision of joint bodies faded away.

Instead, the ideas were taken up by the employers in a relatively one-sided effort at change. Numerous company programs have surfaced in Swedish industry, some with consultative support from the technical department in the Swedish Employers Confederation. Diffusion in Sweden was faster and more far-reaching than in Norway. This diffusion has yielded valuable experiences and concretizations. It must, however, be underlined that what was and is being diffused is something different from what was originally intended. While the programs originally were designed to do something about the basic problems of participation on the shop floor, as part of a strategy for developing employee participation also in the settlement of broader organizational issues and policies, the development in Sweden has been characterized by the "shop floor issues" being considered of exclusive importance rather than as stepping stones to other changes. There has also been a clear shift away from human and social considerations toward such goals as improved productivity and reduced turnover and absenteeism.[1]

Moreover, the experiments often took place in close cooperation between management and the union local, but without changing the basic power structure. Through this strategy, management threatened to weaken the influence of the central trade unions. Under the traditional legal superstructure, management alone has control over issues of work organization. Therefore, any development, any contribution from the employees, would lie outside the domain where the central unions have any statutory authority or possibilities of safeguarding any progress. The fact that the central trade unions found it difficult to establish a reasonable relationship to these changes was one of the major factors behind the changes in the legislation regulating the Swedish Industrial Relations System that took place in the late 1970s.

The Act of Co-determination, made effective on January 1, 1977, opened up all areas of company life to trade union influence. It is a framework law that is supposed to be followed by central and local agreements between employers and the trade unions. Central agreements have been reached in the public sector, the cooperative sector, and the state-owned industries, but not in the private sector (except for banks and insurance companies). These agreements on co-determination cover such areas as personnel policy, work organization, and use of computers.

The Act of Co-determination has been put to practical test for only a few years, so it is too early to draw any conclusions. However, the application of the Act and its agreements until now show every sign of the trade unions' falling back on well-established collective bargaining traditions at the expense of building up knowledge and competence in the field of work organizations. Although a government sponsored but trade union-controlled research institute was created on the basis of the Act of Co-determination—the Swedish Center for Working Life—and although this institute was given large resources compared with other research organizations in Sweden, it has been very difficult for the trade unions to start concrete field experiments or to otherwise initiate research that deals with alternative models of work organization at the plant level. There are several circumstances that may partly explain this lack of development.

First, coinciding with the new Act, Sweden was hit by an economic recession; co-determination and its research resources became to a great extent fully preoccupied with plant closings, mergers, and restructuring of whole industries. Second, the employers have been reluctant to have researchers work at the plant level for the trade unions only; they have not been willing to experiment with the application of new technology or other forms of work organization under conditions outside their control. Third, the lack of trade union-inspired shop floor-level experiments is also a result of a centralized trade union structure and the fact that most central trade unions are only moderately interested in issues that cannot be handled through traditional methods of collective bargaining.

---

[1] From the management's point of view, worker influence limited to the shop floor may be of interest since it presumably leads to greater motivation and increased productivity. This strategy can, in fact, be said to underlie most organizational changes launched in Japan under the rubric "humanization of work" or "quality of working life" (10). There has often been little interest on the company's part in developing forms of decision making that give employees influence over larger issues.

The Act of Co-determination means influence for trade union representatives and not for the rank and file on the shop floor. The trade union representatives probably feel that their time is completely absorbed with negotiations in the field of co-determination and that there is little or no time left over for creative work at the shop floor level. So, ironically enough, legislation and negotiations based on these agreements seem to have absorbed the main part of trade union resources for work reform. Few resources have been left for initiatives on shop floor changes related to the organization of work and the application of new technology. To be sure, this reflects the priorities of the trade unions. However, it is to be expected that joint efforts on work organization will develop as soon as central agreements on co-determination are reached. The trade unions will then be in a quite different position compared to the situation in the 1960s and early 70s. In contrast to that earlier period, they will probably find it easier to relate to developments that encompass both participation through the system of representative democracy and various forms of changes in job content and worker influence on the shop floor. Large investments in training for this purpose are also being made.

The Need for a Multilevel Strategy for Worker Participation

A summary and discussion of research relevant to the discussion of a "participatory work environment strategy"[2] was presented to the 1976 Congress of the Swedish Confederation of Trade Unions (5).[3] In this summary, it was stressed that representative influence in various formal bodies and influence for the rank and file in their daily work must be regarded as two parts in an overall trade union strategy for industrial democracy.

Worker participation is a political goal, but also a means to come to grips with bad working conditions. Future efforts in the area of worker participation should therefore focus on efforts where these levels of influence are deliberately tied together. If the trade unions do not succeed in such efforts, there is a risk that the development of worker participation will be split into two separate parts: one bureaucratic part based on legislation and collective bargaining that seeks to increase the influence for the trade union as an organization in economic life, and another part dealing with worker participation at the shop floor level that concerns the ordinary worker in his daily activities.

Following only the first line of development, the trade unions will soon run into the same problems found with the German Mittbestimmung and the Yugoslav Self-Management. That is, they will be regarded by the rank and file as part of the control system of the company without any basic possibilities—or even interest—to look after the everyday working conditions of the rank and file. This will create great difficulties in relation to their members.

---

[2] The term "participatory work environment" was introduced to the author by Professor Hy Kornbluh of the Institute of Labor and Industrial Relations, University of Michigan, Ann Arbor. The term encompasses both work environment and worker participation issues, and focuses on worker participation as a means of dealing with work environment problems.

[3] The Congress is the highest decision-making body of the Confederation of Trade Unions. It meets every fifth year and determines policy issues for the coming five-year period.

The shop floor-type of development is of interest to management particularly because of the increased intrinsic rewards and increased motivation to work that might follow from increased participation in matters related to one's job and working conditions. If management alone is allowed to control this development, its psychological forces will be used primarily for productivity purposes and not for purposes of creating a more democratic working life. As indicated earlier, many signs show that this split in worker participation strategies is exactly what is going on in Sweden right now.

The Almex case, on which we shall report and comment here, constitutes an example of a trade union-based strategy for the development of a democratic work organization where co-determination in representative forms and autonomous production groups have been united. It is a local initiative which demonstrates an understanding of the need to "marry" shop floor influence and influence for the trade union to each other. Through this multilevel strategy, it represents an answer to some of the limitations of the shop floor-level approach at the same time as it creates a functional relationship between co-determination and direct democracy on the shop floor through a system of autonomous groups. The Almex case demonstrates what might be achieved in many companies under a legislation on co-determination, provided the workers want to push the development of a democratic work organization on the shop floor. The fact that the changes taking place at Almex started and reached their present state before the Swedish Act on Co-determination shows that far-reaching developments in industrial democracy can be reached without any legal support under especially favorable conditions. But society and wage earners cannot rely on benevolent management and unusual local competence for industrial democracy to develop. It is obvious that legislation on co-determination might stimulate and facilitate similar change processes elsewhere. Moreover, legislation and/or agreements on co-determination would probably have helped speed up the changes in this case. It should also be stressed that local developments without any anchorage in the legal superstructure are very vulnerable and often dissolve when the first enthusiasm has cooled off. As soon as a central agreement on co-determination is reached, it would therefore seem necessary and natural to attach the local agreement at Almex to this agreement as a support and shelter for what has been achieved.

Thus, we believe that legislation and/or collective agreements are necessary conditions for a more widespread development toward industrial democracy to take place. At the same time, however, we feel that the main lesson to be learned from the Almex case is that the most important conditions at the workplace are related to the will and effort that can be mobilized among the workers themselves to create their own change process. To involve ordinary workers in a change toward increased control over production, and more challenge and more learning opportunities in their work, takes a much deeper effort than the changes that can be laid down by legislation and collective agreements. A variety of means must be applied, and these means must be interrelated in a consistent and meaningful way. The Almex case points to the importance of changes in work organization being engineered by the workers themselves. In this case, no outside experts or "change agents" were used. Our role as researchers has been only to describe and analyze what had already taken place in order to make it possible for people outside Almex to learn from the experience.

Brief Description of the Company—AB Almex

Before examining the system for a democratic work organization at Almex more closely, it may be useful to have some details about the company, its products, size, economy, and so forth. Almex started as a family company in 1946, producing a portable mechanical ticket machine for use on buses and other forms of public transportation. In 1946, serial production began (Model A). Since this time, new models have been developed, including a ticket-cancelling device which checks tickets electronically (Model A). Annual sales exceed 2 billion Sw. crowns. Over 90 percent of total production is for the export market, the active marketing area being some 40 countries. The company has been expanding both in sales and personnel every year since 1973, and is presently regarded as one of the most profitable companies in Swedish industry.

The company is divided into sales, technical, and administrative divisions. The technical division consists of production, material control, service, and three research and development departments. The autonomous departments are found primarily on the production and service sides.

Autonomous work groups have been introduced into the following departments: M-assembly (April 1976), Service shop (October 1976), Inspection (November 1976), Tool shop (January 1977), Packing (March 1977), Planning group (white-collar workers) (May 1977), Experimental shop (September 1977), and A-assembly (November 1977). In addition to these departments, Electronic parts, Electronic testing, and a subdepartment of the engineering shop function similarly to the autonomous departments, although they lack a formal agreement.

DEMOCRATIC WORK ORGANIZATION AT ALMEX

The organization of work at Almex is characterized by employee influence at all levels of the company. The strategy for development of a democratic work organization is based on the principle that true autonomy at the production group level requires that employees have the right of co-determination when it comes to the more sweeping decisions made by the company, such as those involving finances, technology, personnel policy, work organization, and production planning. Employee co-determination in these more general matters is seen as an essential condition for autonomy at the production group level, which would otherwise be limited to mere job details. The soundness of this principle is supported by evidence from various experiments with autonomous work groups, where employee influence most often extends only to certain aspects of the way each person carries out his own job (6).

Almex is an example of what could be called a multilevel effort. Changes in the work organization have been initiated from below by the Metal union local. The aim has been to link together representative co-determination in strategic decisions and autonomy at the shop floor level.

Co-determination constitutes the framework and prerequisite for autonomous work groups. Through the system of autonomous work groups, all employees become directly involved in the democratic organization of work. The connection between co-determination in strategic management decisions and the autonomous group system therefore becomes a crucial feature of the attempt that Almex represents. It is this feature that distinguishes Almex from a number of other companies that have autonomous work groups. From the outset, this connection was assured by the fact that elected union stewards also served as "contact people" in the autonomous departments, i.e., they represented the group in its contacts with other parts of the company. Due to the gradual increase in union involvement on the part of most of the workers, however, it has been possible to elect contact persons from outside the group of elected union stewards without jeopardizing the connection between the autonomous production groups and the union.

Co-determination

Co-determination at Almex takes both a representative form and a less organized form. The representative form is reflected in the following three bodies: the board of the company, which meets about five times a year; the financial committee, meeting five to ten times a year, where not only economic questions but also topics such as efforts in other countries and incoming orders are discussed; and the health and safety committee,[4] meeting four to eight times a year, where the employees are in the majority and where questions concerning the work environment, machine acquisitions, rebuilding, etc. are taken up. The less organized form involves informal contacts between elected union stewards and management in the course of the day's work. It is this informal day-to-day type of co-determination that is most important and that proves the strong position of the Metal local in the company. The formal aspect of union influence does not differ significantly from that found in most other companies in Sweden today under such laws as the Act of Board Representative, the Work Environment Act, and the Act of Co-determination. Undoubtedly, however, the workers at Almex have a greater say in these formal bodies than is normally found in Swedish companies due to the strong position the Metal local has in the company.

It is difficult to briefly describe how co-determination works. Instead, we shall cite some examples that illustrate how co-determination manifests itself in the areas of personnel policy, foreign investment, and technology development.

In contrast to the official policy of the Swedish Confederation of Trade Unions (LO), the Metal local at Almex has all along considered it very important not to make any distinction between work organization and personnel matters. Recruiting, transfers, and the creation or elimination of positions are regarded as aspects of work organization. Thus, within the framework of union influence on work organization, a written agreement has been adopted that sets the rules for employee influence over what are traditionally viewed as personnel matters. This agreement is formulated as follows: "Representatives from the trade union locals are to be included when deciding on issues involving personnel management, such as personnel planning, recruiting, introduction of new employees, training transfers, staff development and internal information" (November 1977).

---

[4] Health and Safety Committees are required at every Swedish workplace exceeding 25 employees under the 1978 Act on Work Environment. Under this Act, workers have the right to be informed and to check plans, drawings, and regulations for buildings and machinery.

The reasons behind not accepting any distinction between personnel policy and work organization are several. Among the most important is the fact that the Metal local wishes in this way to work against "elite recruitment" to production groups, and to prevent these groups from eliminating people who for some reason are not able to live up to the group norms for achievement or cooperation. This is a criticism often directed against autonomous work groups, which is sometimes justified (11). There is another important reason for maintaining the connection between personnel policy and work organization. Otherwise, the company can—either intentionally or not—start recruiting people for executive positions who do not accept a strong influence from the employees and may therefore systematically work against the development of a democratic work organization. This has happened in some places where autonomous work groups have been formed (9). The company can also, by establishing new positions in the organization, increase its control over production. On one occasion, both of the union locals at Almex (Metal, SIF) jointly opposed the creation of a new administrative managerial post. At first the position was not filled, and later the job description was changed to take into account the specific features of the autonomous group system. It was also decided—in accordance with Metal's wish—that the duties of the production manager were to be "tuned up" (i.e., reassessed) after six months.

When new workers are being hired, representatives from the Metal local are always involved. When there have been more applicants than vacancies, the union has played a decisive role. The contact person and other employees from the affected production departments are also involved. Orientation to the autonomous groups system and its relation to co-determination, as well as training in union matters, is organized by the union and performed during paid working hours.

Another issue in which the Metal local has been able to exert influence concerns investments abroad. Metal's policy is to maintain employment in Sweden. Thus the union local is very critical of plans to take production abroad and has in several instances been able to alter the company's investment plans in this respect. At the same time, Metal is aware of the necessity of expanding into new markets and has in fact stimulated such development in cases when management did not believe deadlines could be met. The critical factor here seems to be the workers' better knowledge of the actual situation in the production departments and the flexibility created by the autonomous group system.

The workers are also aware of the necessity of keeping pace with technological development. This pressure from the workers has contributed to a product development where the company today is well ahead of its competitors. The workers are also closely following developments in production technology and are in a position where they have access to all relevant information about computers and other forms of new work methods. Through co-determination, they will be part of the decision making on these issues.

The Autonomous Group System

In negotiations between the Metal local and the company, an agreement on autonomous groups was reached in 1976. The rights and power of decision making in the autonomous work group were outlined in 11 points, among which the following are the most important:

- After internal discussions, the group makes all decisions within its area of competence that do not interfere with the decision making of other groups.
- Each production group is collectively responsible for production assignments.
- A supervisor appointed by the employer is replaced by a "contact person," a member of the group, elected by and responsible to the group.
- Supervision and the internal distribution of work are decided by the group.
- The production group must cooperate in all directions. Technical experts and sales personnel cannot give orders to the group, but should reach joint agreements.
- The group is responsible for the training of its members, job rotation, and development of production methods. Technical experts should be asked to assist the group in these matters.
- The group must consult the production manager if agreed upon production plans are in danger of being jeopardized, or if there are serious disturbances in production flow, supplies, etc.
- If the group cannot solve its internal conflicts, any group member is free to bring the problem to the trade union local and/or the production manager.

This agreement was applied initially only to a single department. It was understood, however, that other departments could reach similar agreements if and when they wanted to. Since that time, similar agreements have been negotiated for eight out of 11 production departments. Local trade union policy is that the initiative to join the autonomous group system should come from the workers in the various departments. The trade union then helps to negotiate an agreement with management.

Although not part of the agreement, there are also ideological and other important features of the democratic work organization. Among these are the following principles:

- The autonomous group system is a collective work form based on equality of membership and entitlement. It is accepted that people are different and that some people produce more than others. No comparison should be made between individuals, and existing wage differences should be abolished.
- The autonomous group system is based on group work and collective responsibility. People are developing through their relations to other people at a pace they determine themselves.
- Every member should be given the opportunity to learn all the tasks within the group's working area. This increases the flexibility, overview, and strength of the group, at the same time as it makes work more intrinsically rewarding.
- The group cannot recruit new members and replace workers without the consent of the union. The group should be encouraged to give shelter and support to members with social or other types of problems.

The Functioning of the Autonomous Groups

Planning. Planning and purchasing may involve difficulties for the autonomous work groups because of the large number of individual items produced and the many variations that exist for each type of machine. Production planning takes place primarily through informal contacts (in A-assembly through regular meetings) between the production manager, the planning department, and the contact people in the assembly department. The contact people approve the production schedule which the planning department has drawn up. In the case of unusual orders, or when the question of overtime comes up, the production group involved is always to be contacted before the production schedule is prepared. Sometimes a production group is consulted before certain orders are accepted, since it is the group that has the best overview of the situation.

Organization and Distribution of Work. The functioning of the autonomous groups varies according to the nature of their tasks, their size, and their "history" within the autonomous group system. M-assembly has been built up around the idea of autonomy. The organization of work is very flexible and varies depending on the size of an order and the number of different types of machines involved. This flexibility has been made possible by the fact that practically all of the nine people in the group are able to perform all the tasks. A-assembly, with 16 people, is a relatively large department where people have worked at the same tasks for a long time. They have not yet succeeded in achieving an organization of work as flexible as that in M-assembly. Some people in A-assembly have shown a certain reluctance to "let go" of what they consider as "their" job, and they also feel a certain amount of insecurity about learning something new. It seems obvious that the size of the department has contributed a great deal to the somewhat slower pace of progress. New hires, however, are taught to assemble the whole machine. Eventually this goal will be reached for all employees.

The inspection department performs two roles: checking incoming details from subcontractors and checking complete machines ready for delivery. Before the department joined the autonomous group system, more qualified measurement was performed by a few specialists. The group organized early on a technical school using technical experts as teachers. Today all 12 workers are able to perform all tasks, which has meant increased capacity and increased quality of work. The service department maintains and repairs machines sent in by the customer. The degree of skill and independence has remained relatively great. The department has also taken over customer contact with all Swedish customers.

Further Development of Work Methods. Working in an autonomous group means a process of constant learning for the employees. However, formal training in connection with autonomous work groups has taken place only in the service shop and in inspection. In inspection, a comprehensive training program was carried out on the initiative of the employees and the union local. Union representatives underscore the fact that a prerequisite for autonomy in inspection was that the employees there received some formal training so they would be able to handle the more difficult inspection tasks. In the earlier supervisor-type of organization, the skilled tasks were assigned to only a few people. The training was arranged by the Metal local in cooperation with the employees of the department, and drew upon the knowledge about testing techniques that technical experts possessed. From the beginning, this training was conducted partly during free time; despite that fact all employees participated. The program demanded a considerable effort from many workers, especially since they had not taken part in any similar training previously. The course included both a theoretical review of testing techniques and practical exercises in the use of various measuring instruments, e.g., microscope, projector, electronic clock. One result of this training is that inspection work has become more comprehensive and skilled and—according to the employees in the group—more careful. In M-assembly, the testing of machines has been made a part of the autonomous work group's responsibility. The group, in cooperation with the engineers, has worked out a test program for all machines. Other changes made by the employees include organization of an intermediate supply depot, revised work routines, and administrative simplification.

Contact Persons. An important part of the agreement on autonomous groups was the replacement of the traditional supervisor with a contact person selected from among the group members. A contact person is appointed only in the larger autonomous departments (A- and M-assembly and inspection). Rotation of this office has occurred in two of these departments. In the future, the group members will review the duties of the contact person twice a year, and perhaps select a new one. Should special reasons arise, a new contact person can be appointed at any time during the term of office.

The contact person has primarily played a unifying role. His or her assignment includes keeping in touch "upwards" in the company—particularly with planners, the production manager, design engineers, and purchasers—on those matters that are *common* to everyone in the group. This does not preclude any employee in the group from making such contacts himself. The contact person conveys the information he gets "downwards" to the employees in the department. Since the contact people have usually been elected union stewards, they have also answered for union information and for contacts between the production group and the union board.

The union representatives emphasize that the importance of the contact person in an autonomous work group should not be exaggerated. They agree with management that there should be such a person in all the later autonomous departments to assure a desirable degree of order in the group's transactions with its environment. But it is also important that this duty rotates, and that the contact person not act unnecessarily as a channel for those contacts that could as well be taken directly with or by the worker involved. As the others in each autonomous work group have become more knowledgeable and involved, and as the white-collar employees (often at the urging of the contact person) go directly to the workers of a department, the function of the contact person has gradually become less critical.

The tasks of the contact person are in some respects similar to those that have traditionally been assigned to a supervisor. One may therefore ask what the difference is, and whether it is not irrelevant to an employee if he has a contact person or a supervisor. The latter view is one that some white-collar workers—in particular the former supervisors themselves—express. Nearly all employees in the autonomous departments (but significantly fewer in the other departments) perceive a distinct difference between the role and function of a contact person and a supervisor. The difference they point to can be summarized as follows: (*a*) a contact person is chosen— and can be dismissed—by the workers in the department, whereas a supervisor is appointed by management; (*b*) a supervisor has closer ties to management; and (*c*) the supervisor's assignment consists of checking up and monitoring, making it difficult to include him in the group on the basis of equality.

The job of contact person has until now meant a lot of extra work and stress, and is therefore regarded as a demanding one. One reason for this is the service function that the contact person performs for the employees in his work group. However, the job of contact person also means a vote of confidence from the others in the group, as well as interesting, important assignments. Thus, serving as a contact person involves not only strains but also significant social rewards. There are no material rewards.

THE PROCESS OF GROWTH TOWARD
A DEMOCRATIZED WORK ORGANIZATION

The autonomous groups and co-determination were introduced and developed out of a situation that was characterized by the following features: a paternally ruled enterprise with a low-wage policy and a small number of skilled workers; a piece-work system, which created arbitrary wage differences both within and between the various departments; worker dissatisfaction with the trade union local, the affairs of which for the most part were handled by a single person; and no employee influence on personnel policy, transfers, or the like.

Prior to the development of autonomous groups, solutions to these problems were sought by each worker individually. Through good contact with the foreman, some people succeeded in getting better jobs and better pay, but that did not solve the problems for the workers as a group. What has been termed the "workers' collectivity" (1)—that is, a set of generally accepted norms that emerged from the workers' need to protect themselves from the pressure of the technical/economic system—was very weak.

Primarily as a result of a strong sense of dissatisfaction with the union's role, some workers began in the early 1970s to spend more time together on the job and to discuss union matters. They soon found out that the problems were not individual but rather collective problems. These workers decided that something had to be done about the situation, and support was quickly forthcoming from other employees. The result was that, in 1972, a new board was elected to lead the union local. A strong workers' collectivity was beginning to emerge which saw the trade union as its leadership and as an instrument for change.

Due largely to greater confidence in the new union stewards, interest in the union grew rapidly. This was evident in increased participation in union meetings. At the same time, the union stepped up its level of activity; among other things, study circles were arranged and union assignments were distributed more widely. This increased interest in the trade union can be attributed mainly to the democratization of the union's work and the increased strength and influence of the union in management questions, especially personnel matters. Democratization of the union's work involved a wider distribution of union assignments and also meant that the union stewards regularly went around to the various departments and talked things over with the workers. The union thus became better informed at the same time as confidence in the union among the workers increased. Negotiations were carried out by a "trojka" whose composition was changed from time to time in order to maintain the confidence of the rank and file. The increased influence of the union in management questions proved to the employees that the union was now better able to represent their interests. This greater influence was due to several interrelated factors, including better knowledge among union stewards acquired both through training organized by the national union and through informal study groups, the experience of sitting on the company board, and several strikes or open conflicts with management through which the trade union was able to advance the cause of the workers. Practically all the workers were involved in these conflicts, and for many it was their first collective action. Since the outcomes of these conflicts were favorable to the workers, they also demonstrated the strength of the trade union and of the workers' collectivity.

It is difficult to determine how and when the idea of autonomous work groups arose. However, the increase in the level of union activity and the democratization of union work must be regarded as essential prerequisites for the development that took place at Almex. Increased solidarity and a greater feeling of unity among the employees were also very important. Between 1972 and 1975, the Metal local arranged several study circles in which a nucleus of active workers participated. The circles dealt with industrial democracy issues and helped the workers to analyze their own work situation and—most importantly—develop a sense of community. Through this study, they began to see alternatives to the existing work organization and understand the ways in which they must operate for changes to get under way.

When these active union members had agreed to try to create a more democratic work organization, and when support for this was forthcoming from the locals of both the union of Clerical and Technical Employees in Industry (SIF) and the union of Foremen and Supervisors (SALF), the next step was to take these ideas to the company.

Early in 1976, following a decision in the Work Council,[5] a task force was formed to discuss the possibility of a new work organization. The task force consisted of two people from the SIF local, two from the Metal local, one from SALF, and two company representatives. The Metal local was strongly supported in this task force—as it was later in the implementation of autonomy—by the representatives of SIF. This united front on the part of blue- and white-collar workers was very unusual at the time and has probably been of great importance in the development of autonomy at Almex. The most significant result of the efforts of the task force was the decision to introduce autonomous production groups in the assembly departments. This effort was to follow the guidelines for autonomy that had been discussed and agreed upon in the task force.

When the representatives from the Metal local saw an opportunity to introduce autonomy in one of the assembly departments, it became obvious that some form of organized training involving people from various levels in the company was going to be necessary. This training should focus on organizational principles and show management and white-collar workers that an autonomous group system could be advantageous not only to the workers but to the company as a whole, including middle-management and technical experts. The training package, prepared and administered by Metal local, contained the following items: a review of different theories of organization; a discussion of the current work organization at Almex; a discussion of the wage system,

---

[5] The central agreement on Work Councils is today replaced by the Act of Co-determination and its various agreements.

planning, and leadership; an outline of a new work organization for the company; and a discussion of the role of the union in this new work organization.

Autonomy was first introduced in M-assembly and then extended to other departments step-by-step, with the employees in each department setting the pace and playing an active role in the change. Although active union members try through discussions in the various departments to stimulate an interest in and push for autonomy, it is the workers themselves who decide if and when autonomy is to be introduced. Once a department has decided that it wants to be organized into an autonomous production group, the union stewards participate in the negotiations with management and help to draw up an agreement on autonomy in keeping with the wishes of the department. In this way, the union has succeeded in combining active guidance and coordination of the development of autonomy with letting each department act independently in this matter.

This has important consequences for both the form and the future of autonomy. But it is no doubt a problem that the autonomous group system does not comprise all production departments in the company. The conditions for autonomy and for choosing not to join the system of autonomous groups are dealt with in the next section.

CONDITIONS FOR A DEMOCRATIZED WORK ORGANIZATION AT ALMEX

In addition to the circumstances and activities already described, the possibility of developing a democratic work organization is dependent on the technical/economic as well as the social-psychological conditions that exist in each particular case. The technical/economic conditions include the following factors: nature of technology and production; organizational structure; company size; degree of planning and control; marketing situation and dependence on customers; owner structure, competitive and financial situation; and the composition of the worker population in terms of education, nationality, and so forth. The social-psychological conditions affecting the development of a democratic work organization include factors such as people's outlook, attitudes, and opinions.

The Technical/Economic Conditions

Among the more important overall conditions existing in the company in the early 1970s, several deserve particular mention. The company has gradually succeeded in strengthening its position with respect to its competitors, and has been continuously growing since its start. Production is to a large degree determined by customer orders. It is essential to be able to accept quick orders and to adapt production to customers' wishes. Both of these factors necessitate a flexible production apparatus. In addition to these general conditions, it is important to take a look at the impact that certain special conditions (such as those relating to technology, planning, wage policy, and customer demand) have had on the development of a democratic organization at Almex. The possibility of implementing such an organizational form can be limited or even precluded by centralized, detailed planning and firmly steered production, whether this stems from management, the wage system, technical considerations, or a combination of these factors.

The conditions at Almex with regard to planning and production control are favorable for the introduction of autonomous work groups. Technical control of production at Almex has never been strong. The low level of mechanization and the manual "craftmanship" involved in much of the work has made it impossible up to now to impose a detailed control system in accordance with the traditional methods of scientific management. It is also difficult to determine exactly how much time each work operation takes, since assembly requires constant fitting and adjusting. Moreover, due to customers' demands, a large number of machine variants are produced. These conditions—together with a poorly organized piece-work system—are the main reasons why piece-work wages were dropped in 1972 and replaced with hourly wages for all blue-collar workers. Time wages—in contrast to piece rates—are probably an essential prerequisite for group work based on cooperation and the sharing of experience. In many experiments with worker participation, in Scandinavia and elsewhere, the wage system has proved to be an obstacle to flexibility and cooperation within the group. Group piece rates or bonus systems may also lead to group pressure to get rid of weaker members who do not contribute as much to group efficiency.

The impact of the wage system for autonomy is confirmed by the workers. In our interviews, 65 percent of workers were of the opinion that equal salaries are a necessary prerequisite for creating autonomous work groups. There are still wage differentials in the autonomous departments—even if they are decreasing—but these are relics of the era before autonomy.

Customer determination, which leads to a large number of variations of each type of machine, together with differences in the size of orders, makes detailed planning difficult. In addition, shortages of items provided by subcontractors often arise and cause planning problems. All this means that production must be flexible.

The nature of the work has meant that many employees—even though they are not skilled workers in a formal sense—have acquired both skills and an ability to view production as a whole. These skills and abilities have been an important prerequisite for participation in the planning of production and therefore for the democratization of the work organization.

Social-Psychological Conditions

The social-psychological conditions for autonomy include self-confidence, interpersonal relations, and a sense of responsibility. Virtually every worker interviewed was of the opinion that good relations with one's fellow workers are a necessary condition for autonomous work groups to function. This already existed in those departments where autonomy has been introduced; in addition, the feeling of unity was strengthened by the discussions that preceded the changeover.

There are several departments at Almex that are not autonomous. When one takes a close look at the resistance to and doubts about autonomy that exist among these departments, the psychological factors seem to be the most significant. The reasons for opposition to autonomy can be summarized as follows: (a) fear that the work group will not function democratically and that a few people will dominate the department; (b) fear that conflicts will arise in the work group; (c) concern that certain people will misuse the freedom implied in autonomy; (d) personal insecurity due to a lack of technical skills and self-confidence, which means that people are afraid to take responsibility and make their own decisions; and (*e*) a sense that the present work organization is something that cannot be changed.

Naturally the employees in the nonautonomous departments are influenced by the experiences of their fellow workers in autonomous work groups. We shall therefore turn now to an account of the consequences of the democratized work organization in order to understand what it has meant to the workers as well as to the company.

CONSEQUENCES OF THE DEMOCRATIZED WORK ORGANIZATION

Introductory Methodological Remarks

The theoretical and metascientific basis of our approach implies that the change process at Almex cannot be regarded as an "intervention" whose effects in various areas can be easily read off from interviews and statistics. Both the autonomous groups and the company must be regarded as open systems which interact with the environment and adapt to new realities in a dialectic and unstructured way.

Nevertheless, our task is to analyze this process in a way that can give some understanding to others of what has happened, why it happened, and what main consequences can be traced back to the change process or some aspect of it. In doing so, we have turned to the literature in a fairly open search process, looking for those theories and concepts that we believe contribute to an understanding of what has taken place at Almex. This method contains an inescapable element of subjective choice in conceptualization. Other observers of the same organizational events might have preferred to use other concepts and to stress other outcomes or aspects of the change process. The analysis presented herein is also incomplete in many ways, not the least with respect to explicit reference to earlier research. For a more comprehensive account of our theoretical anchorage, readers are referred to the main report (12).

Data have been collected basically on a qualitative basis, through interviews, group discussion, and informal observation virtually every day during one year. In the first round, workers who had joined the autonomous group system were interviewed. These interviews were open-ended, following only a checklist prepared in advance. Issues brought up during the interviews that were not foreseen were recorded and added to the checklist for the next interview. Working reports were prepared on four different occasions and shown to the workers for their comments and suggestions.

The second round of interviews was built on the first. From these results and earlier research considered relevant, a questionnaire was constructed which was used in personal interviews with all workers in the production departments. These interviews were designed to capture—both in qualitative and quantitative terms—the possible differences in attitudes and evaluation between workers who had joined the autonomous group system (60 workers) and those who had not (40 workers). In this way, we felt it would be possible to get a somewhat clearer understanding of the autonomous group system as part of the democratized work organization, whose other part—co-determination—is valid for the whole company. Existing differences between workers in autonomous and nonautonomous departments cannot, however, simply be interpreted as effects of the autonomous group system owing to various types of selection mechanisms operating in this case. We shall discuss these problems at various points in the text.

Our analysis dealt with three different areas: consequences for the workers; consequences for middle-management and technical experts; and consequences for the effectiveness of the company. [We will comment here on the role of middle-management and technical experts, but will not analyze the new work organization from their perspective. This is a substantial part of the main report (12), however.]

Consequences for the Workers

Our analysis deals with outcomes on three different levels: the worker as an individual, the worker as a group member, and the worker as part of a collectivity.

The analysis of the worker as an individual is based on two main concepts: identity and self-confidence. The concept of identity was never referred to explicitly by the workers. We use it, however, since we believe it is a concept that captures changes in the perceptions about oneself that many but not all workers displayed. It is a cognitive concept that answers the question: Who am I? And we will try to show that many workers changed their answer to this question in the course of the growth toward democracy at the workplace. The concept of self-confidence is an affective concept. It was very often referred to by the workers in describing how they felt since becoming part of a democratized work organization.

Identity. Changes in identity or perception about oneself touch upon several different aspects of the democratized work organization. First are identity changes related to an increased area of competence due to the autonomous group system. Among other things, this means workers have acquired technical skills of greater depth and variety, since all group members are invited to learn all jobs within the group's working area. In addition, there has been increased participation in planning for production and personnel, and increased participation in decision making on the group level as to volume, pace, internal distribution of work, and the solution of various production problems arising during the day. Second are identity changes related to membership in a group with new and enlarged functions. The autonomous groups have meant increased group influence in relation to higher hierarchical levels. Technical experts can no longer give orders but must act as advisors and seek joint agreement. Moreover, the entire production group, not the individual worker, is responsible for production volume and quality. Responsibility for production in this case does not mean that the group has to fulfill a certain quota as a result of negotiations. Instead, group responsibility for production is generally accepted by the workers as an integral part of the autonomous group system.

A third identity change is related to membership in the trade union. This is due to the trade union's role in the change process and the fact that the union is regarded as an instrument for expressing the values and needs of the rank and file. The following aspects of the change process and its monitoring seem to have been of special importance for the identification of the democratized work organization with the trade union: (*a*) the development toward democracy at the workplace was originated and has throughout been engineered by a democratized trade union local, in close contact with the members; (*b*) as part of making the union local more democratic, trade union procedures have been simplified and assignments spread among a greater number of people; (c) union stewards were elected contact people for the first autonomous groups in order to keep a close relationship between autonomy on the group level and co-determination in management decisions; (d) autonomy on the shop floor is viewed as part of a trade union strategy for increased worker say in the company as a whole; (e) various collective actions demonstrated the strength of the trade union and of the workers' collectivity to both management and individual workers; (f) the trade union organized training activities on the job, including both general training in democratic work organization and technical training for some of the departments; and (g) the union organized study circles in leisure hours that have been of great importance for self-esteem and fellowship among the workers. The best illustration of this aspect of identity change is the increase in attendance at trade union meetings from 3 to 4 percent in 1972 to 70 to 80 percent in 1977. Because of this large attendance, workers have been able since 1978 to negotiate five union meetings per year during paid working hours. Everyone present at work that day participates in the meeting.

Self-confidence. This was the most commonly used expression when workers tried to describe how they felt about the change and what the increased autonomy has meant for their personality. By self-confidence, they meant the following: you feel confident about yourself; you know what you want; you feel you are able to do things yourself; and you feel that you are not inferior to other people "higher up" in the organization.

This increased sense of self-confidence was observed in three ways. First, fellow workers and technical experts reported that workers take more initiative, act more independently, and are generally more active since the introduction of autonomous production groups. Second, this was noted in interviews in which virtually all the workers reported greater self-esteem. The major reasons given for increased self-confidence (as compared with the nonautonomous departments) were the following: you are a member of a group which discusses production problems, makes joint decisions, and takes responsibility for its work; you are supported by a strong union that has influence on the running of the company; and you are not supervised or controlled in a detailed manner. Third, researchers observed that workers explicitly want to take increased responsibility for production. The increased influence through the autonomous group and through union co-determination makes increased responsibility appear not as a burden but as a means to increased freedom and self-esteem. One-third of the workers said increased independence and responsibility were the most important aspects of the change: "It is we, the workers, who make the decisions about production." "We are responsible now." "We are on our own." "Nobody tells us what to do. Of course that leads to increased self-esteem."

Job Satisfaction. In the previous sections, several aspects of increased job satisfaction have been demonstrated in relation to the democratized work organization. These aspects are above all increased "craft pride" and a sense of increased satisfaction with the fact that the production group is capable of taking responsibility for "its own work." Both these aspects show that the democratized work organization has increased workers' sense of worth and dignity. This section briefly touches on another aspect of job satisfaction—the value work has for the individual worker.

We tried to get an understanding of the value of work to each worker by asking people if their job in general provides financial rewards only, or if one also feels that some personal satisfaction can be gained from the job. This question has been asked in a number of other studies of industrial work. These investigations found that, on the average, 60 to 65 percent of Swedish industrial workers have an instrumental attitude toward their present job, that is, they value their job only for the earnings it provides. The more predetermined, controlled, and repetitive the work is, the more widespread is this instrumental attitude (4).

At Almex, we compared autonomous and nonautonomous departments. Our expectations were that the instrumental attitude toward work would be significantly less common in the autonomous departments. This did, in fact, prove to be the case. Only 20 percent of the employees in the autonomous departments, compared with 50 percent in the other departments, felt that the benefit from their job was mainly the money earned. We cannot be sure, however, if this difference depends on the fact that people's outlook has been changed by autonomy, or if those with a noninstrumental orientation toward work to a greater extent have sought employment in the autonomous group system. Qualitative data from the interviews, however, clearly support the conclusion that autonomy does change people, and that in the course of this process people start to view their work and what it means to them in a different way. We have also found support for this interpretation from studies in other companies. The same question about job satisfaction was asked in connection with an experiment in autonomy in some departments of the Swedish Tobacco Company (13). After a four-year-long experience with autonomy, most workers in these departments changed to a less instrumental view of their job.

Stress. In this section, we shall make use of Frese's treatment of the phenomenon of stress in working life (14). Frese gives a very general definition of stress, viewing it as something caused by conditions that the individual experiences (evaluates) as threatening and "repugnant" (aversive). He argues, like many others who write about stress (15, 16), that the consequences of stress depend on the degree to which the individual can control the stress-creating conditions. Frese stretches the notion of control to include the individual's influence over such company matters as personnel policy, production policy, investments, company formations, and marketing mechanisms.

Our main concern was whether, and to what extent, autonomy has increased the psychological pressures on the individual worker. This has been shown to be the case elsewhere (13). Democratization has unquestionably meant that the autonomous production groups, together with the local Metal Worker's Union, bear a greater responsibility for production quality and output, personnel policy, employee training, and coordination of the work of the various departments. This increased responsibility is a challenge, but it also puts greater demands on individual workers to take the initiative in contacting people and to cooperate with others. It further involves some additional work (administration, replenishment of parts and materials, etc.) and, in certain situations, a work speed-up. The fact that production is stressed by the customers' orders also causes an extra strain, since delays can result in the company's losing future orders or being subject to claims for damages.

The increased stress that we have been able to detect has mainly been associated with periods when the autonomous groups have had difficulties meeting their production commitments. Problems have been caused, for example, by inadequate planning, defects in materials, and delivery problems, which in turn have led to production delays. The workers' strong sense of responsibility and desire to prove the effectiveness of the autonomous group system have meant that everyone has tried hard to meet the production deadlines anyway. Certain "pressures" from production management, especially in the form of insinuations about the inefficiency of autonomy, have also tended to lead to a certain work speed-up in such situations.

For the shop stewards and contact people, democratization has often entailed great psychological pressures, not only because of the additional work load which their assignments involve, but especially because of their increased responsibilities in such areas as personnel. In the case of the local union board, collective leadership has helped counteract the psychological pressures associated with negotiation situations. As for the contact people, they have often received support from some of their co-workers in their dealings with company representatives.

To determine whether autonomy has led to increased psychological stress, we had to rely primarily on the workers' own feelings. A comparison was made between the autonomous and nonautonomous departments, but these results must be interpreted with caution since there are differences in the working environments in the departments, e.g., noise level and monotony, that may impact on stress. In the autonomous departments, 16 percent of the workers said they felt very often or quite often that they had too much to do, while the comparable figure for the nonautonomous departments was 10 percent. Nonetheless, the latter workers experienced the most psychological stress: 18 percent of those in the nonautonomous departments reported experiencing stress very often or quite often, compared with 7 percent in the autonomous departments. This apparent contradiction may possibly be explained by reference to the meaning of autonomy in this case. The fact that one occasionally has a high work load is seen as an inevitable consequence of the autonomous group system, i.e., autonomy has a price in terms of increased responsibility for production. Through autonomy, however, this increased responsibility and temporary periods of stress and overtime are perceived not as something imposed on workers by an authoritarian system, but as part of the pride in being able to manage production oneself. There is a trade-off between autonomy and responsibility for production. Through the joint system of co-determination and autonomous groups, the workers and their union are able to control where that trade-off is going to be.

Another way to gain an understanding of job-related stress is to study its effects off the job (17, 18). Only 2 percent of those in the autonomous departments reported having trouble relaxing after leaving work, while the corresponding figure for the other departments was 9 percent. Similarly, 72 percent of those in the autonomous departments reported never having trouble relaxing, compared with 51 percent of the others.

The same trend is suggested by the answers given to the following question: Does it ever happen that you are so tired after the day's work that you have trouble doing something else like getting together with friends or spending time on some hobby? This statement was considered true very often or quite often by only 2 percent of those in autonomous departments, compared with 22 percent of the other workers. This was *never* true for 54 percent of those in the autonomous departments but for 31 percent of other workers.

All of the figures cited above confirm what we were able to ascertain qualitatively from our interviews and observations: namely, that autonomy has *not*—except on a few specific occasions—resulted in increased psychological stress. On the contrary, it appears that psychological stress has decreased as a result of autonomy. There seem to be several reasons for this. The autonomous group can influence both production output and planning, and this has given workers a better understanding of the production process as a whole and made it possible for them to organize and plan their work better. "It has been calmer now when we can work at our own pace," reported one worker. "When we are missing parts, we can redistribute the work and get ahead with pre-assembly or something else. . . . This makes things less hectic," said another. According to a third, "At the end of a period there's always a lot of stress, but we try to plan things so it won't be that way." Moreover, the autonomous production groups, in cooperation with the local union, can regulate the assignment of both production work and personnel among the departments. This makes it possible to get help during peak periods and to avoid having to sit around with nothing to do when lengthy production delays occur. As one worker commented, "When we had little to do here and A-assembly had a lot to do, we could help them out."

Autonomy further provides more chances for individual self-determination when it comes to planning one's own work and choosing work methods, for example. "It doesn't matter so much if you have a lot to do as long as you get to decide yourself how to do it and have an overall idea of what's going on," said one worker. "I know roughly how many machines I've got to make, and therefore I know when I have time to take a break," commented another. Autonomy has made the work more challenging, thus it is experienced as less monotonous. For this reason, autonomy has reduced the feeling of being understimulated (underutilized), which can also give rise to stress.

The greater strength and increased influence of the local union has made all employees feel more secure with respect to such changes as cost reduction measures, technical development, personnel lay-offs, and transfers. One of the workers interviewed observed, "I think that the company would find it hard to put through something that the union opposes. This gives us some security." The greater strength of the union, together with the system of autonomous groups, has meant less supervision and control by management, even for the employees in the nonautonomous departments. Another worker pointed out, "You notice that complaints about us come through the union now. . . . That's good since it's easier for the union to stand up to such things. And we also get a chance to come up with an explanation." Less supervision has also given the workers more chance to move about freely in the company.

Furthermore, cooperation and collective sharing of responsibility in the production groups has led to greater solidarity, which in turn affords added support to the individuals in the group. This support has been especially important to those who found it hard at the beginning to work independently, and to those who have made technical mistakes in their work for which the group has had to take collective responsibility. Autonomy has also made it easier for people to cooperate and to organize the practical details of the work. This point was made in one of the interviews: "The worst thing is when someone sitting ahead of you keeps on snatching the machine you have just finished. We have agreed that we won't do this. We don't want to make anyone feel a lot of pressure unnecessarily."

The notion of stress can also be related to both identity and self-confidence. A professional identity based on skills, experience, and self-determination results in a feeling of self-assurance, which in turn diminishes the feeling of stress. Knowing that one can manage the job at hand is a characteristic of skilled workers. It is easy to observe this sense of assurance—of "mastery"—among true craftsmen. Such a feeling of confidence that they can manage the production demands is also clearly discernible among the workers in the autonomous departments at Almex. A strong degree of self-confidence counteracts stress. One feels less anxious about making a mistake, and better able to stand up to criticism for those mistakes one does make. This self-confidence and the consequent decrease in stress it brings with it has been expressed by the workers in the autonomous departments at Almex as a feeling that "people dare to stand by what they do" and that "everyone has a right to make a mistake."

The Democratized Work Organization and the Union

Autonomy, union consciousness, and union power are complex relationships that mutually reinforce each other. For example, it is clear from the material already presented that it was increased union consciousness, in combination with the democratization of union work, that paved the way for the autonomous group system. However, once autonomy has been introduced and becomes understood as part of a trade union strategy for increased worker influence, the idea spreads and further deepens people's interest in the union.

While we are aware that union consciousness and autonomy affect each other profoundly, we shall concentrate here on only one aspect of the interrelationships—how autonomy influences workers interest in union policy. The workers in both the autonomous and nonautonomous departments were asked about their interest in union matters. Their responses are given in Table 1. The table shows, first, that there are few people who claim to lack all interest in the union, and, second, that interest in the union is greater in the autonomous departments.

Union involvement can be assumed to have increased in the entire company as a result of co-determination and the introduction of autonomous groups. As was pointed out

Table 1

Interest in the union among Almex workers, autonomous and nonautonomous departments

Department	High level of interest (%)	Some interest (%)	No interest (%)
Autonomous (N = 55)	36	61	4
Nonautonomous (N = 27)	11	78	11

earlier, participation in the meetings of the Metal local increased over a five-year period from a few people to a regular attendance of about 70 percent. Since 1978, the Metal local (and since 1979 the SIF local as well) have been granted the right to hold union meetings during paid working hours. The local agreements give both Metal and SIF the right to five meetings a year. Both the local and the company stress that this is a shared interest, since it is one way to be sure that information gets out to all employees. For the Metal local, it is regarded as a great strength that decisions can be made at meetings where virtually all the workers are present. For some years, the Confederation of Trade Unions in Sweden has been demanding the right to hold meetings on paid time. Almex is one of the first companies in which this right has been granted. It should be emphasized, however, that increased involvement in union affairs is connected not only to autonomy, but also to the union's role in co-determination. Successful worker participation in strategic decisions through co-determination has stimulated curiosity and interest among the rank and file in matters that are broader than those directly connected to daily work in the production group. Once again, the dynamics of the multilevel approach which Almex represents are demonstrated.

As noted, union interest is greater in the autonomous departments. This manifests itself among other things in the fact that workers from the autonomous group discuss union matters and, according to the union stewards, ask for union information more often. This difference in level of interest cannot be viewed solely as a result of autonomy, however, since autonomy has been introduced in precisely those departments where interest in union matters was greatest. Moreover, in certain cases, people involved in the union have applied for jobs in the autonomous work groups. The following aspects of the autonomous group system can nevertheless be assumed to have had a positive influence on union interest. First, the autonomous group system is often experienced by the workers as part of the union's effort to increase industrial democracy. This almost daily experience makes the relation between the autonomous group system and the overall trade union strategy very clear. Second, workers in the autonomous groups take part in decisions involving production planning. Through this participation on the group level, their interest in influencing more sweeping company decisions is increasing, since they come to learn how these larger issues affect their immediate work situation. Third, the autonomous group system is an expression of the union's power. Through the close relations that exist between the groups and the trade union board, the union's role in co-determination is made very clear to the ordinary worker. And fourth, participation in union-organized courses among workers who come from the autonomous departments has strengthened the union's image. During 1979, two study circles were arranged with a total of 30 participants. There have also been educational activities over the weekends, where people have performed plays, read worker literature, and discussed union problems.

A genuine interest in union matters does not necessarily lead to active involvement in the form of taking on union assignments or participating in the union's educational program, however. There are many obstacles to participation, including lack of self-confidence, unfamiliarity with speaking before a group, and a feeling of not knowing enough, either about the trade union or in general. Autonomy has proved to be especially effective in removing these more "personal" obstacles to participation in union activities.

There are large differences between the autonomous and nonautonomous departments in the way the union is perceived and evaluated. In the nonautonomous departments, a more "traditional" understanding of the union's main responsibilities—wages and working environment—predominates. The reasons employees in the nonautonomous departments give for membership in the union often have to do with the security that membership affords. In the autonomous departments, people are more inclined to emphasize the collective strength and solidarity that union membership represents. Among these people, being a member of the union is regarded as natural for workers. This is not always the case among those working in nonautonomous departments, however. One can say that the union is perceived by those in the autonomous departments as being more of an offensive instrument for influencing the general conditions in the company.

The union local at Almex has been involved in a long cooperative effort with management related to the development of autonomy. At the time autonomy was introduced, management had an open attitude toward the demands for a more democratic work organization. Support for these demands came especially from the president. This interest in autonomy still exists, and, if anything, seems to have deepened over the years.[6] Are there not risks from the workers' standpoint in such close collaboration? In the general debate on industrial democracy, the following reasons are among those given for unions not to take part in such collaboration: (a) it is a way for management to split the union or assure higher profits; (b) if the changes succeed, management takes the credit, but if they do not succeed, then the union gets the blame; (c) there are no guarantees that the results will be lasting, since management can break agreements when it wishes; and (d) cooperation will erase the boundaries between workers and managers, in that the union officials will lose their identity and come to be regarded more as a part of the company's control apparatus.

Only one of these objections can be said to have had any relevance to the situation at Almex—namely, that the change has meant lowered costs for the company. Union representatives feel that there has been a corresponding gain in the form of increased interest in the union; moreover, they feel that it is wrong to use promises of higher pay to interest workers in autonomy. Furthermore, the union local has emphasized that cooperation takes place on the basis of each side's own interests and does not preclude conflicts or offensive actions. Nor is it likely that the autonomous group system can be abolished by management, at least not in the short run. For one thing, there is a local agreement underlying the system of autonomous groups. For another—and this is surely more important—a majority of the employees in the autonomous departments say that they would be prepared to go on strike to preserve autonomy. The risk that cooperation will bring about a split between union officials and members has been counteracted at Almex by democratizing union work and making extensive information available. In terms of the latter, the agreement to hold union meetings during paid working hours is considered a big help.

---

[6] Since this was written, Almex has taken on a new managing director and a new production manager. It remains to be seen whether these leaders will be able to understand the benefits of the democratic work organization.

Most of the workers, and indeed all of those in the autonomous departments, are in favor of the form of cooperation that the union has had with the company. The workers' opinions are mirrored in the following quotation from a worker: "It is obvious that if both sides are on the same track, then there isn't anything wrong but if the company wins advantages at our expense, then it is another thing!" In the nonautonomous departments, however, there are a few workers who are critical of the union local's close collaboration with management. The reason for this difference in attitude is probably that the employees of the autonomous departments can see more clearly how union co-determination influences and is a prerequisite for autonomy in their own department. In the nonautonomous departments, on the other hand, people are less interested in—and in a few cases directly opposed to—the autonomous group system and union co-determination affecting their own work situation.

About 80 percent of workers agree that the union at Almex has become stronger as a result of the development of a more democratic work organization. Autonomy and the changes in the union's role in the company have contributed to a heightened trade union/political consciousness among many employees. Autonomy is important not primarily because of an increasing interest in and motivation for work, but because it has made it possible for many people to identify positive changes at the workplace with trade union policy and power. One manifestation of increased union consciousness is greater demand for increased worker influence.

Demand for Increased Worker Influence

We have tried here to underline the dynamics of the multilevel strategy and to show that co-determination and autonomy are viewed as parts of the same ideology, mutually reinforcing each other. We have also stressed that the autonomous groups are learning organizations. Through the demands and responsibilities of the group, workers increase their technical and social skills. But the autonomous group system is also helping people to see the relation between their immediate work situation and more sweeping issues in the company, and teaching them to see how they can influence strategic decisions on these issues. In this section, we shall look at the perceived relationship between these various levels of worker participation, concentrating on the demands for increased worker influence created by the autonomous group system.

Table 2 shows what demands the workers make for increased worker influence, including both the issues that they want to influence themselves (level of the individual) and those they want the union to help decide (collective level). According to Table 2, the demands for worker influence in practically all areas are greater in the autonomous than in the nonautonomous departments. This is true for demands for individual influence as well as collective influence through the board of the union local. The only exceptions are input on new appointments and the choice of an immediate boss; here, those in the nonautonomous departments are more interested in individual input than in increased influence through the Metal local. In the autonomous departments, where union say on new hires is already strong, people are much more interested in a union board influence. Those issues in which workers in the autonomous departments want to have a greater say themselves are all related to the job and the work environment, e.g., issues

Table 2

Demands for worker influence, autonomous and nonautonomous departments

	Autonomous departments[a]		Nonautonomous departments	
Issue	Want to influence themselves (%)[b]	Want union board to influence (%)[b]	Want to influence themselves (%)	Want union board to influence (%)
Rebuilding, furnishing	84	16	43	6
New appointments	9	84	14	17
Internal recruitment to the department	58	40	31	14
Selection of immediate boss	—	—	34	11
Selection of higher managers	29	51	14	29
Training	55	36	26	11
Finances, investments	9	82	3	26
Planning material supplies	73	18	31	0
Choice of machines, tools	82	15	40	6
Production volume	76	11	17	6
Production development	7	47	3	26

[a]Dashes indicate not applicable. An immediate boss in the sense of a supervisor appointed by the employer does not exist in the autonomous departments.
[b]Percentages refer to positive responses to each alternative. Workers may check both alternatives.

concerning the work premises, planning and material supplies, recruitment and training, selection of machines and tools, and production volume. Even in the nonautonomous departments, a relatively large percentage of workers want to be able to influence these conditions themselves, but roughly twice as many in the autonomous departments demand such influence.

When it comes to demands for worker influence on more general issues, two important aspects may be underscored. First, with a few exceptions, workers in both autonomous and nonautonomous departments transfer their demands for worker influence to the trade union (collective level). Workers in the autonomous groups to a somewhat greater extent want an increased say as individuals in these issues, but it is not a very clear and strong tendency. On the basis of an earlier hypothesis (18), it had been reasonable to assume that increased influence on the shop floor would have increased demands to participate in more sweeping decisions, not only for the workers as a collectivity but also for oneself, because of the greater understanding created by autonomy of the relations between more sweeping issues in the company and one's own immediate work situation. Even if the results are not contrary to this hypothesis, it seems reasonable to interpret the findings to mean that the trade union local in this case has succeeded in tying co-determination and autonomy to each other in a way that is satisfactory to the ordinary worker in his day-to-day activities. He feels that the trade union local is really arguing his case. Using an earlier terminology, the trade union local is perceived as a true representative of the workers' collectivity.

The second important aspect is that demands for collective worker influence on more general issues are only weakly developed among the nonautonomous compared with the autonomous departments. A good illustration is the way people view finances and investment: only one out of four workers in the nonautonomous departments wants the union to have an influence on these issues, compared with about four out of five workers in the autonomous departments.

By and large, we feel that these results support the assumption that worker say on job-related decisions creates increased demands for the workers to be able to exert influence on more comprehensive decisions (7, 18). Whether these demands are expressed in demands for oneself or for representatives for the workers seems to depend on the intricate relationship among factors such as technology, company size, trade union efficacy, and—in this case—the relations between the trade union local and rank and file through the autonomous group system.

Effectiveness of the Company

One of the aims of this report, agreed upon by the steering group, was to see how the changed work organization has affected productivity. It was agreed that this task should be assigned to a joint management-worker task force. No reliable statistics have been produced, but there is consensus between management and workers that productivity has not declined. Instead of talking about productivity, we shall use the broader term "effectiveness," which relates to the company's general goals, including quality and service, and its informal and flexible way of working. Effectiveness can thus be regarded as a composite of the following factors: product quality, customer service, flexibility, initiative taking by the employees, and capacity to meet deadlines. The results presented below are based on the judgments and assessments of the managers responsible for production. The workers' own evaluations of the same phenomena are in general more positive.

The responsible managers judge that the quality of the work done has not deteriorated as a result of autonomy. They think it is too early, however, to judge whether the quality has improved, since such a judgment must be based on complaints from customers, need for repairs, and so on. In statements made six months later, top management admits that product quality is likely to have increased. Customer contacts in the service department, which is the department that has the most contact with customers, have also improved, in the opinion of the department manager. The production manager feels that flexibility has increased, both within and between departments. The ability and desire of employees to take the initiative seem to have increased following the introduction of autonomous work groups. There are a number of examples of how employees in the autonomous departments have taken the initiative in order to avoid production delays, and of how they have put into effect improvements and administrative simplifications of various kinds. Also, the workers' general attitude to the company seems to have become more positive as a result of the democratic work organization. There are, for example, considerably more people (94 percent) in the autonomous departments who would advise a friend to work for Almex than in the other departments (55 percent).

SUMMARY AND CONCLUSIONS

We have tried here to summarize a report on a trade union-based strategy for democracy at the workplace. From this larger report we have chosen to describe and comment upon: (a) a local co-determination system that is more far-reaching than the central agreements in Sweden based on the Act of Co-determination of 1977; (b) the ways autonomy (direct democracy) and co-determination (representative democracy) in combination have led to important changes for the employees in their daily work and to important changes in the relation between workers, the union, and management; (c) how the change process came about and was engineered; and (d) how this has been a positive experience for almost all employees in the autonomous production groups.

We have described an effort, comprising all organizational levels, to democratize a work organization, and we have stressed the interdependence between worker influence at the levels of co-determination and autonomous work groups. Also, we have stressed the importance of democracy and high member involvement in union work. However, Almex shows certain conditions that make it impossible to automatically transfer the experiences to other companies. These conditions include: customer-ordered production; a low degree of mechanization in combination with little dependence on traditional time and methods studies; complex manual work with a good overview on the part of the workers of the entire production process; and a successively strengthened position on the international market. The importance of continuing profitability and growth must also be stressed. While these conditions are not necessary for the introduction of autonomous work groups, we think that the actual structure of the autonomous production groups is influenced by these facts. There are other conditions in other enterprises, and the structure of the autonomous groups must be based on these conditions. Nonetheless, Almex's development toward a more democratic work organization has many characteristics that seem to be important for other unions to observe and possibly to even copy under very different circumstances.

Based on the Almex experience, we conclude that the following factors are necessary for democracy at the workplace to grow: (a) union co-determination in strategic decisions in the company; (b) introduction of a system for autonomous production groups; (c) a conscious connection between co-determination in strategic decisions via the union representatives and direct participation by all workers in the autonomous production groups; (d) constant opposition to unnecessary hierarchies and unnecessary formal means of contact; (e) democratization of the union administration; (f) trade union education, partly to build up knowledge but also to establish solidarity against elite recruitment and tendencies to push out nonconformist workers; (g) a training program inside the company but run by the unions to propagate the value and nonthreatening character of a democratic work organization throughout the firm; (h) good cooperation between the different unions in the plant; and, finally, (i) active participation of all workers in the change process.

Acknowledgments — This report was written during a research period at the Institute for Social Research, University of Michigan, Ann Arbor. Valuable comments on the draft were made by Robert E. Cole, James S. House, Robert L. Kahn, Daniel Katz, and Hy Kornbluh.

REFERENCES

1. Lysgaard, S. *Arbeiderkollektivet* [Workers' Collectivity]. Universitetsforlaget, Oslo, 1961.
2. Roethlisberger, F. J., and Dickson, W. J. *Management and the Worker.* Harvard University Press, Cambridge, 1950.
3. Dahlström, E., Gardell, B., Rundblad, B., Wingårdh, B., and Hallin, J. *Teknisk förändring och arbetsanpassning* [Technological Change and Worker Satisfaction]. Prisma, Stockholm, 1966.
4. Gardell, B. *Produktionsteknik och Arbetsglädje* [Technology, Alienation and Mental Health]. Personaladministrativa Rådet, Stockholm, 1971.
5. Gardell, B. *Arbetsinnehåll och Livskvalitet* [Job Content and Quality of Life]. Prisma, Stockholm, 1976.
6. Gardell, B., and Gustavsen, B. Work environment research and social change—Current developments in Scandinavia. *J. Occup. Behav.* 1: 3–17, 1980.
7. Thorsrud, E., and Emery, F. E. *Form and Content in Industrial Democracy.* Tavistock, London, 1969.
8. Thorsrud, E., and Emery, F. E. *Democracy at Work.* Nijkoff, Leiden, 1976.
9. Gulowsen, J. *Selvstyrte Arbeidsgrupper* [Autonomous Work Groups]. Tanum, Oslo, 1971.
10. Cole, R. E. *Work, Mobility and Participation: A Comparative Study of American and Japanese Industry.* University of California Press, Berkeley, 1979.
11. Gardell, B. Missnöjes—och tillfredsställelsefaktorer i arbetssituationen [Sources of job satisfaction]. *Sociologisk Forskning* 4: 57–68, 1967.
12. Gardell, B., and Svensson, L. *Medbestämmande och Självstyre. En lokal facklig strategi för demokratisering av arbetsplatsen* [Co-determination and Autonomy. A Local Trade Union Strategy for Democracy at the Work Place]. Prisma, Stockholm, 1981.
13. Andersson, A. Företagsdemokrati vid Tobaksfabriken i Arvika [Industrial Democracy at the Tobacco Plant at Arvika—An Evaluation]. Mimeograph. Industridepartementet, Stockholm, 1976.
14. Frese, M. Partialisierte Handlung und Kontrolle: Zwei Themen der industriellen Psychopathologie. In: *Industrielle Psychopathologie,* edited by M. Frese, S. Greif, and N. Semmer. Verlag Hans Huber, Bern, 1978.
15. Frankenhaeuser, M. Coping with job stress—A psychobiological approach. In: *Working Life: A Social Science Contribution to Work Reform,* edited by B. Gardell and G. Johansson. Wiley, New York, 1981.
16. Gardell, B. Scandinavian research on stress in working life. *Int. J. Health Serv.* 12(1): 31–41, 1982.
17. Rissler, A., and Elgerot, A. Omställning till arbete i kontorslandskap. Betydelsen av arbetets art för psykologiska anpassningsreaktioner [Stress aspects of the open space office]. Report no. 33. Psychological Institute, University of Stockholm, 1980.
18. Johansson, G. Aronsson, G., and Lindström, B. O. Social psychological and neuroendocrine stress reactions in highly mechanised work. *Ergonomics* 21: 583–599, 1978.
19. Gardell, B. Autonomy and participation at work. *Hum. Rel.* 30: 513–533, 1977.

CHAPTER 13

Democratizing Occupational Health: The Scandinavian Experience of Work Reform

Björn Gustavsen

During the 1970s most industrialized countries made efforts to improve workplace health and safety. This took place because of pressure from various sources, such as the growing recognition that the aims of the welfare state were still far from being fulfilled in the workplace (1), the increasing concern about the chemical complexity of our environment, and the emergence of "new" issues such as stress. Sweden and Norway were no exceptions to this trend. In both countries the work on major national reforms started in the early 1970s. Bertil Gardell and I became involved in this work and developed a close collaboration. While at the Work Research Institute in Oslo we had worked on the question of strategies for changing working life; Gardell had been leading the development of an empirically strong research tradition that could function as a knowledge resource. However, to bring together descriptive research and action research into one line of thought and action is no easy task. The extent to which we succeeded in taking some steps in this field must be left to others to judge. In this chapter, the intention is to present some of the points and arguments that played a role in the construction of a democratically oriented work environment strategy to which Gardell and I contributed.

PSYCHOSOCIAL ISSUES IN WORK

A main characteristic of Scandinavian workplace health and safety reforms is the effort to deal with "social" and "psychological" issues in work. To catch some of the salient features of "the social" and "the psychological," a number of concepts had been introduced long before the 1970s, particularly dissatisfaction, alienation, and stress. Concepts such as these seemed to open new ways of understanding the relationship between humans and work, and new possibilities for reconstructing working life toward a socially and psychologically better situation for workers. To what extent had this promise been fulfilled? When we started to look into whether strategies existed upon which to build the emergent Scandinavian reforms, we found a mixed situation. A large number of research reports had accumulated in a number of countries, but it was hard to find examples of practical action, specifically of reform programs of meaningful scope. Stress had fared somewhat better than the other concepts in terms of practical impact, but this impact was largely limited to individually oriented diet and exercise campaigns. Why was there such a lack of larger efforts involving whole enterprises, not to speak of the whole of society? To answer this question it was necessary to look into the ideas and principles underlying the traditional approach to workplace health and safety.

THE TRADITIONAL APPROACH TO WORKPLACE HEALTH AND SAFETY

Western industrial society was shaped by a merger of two main ideas: economic liberalism and participative democracy. In the type of society arising from this merger, certain principles came to stand out. One of these principles is a distinction between a "public" and a "private" sphere: between a sphere that is open, transparent, and subject to democratic discussion, and a sphere that is withdrawn from public scrutiny and democratic discourse. A typical example of the private sphere is the family. It was thought that for democracy to be possible, those who are to act in the democratic arena need resources, but these resources are not themselves part of the arena (2, 3). Consequently, a support system was developed for society's democratic actors; during the early phase of democracy these actors constituted a very small part of the total population, generally those who owned something of a certain economic magnitude.

While the idea of a public and a private sphere was drawn from democratic thinking, economic liberalism entered the scene when the question emerged of where the boundary between these spheres should be drawn. In addition to the family, economic enterprises came to be defined as falling within the private sphere. This happened through the following line of reasoning. A cornerstone of liberal democracy is the right of the citizen to privately own physical resources such as land and tools. The formation of enterprises was seen as a way of using the ownership rights to the assets that were placed at the disposal of the enterprise. Establishment of an enterprise also involved the formation of social relationships, for example through the hiring of people, and these relationships were seen as also falling within the private sphere.

The private nature of both the enterprise and its internal matters has exerted a substantial influence up to the present. When legislation started to emerge to protect workers from health damage due to their work—which in Scandinavia happened toward the end of the last century—this legislation was seen as an encroachment on the freedom of the enterprise, a penetration of the constitutionally protected private sphere. This did not make legislation in favor of the workers impossible, but it made it subject to certain restrictions:

- Any such encroachment should preferably be defined in terms of rules applying equally to all enterprises, otherwise the idea of competition on equal terms would be disturbed.

- The rules must state clearly what is allowed and what is not: a threshold limit value is a typical example of an acceptable norm.
- Rules to protect the workers should be based on a demonstrable need, and rules that cannot be documented as necessary should not be issued.

In a pure form, these principles belong to the early phase of liberal democracy. By the 1970s a number of exceptions had been introduced. Nevertheless, these principles continued to exert a considerable influence. It was also clear that insofar as these principles were adhered to, it would be difficult to introduce "psychosocial" issues as part of health and safety reforms.

At first health and safety reforms tended to be restricted to those areas for which rules fulfilling the above criteria were possible. This gave a preference to such issues as technical prerequisites for safety, and for those areas of occupational medicine in which threshold limit values could be developed. Areas that do not lend themselves to this relatively "mechanical" form of legal effort will remain untouched by publicly initiated activities. This pertains not only to issues such as job dissatisfaction and stress, but to other major aspects of the work situation such as the field commonly referred to as "ergonomics."

Furthermore, the classical approach demands that advances in the work environment field rest on solid evidence. Ideally, a regulation is seen as the prohibition of an activity or a technology, and such a prohibition should occur only when positive evidence unequivocally supports a direct causal link between what is to be prohibited and specific negative effects on health. It has been difficult to operationalize and develop knowledge on psychosocial issues on a sufficiently unequivocal level to bring these issues within a legislative structure. This principle also becomes problematic in relation to other issues. In general it means that "the burden of proof" lies with the workers; they must accept exposure until it can be positively documented that the exposure is harmful and should not take place. As long as doubt prevails, it is the workers who carry the risk.

A third aspect of the traditional approach is that it transforms work environment problems into a relatively narrow concern with technical issues of measurement within the context of the legal enforcement system. Workplace health and safety has become an issue for experts and inspectors, while the workers themselves play a passive role. This turns workers into objects whose welfare is the responsibility of others.

A number of other points could be added (for further discussions, see 4; 5; and 6, pp. 115-129), which all lead to the conclusion that the traditional strategy for workers' protection is unable to include psychosocial issues. What, then, should be done? An alternative approach needed to be developed. Such an alternative could be generated by taking different points of departure. Here, we will start by looking at some alternative views on the relationship between the way work is organized and the emergence of occupational disease.

DISEASE AND THE ORGANIZATION OF WORK:
DIFFERENT PERSPECTIVES

The relationship between the way work is organized and disease is essential to the psychosocial concept. Among the various efforts to identify this relationship, five different positions can be found. These positions will be briefly sketched here, since the relationship between them provides a bridge to the issue of an alternative strategy.

With roots in the introduction of the human relations perspective on work (7), job dissatisfaction has been the most widely applied concept in efforts to define and trace the psychosocial impact of work on people. It has given rise to a vast number of studies and consequently to a wide range of operationalizations and research approaches. Although the studies differ, we can identify some trends in the concept of dissatisfaction as a key to understanding the impact of work on people.

In spite of a great number of empirical studies, it has not been possible to generate a clear, stable, and practically efficient picture of job dissatisfaction—certainly not on the level of national reform strategies. When applied to broad surveys, the concept of dissatisfaction does not discriminate very well. Generally, about 85 percent of the respondents declare themselves satisfied with their work. Those who declare themselves dissatisfied form a very small group; strong dissatisfaction is generally expressed by less than 5 percent (8, 9). On this basis, Wilensky (10) argues that no general work reform is called for within the psychosocial field because those "pockets of alienation" that exist can be dealt with at the local level. Correlations can be found between job dissatisfaction and other dimensions of work, such as lack of productivity, certain types of disease, etc., but they tend to vary from study to study and generally are weak (11).

The theoretical foundation for the idea of satisfaction or dissatisfaction is based on humanistic psychology and the idea that "man enters the world" with a reasonably well-structured system of needs. Maslow (12) developed the most widely applied example of this theory. Satisfaction is thought to indicate need fulfillment, while dissatisfaction indicates the reverse. Furthermore, lack of need fulfillment is thought to lead, through various processes, to the development of certain types of disease, at least if the dissatisfaction is strong and lasting. However well meant the "theory of man" found in this type of psychology may be, it is nevertheless difficult to substantiate empirically that people actually "have" such specific needs independently of the situation in which they happen to find themselves (13). Such need theory is a normative stipulation rather than an empirically substantiated picture of reality. When looked at from this perspective, such theory can be applied just as easily to the creation of social cleavages between people as to the promotion of humanistic or democratic ideals. Consequently, the concept of job dissatisfaction has received a broad range of critical remarks in recent years (14–16; for critical comments on need theory in general, see for instance 17 and 18). Similar problems pertain to alienation in its "Western" interpretation (e.g., 19): as a sociopsychological state that can vary between workers. A Marxist approach to alienation is not sufficient either, for according to this view all workers in capitalist society are alienated. Hence, we are still short of a concept that can help us identify those who actually acquire an illness.

The concept of stress seems to lack some of the shortcomings of job dissatisfaction. By linking the psychosocial and the physiological to each other, we are able to give psychosocial issues a physical health correlate that makes them more easily definable, diagnosable, and subject to preventive as well as therapeutic action. It should also be possible to engage the resources of the sizable medical establishment and its associated disciplines such as chemistry and biology in the pursuit of a better psychosocial world. Even though the concept of stress may have this potential and has proved to be fruitful for doing fairly precise studies of small groups of employees, it has a number of problems. While the concept of stress is clearly potent in cross-disciplinary studies of small samples, it is difficult to carry this methodological strength into broader investigations. When one must rely on questionnaires and relinquish the physiological parameters, the concept almost automatically inherits the problems of job dissatisfaction. It becomes vague and subject to competing definitions, and has varying and generally weak correlations with other concepts, whether pertaining to conditioning factors or to consequences for health. As a backbone of practical action, stress has proven about as difficult as job dissatisfaction.

Job dissatisfaction and stress have, from a theory of science point of view, a number of elements in common:

- They are both based on the idea that it is possible to define humans in terms of a number of "internal states" that can be made subject to measurement.
- They approach the human environment in the same way: as another set of measurable states.
- These states of people and environment can be linked to each other by cause-and-effect relationships, or at least correlations, which are sufficiently strong to form the basis for ameliorative action.
- The relationship between the person and work can—and should—be split up into a series of two-factor cause-and-effect relationships, e.g., between noise and its effect, between organization of work and its effect, etc.
- Last but not least, the above-mentioned points generally imply a naturalist view: that humans can be understood and described in roughly the same way as physical nature.

However, studies of the relationship between humans and work do not stop with these efforts. Particularly during the 1970s, with the mushrooming interest in workplace health and safety, there emerged studies that approached the problems in other ways. Here three such approaches will be indicated. Together they merge into a view of the person at work as subject.

For instance, in a study done at the Work Research Institute on the work and health problems of hotel and restaurant workers, generally the occupational group with the shortest average life span, the work environment was analyzed in holistic terms: as a system of factors, most of them rather "innocent" when looked at separately, that together produced a dramatic impact on health in the form of synergistic effects (6, pp. 121-122; 7; 20). Patterns of interaction were found to exist between such seemingly disparate conditions as the lifting and carrying of heavy loads, work organization, wage system, work time system, temperature, noise, lighting, air pollution, etc. Factors that at first glance do not seem to have much to do with each other can unite to form a whole with a very strong impact on health. Restaurant workers have higher than average scores in all three major illness categories: cancer, coronary heart disease, and wear and tear on the body.

In terms of theory of science, this holistic approach meant the abandonment of the method that splits up the human work situation into a large number of pairs of factors, in favor of stressing the whole. The worker is viewed as being embedded in ecological processes rather than as being at the receiving end of a large series of disconnected cause-and-effect relationships. On the other hand, the ecological frame of reference can be said to maintain the idea of humans as "nature" in the sense that the worker is embedded in processes that are essentially seen as naturalistic, although the frame of reference for understanding them differs.

One possible argument against this holistic perspective is that it is impractical from a reform perspective; however solidly founded it may be in theoretical terms, it can be argued, practical action demands a splitting up into pieces since one cannot deal with everything simultaneously. This argument appeared during the discussions of the 1970s. An answer emerged out of experience that had, by that time, already been gained. Hotel and restaurant workers were mentioned above as an example of a high-risk category of employees. If we look at what had been done by the mid-1970s to correct this by the Labor Inspection and other bodies proceeding from a factor-by-factor perspective, it amounted to very little. Insofar as significant improvements had occurred, they had emerged as part of organizational development projects such as that occurring in Hotel Caledonien in Norway (6, particularly pp. 51–66). Here, however, the approach had been along a holistic line in the sense that changes were not restricted to one or a few factors but included a broad range of issues: organization of work, wage systems, shift plans, worker participation in design of restaurants, physical improvement programs, etc. These efforts were reasonably successful, it seemed to us, just *because* they were broad and covered a range of factors.

This leads to a further point about the relationship between work organization and disease. In projects such as that in Hotel Caledonien, a number of different factors were included—physical ones such as noise, lighting, the lifting and carrying of heavy loads. However, the main lever in these projects was the organization of work. Wear and tear on the body was, for instance, attacked through changing patterns of work organization toward a system in which the waiters could help and support each other and in which the wage system emphasized collaboration rather than competition. Another example occurred in a ship-building company in Bergen. In this facility it was possible to solve a problem of exposure to cold through changing the system of production planning so that operators working out of doors during the winter were automatically recalled if they were kept idle for more than a quarter of an hour because of lack of parts (21). It would, of course, have been better to enclose the whole yard and heat it, but this was economically impossible.

From these experiences with using the organization of work as a main lever in change, a broader perspective emerged: work organization can be seen as a *meta-condition*. The way work is organized can be seen as the factor that decides exposure to *all* work environment hazards since it is the organization of work that determines who is to do what for how long. It is the organization and division of work that lead some people into operator jobs and exposure to, for instance, noise and high speed requirements; other people are brought into managerial positions which may have their exposure patterns too, but at least these are different from those on the shop floor.

This perspective on work organization as a meta-condition merged into the last position to be mentioned here, which grew out of a study of how enterprises deal with issues of workplace health and safety (6, 22). The point of departure for this study was the question: what characterizes those enterprises that have an efficient approach to improvement within the field of health and safety? It was found on the first level of analysis that an effective approach to health and safety was dependent upon an active interest in these matters from management as well as from the workers. This finding may seem somewhat trivial, but it implies a point of major importance: the Labor Inspection was of little significance in this respect, as were the industrial occupational health services insofar as they existed at all. The question to emerge, then, was what factors are linked to an active interest in issues of health and safety on the enterprise level and a commitment to improvement? It was found that management activity was largely the result of worker activity. Unless the workers showed an active interest in health and safety and pursued these issues, management tended to be passive. Although management commitment to improvement is, of course, crucial to getting anything done, worker activity could still, through its initiating function, be singled out as a chief condition. On what, then, did worker activity depend? The answer was found to depend on the type of work. To the extent that the work role provided people with possibilities for taking initiatives, making judgments, and developing skills and contacts with fellow workers, the workers became active.

In terms of theory of science, this study represented a further step toward seeing people as subjects: the work environment and its impact no longer appear as a metaphysical destiny but as something that was open to change and reconstruction by those concerned.

At this point some of the ideas and perspectives of Bertil Gardell and associates entered the picture. Gardell had started out in the job satisfaction tradition, and to some extent felt loyal to that tradition. However, he had also transcended this tradition in a major respect. Through a number of empirical studies, Gardell had consistently found that if workers have some degree of *control* over their work situation, they seem to fare better in a number of different respects. Control, in turn, can be said to be constituted of three main dimensions (23):

- Freedom to make decisions.
- Competence, or knowledge, which enables the worker to use this freedom.
- Contact with fellow workers, which enables the worker to coordinate activities in relation to others and to develop joint learning processes, relationships of social support, etc.

Gardell had developed this view on the basis of empirical investigations with a naturalistic foundation. The successive emergence of the idea of control, which was brought a major step further when Karasek (24) conceptualized the demand-control model, did, however, also imply a change in the theory of science implicit in Gardell's work. Why is control important? Control is important because it is equal to activity, to the worker being able to develop and choose between *different* courses of action to meet workplace problems. When the possibility of worker action is brought into focus, the worker changes from being an object to becoming a subject, someone whose actions shape his or her own fate.

This position, of course, raises a series of problems. What happens, for instance to the idea of "social laws" which Gardell saw it as one of his main tasks to "uncover"? When such "laws" can be changed by those who are supposed to be under their control is it then reasonable to talk about "laws" at all? Furthermore, to see the worker as an acting agent can, under certain circumstances, undermine welfare policy since it can locate the onus of responsibility on the worker. How should one deal with such issues? One effort was made when four researchers with different backgrounds—Bertil Gardell with his background in empirical, originally fairly "positivist" research; Sverre Lysgaard, with a background in hermeneutic, or interpretative, sociology; Ragnvald Kalleberg, with a background in critical theory; and myself with a background in action theory—formed a group to start working on these issues. This effort had to be abandoned when Gardell became ill. We hope that it can be resumed sometime in the future, even though Bertil Gardell will no longer be there to argue his views. Let it be added, although the point cannot be elaborated here, that though the subjectification of the worker raises major problems, there are possibilities for working out answers to these problems. Under no circumstances can the problems be dealt with by a reversal to the objectified workers of proletarian sociology, who, for their salvation, are dependent upon the social sciences to get their case argued. The whole idea of workplace democracy rests on the possibility of the workers' taking on the role of subject. Furthermore, on the practical level, by the mid-1970s society had moved so far in defining the worker as a passive entity subject to welfare policies designed by others, that a substantial reconstruction could be done without having to start considering the "limits of subjectivity."

AN ALTERNATIVE STRATEGY

The line of reasoning presented above led to the conclusion that an approach to workplace health and safety that would include psychosocial issues had to have workplace action as a core element, since only through activity would it be possible for the workers themselves to become subjects. Workplace reconstruction based on inspectors, experts, and researchers, however well meant it may be, would only contribute to the dependence and hence the lack of control that seemed to lie at the core of the problems of the workers. The next issue was to convert this point of departure into a practical, legislatively based, work environment strategy. The best opportunity for doing this appeared in Norway, where I was given an opportunity to influence the legislative process through participating in a work group that developed the first proposal for a new Work Environment Act.

The first step in moving from social principles to legal reform was to convert the conclusions stated above into a series of principles that could form the basis for legislative development. In this context the following principles were developed:

- There must be a broad obligation to act within the field of health and safety on an enterprise level.
- There must be a broad right to raise work environment issues on the level of the enterprise and workplace.
- The workers must have the right to participate in all phases and aspects of the work with work environment issues.

- Workers and management on the level of the enterprise must have a broad right to exercise their own judgment about definition of problems, setting of priorities, and development of action plans.
- Public power should be applied to further local activity on health and safety issues in general rather than to focus only on the correction of specific work environment factors.

These principles were of course not wholly new; elements could be found in older legislation. To some extent they may also seem rather self-evident. However, when compared with existing legislation and practice, they deviated quite substantially. Even the old legislation declared workplace health and safety to be a responsibility mainly resting with the enterprise, but the law and its corresponding by-laws and prescriptions dealt mainly with those aspects for which public authorities were responsible and consequently created the impression that even though local responsibility was declared, this was mostly for reasons of principle. Furthermore, there were no legislatively expressed views on how local efforts should be organized and carried out. Under the older legislation, the raising of work environment issues was identical to putting forth a complaint and arguing that things were not according to law. This made it difficult to raise issues since it tended to lead to defensive reactions and to debates about the legality of the existing situation rather than efforts to improve it. Worker participation in workplace health and safety was largely limited to the right to elect safety delegates. The Labor Inspection was thought to represent the highest level of insight and competence in the field and was given a broad right to enforce its own judgment on other actors such as workers and management in individual enterprises, even when they had developed their own improvement programs, based on their own evaluation of the situation.

The next step was to take the broad principles a step further and convert them into specific legal and administrative requirements. At this stage, a broad range of legal issues and considerations entered the scene. These issues covered such topics as the introduction of developmentally oriented standards in addition to threshold limit values; the demand for a total, or holistic, evaluation of the work environment; and questions pertaining to causality and evidence (for a more detailed analysis, see 4). One point should be emphasized: the need to include the issue of organization of work in the reform. If worker participation in the development of solutions to problems of health and safety is to take place, certain prerequisites must be fulfilled in terms of what type of work people have. As indicated above—a point that was particularly well covered in the research of Bertil Gardell—work must be organized so that it allows for the development of competence, social contacts, and ability to make decisions. Against this background the Norwegian Act came to include the following article (Article 12 of the Act):

Planning the Work

1. General requirements
   Technology, organization of work, working hours and wage systems shall be designed so that the employees are not exposed to undesirable physical or mental strain and so that their possibilities for displaying caution and observing safety measures are not impaired.

Conditions shall be arranged so that employees are given reasonable opportunities for professional and personal development through their work.

2. Arrangement of work

The individual employee's opportunity for self-determination and professional responsibility shall be taken into consideration when planning and arranging the work.

Effort shall be made to avoid undiversified, repetitive work and work that is governed by machine or assembly line in such a manner that the employees themselves are prevented from varying the speed of the work. Effort shall be made to arrange work so as to provide possibilities for variation and for contact with others, for connection between individual job assignments and for employees to keep themselves informed about production requirements and results.

3. Control and planning systems

The employees and their elected Union representatives shall be kept informed about the systems employed for planning and effecting the work, and about planned changes in such systems. They shall be given the training necessary to enable them to learn these systems and they shall take part in planning them.

4. Work involving safety hazards

Performance premium wage systems shall not be employed for work where this may materially affect safety.

Here, it is not possible to move beyond stating the text of the article; for further analyses pertaining to interpretation and implementation, see references 6 and 25 (see also comments in 16, 26, and 27).

This particular way of defining work environment problems and designing reform policy is of course peculiar to Norway. Even in Sweden there are substantial differences, although the overall aims of the reforms were fairly parallel, as were the institutional contexts out of which they emerged. However, there were, and are, points of contact beyond Scandinavia, of which three will be mentioned here. In the province of Saskatchewan in Canada at the time when Robert Sass was Deputy Minister of Labor in the provincial government and head of the health and safety branch, a health and safety reform based on activating the workers was developed, which in many ways differs from that in Scandinavia but which also shares a number of basic ideas (28). The tradition of worker medicine in Italy is also worth mentioning (29); even though it has a stronger element of labor-management conflict built into it than is the case in Scandinavia, there are points in common. Lastly, a series of analyses of work environment problems and ameliorative efforts were done at the Science Center in Berlin (e.g., 30–32).

EFFICIENCY OF THE PARTICIPATIVE APPROACH

What happened when the Norwegian Work Environment Act went into force and its corresponding training programs were launched? This issue has been dealt with in several publications (e.g., 25, 33–35). In this context, only a brief review is possible. First, however, a few words about the Work Environment Act of 1977 as a whole.

The participation strategy influenced the Act, but it was not the only determining factor. Being new, the participative approach confronted several of the more conventional ways of dealing with issues of workplace health and safety; out of this confrontation came a law with a number of different elements and regulatory principles. The participative approach constituted too much of a break with tradition to fully penetrate the new Act. Consequently, the reform work was started in a situation characterized by mixed, and conflicting, legal and administrative principles. This was also very much the case in Sweden, where a participative strategy had somewhat less success in penetrating the Work Environment Act than was the case in Norway, but where a broad act on co-determination based on the extended use of collective bargaining also appeared in the same period. In principle, these acts could support each other (36). This, however, happened only to a limited extent.

Turning to the more specific actors and processes in Norway, the Ministry of Labor, under which issues of work environment and worker co-determination belong, was in favor of the participative strategy from the start. This was clearly expressed in a policy document on the implementation of the act issued in 1981 (3).

However, the Labor Inspection, which is organized as a directorate under the Ministry of Labor, is a different matter. When I had the occasion to present some of the elements of the new law to the head administrators of the Labor Inspection Board (centrally and regionally) in a conference organized by the Ministry of Labor in connection with the Act's going into force in 1977, the reactions ranged from silence to strongly negative comments. Clearly, the participative approach was seen as a threat to its traditional expert status.

In principle, three roles are possible for the Labor Inspection Board:

- As a body relying on legally defined power to enhance technical standards.
- As a consultant.
- As a body that applies public power to compel local activity where this does not otherwise emerge.

On the level of the field inspectors all three positions have been and are represented; one and the same inspector sometimes applies all three approaches. However, the third role, which is crucial to the participative strategy, is clearly the one least applied. The central directorate has based its policy on a mixture of the first and the second roles and has generally avoided promoting the third. One may ask why the Ministry of Labor has not been able to force a different view on the directorate. This is an interesting question. In Norway, as in Sweden, the public sector has seen, during the post-World War II period, the emergence of a number of fairly large, resourceful, and powerful public bodies outside the ministries. The directors general of these bodies, as they are generally called, are often picked from among political people. They tend to have independent power positions and are not easily controlled by the ministries. In addition, the directorates often have boards with high-level representation from those concerned, e.g., the labor market parties, and these boards tend to constitute independent policy centers. Furthermore, even in the 1970s, issues of workplace health and safety never seem to have had an absolute first priority in the ministries of labor in Norway or elsewhere. On the whole, the income settlements tended to hold first place. There was, consequently, a limit to how much effort and force the ministry was willing to spend on the issue of health and safety and on an appropriate strategy for dealing with these issues.

The occupational health services were relatively undeveloped in Norway at the time when the new Act went into force. The succeeding substantial build-up in this field has also led to an influx into these services of new and relatively young people who have often shown an interest in exploring more participation-oriented professional roles. There is little doubt that the occupational health services to a large extent have become proponents of the participative line.

The main labor market parties have followed a mixed line on work environment strategy. The employers, as represented by the Norwegian Employer's Confederation, wanted to keep the reform "low-profile" and limited in terms of costs. However, a number of employers, not least in the larger industrial companies, have favored the participative line since they have seen this as better from an employer perspective than a line based on heavy application of public power. On the other hand, although there are exceptions, employer support for the participative line is often subject to the proviso that worker participation should be pursued, but not at the expense of the power of the employers. Since real worker participation cannot be pursued without consequences for the power position of the employers, this constitutes a dilemma. The Federation of Trade Unions has generally supported the participative line as well as the centralist/expert line, without quite recognizing, at least not explicitly, that these lines can come into conflict with each other.

When the Work Research Institute did a survey of three samples of enterprises and public institutions in about 1980, (e.g., 33), it was found that only among larger industrial enterprises had a reasonable number developed local action programs that involved organization of work: about 20 percent. In nonindustrial sectors and in smaller firms, about 5 percent had developed such programs at this stage. In a survey conducted in 1983 on a sample representing the working population, it was found that about 15 percent of all employees were involved in, or touched by, changes emerging out of Article 12 of the Work Environment Act (37). Since 1983/84 there has been a shift in the context of work environment efforts; after the labor market parties made an agreement on development in 1982 (38), many of the efforts that concern work environment issues have been integrated with issues pertaining to productivity and industrial democracy and brought under the umbrella of this agreement. The number of enterprises that participated in this development directly or through branch programs at the end of 1987 was around 300. There has been a growth after the 1983 survey was conducted. Consequently, it is a reasonable estimate that 20 percent of the work force in Norway is involved in, or at least touched by, efforts to make work provide possibilities for developing competence, social contacts, and the ability to make decisions. It must be added that such a figure is somewhat uncertain. It covers, for instance, a lot of different efforts ranging from deep and highly significant workplace reconstructions to superficial exercises such as management-controlled job rotation schemes. On the other hand, large groups of employees do not need reconstructions of the type dealt with in Article 12 since their work generally already gives them these possibilities.

While the work environment reform of the 1970s was not an unequivocal success in the sense that all workplaces were efficiently reached by the reform after, let us say, five years, it has nevertheless exerted a substantial impact. Work organization and the field of "psychosocial problems in work" not only have been recognized as important topics but have been made subject to remedial action on a *relatively* broad front. Even though "the 20 percent level" is limited compared with working life as a whole, it nevertheless far exceeds that in earlier periods when the issue of organization of work was hardly dealt with beyond a few field experiments or some "star cases" such as the Volvo Kalmar plant in Sweden. The work environment reform brought the issue of organization of work and the psychological and social aspects of work from the margin of society and toward the center. It did not succeed in going all the way, but it definitely made a jump from the margin to become a force of a considerable magnitude.

CONCLUSIONS

To move "from theory to practice" within the field of the psychosocial work environment is to move into a terrain where a number of difficult issues emerge. The tradition within the Western industrialized world has viewed psychosocial problems associated with work as semi-private problems to be posed and dealt with on the level of the individual enterprise. However, society cannot rely on enterprise intitiative to carry the burden of broad change. Left to themselves, the enterprises will move slowly, often not at all, and in a number of different directions, making joint learning processes and cumulative development of knowledge difficult. A certain element of pressure must be established by society, along with some guidelines on the direction that the efforts should take. Traditional rule-making, on the other hand, will not be a very efficient approach either, since it is very difficult to make psychosocial work environment problems subject to threshold limit values or similar types of legal regulation. Consequently, we need to seek a certain type of balance between society and the enterprise; between the central and the local; between what is regulated in law and what is made open to judgment and decision on the local level. One way of solving this problem of balance emerged with the Norwegian work environment reform of the 1970s.

Experience from efforts to create change and reform in working life has demonstrated that this is not a question of "application" of knowledge generated in descriptive or evaluative research. In the social field, the process of work reform places such demands on this type of knowledge, in order to make it effective for the purpose of change, that a radical revision of the idea of knowledge itself is necessary. Knowledge that is to be made operational in the workplace must, in principle, be created jointly between researchers and those concerned.

When traditional research and the demands emerging out of the need for practical reconstruction of working life confronted each other in Scandinavia, there emerged a need for rethinking and change on both sides. This involved both the way we understand and work with change as well as what kinds of knowledge were relevant to this process. In building this bridge Bertil Gardell played an important role. He left his mark not only on social theory but also on social practice.

REFERENCES

1. Ashford, N. J. *Crisis in the Workplace: Occupational Disease and Injury. Report to the Ford Foundation.* MIT Press, Cambridge, Mass., 1976.
2. Gustavsen, B. Workplace reform and democratic dialogue. *Econ. Industr. Democr.* 6(4): 456–480, 1985.

3. KAD. Oppfølgningen av Arbeidsmiljøloven (The Ministry of Labour: A follow-up study of the implementation of the Work Environment Act). Oslo, 1981.
4. Gustavsen, B. Improvement of the work environment: A choice of strategy. *Int. Labour Rev.* 119(3): 271–286, 1980.
5. Gustavsen, B. Direct workers' participation in matters of work safety and health: Scandinavian strategies and experiences. In *Work and Health in the 1980s*, edited by S. Bagnara, R. Misiti, and H. Wintersberger, pp. 131–185. Edition Sigma, Berlin, 1985.
6. Gustavsen, B., and Hunnius, G. *New Patterns of Work Reform. The Case of Norway*. The University Press, Oslo, 1981.
7. Mayo, E. *The Social Problems of an Industrial Civilization*. Macmillan, New York, 1933.
8. Brayfield, A. H., and Payton-Miyazaki, M. The good job and the good life: Relation of characteristics of employment to general well-being. In *Measuring Work Quality for Social Reporting*, edited by A. D. Biderman and F. T. Drury, pp. 125–150. Halstead, New York, 1976.
9. Thurman, J. E. Job satisfaction: An international overview. *Int. Labour Rev.* 116(3): 249–267, 1977.
10. Wilensky, H. Family life cycle, work and the quality of life: Reflections on the roots of happiness and unhappiness in modern society. In *Man and Working Life: A Social Science Contribution to Work Reform*, edited by B. Gardell and G. Johansson, pp. 235–266. Wiley, Chichester, 1981.
11. Seashore, S. E., and Taber, T. D. Job satisfaction indicators and their correlates. In *Measuring Work Quality for Social Reporting*, edited by A. D. Bidermand and T. F. Drury, pp. 89–124. Halstead, New York, 1976.
12. Maslow, A. H. *Motivation and Personality*. Harper, New York, 1954.
13. Silverman, D. *The Theory of Organizations*. Heineman, London, 1970.
14. Fox, A. The meaning of work. In *The Politics of Work and Occupation*, edited by G. Island and G. Salaman, pp. 83–95. University of Toronto Press, Toronto, 1980.
15. Gustavsen, B. From satisfaction to collective action: Trends in the development of research and reform in working life. *Econ. Industr. Democr.* 1(2): 147–170, 1980.
16. Lewis, G. A. *News from Somewhere. Connecting Health and Freedom at the Workplace*. Greenwood Press, New York, 1986.
17. Maccoby, M. *The Gamesman*, Swedish translation. Askild and Kärnekull, Stockholm, 1978.
18. Rose, M. *Industrial Relations*. Penguin Books, London, 1985.
19. Blauner, R. *Alienation and Freedom*. University of Chicago Press, Chicago, 1964.
20. Karlsen, J. I., and Naess, R. *Arbeidsmiljø i Hotell- og Restaurantnaeringen*. Work Research Institutes, Oslo, 1978.
21. Ødegaard, L. A. *Arbeidsplasskartleggingene i Miljøarbeidet*. Work Research Institutes, Oslo, 1978.
22. Karlsen, J. I., et al. *Arbeidsmiljø og Vernearbeid*. Tanum-Norli, Oslo, 1975.
23. Gardell, B. *Arbetsinnehåll och Livskvalitet*. LO-Prisma, Stockholm, 1976.
24. Karasek, R. A. Job socialization and job strain: The implications of two related psychosocial mechanisms for job design. In *Working Life: A Social Science Contribution to Work Reform*, edited by B. Gardell and G. Johansson, pp. 75–94. Wiley, Chichester, 1981.
25. Gustavsen, B. The Norwegian work environment reform: The transition from general principles to workplace action. In *Organizational Democracy and Political Processes*, edited by C. Crouch and F. Heller, pp. 545–564. Wiley, Chichester, 1983.
26. Blackler, F., and Brown, C. The law and job design: Comments on some recent Norwegian legislation. *Industr. Rel. J.* 13(4): 73–83, 1982.
27. Sass, R. Work environment developments in Scandinavia. A beacon for Saskatchewan and elsewhere. *Working Environment*, 1987 issue, pp. 38–40. The Swedish Work Environment Association, Stockholm, 1987.
28. Sass, R. The Saskatchewan approach to workplace health and safety. In *Work and Health in the 1980s*, edited by S. Bagnara, R. Misiti, and H. Wintersberger, pp. 195–206. Sigma, Berlin, 1985.
29. Misiti, R., and Bagnara, S. Participation in health control at the workplace. In *Work and Health in the 1980s*, edited by S. Bagnara, R. Misiti, and H. Wintersberger, pp. 31–50. Sigma, Berlin, 1985.
30. Friczewski, F., et al. (eds.). *Arbeitsbelastung und Krankheit bei Industriearbeiten*. Campus, Frankfurt am Main, 1982.
31. Maschewsky, W., and Schneider, U. *Soziale Ursachen des Herzinfarkts*. Campus, Frankfurt am Main, 1982.

32. Rosenbrock, R., and Hauss, F. (eds.). *Krankenkassen und Prevention*. Sigma, Berlin, 1985.
33. Gustavsen, B. Regulating organization of work: The Norwegian example. In *International Institute for Labour Studies: Changing Perceptions of Work in Industrialized Countries: Their Effect on—and Implications for—Industrial Relations*, Research Series, No. 77. International Labor Organization, Geneva, 1983.
34. Gustavsen, B. Hvor lang kan lovgivningen reformere arbeidslivet? In *I virkeligheten*, edited by D. Gjestland and T. Hanisch, pp. 86-102. The University Press, Oslo, 1984.
35. Gustavsen, B. Training for work environment reform in Norway. In *The Organizational Practice of Democracy*, edited by R. N. Stern and S. McCarthy, pp. 125-140. Wiley, Chichester, 1985.
36. Gardell, B., and Gustavsen, B. Work environment research and social change—current developments in Scandinavia. *J. Occup. Behav.* 1(1): 3-17, 1980.
37. Lafferty, W. M. Workplace democratization in Norway: Current status and future prospects with special emphasis on the role of the public sector. *Acta Sociol.* 27(2): 123-138, 1984.
38. Gustavsen, B. Technology and collective agreements: Some recent Scandinavian developments. *Industr. Rel. J.* 16(3): 34-42, 1985.

CHAPTER 14

A Democratic Strategy for Organizational Change

Lennart Svensson

The basic assumption is that workplace democracy is of crucial importance to employees. Democracy is, of course, a basic value in itself. This was stressed by the classical democrats (J. S. Mill, Rousseau, Cole, and others). Participation in direct democracy at work has been seen as an important educational experience and as a ground course to prepare the individual for political participation in general (1). A vast body of research and practical experience has demonstrated the positive effects of democratized work organizations; the benefits include healthier working conditions, a reduction of stress, more stimulating and demanding work, better opportunities for social support, the "smoother" introduction of new technology, and greater equality for women.

If workplace democracy has such definite advantages for the employees, why are there so few instances of it? And how can we explain the failure of so many of the best-known experiments? Why is it so difficult to introduce workplace democracy and to keep it alive? The purpose of this chapter is to discuss the manner in which workplace democracy can be introduced and developed. The involvement and mobilization of the employees is of central importance. I also refer to the role of research and the researcher in this process. These voluntaristic themes need to be balanced by a more structural perspective, from which obstacles to and opportunities for workplace democracy can be discussed.

A NOTE ON THE ROLE OF VALUES IN SCIENCE

This chapter, as well as my research, is based on a worker's and female perspective. It expresses a clear ideological standpoint. But can it be considered scientific? All research—at least any of practical importance—is ideological by nature. Traditionally, working life research has been conducted from a management and male perspective. This, however, is seldom acknowledged or openly stated. It is important to make the values and basic assumptions of the research manifest and to provide the reader with the opportunity to reflect on them. In this way, it is easier to see how values

241

are intertwined with the way the research is conducted and to be critical of these values.

The research referred to here has been action-oriented, i.e., it is intended to promote change. Again, can this be considered scientific? A researcher—at least one involved in working life research—always affects what he or she is studying. To confirm and not to change the existing power structure is one way of affecting the situation. Action research is an established procedure, and is particularly prevalent in working life research in the Scandinavian countries. It has some definite advantages, especially when processes of change are the object of study or when relevant knowledge from "inside" is required. In action research it is necessary to maintain a dialogue with the participants, to receive a continuous feedback and to present the results in a less conventional way than is normally the case. For me, action research primarily means taking part in a process of change as a discussion partner and present-ing facts, new interpretations, and different perspectives. The methods used can vary from case to case. I have used a combination of qualitative and quantitative methods: interviews, surveys, participant observations, statistical analysis, the keeping of diaries, etc. The rules of reliability and validity are, of course, as strict as in other kinds of research, but sometimes they can be applied differently. The action researcher has the advantage of being able to obtain the validation of research results from the reality he or she experiences in the research process itself.

WHAT IS WORKPLACE DEMOCRACY?

Workplace democracy is an ambiguous concept and, in some ways, a misleading one. The principle, for example, of "one person, one vote" cannot possibly apply in privately owned firms whose main—and, for the employees, equivocal—goal is to maximize shareholders' profits. It is also impossible to conceive of the idea of pure workplace democracy in the public sector, because of the conflict of interests between workers on the one hand and consumers and taxpayers on the other. We can, however, retain the concept and use it in a weaker sense, i.e., to mean *democratization*. Even if workplace democracy cannot be fully realized, it is still possible to make considerable progress. This can be illustrated by a case study that Professor Gardell and I made of a medium-sized production plant in Stockholm between 1978 and 1981 (2, 3).

The case study demonstrates the necessity for workers to make a real impact on decision-making at all levels of a company. Democratic change could, in this sense, be called a *multilevel strategy*, which involves the development of a combined—an interdependent and mutually reinforcing—influence at different organiza-tional levels. In our case study, the workers' influence had the following three elements:

- *Codetermination* in decisions made at higher levels in the company. This included questions of the company budget, personnel policy, work environment, production planning, location of production, recruitment of management, technical change, etc.
- *Autonomous groups*. More than half of the workers (about 70) were organized in autonomous groups. This applied in seven of a total of 11 departments. In the

autonomous groups, workers made the decisions jointly and also took joint responsibility for them. They organized and planned the work themselves. Each group appointed a contact person, whose role was mainly to provide information, but who had no formal or privileged position within the group.

- *Individual self-determination.* The work process was based on rather separate work roles. The individual worker had the freedom to organize and plan his or her own work, to make contact with other departments, to carry out certain administrative tasks, etc.

Codetermination represented the framework and prerequisite for autonomy in the work groups, and through autonomy and self-determination *all* employees became directly involved in the democratic organization of work. The connection between codetermination in strategic management decisions and the autonomous group system therefore came to be of crucial importance. A multilevel strategy for democratic change demands a combination of *representative* democracy (union codetermination) and *direct* democracy (autonomy and self-determination). This perspective on democracy was essential to Gardell's work and to his attitudes to human interaction in general.

Many critics of workplace democracy have pointed to cases of failure. They have argued that it was the introduction of democracy itself that caused the failures. In 1984 I made a follow-up study of 25 well-known local cases of organizational change (4). Many of them could be classified as failures, but my explanation was, by contrast, that it was a lack of democracy that explained the failure in most cases. The degree of democracy was usually very limited, amounting to little more than an extension of influence at the individual or the group level. Only in a very few cases was a multilevel strategy applied, and these cases were the only successful ones, from the perspective of both workers and management.

Management and owners seem consistently to have resisted a multilevel strategy for workplace democracy. This can be explained by their interest in maintaining their position of control (5, 6). However, it has also been claimed that workers, who clearly do not share this perspective, are themselves not interested in decisions made at higher levels in the company. According to this view, workers are more interested in decisions that concern their own jobs, social relations at work, the style of leadership, etc. Recent research, however, has shown the opposite to be the case (7). Employees are, in fact, most interested in influencing the "higher" decisions of companies. These include decisions with consequences for employment security and those concerning the introduction of new technology, new forms of rationalization, and the structure and level of wages. Recent structural changes within companies that have had immediate consequences for the employees have made the importance of these decisions obvious (7).

HOW CAN WORKPLACE DEMOCRACY BE INITIATED AND ITS GROWTH ENCOURAGED?

Workplace democracy involves a change in power relations within companies themselves. To initiate, develop, and defend democratic changes, it is necessary to mobilize the employees. *The way* in which a work organization is changed is important, especially when the objective is a *democratic* work organization; the means must be consistent with the goal. The employees concerned must be actively involved in the process of change and have control over it. Too often, democratic changes in work organization have been implemented in a technocratic way both from above and from outside (4). It is paradoxical and pseudo-democratic to tell workers that others have decided for them that it is, in fact, they (these others) who should be making the decisions. In these cases the employees have no control over the changes, nor do they identify themselves with the ones that take place. In many cases the changes are restricted to one or a few departments and disappear under pressure (from a new management, changed market conditions, or the introduction of a new technology). The new organization has no flexibility because the process of change does not contain the participative and educational elements that the employees require (8).

In this section I will try to sketch out a strategy for democratic organizational change. It is not meant, however, as a recipe that can be applied indiscriminately. The propositions presented below are of a tentative and exploratory nature and represent a starting point for discussion. They are based on my own experience—of more than ten years—as an action-oriented researcher. Cases from both private industry and the public service sector are included.

A Strategy for Organizational Change

My conception of a democratic strategy for organizational change can be summarized in ten propositions.

1. It is necessary to take a long-term perspective on the *continuous process* of change. Workplace democracy cannot be implemented at one time, all in one go. The employees must learn collectively and undertake a continuous and critical evaluation of the ongoing changes. It is this that provides the basis for future change.

2. The changes should be developed from "inside" and from "below." The employees should organize the changes from the very beginning. Although it is possible to make formal or administrative changes from "above" and "outside," our evidence suggests that this is not the right way to introduce organizational changes, the very purpose of which is to increase the responsibility and influence of the employees. This can be illustrated by two examples.

The first concerns a study of home services for the elderly in two large Swedish municipalities (9). One municipality was known for its progressive organizational program. The change program was organized into projects (nine at that time), which involved a large number of central personnel and considerable expense. Meetings with home workers and consumers of the services suggested that the impact of the program had been minimal. It had an artificial character and seemed to "live a life of its own," isolated from the daily lives of the people at the bottom of the organization. The second example is provided by an ambitious organizational development program in a large Swedish insurance company. The management wanted to create a more customer-orientated organization and, at the same time, to improve the working conditions of its employees. Consultants had a central—and expensive—role in the program. A number of task groups, consisting of people from middle and top management, were organized in order to implement the new ideas. The ideas themselves were expressed in large quantities of written material and in some visionary speeches from the new managing director. Our evaluation, however, revealed that very few changes that would further the interests of either employees or consumers had, in fact, occurred (10).

In both these cases, failure can be explained in terms of a lack of democracy in the process of change. The employees knew very little about the changes; in fact, for many, they were a source of anxiety and strain. The employees expressed no feeling of participation in or sense of control over what was going on. The changes were organized from above. Although democratic ideas can come from outside (from other workers, central union representatives, researchers, etc.), it is essential that the employees themselves control the change process. Also, the changes must be accepted by management and the owners (in the public sector the government authorities). This is essential because of the power structure that prevails in this type of organization. Management can be "socialized" into the new democratic ideas, but this will be a result of the process itself. There are times when management initially resists democratic change, but later encourages the process when it sees the positive economic effects that the new form of organization has had. Often the strongest opposition comes from foremen, supervisors, and middle management; since their roles will be made redundant, this is hardly surprising. (It is therefore important to create new and better qualified jobs in the new organization for the people affected.)

This element of the strategy for change can be summarized as follows: pressure and struggle from below plus support from above.

3. "Horizontal networks" between employees from different companies must be created. This is important for a number of reasons: to exchange experiences and learn collectively; to obtain support and help from people in similar situations; and to create more wide-spread pressure from below, which may promote legislative change through its effect on public opinion.

It takes time and a lot of effort to develop a democratic organization. The process can be facilitated if horizontal learning becomes a reality. In Sweden, we have a tradition of workers' study circles that can help to initiate change. Study circles are based on the principles of solidarity and democracy. Workers come together in small groups (five to ten people), without a teacher, to collectively acquire and produce knowledge that is useful for them. Study circles were an important element in the introduction of the democratic work organization at the production plant described in the first section of this chapter (2, 3). Study-visits, "search-conferences," job exchanges, and arrangements for work experience in other companies are other ways of facilitating and speeding up a process of democratic change. What is crucial is that employees can themselves meet, in an informal and unrestricted way, to formulate their ideas and develop their interests, goals, and strategy for change. It is then easier for the employees and the union to cooperate with management on the question of a new work organization. Negotiations will then take place on more equal terms.

4. We should start with *practice*, not with theory. For the workers to mobilize and be activated, their immediate problems at work must be articulated. Contacts with workers from other companies—who have succeeded in introducing some democratic changes—will provide evidence of the possibility of change. Small, but immediate,

changes in work organization can both provide illustrations of the opportunities available and be important sources of motivation. The changes can then be carried out "step-by-step" as part of a larger strategy, while the reality of power relations both inside and outside the company is still recognized. With this theory, workers can obtain a critical perspective that enables them to make comparisons with other similar situations, to analyze the power structure, and to make realistic judgments on the possibilities of new developments, etc. From my experience, as a part of this process, the workers are fully capable of doing this themselves without any help from outsiders (4). There are, however, some examples of fruitful dialogue between researchers and local unions (11-13). The action-orientated tradition that Bertil Gardell represented can be seen as an example of this type of cooperation.

It is important to try to cooperate with employees on their own terms, to take a stand, to be close to the production process, and to take time to get to know the people involved. If we do not succeed in this, we run the risk of meeting a reaction similar to that received by some sociotechnical researchers in Norway when they presented their project (14, p. 38; author's translation):

> Even during the first meeting the research group got to know how little information had reached the workers. Nobody showed any positive interest, apart from the union representatives. While the project leader was telling the employees about the project, which was not easily done without using technical terms, the 50 workers sat silently, looking at the floor or through the windows. Only one real question was asked after the presentation. A worker, well-known for his sharp tongue and his critical frame of mind, asked the following question: "Can you tell me if one thing is true. Are you the new committee which has come to rationalize the company and make some of us redundant?" The union leader's answer did not change attitudes to the project very much, but it had the effect of making the time department skeptical about the project.

5. *Local leaders* among the employees are very important in the change process. Behind many successful democratic changes there seems to be a local enthusiast who strongly advocates and believes in the idea of democracy. A local leader must be able both to convince his or her fellow workers—which is often a hard task—and to resist pressure from management. He or she must be a person of action and a theoretician in one and the same person—a natural leader (in Gramsci's terms an "organic intellectual"). Unfortunately, few union officials have such qualities. They are often the victims of their own bureaucratic and professional work, which tends to distance them from their members. Given union support, natural leaders will often be willing to engage in the work of the union, provided this can be done in a free and informal way.

6. *The unions* must make workplace democracy into a central issue, instead of remaining preoccupied with traditional issues such as wages, employment conditions, and safety. The centralized and bureaucratic union structure has been an effective instrument for the introduction of a solidaristic wage policy, but it is an obstacle to progress in new areas, such as workplace democracy and equality for women workers.

The unions should be an important partner in the struggle for workplace democracy, but their role must be new and different. Rather than lead, they should support, coordinate, educate, and inform. Such an approach, however, is alien to the Swedish unions. They are used to vertical contacts and communication, mostly from the "top down." Horizontal contacts have usually been viewed as a way of fractionalizing and splitting their own organization. If internal democracy is improved, and if it becomes easier for ordinary members to take part in union affairs, then strong representative democracy can be complemented by a vital direct democracy. For example, in our case study of the production plant (2, 3), union leaders thought that the union should be democratized before the company. This was achieved by the introduction of a collective leadership (a "trojka") by the rotation of leaders, by the decentralization of union work, and by intensive union training for the members.

In any democratic work organization with strong codetermination, the union will be responsible for some management decisions. This means that the union may lose its identity and be coopted by management in the manner that is customary in Japan. This tendency can be counteracted in a number of ways: the promotion of strong internal democracy in which members have control over their leaders; the maintenance of the clear independence of the union; open criticism of decisions that the union has been unable to influence; and the promotion of a strategy for organizational change that keeps the union "one step ahead" of management.

Unions in Sweden, as elsewhere, are male-dominated; this is the case even where a great majority of the members are women. Few women become union officials, and women are almost nonexistent at higher levels in the union hierarchy. In both scientific and public debate it is common to blame this on women themselves. They are said to be uninterested, passive, and politically unaware (15, 16). There is an alternative perspective, however, in which the political passivity of women is explained by the very fact of male dominance in the unions. Hierarchical organizations, centralization, bureaucracy, and professionalization both reflect and reinforce male dominance (16, 17). Male dominance in the unions can partly explain the lack of union interest in issues of special importance to women, such as the content and quality of work, good relations with customers or clients, a democratic work organization, and a more informally organized union (17, 18). If women strengthen their position within the unions, we should expect workplace democracy to be given a higher priority.

7. The impact of *formal training and education* in organizational development has been overestimated. Management has had exaggerated expectations from expensive courses for management and supervisors; these have had little effect on work organization. The new trend in Sweden is for employees to attend courses that are service-oriented. These courses, however, seem to be designed to promote motivation and to further identification with management, rather than to change the nature of work organization itself. The names of the courses illustrate this: "Cheer Up," "Full Speed Ahead," and "We Shall Be Best" are some examples.

The unions have also exaggerated the role of formal training programs both in organizational development and as a means of implementing change in general. More than 100,000 union-organized workers have attended courses on the Codetermination Law and other pieces of legislation. Very few practical results, however, can be detected. The courses may even have had a negative effect. Union members have been taught how complicated it is to make organizational changes, but they have not been able to express their deep-rooted feelings of moral indignation, subordination, and humiliation. Instead, discussions have centered on the application of the labor laws.

An alternative strategy for change—based on mobilization and activation—would, by contrast, start with the workers themselves discussing their immediate work situations, discovering their common interests, and trying to find common solutions to their problems. Such a process requires a high level of knowledge creation. This, however, can occur in many ways, not only through formal training and ready-made courses, but also by the coordination and critical evaluation of one's own experience, by meetings with other workers from other companies, by a dialogue with union leaders and researchers, and by taking part in programs of practical change that have a direct impact on working conditions.

Training programs of a more formal nature will probably continue to be necessary, if only to increase the competence and qualifications of the workers. The democratization of work means that workers will have to take over new tasks and responsibilities, from supervisors, planners, inspectors, controllers, etc. But the need for training will be felt by the workers themselves as the process of change develops. Many workers, who earlier had no interest in such training, have, in a new democratic situation, felt it natural and necessary to participate. They have usually responded positively afterward, and their self-confidence has increased as a result.

8. The benefits of organizational change should accrue to the employees involved. The employees must continuously experience the positive effects of the changes. Confirmation and evaluation are, in fact, essential parts of the process. In this way the employees' interest in taking part in further organizational changes will increase.

Local changes that receive publicity and become well-known also seem to produce "surplus value." This surplus value is often expropriated by, among others, managers, supervisors, researchers, union representatives, and consultants. They acquire status, money, publicity, and promotion when the change model is "sold" as a commodity on the growing market for organizational development. The employees involved have reacted very strongly against such exploitation, especially when the impact of the changes on their own working life has been very limited. The surplus value produced should accrue to the employees themselves. This should be made clear at the very beginning of the process. The employees should present the changes and their consequences at study visits, at conferences, and in the mass media. This has been tried successfully in some cases (see below).

9. *Funds* must be made available for organizational change. This is costly in the short run, but the investment should pay off in the long run. It is probably wise for a company to use about 5 percent of its budget on continuous organizational change. Today, most of the funds available are allocated to managers, specialists, and consultants, little being reserved for the workers themselves. A first step should be to transfer the money spent on expert advice to the employees involved. They could be "taken out" of production in order to work temporarily on organizational change. The use of its own personnel as "consultants" in this way represents a saving for the company (see below).

10. Involvement in organizational change should be *stimulating* for the employees. It provides them with better knowledge, new contacts, a better overview of the production process, and, most of all, a feeling of satisfaction at being able to affect important aspects of their lives.

Some Applications of the Strategy

My own experience enables me to summarize some attempts to initiate practical change. They should not be seen as strict applications of the strategy described above, although certain aspects of these attempts should be seen in the light of the propositions that comprise this strategy.

Learning from Each Other. Let us return to the study of home services in two large Swedish municipalities. The organization of work differed considerably between these two municipalities. One municipality had a more democratic work organization—operating in small, autonomous groups and permitting the home workers a large degree of influence. Home workers in this municipality felt that their situation was considerably better than that of the home workers in the second municipality.

When we presented the positive results of our study to the home workers in the second municipality, they accepted out conclusions "in principle" but they were not prepared to act on them. Both the union and management defended their own procedures and openly questioned our results. We found it natural that they would be reluctant to accept our findings; they came from outside and—at least in one sense—from above. Under these circumstances we suggested that the home workers should undertake research of their own. We invited four home workers from each municipality to swop jobs with their counterparts in the other municipality for a period of two weeks. The invitation was accepted. They met before the exchange for preparation and afterward for the evaluation of their experiences.

The eight home workers came to a common conclusion. All of them preferred the organization that contained small, autonomous groups. They thought that the home workers in the first municipality had more of a say in what they did and had acquired a greater level of responsibility. The union representatives and the management in the second municipality accepted this conclusion. It would have been difficult for them to question the judgment of a united group of home workers that possessed a high degree of collective credibility and reliability. When the home workers tried to change their work organization, however, they met resistance from a management that was not used to initiatives from below. The home workers were asked to write a proposal for change. They did not feel confident enough to do this and hesitated for a while. Participation in the research project had, however, increased their self-confidence and they decided to make unilateral changes to the work organization in secret (with the help of a supervisor). Large groups were divided into small ones. This enabled the home workers to prepare and plan their work collectively. As a result of this, the consumers of the services—mostly old people—met the same home worker more often, something that was very important for them.

According to the superviser involved, the new organization functioned better in many ways: the home workers were more involved, planning was made more flexible, the rate of absenteeism declined, and the home workers' demands for influence increased. Other groups became interested, and the new organization spread "horizontally" when home workers from different groups met and discussed their own working situations. When management received reports on the positive impact of the new organization, they declared their whole-hearted support. A decision was taken that all groups (comprising about 1,000 home workers) should be reorganized in line with the new model before February 1, 1987. The management, once again, had made the mistake of trying to implement change from above. What had been a means to an end—the small group—became a goal in itself. Many groups did not understand the reasoning behind the organizational change, nor has the new organizational form spread as quickly as the management had hoped.

The example of job exchange illustrates how a democratic change process easily can be initiated, but also reveals the risk that it can be destroyed just as easily. The municipality involved was, in fact, the one that was well-known for its progressive organizational development program. The impact of this program was, perhaps, less substantial than that of the changes initiated by the home workers themselves. The example also illustrates a bureaucratic paradox. Experts on organizational development, whose very job it is to promote change, in practice often prevent people from making changes themselves.

We arranged a similar job exchange for a group of cleaners in 1987 (19). The cleaners were threatened by a rationalization program, jointly developed by management and outside consultants. They intended to reduce cleaning resources in the municipality by about 25 percent. For the cleaners, who already worked under very demanding conditions, this would have meant increased stress and further exposure to risk of injury.

For fear of privatization, the cleaners accepted the principle of rationalization and decided to try to make a proposal of their own. To be able to do this, six cleaners (in sets of two) were invited to visit three municipalities for a period of two weeks. They worked half-time and conducted interviews (with cleaners, with other personnel involved, and with management) during the other half. We helped them to prepare the questions in advance. The six cleaners selected three specific municipalities in order to make the best use of this learning opportunity: one commune had practiced the rationalization model; another had introduced a more democratic organization, in which the cleaners were responsible for economic issues and personnel management; the third municipality had integrated cleaning, along with cooking and maintenance work, into one unit. The cleaners met afterward on different occasions to evaluate and to present the results of their experience to the other cleaners in their municipality (about 450). During 1988 they were to visit different groups of cleaners and make a more thorough presentation. The groups should be encouraged to engage in discussion and make suggestions of their own on the subject of a new work organization.

This example illustrates how the idea of learning from each other can be extended and made more systematic. It is important, especially if management is to be convinced, to have some hard data to present on the positive effects of a democratic work organization. It is too early to say anything about the organizational consequences in this case, but the cleaners are now more on the offensive and are more active in the change program.

How Conferences Can Be Used

In my experience there are two different ways in which conferences can be used as a way of initiating organizational change (20). The concept is the same in both cases: employees are encouraged to gather together and exchange experiences. Conferences have the advantage that large numbers of people can be involved in short periods of time.

One set of conferences concerned home services. After the completion of the study of home services in two municipalities, I received a number of invitations to present my results to other communes (9). Such presentations, however, seem to have almost no practical consequences; home workers and consumers are generally absent on such occasions. To remedy these defects I tried to arrange conferences at which the home workers from the two municipalities specifically involved in the study could present my research results and give an account of their own experiences to other home workers. In this way, two different models of work organization could be presented; we hoped that this would enable home workers to question the structure of their own organizations and that they would try to initiate some changes on their own. Eight home workers from the two municipalities—some of whom had earlier been involved in the job exchange—were given a summary of my results, which were also presented on video tape. The Central Municipality Office, as well as the two municipalities themselves, were formally responsible for the organization of the conferences. Six conferences were held in different parts of the country; they all lasted two days, and there were about 70 participants on each occasion.

We have made a preliminary evaluation of the conferences. The participants were satisfied with the conferences, but so far they do not seem to have promoted organizational change. From this point of view the conferences can be seen as failures, even if it is rather too early to draw such a definite conclusion. There are, however, some explanations for their apparent lack of success. Only about half of the participants were home workers. As a result, home workers were not at the center of the discussions in the way we had hoped. There were too few group discussions, in which it would have been easier for the home workers to take an active part.

The second type of conference we have organized could be called a kind of "search-conference," in which employees from different companies come together and try to learn from each other. These conferences lasted for a day and about 50 to 100 people were present. It was hoped that workers who had made important changes in their work organization would communicate their experiences to others. Each presentation— about four altogether—took about half an hour. In the afternoon sessions, participants from other companies or municipalities played the central role. In small groups, they discussed how their own organization could be changed. The workers who had earlier made the presentations were to act as "consultants" as well as partners or leaders of the discussions.

These conferences functioned well. An efficient, honest, and concrete learning situation was established. The type of "showing off" that often takes place in public meetings was very little in evidence. One problem was that a number of supervisors, who were also present, tried to take over the discussions. Most importantly, however, employees were shown that changes in work organization are possible and do have positive effects. Many workers were encouraged and wanted to make changes to their own organization as a result. These changes were almost universally opposed by foremen and supervisors. The unions did not try to mobilize the employees in a struggle for workplace democracy. There was a clear lack of institutional and legal support for democratic change. I consider this to be one of the biggest problems in the democratization of working life. We will turn to this in the next section.

OPPORTUNITIES AND LIMITS AT A SOCIETAL LEVEL

The discussion must now be extended from a purely organizational to a wider societal level, since societal factors also determine the possibilities for and limits of workplace democracy.

Little has been said about the interests of management and owners. They aim to achieve a high level of control over production (including their employees) and high levels of profit. Managers and owners will not relinquish part of their control freely unless they have some specific incentive, e.g., they believe that they can increase profits in this way. A democratized work organization can be more efficient than a traditional one in a number of ways: it can increase flexibility, speed up the decision-making process, improve product quality by making production more customer-oriented, and reduce absenteeism and turnover. Above all, it can alleviate the acute and growing problem of the recruitment of new personnel.

The employees, in general, have their own specific way of changing work organizations. Their principle involves the decentralization of minor decision-making with, at the same time, the centralization of higher level decisions. For the employers this provides stability and flexibility, self-determination and control, independence (for production departments) and unity. Employers are certainly not interested in the multilevel strategy for democracy discussed above. Their "democracy" has, by contrast, been used to counteract the more far-reaching claims of employees. The division of the work organization into small, autonomous units, when not combined with union codetermination, is a way of fractionalizing the workers. A "new" work organization is often introduced in combination with profit sharing, fringe benefits, private share-ownership, and other ways of integrating the employees into the company. Then there is less risk that employees will use their new autonomy in a way that is not in the interests of the company. This management strategy is most common in the new knowledge-intensive companies and in large, profitable, and export-oriented companies in Sweden. Their complicated patterns of ownership and the nature of their international business also make it difficult for the unions to exert pressure on them (21, 22).

If the employers will not accept workplace democracy voluntarily, the employees have the alternative of enforcing it through legislation. This strategy was adopted in the 1970s when several new labor laws were introduced. These laws, however, have had only a very limited impact on power relations between labor and capital (23). One recent evaluation has shown that 90 percent of influence in the area of strategic decisions remains in the hands of management (24). The laws are simply too weak. The Codetermination Law, for example, only gives the local union the rights to obtain information and to negotiate. What is needed is stronger labor legislation that would give employees the right to participate in decision-making at all levels. But it is difficult, today, to see how such legislation might come about. The Social Democratic Party and the unions do not give high priority to workplace democracy. By contrast, they adopt a defensive stance, favoring traditional policies that include economic growth, industrial expansion, technological change, a reduced budget deficit, low inflation, full employment, and social security.

Economic goals have a high priority, and to achieve them the labor movement is dependent on cooperation with employers. This mutual dependence can be illustrated by the "Volvo-ization" of the Swedish economy. Volvo has such a key position in the economy that no government, Social Democratic or bourgeois, could act in a way that is contrary to the company's interests without affecting the whole economy. Consequently, the Swedish government has formed a partnership with Volvo (25, p. 10; 26). Under the circumstances, it is difficult to see how the labor movement can lead a political struggle for workplace or economic democracy. During the last decade, capitalist strength has grown as a result of the concentration of capital, the internationalization of the economy, higher profits, new forms of company structure, and favorable political and ideological conditions. Workplace democracy cannot simply be introduced through stronger labor legislation. Legislation must be accompanied by a widespread shop-floor struggle for democracy, which will create strong and continuing pressure for further institutional change. The absence of such an interaction between shop-floor activism and legislative reform can to a great extent explain the failure of workplace democracy in Sweden.

In the public sector, opportunities for workplace democracy and for the mobilization of employees are much better than in the private sector. It is not a coincidence that the examples referred to are almost exclusively taken from the public sector; the most interesting changes in work organization have occurred in care for children and the elderly, in hospitals, in public cleaning, and in state production plants. There are a number of reasons why this is the case. The public sector in Sweden, as elsewhere, is threatened by privatization and the associated risk of poorer working conditions. As a result, public employees are more prepared to engage themselves in organizational change. Democratic changes are possible, because they can satisfy the needs of the employees, consumers, and tax payers alike. A democratic work organization can increase flexibility, responsibility, and efficiency (27). Managerial opposition can be overruled by the political authorities (28).

Workplace democracy in the public sector, however, is not without problems of its own. Employees cannot affect budget decisions, which are politically controlled. Other decisions—for example over working hours—must be taken jointly with consumers. A new and more democratic organization of the entire public sector requires close cooperation between employees, consumers, and politicians. Much of the bureaucracy could be disposed of in this way (9). Democratic reform of the public sector will have important consequences for society as a whole. More than one-third of all employees in Sweden work in the public sector and most of them are in a subordinate position (29). The democratic organization of the public sector could represent a model for the democratization of society as a whole. Such democratization will be of special importance to women, for almost two-thirds of all employees in the public sector are women.

In the examples discussed earlier—in home services and cleaning—women predominate. This is one indication that the pressure for workplace democracy today is strongest among women (4). Women seem to prefer to work in a more informal and democratic way. They seem to be less interested in making careers of their own, and they seem to prefer collective and solidaristic solutions to work problems (30, 31). There is a material explanation for women's interest in this issue and their consequent political offensive. Women tend to be subordinated to male workers, holding the most menial and lowest paid jobs. They are also victims of the most intensive control and supervision. Their opportunities for promotion are limited (30, 31). In these respects women can be said to have the traditional characteristics of a working class, and may be said to be the new working class (32).

The number of women on the labor market has increased rapidly and is continuing to increase; Sweden leads the world in this respect. In qualitative terms, women have gained a stronger position on the labor market; they have increased their number of working hours and have adopted a long-term perspective with regard to their participation in wage labor. These circumstances place women in a position of strategic importance. Their situation at work is reflected in Swedish elections; women are more inclined than men to vote for socialist parties. Very few researchers or union leaders have understood the political and strategic importance either of the situation of women on the labor market or of their subordination within work organizations. Interest has mainly focused on men in the private sector—especially men in the metal industry—who are often thought to constitute the vanguard in the struggle for workplace democracy and for political change in general. It is, of course, not a question of "either/or"; there should be cooperation between different groups on the labor market.[1] But, in my experience, it is women from the public sector who have led and controlled the joint teaching experience. A priority for the future should be to encourage this kind of horizontal learning and mobilization across different groups.

SOME COMMENTS ON THE GENERALIZABILITY OF THE SWEDISH EXPERIENCE

The results of our research can be summarized as follows: we have found it rather easy to initiate democratic changes in work organization—when the workers are allowed to be in control, when they have the opportunity to learn from other examples, when they get union support, etc. It seems, however, to be very difficult to carry through these changes at all levels in a company, to consolidate and protect them, and to spread them to other companies. One important conclusion of our research points to the necessity of analyzing the obstacles to the democratization of work organizations from a power perspective on a societal level. For a number of reasons, the opportunities for workplace democracy are best in the public sector.

What in this strategy can be generalized to other countries? At a "micro-level" and in a restricted (technical) sense, some of our propositions can be useful in specific cases of organizational change. The idea of allowing the employees concerned to be more active in the change process (by job exchange, by defining their own training needs, in evaluating and presenting the outcome of the changes, etc.) is acquiring

[1] I have used the terms workers and employees interchangeably. I do not think it is necessary to provide a strict definition in terms of class interest. Those I have in mind are blue-collar workers and lower level white-collar workers. These groups can be seen as the main actors in the struggle for workplace democracy. They have the most to gain from collective and solidaristic solutions because of the way in which they are subordinated within the work organization.

growing acceptance. I have been contacted by many managers and consultants who are very interested in aspects of the collective learning process outlined above. This, however, should be seen as a technical and pseudo-democratic use of the strategy for organizational change. The means (the strategy for change) must be part of and consistent with the goal (a democratization at all levels in the company).

The opportunities for the democratization of work organizations may be better in the Nordic countries than elsewhere. A judgment on what is possible in other countries would, first of all, require an assessment of the power structure in the society in question: the strength of the working class; the role of the unions; the degree of union organization; the internal organization of the unions and the extent of their presence at the work place; the type of labor legislation; the degree of segmentation of the labor market; the strength of workers' culture in general and, specifically, at the shop-floor level; the role of the employer associations; and the existence of a corporate culture in the companies. Such an analysis would probably produce a pessimistic forecast in most countries. Left parties and unions are on the retreat in most countries and are not pushing for democratic change. But the objective conditions are there: a perceived need for better working conditions; increasing competition, which necessitates more efficient work organizations in which all the employees have a central role to play. In many countries, the best opportunities for a democratization of work organization are probably in the public sector, for the same reasons that apply in Sweden.

What is possible cannot be decided in theory, but only tested in practice. Above all, it is a question of the mobilization of the employees. The shop-floor activism of the 1970s in Italy provides one example of such mobilization; this involved claims for a better working environment and for workplace democracy. In most countries there are some cases of workplace democracy. It is of great importance to protect and consolidate them, to use them as "learning examples," and to spread them horizontally. The strategy outlined in this chapter may be of some help in this arduous and long-term struggle. As researchers, we can contribute to this struggle, partly by providing practical support, but most importantly through critical evaluation and analysis. It is in this arena that Gardell's work and the methods he used remain of great value.

REFERENCES

1. Pateman, C. *Participation and Democratic Theory*. Cambridge University Press, New York, 1970.
2. Gardell, B., and Svensson, L. *Medbestämmande och självstyre*. (Codetermination and Autonomy.) Prisma, Stockholm, 1981.
3. Gardell, B. Autonomy and participation at work. In *The Study of Organizations*, edited by I. D. Katz, R. Kahn, and J. C. Adams. Jossey-Bass, San Francisco, 1980.
4. Svensson, L. *Självstyrande grupper*. (Autonomous Groups.) Arbetslivscentrum, Stockholm, 1984.
5. Braverman, H. *Labor and Monopoly Capital*. Monthly Review Press, New York, 1974.
6. Edwards, R. *Contested Terrain: The Transformation of the Workplace in the Twentieth Century*. Basic Books, New York, 1979.
7. Karlsson, L.-E. *Work Satisfaction, Demands for Change and Alienation in a Swedish Factory*. University of Luleå, Luleå, 1985.
8. Leymann, H. Towards a new paradigm of learning in organizations. In *Socialization and Learning at Work*, edited by H. Leymann, and H. Kornbluh. Gower Publishing Ltd., Aldershot, 1988.

9. Svensson, L. *Grupper och kollektiv.* (Groups and Collectivities.) Arbetslivscentrum, Stockholm, 1986.
10. Karlsson, L.-E., Svensson, L., and Westerstrom, A. *Företaget och facket.* (The Company and the Union.) University of Luleå, Luleå, 1988.
11. Andersson, A. *Företagsdomakrati vid Tobaksfabriken i Arvika–en utvärdering.* (Industrial Democracy at the Tobacco Plant in Arvika–An Evaluation.) FÖDD, Stockholm, 1976.
12. Sandberg, A. (ed.). *Computers Dividing Man and Work.* Arbetslivscentrum, Stockholm, 1979.
13. Barklöf, K. Arbetsorganisatorisk förändring och förnyelse–en fallbeskrivning från svensk lokaltrafik. (Organizational change–A case-study of local transport in a Swedish city.) In *Forskning för Framtidens Arbetsliv* (Research for the Working Life of the Future. A book in memory of Bertil Gardell), edited by H. Leymann, and L. Svensson. Prisma, Stockholm, 1987.
14. Thorsrud, E., and Emery, F. *Medinflytande och engagemang i arbetslivet.* (Influence and Involvement at Work.) Utvecklingsrådet, Stockholm, 1969.
15. Baxandall, R. Women in American trade unions: An historical analysis. In *The Rights and Wrongs of Women*, edited by J. Mitchell and A. Oakley. Penguin, New York, 1979.
16. Coote, A. *Hear This Brother: Women Worker–And Union Power.* New Statesman, London, 1980.
17. Gonegai, B., and Thorsell, B. *Kvinnorna i facket.* (Women in the Unions.) Gothenburgh University, Gothenburgh, 1985.
18. Baude, A. *Kvinnorna i facket.* (Women in the Unions.) A project proposal. Arbetslivscentrum, Stockholm, 1984.
19. Höglund, S. *En studie av lokalvården.* (A Study of the Cleaners Organization.) The University of Örebro, Örebro, 1988.
20. Aronsson, C., Höglund, S., and Svensson, L. *En demokratisk förändringstrategi.* (A Democratic Strategy for Change.) Prisma, Stockholm, forthcoming.
21. Sandberg, A, (ed.) *Ledning för alla?* (Management for Everyone.) Arbetslivscentrum, Stockholm, 1987.
22. Laestadius, S. *Produktion utan gränser.* (Production without National Limits.) Liber, Stockholm, 1980.
23. Broström, A. *MBL:s gränser. Den privata äganderätten.* (The Limits of the Codetermination Law–Private Ownership.) Arbetslivscentrum, Stockholm, 1982.
24. Berggren, C. *Fack, företagsledning och besluten om företagens framtid.* (Unions, Companies, and Strategic Decisions.) Arkiv, Lund, 1987.
25. Israel, J. De-alienation under Capitalism–Alienation under Socialism. Paper presented at the Dubrovnik Meeting on Alienation, March 1985.
26. Kjellberg, A. Klassamhällets omstöpning. (The restructuring of class society.) *Zenit* 91, 1986.
27. von Otter, C. *Worker Participation in the Public Sector.* Arbetslivscentrum, Stockholm, 1983.
28. Ressner, U. *Vårdarbetarkollektivet och facket.* (A Workers' Collectivity in Care-work and the Union.) Arbetslivscentrum, Stockholm, 1981.
29. Ahrne, G., and Leiulfsrud, H. De offentligt anställda och den svenska klasstrukturen. (The public employee and the Swedish class structure.) In *Häften för kritiska Studier* 1, 1984.
30. Ressner, U. *Den dolda hierarkin.* (The Hidden Hierarchy.) Rabén & Sjögren, Stockholm, 1985.
31. Gunnarsson, E., and Ressner, U. *Från hierarki till kvinnokollektiv?* (From Hierarchy to Women's Collectivity.) Arbetslivscentrum, Stockholm, 1983.
32. Hoel, M. *Den kvinnelige arbeiderklassen.* (The Female Working Class.) Universitetsforlaget, Oslo, 1982.

CHAPTER 15

Action Research on Occupational Stress: Involving Workers as Researchers

Barbara A. Israel, Susan J. Schurman,
and James S. House

In this chapter we describe the design and selected results of a research and intervention project in which workers and researchers collaborated for the purpose of reducing occupational stress and strengthening psychosocial factors that may mediate the negative effects of stress on health and quality of worklife. The project is intended to address a number of gaps and weaknesses in the existing research and intervention literature in the United States by drawing on the action research approach more common in Sweden and Norway that is aimed at improving the work environment. Results thus far suggest that the design is workable and can improve on more conventional approaches in both research and interventions regarding job stress and health.

Our review of the relevant literature indicated to us (and others) a number of limitations. On the *research* side, most prior studies are cross-sectional, based solely on self-report survey data, lack conceptual clarity on many of the variables examined, and are seldom linked to a meaningful, longer-term effort to understand and ameliorate adverse health consequences of stress in actual worksites. This means that (*a*) causal inferences are often difficult regarding the impact of stress on health or vice versa, (*b*) the role of environmental versus personal factors in producing stress is not adequately understood, and (*c*) research has, at best, limited impact on applied efforts (1-6). Furthermore, there has been an overreliance in this research on single-method approaches to data collection (usually quantitative) that often raises questions about validity, comprehensiveness, and process evaluation (7-9).

Occupational stress *interventions* are often either not firmly based in research, or not adequately evaluated, or both (10); and they focus almost exclusively on altering

Preparation of this chapter was supported by grant no. 501 AA06553 from the National Institute of Alcohol Abuse and Alcoholism. Parts of this chapter were presented at the Annual Meeting of the American Public Health Association, September 1986, and appeared in the proceedings of the IFF/WHO-Europe Workshop on "Cultural Factors in Worksite Health Promotion," June 1987.

individuals' perception of and reactions to stressful situations, despite growing evidence that social and environmental factors are important contributors to job stress and its effects (2, 6, 11, 12). Additionally, the effects of interventions are often small to begin with and seldom sustained over time (10-12), often because the interventions are insufficiently tailored to the values, attitudes, and needs of the employees and organization (13-15).

The design of the present study addresses these gaps and weaknesses in three major ways: (a) the project has been implemented within an *action research framework*; (b) it *combines research and intervention* in a single *longitudinal* study; and (c) it employs *multiple methods* of both research and intervention. In this chapter we explicate each of these aspects of the design, show how the design has effectively been put in operation, provide evidence of ways in which these features have improved the project over conventional approaches, and address limitations in terms of effectiveness and efficiency.

CONCEPTUAL FRAMEWORK AND EMPIRICAL EVIDENCE

There has been a failure in the occupational stress literature to adequately define and conceptualize the stress phenomenon (1, 16), which has been pointed to as a key factor in much of the confusion and contradiction in the field (17-20). Recent evidence suggests that conceptualizing stress as a process in which individual and environmental characteristics interact to produce a variety of outcomes offers the greatest potential for intervention strategies (e.g., 2, 6, 21). Thus, in the present research, occupational stress is defined as a *process* that includes not only the environmental sources of stress and the individual's perception of them, but also short-term and long-term physiological, psychological, and behavioral responses, and a number of moderating factors that influence the relationships among variables in the stress process. The specific manner in which this process is hypothesized to unfold is shown in Figure 1.

Based on this conceptual framework, a preventive approach to occupational stress might be aimed at numerous factors; that is, reducing organizational sources of stress as well as strengthening those factors thought to be especially significant in their potential to moderate the negative effects of stress (e.g., social support, participation in and control over decision-making). The intervention model employed in this study incorporates both of these aims.

The present study builds upon the extensive empirical evidence that substantiates this conceptual framework. In the last 15 years, considerable research has identified numerous sources of stress at work that are related to diverse physiological, psychological, and behavioral outcomes (e.g., 1, 3, 6, 17, 20-32). This research has found not only an association between work stress and health and quality of working life, but also that numerous psychosocial factors play a significant role in moderating this relationship. Among these, social support and participation in and control over decision-making have been selected for examination in our study, based on the significance of their role in previous research (1-3, 17, 21, 25, 27, 33-42), and their relevance to an action research approach (14, 15, 43-51).

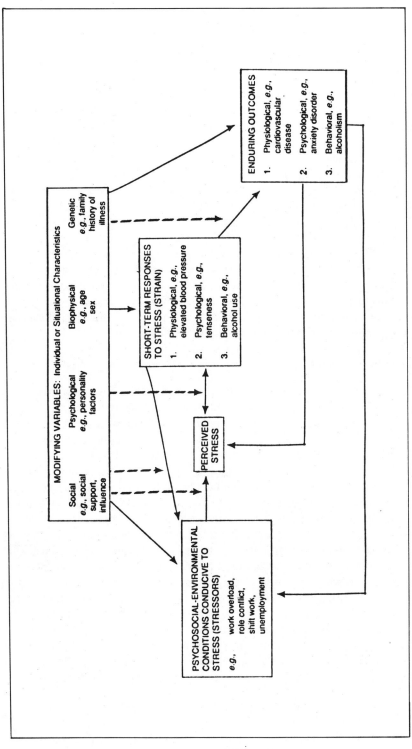

Figure 1. Conceptual framework of the stress process (2, 29). Solid arrows between boxes indicate presumed causal relationships (direct effects) among variables. Broken arrows intersecting solid arrows indicate an interaction between the modifying variables and the variables in the box at the *beginning* of the solid arrow in predicting variables in the box at the *head* of the solid arrow.

OVERVIEW OF THE STUDY

Study Site and Sample

The study is in the third year (in 1988) of a four-year project, conducted in a component-parts plant of a major manufacturing corporation located in a medium-sized urban area in Michigan. The plant resembles a collection of small businesses, each producing a distinct and unrelated product line with a diverse array of processes, technologies, and managerial practices ranging from the traditional manufacturing organization of the 1950s to a more modern, flexible approach to manufacturing.

At the beginning of the project, the plant employed 1,036 people; 99 salaried and 937 hourly. Because of economic difficulties within the industry as a whole, approximately 250 employees have been laid off, but the distribution of hourly and salaried employees has remained about the same. Approximately 95 percent of the employees are male and 80 percent are white. Because the plant is predominantly a machining rather than assembly operation, jobs are viewed as desirable. Consequently the workforce is older (only 8 percent are under 30 years old) and employees have higher seniority than those in an assembly facility. The hourly workforce is represented by a major industrial union, and the plant is part of a large multi-plant local. Relations between the plant union and management are relatively cooperative.

Research and Intervention Goals

This study involves an action research approach in which researchers from the University of Michigan and organization members are engaged in a collaborative effort aimed at both increasing our understanding of the stress process (research objectives) and meeting the immediate needs of the organization (intervention objectives). This approach precludes the complete specification of a research and intervention agenda prior to the involvement of organization members. However, at the beginning of this project we were able to specify research and intervention objectives and questions that can be categorized into four general dimensions: (*a*) evaluating the action research strategy, e.g., to what extent is the research team able to implement the action research strategy as planned?; (*b*) examining cross-sectional relationships, e.g., to what extent are social support and participation and influence negatively associated with levels of stress and adverse behavioral and health outcomes?; (*c*) monitoring intervention effects, e.g., to what extent do varying degrees of exposure to the intervention result in different impacts; that is, can changes in social support, participation, stress, and behavioral and health outcomes be attributed to the intervention?; and (*d*) examining change-oriented research questions, e.g., to what extent do changes in social support and participation result in changes in stress or behavioral or health outcomes? These objectives are presented as examples of research and intervention questions of this action research project, and should not be considered as exhaustive.

THE ACTION RESEARCH APPROACH

As described above, an action research approach in a work setting involves researchers and organization members in a joint process aimed at meeting both research and intervention objectives (14-15, 43-51). The conduct of action research involves a cyclical problem-solving process with five phases: diagnosing, action planning, action taking, evaluating, and specifying learning. Organization members and the research team collaboratively carry out the process (15).

In addition to action research, there are other similar alternative approaches to social science inquiry that have also been drawn upon in the present study. These approaches include "empowering participation" (52), "participatory research" (45), and "participative research" (53-54). It is beyond the scope of this chapter to address the similarities and differences across these models; rather, the following presents several of the key characteristics of the action research approach used here, which was augmented by elements of these other models. In the literature, there are actually many somewhat different conceptualizations of action research itself [see Peters and Robinson (49) for an excellent discussion], as well as comparisons between action research and participatory research (45). Thus, the characteristics listed below highlight the combination of elements of these models that are most germane to this study.

Several of the key characteristics of action research include:

1. It is *participatory*, both in the sense that organization members are involved in all phases of the research and action, and that the issues addressed include those generated by organization members and are not just the theoretical problems identified by researchers (15, 47, 49, 52-54).
2. It is *collaborative*, in that action research involves organization members and researchers in a joint, cooperative process in which both have needs and expertise that they contribute (15, 47, 49).
3. It is a *co-learning process*, in which researchers involve workers in developing local theory that explains their own situation, and such knowledge in turn is used by workers to change the organization (52, 54).
4. It involves *system development*; that is, the action research process creates the competencies within a system (e.g., organization) to engage in the cyclical process of diagnosing and analyzing problems, and planning, implementing, and evaluating interventions aimed at meeting identified needs, such as reducing work stress (15, 47).
5. It is an *empowering process*, in which, through participation, organization members gain increased control over their own lives (52).

Rationale for Why Action Research

There are several reasons why action research was selected as the most appropriate strategy for the present study. First, as has been convincingly argued elsewhere (15, 53, 55-56), the traditional, positivist science model—with its emphasis on value neutrality, treating subjects as objects, and with research objectives and design viewed as well-specified, unchanging, and controlled—is at odds with the diverse parties, multiple objectives, and partial researcher control that best describes the often turbulent and ever-changing organizational setting. Action research, with its emphasis on participation and collaboration, in which researchers and workers are co-learners in an empowering process, is a more appropriate approach for generating knowledge and change in the organizational context (15, 53, 55-56). Second, employees, especially those belonging to or represented by labor unions, are often unwilling to participate or misrepresent their opinions when involved with conventional research projects, because they associate researchers with management and the existing hierarchical structure (57). Through its emphasis on close collaboration with workers and developing an atmosphere of mutuality and trust, action research represents a promising strategy for overcoming this mistrust. Third, such a collaborative research effort has the potential to provide new insights for the researcher that might not be obtained in a more detached role (48). Fourth, given that a reduction in stress is brought about by the ability of the individual to take actions that increase the "fit" between actual and ideal situations (58), the action research focus on participant involvement and control of decisions and actions makes such a strategy especially appropriate in addressing stress-related factors in organizations (14).

A fifth reason for choosing an action research strategy is that planned change programs have often failed to diffuse new ideas, change behaviors, or achieve long-term program acceptance because such programs did not obtain the participant's "inside" understanding of attitudes, needs, and the environment (52, 59-61), nor was there a sense of similarity between those introducing the change and the participants themselves (62), nor were the participants involved in the management and control of the research and change process (59). The active, ongoing involvement of employees in the action research process increases the potential of minimizing these previous shortcomings. Finally, as was presented earlier, there is a link between participation and control and health status and quality of working life, and hence, the action research process may be considered health enhancing in and of itself. Thus, in implementing this project, particular emphasis is being placed on establishing a relationship between researchers and organization members that is characterized by coequal status and interdependence, with the long-run aim of transferring ownership and control of the process to the employees themselves.

In summary, action research represents a strategy that is consistent with Levi's (6) principles for improving the work environment and promoting and protecting workers' health. These principles are (a) a *comprehensive* view of workers and work that considers physical, mental, social, and economic aspects; (b) an *ecological* strategy that considers the interaction between all aspects of the individual and the environment within a complex system; (c) a *cybernetic* strategy that involves ongoing evaluation of the multiple effects of the work environment and making changes as necessary; and (d) a *democratic* strategy that gives workers the greatest possible influence over their work situation (6, pp. 82-83).

Phases of This Action Research Project

The particular action research approach employed in this study is based on a model similar to Cunningham's (46) procedural model. In this approach, action research is viewed as a cyclical process that involves three basic sequences of activities: group development, research, and action—with evaluation as a crucial ongoing component in each of the sequences. A description of each of these sequences is presented below, including an analysis of some key project activities. These activities demonstrate our attempt to adhere to the principles and processes of action research that we consider to be the strengths of this strategy over more conventional approaches to research and intervention.

Sequence I: Group Development. This sequence is comprised of a series of steps aimed at achieving acceptance of the action research project by the organization's decision-makers and preparing the action research group for its role in the project. Activities in this sequence include, for example, entry, group formation, training, and development of group goals.

After completing the initial entry discussions with both divisional and plant management and local and plant union officials, the first stage of this investigation involved organizing a representative group of employees to participate in the research. The plant already had experience with employee participation since it had previously implemented employee participation in a joint union-management decision-making program, and other jointly administered programs (e.g., health and safety, sports, and community service). Thus, the concept of a jointly sponsored program was familiar to them, and we were able to draw on this experience in the early group development stage of the project.

Our original plan was to form a group comprised of 10 to 15 volunteers interested in the issues of stress in the workplace, which included representatives from each product area and shift in the plant; men, women, and minorities; and union and management leaders. Initially, two persons (one hourly and one salaried) were selected by the union and management to work with us in identifying potential committee members. During several meetings, they made it clear that we could not achieve the degree of representativeness needed without a larger group, and that the final selection criteria for group membership also needed to include people knowledgeable about the plant, people who are trusted and respected, people who communicate well with others, and a substantial number of hourly employees who work on the shop floor. The initial list of potential committee members included over 40 names, which we were able to reduce to a list of 26 through a process of discussion and consensus between the University and site teams. Although the Stress and Wellness Committee (the name the committee members have chosen to call themselves) is larger than we had originally intended, we have benefited from the local knowledge and expertise of the employees in developing a group that is appropriate for their organization, rather than trying to meet some standards set by outside researchers. This process of committee selection illustrates the nature of the participatory, collaborative process that we tried to establish, one in which ownership and control are transferred as soon as possible to the people involved.

The establishment of mutual influence and ownership was further enhanced as the study evolved. During the early meetings of the Stress and Wellness Committee, the University-based action research team played an active role in facilitating the process, but this did, by design, diminish as employees assumed more responsibility for the group's actions. The success of our efforts to institutionalize a collaborative process is substantiated by the results of an evaluation questionnaire completed by all committee members at the end of year one. In this assessment of the committee's efforts and the project as a whole, almost all committee members state that they are, for example, "somewhat" or "very" satisfied with the way the decision-making process is working and their influence over decisions made; and that it is "somewhat" or "very" true that everyone has a voice in the decisions, and that the Stress and Wellness Project is a good example of union and management working together in a joint project.

Sequence II: Research. According to Cunningham's model (46), research involves joint problem definition by the researchers and action research group, development of data gathering approaches, data analysis, planning and implementing feedback of the data to organization members, and formulation of action hypotheses based on the data. In the present study, data collection began concurrently with Sequence I. During the first working session of the Stress and Wellness Committee, the research team involved the group in an experiential activity designed to obtain the "inside view" from the employees of what it is like to work in the plant, which would in turn illustrate as well as test the model of stress described earlier (Figure 1). Pairs of individuals interviewed each other to discover (*a*) personal sources of job stress, (*b*) perceptions and feelings about the stress, and (*c*) typical ways of responding to or coping with the perceived stress. During a series of meetings, the committee generated a model that overall looks quite similar to the one presented here, but also contained elements specific to the local situation. This exercise began the process of group formation and development as well as data collection and learning. That is, the activity provided the group with a better understanding of stress and its effects, and provided the research team with a rich preliminary overview of the organizational context and sources of stress, data on the variables of our conceptual framework, and an informal test of the framework's utility.

We also recognized that in order to engage in research and action strategies that were relevant and culturally appropriate, we needed to be more knowledgeable about the history of the organization, its structure (e.g., decision-making processes, communication patterns), as well as sources of stress that other people in the plant might experience. Therefore, as an organizational diagnosis, we conducted in-depth semistructured interviews with each committee member, the plant union committee, and upper management. Not only did these interviews provide an important data set, but they also served to establish trust and rapport between the researchers and plant members through sharing information about the project. On several occasions people stated that prior to the interviews they had not been clear about the purpose of the project and now they were, or that they really appreciated the opportunity to share their opinions.

In order to obtain more widespread input throughout the plant, a major concern of the Stress and Wellness Committee, a plantwide survey was conducted. This survey served both as a broad-based needs assessment for defining problems for potential action, as well as a quantitative baseline data set for research purposes. Here again, the active role of the committee was essential to the success of this effort.

First of all, the design of the survey instrument, in addition to using standardized items with proven reliability and validity, included questions based on the committee's input that were specifically tailored, in both language and content, to the plant situation. At the committee's request, we added questions on sources of stress outside of work, and the extent to which work interferes with life outside and vice versa.

After pretesting the survey with the committee, we made many revisions in item wording, response categories, and formatting, based on suggestions from committee members. This strategy adhered to Elden's (54) critique of the use of prepackaged surveys in action research, in which he argues that if organization members are to learn from and use research, then it needs to be in their language and address issues that they consider to be important. Elden further states his objections "to a change-oriented social science that would attempt to increase the control of people over their own lives but at the same time use alienating methods" (54, p. 266).

The data collection process also benefited from the committee's involvement in activities concerning survey administration. The committee decided by consensus that the best way to obtain participation was to schedule sessions during working hours, at which time employees could voluntarily take the survey. Since this involved shutting down production, we had not considered this as a potential strategy. However, several members representing the committee met with upper management and obtained approval for this approach, and they subsequently met with department managers and established the time schedule for conducting the survey. The committee also, completely on its own, informed employees about the survey and asked for their participation. The committee members wrote an article for the plant newsletter, distributed flyers in everyone's paycheck, made announcements at meetings, and posted large banners throughout the plant. During the survey administration, members of the committee and research staff worked together to distribute surveys, to explain confidentiality and voluntary consent procedures, and to answer any questions.

These examples indicate that both the content and process of collecting data were enhanced by the use of a collaborative, participatory action research approach. The committee members and researchers each have expertise and access to information that are different but complementary, with one party often better able to accomplish a given task successfully. The result of these efforts was a 68 percent response rate—the highest response to a survey the plant has ever achieved (almost twice as high as previous surveys).

The results of the survey have both contributed to our knowledge about the stress process and provided guidelines for interventions. This is depicted in the following summary of some of the major findings.

In one major set of analyses we tested the conceptual model presented in Figure 1 (63). We examined both the independent and joint impact of psychosocial factors—personal resources (self-esteem, mastery), interpersonal relationships (social support and negative relationships), participation in and influence over decision-making, and coping behaviors—on occupational stress, job strains (job satisfaction, negative feelings about work), and physical and mental health (global health symptoms, general health, depression).

Considered one at a time, all of the potential moderators were found to have significant and usually substantial association with the dependent variables. In addition, an examination of their combined effects indicated that all of these psychosocial factors (with the exception of satisfaction with participation) have substantial independent effects on some of the stress and health outcomes. The effects of participation are mediated almost entirely by satisfaction with influence, suggesting that it is the influence that results from participation rather than participation per se that is consequential for job stress and health. Thus, there is evidence, as hypothesized, that these psychosocial variables have both direct and indirect effects on the outcomes and that their moderating effects differ depending upon the outcome being investigated. Of particular importance to the action research approach is the confirmatory finding concerning the crucial role that influence plays in this process.

We conducted another set of analyses of the frequencies and correlations of the major variables in the survey, as well as the interview data. The findings were presented in a report prepared for the Stress and Wellness Committee to use as a basis for intervention. The results of these analyses suggested that job strains (job dissatisfaction and negative feelings about work) and physical and mental health are most strongly associated with (a) people problems (lack of information and communication, hassles with supervisors); (b) job demands related to work overload and responsibilities, and demands of other people; (c) lack of job security; (d) supervisory support; and (e) satisfaction with participation and influence. Physical-environmental problems and physical demands of the job were less strongly associated with either job strains or health. In preparing this report and accompanying feedback sessions, we recognized the obligation both to return knowledge in understandable language that is accessible to organization members (55), and to help workers learn to carry out their own research in an effort to democratize and thereby demystify the research process (52, 54–55).

Sequence III: Action. In accordance with Cunningham's model (46), this phase involves the action research group in the formulation of action plans based on hypotheses drawn from the data. This may involve recommendations to organization decision-makers about problems and potential solutions and, depending on the nature of the problem, may involve the group in actually designing programmatic interventions. Based on the findings of the survey and interview data (described above), the Committee identified four top problem areas for stress reduction efforts: lack of participation in and control over decision-making; lack of information, communication, and feedback; problems with supervisors; and conflict between producing quality versus quantity of product. It is important to note that the first three of these major sources of stress are congruent with the psychosocial factors identified in the conceptual framework. The empirical evidence summarized earlier also substantiates that these stressors are significant predictors of physical and mental health.

The Stress and Wellness Committee then formed four subcommittees, each of which formulated initial action recommendations for one of the top four problem areas selected. These subcommittees met for several months in order to obtain an in-depth understanding of the problem (often involving further analyses of the survey or interview data), to examine the barriers and resources that influence the problem and its resolution, to identify alternative strategies for solving the problem, and to develop preliminary recommendations for interventions. These recommendations were presented to union and management leaders for their approval. Examples of action strategies that were implemented include (a) the creation of a daily newsletter that contains up-to-date information on a number of issues; (b) the building and placement of 10 information display cases throughout the plant; (c) the appropriation of time on the job for leaders of existing employee participation programs to follow through on identified problems; and (*d*) modifications of the performance appraisal system for salaried workers.

Based on continuing analysis of the four major problems, the Stress and Wellness Committee concluded that these problems were interrelated and decided to combine the findings and recommendations from the four subcommittees into a pilot project to be conducted in one product area of the plant. Approval for the pilot project was obtained, and a Steering Committee comprised of top union, management, and hourly and salaried employees was established to implement the project. The goals of this pilot project are to improve quality and quantity ratings and eliminate waste, to increase participation in and influence over decisions on the job, to increase trust and improve relationships between supervisors and supervisees, and to identify and document the factors essential to the success of such a project in a process of ongoing evaluation. The project has involved the establishment of a small problem-solving team comprised of a cross-section of employees from the product area. These team members have participated in training, e.g., problem-solving, communication skills, team building, quality control, and have engaged in further problem identification, priority setting, and problem resolution. Based on the recommendations of the Stress and Wellness Committee, this team developed into the first example within the plant of a semi-autonomous work group (64) in which both the multi-level composition of the group and the authority given to it enabled the group members to meet their goals.

Evaluation. Cunningham (46) describes evaluation as a key ongoing activity in each of the three sequences of the action research approach, and provides the basis for determining whether the project is ready to proceed to the next sequence or whether further emphasis is required in the present phase. Evaluation provides the necessary feedback loops to help the action research group determine the appropriate activities to engage in as the study evolves.

As mentioned previously, at the end of the first year of the project all committee members completed a questionnaire designed to obtain their assessment of the committee's functioning, their role, the role of the research team, and the effectiveness of the project as a whole. Overall, the results were very positive for such dimensions as group development, decision-making processes, influence, commitment, trust and openness, working together as a group, amount of direction provided by the research team, and comparison between this project and other programs at the plant. The major frustration expressed concerned the slow progress in addressing the problems that had been identified. Frequently mentioned aspects of how this project is different from other programs included composition, concern, equality, and participation of committee members; longevity of the program; and the problem-solving process that the committee employs.

Obviously, this three-sequence model is an oversimplification. In reality, as depicted here, activities from all three sequences may occur concurrently. Research will commence during group development, and group members will be forming action-hypotheses in advance of the formal step associated with this activity. Furthermore, this is a cyclical ongoing process, in which as action is taken on one issue, the group may formulate new goals to identify and address additional problems.

LONGITUDINAL STUDY DESIGN

In addition to the use of an action research approach, a second major way in which this study has addressed the gaps and weaknesses in the field is through the combination of research and intervention in a single longitudinal study. Over a four-year period, multiple types of data have been and will be collected at numerous points in time. This has provided both longitudinal and quasi-experimental data that enable us to address questions of causality that have been left unanswered by the largely cross-sectional nature of prior research. For example, what are the causal priorities among social support, participation, stress, and health? In addition, these longitudinal data have guided both the design and evaluation of interventions tailored to the study site. The analysis of the second survey indicated, for example, that the top problems identified from the first survey continued to be the major sources of stress in the plant, and thus the Committee felt warranted in continuing with its intervention plan. Furthermore, these longitudinal data allow for the examination of questions such as how do key variables vary over time?; do changes in proximate variables result in changes in behavioral and health-related outcomes?; and to what extent can changes in social support, participation, stress, and health outcomes be attributed to the intervention?

We would argue that a pure two-way panel design may provide little improvement in explaining causality over cross-sectional studies. This is especially true when intervening events are not clearly demarcated. Rather, a larger gain is obtained with three waves of data because it is possible to use the results from the first and second surveys to predict changes in the third survey. The availability of more than two data collections also provides for exploration of direct versus lagged effects and gives two opportunities to observe shorter term effects. Furthermore, it allows analyses that estimate reliability and stability separately for each variable. Finally, the presence of interventions between waves generates a variety of quasi-experimental designs.

MULTIPLE METHODS: RESEARCH AND INTERVENTION

The use of an action research approach within a longitudinal study design does not assure that previous limitations in collecting data and conducting interventions will be overcome. For example, there has been an overreliance in occupational stress research on single-method approaches to data collection (usually quantitative) that often raises questions regarding validity, comprehensiveness, and process evaluation (7-9). In addition, occupational stress interventions, in the United States especially, usually focus almost exclusively on changing the perception and behavior of individuals, despite the growing evidence that social and environmental factors are important contributors to job stress and its effects (2, 6, 11, 12, 65). Therefore, in an attempt to counter these weaknesses, the present study employed multiple methods of both research and intervention. The rationale for taking this approach and examples of results and actions taken are presented below.

Multiple Research Methods

The diverse goals and objectives of this study center on three tasks: monitoring program implementation, assessing impact, and providing causal explanation (9). This diversity of tasks requires multiple sources of data, as well as methods of data collection. It has frequently been argued that "by combining multiple observers, theories, methods and data sources, [researchers] can hope to overcome the intrinsic bias that comes from single-method, single observer, single-theory studies" (66, p. 313). Thus, our research strategy used both quantitative and qualitative methods.

Although the use of multiple methods within a single research strategy has been frequently advocated (e.g., 7-9), few studies have actually used such an approach and to do so presents numerous difficulties. Constraints in the form of limited resources, inadequate training in both methods, and different scientific ideologies present obstacles that must be overcome (9). We have minimized these problems through the use of a clearly specified research plan that describes the particular manner in which different methods are used.

The multiple data collection methods that we carried out include (a) ethnographic field notes of all major contacts with the research site (e.g., telephone conversations, meetings with individuals, Stress and Wellness Committee meetings); (b) in-depth, semi-structured interviews with all members of the Stress and Wellness Committee, top management, and union committee body (total of 44 interviews, average length 1½ hours, tape-recorded and reconstructed detailed notes written for each interview); (c) participant observations of activities in the plant; (d) content analysis of organizational newspapers and other documents; (e) a plantwide survey administered to all hourly and salaried employees on a voluntary basis at three points in time over the four-year study; (f) pre- and post-tests administered to members of the product area in which the pilot project was conducted; (g) collection of business data on the pilot project product area, e.g., cost of scrap, quality audit; and (h) focus-group interviews with various groups in the plant (e.g., supervisors, engineers).

These multiple data sources provide different perspectives on the research and intervention, and help to correct against the limitations of any particular methodology. In accordance with Ingersoll-Dayton's (8) suggestion, we used qualitative and quantitative methods for the multiple purposes of problem definition, illumination of meaning, cross-validation and triangulation, and enhanced generalizability. The following discussion presents examples of how we tried to meet these aims; a more in-depth treatment is provided elsewhere (67).

Problem Definition. Qualitative data collection techniques were used in the early stages of this study as part of the exploratory process of defining the problem areas. In-depth ethnographic interviews, conducted during the initial stages of the project as a part of the organizational diagnosis and assessment of needs, were coded and analyzed. The results indicated several categories of major sources of stress at work: equipment problems (e.g., breakdowns, lack of preventive maintenance); problems with supervisors (e.g., lack of concern, style and decision-making procedures); quality issues (e.g., poor quality parts, conflict regarding quality versus quantity of parts); problems related to management (e.g., style and decision-making, organizational structure); job demands (e.g., too much work and too little time, lack of control); lack of job security; and communication problems (e.g., not being adequately informed). This is an oversimplification of the qualitative data obtained from these interviews, but initially we used these major problem areas to guide the construction of survey questions in order to determine the extent to which these were important issues for employees throughout the plant.

Illumination of Meaning.   The qualitative data were used to help us understand the meaning of the quantitative data. In some cases the findings of the baseline survey were not readily understandable, and examination of the interview data clarified the meaning. For example, several questions were asked on the survey about job satisfaction and positive feelings about the job. The frequency distribution for the index constructed on job satisfaction (alpha = .84) indicated that over 60 percent of hourly employees and 50 percent of salaried employees were "often" or "almost always" satisfied with their jobs. Given the numerous sources of stress also reported in the survey, members of the Stress and Wellness Committee were surprised and puzzled by these positive results. However, in analyzing the responses in the qualitative interviews regarding positive aspects of work, we identified several dimensions. These included salary benefits; a sense of accomplishment and challenge; a sense of making a contribution to the plant; satisfaction from working with others; and a feeling of familiarity with the environment. In sharing these open-ended interview data with the committee, we were able to better understand the meaning behind the survey responses concerning job satisfaction, thereby recognizing that people could be satisfied in general and still experience stress.

Cross-Validation and Triangulation.   We used a triangulation approach (7, 9) that includes the combination of quantitative and qualitative methods concomitantly. This technique involves the simultaneous but independent use of both methods, which allows each method to serve as a check and balance for the other; providing cross-validation of and increased confidence in the results.

We used such a triangulation approach to delineate and understand the major sources of work stress. We listed earlier some of the stressors identified through the in-depth interviews. In addition, there was one open-ended question on the first survey regarding the respondents' "biggest problem or source of stress at work." A total of 450 responses to this question were coded and grouped according to similar responses. The most frequently mentioned biggest source of stress for hourly and salaried employees combined were, in rank order, problems with people (e.g., lack of cooperation and communication with supervisors and top management); job demands and pressures (e.g., rush assignments, too much to do and not enough time); materials and equipment (e.g., equipment breakdowns, delay in getting machines repaired); physical work environment (e.g., noise, ventilation); organizational practices and policies (e.g., scheduling, reorganization); and lack of job security.

As is readily apparent, these sources of stress are quite similar to those identified in the in-depth interviews. Additionally, in analyzing the closed-end questions on the survey, we compared across single items that asked respondents "how often they were bothered by" certain situations at work. In examining the percentage reporting "often" or "almost all the time," the sources of stress, in rank order, were hearing about possible layoffs, not having enough information to do the job, having to deal with or satisfy too many different people, having to work with equipment that breaks down, feeling that people are not adequately trained, and having too much work to do and not enough time to do it.

Additionally, we analyzed the sources of stress measures from the survey (single items and indices) in relation to several dependent variables, i.e., positive and negative feelings about the job, overall self-reported health, depressed feelings, and sleep problems. Those stressors most strongly related to these outcome variables were supervisor hassles, communication and information problems, too much work and responsibility, and demands from other people.

Thus, in using qualitative and quantitative data for triangulation purposes, considerable convergence was found on the major sources of stress within the plant. Given this convergence, the research team and Stress and Wellness Committee felt more confident that they were indeed tapping the important issues.

Enhanced Generalizability. The fourth reason for our use of multiple methods is that the use of survey data, in combination with qualitative methods, increases generalizability and provides a focus and specificity. The survey data allowed us to identify problems and associations with greater confidence than we could have with the interview data alone. In addition, in this particular research setting, we have used a quasi-experimental design for the pilot project, collecting appropriate quantitative data, thus helping to overcome the limitations of a single case study design.

Multiple Intervention Approach

Of particular importance to the present study is the conceptual framework (Figure 1) and research evidence suggesting that there are multiple determinants of disease in the stress process, and that it is unlikely that any one stressor or psychosocial process will be etiologically specific for a particular disease—mental or physical (68). Therefore, a given intervention may be aimed at any one of numerous factors in the model, and it is advantageous to examine both physical and mental health outcomes.

Despite this conceptual perspective and research evidence, most occupational stress programs in the United States focus only on altering individual behavior and do not attempt to modify or eliminate the organizational and environmental factors that are frequently beyond an individual's ability to control. Recent reviews of worksite health promotion programs in general (10, 69), and job stress programs specifically (11, 12, 70), suggest that a majority of such interventions are aimed at changing individual behavior and lifestyles (e.g., smoking, exercise, nutrition, relaxation) and have had limited positive results. In a review of 19 evaluation studies of work stress interventions (11), only one study used an organizational change approach.

These findings suggest a need for a more comprehensive approach to preventing the onset of job stress-related problems and illness, which focuses on changing both individual characteristics as well as characteristics of the social and physical environment (2-3, 6, 11-12, 65, 69, 71-73). Thus this study has focused on developing a diversity of interventions, as mentioned earlier, that aim at both reducing sources of stress through change at the organizational level (e.g., conflict between quality and quantity, lack of participation and control) and interpersonal level (e.g., negative relations with supervisor), as well as strengthening psychosocial resources (e.g., communication skills) through individual change strategies aimed at managing stressful situations.

ISSUES AND LIMITATIONS

As with any research effort, there are numerous issues and limitations of this action research project that need to be recognized and addressed. It is beyond the scope of this chapter to present and respond to each of these issues; rather, it is our intent to highlight a few of the major ones. (The earlier section on the rationale for action research provides a counter-argument to many of these issues.)

Given the cyclical process involved in action research, with emphasis on data collection and analysis, documentation, communication, feedback, and action, this approach requires a significant amount of personnel time and diverse human resources (74). The method requires a multi-disciplinary team with competencies in varied content and process areas, as well as skills in both quantitative and qualitative research methods.

Another issue in conducting this type of research is the long time period that is needed. As indicated here, several years of active work are initially required to implement such an approach, and it may be closer to a total of five to eight years from the inception of an idea to achieving a full sense of the results and outcomes (53). This longer-term perspective is often advocated in both research and organizational practice, but the actual organization of the academic/research world and the corporate sector often push for a much shorter time frame (56).

In carrying out an action research effort such as the one discussed here, the research team is faced with multiple issues concerning relationships to the research site. Such issues include the need to obtain "simultaneous" joint union and management sponsorship and support; the possibility that there may be different agendas and interests of the parties involved; the possibility that the objectives and demands of the research may come up against the objectives and demands of the workplace; the reluctance of some people to endorse such an effort because it addresses the need for organizational change as well as individual behavior change; and the difficulty of obtaining support for such an open-ended process as action research.

From the perspective of more traditional research designs, action research is criticized for the bias introduced as a result of its emphasis on active participation and collaboration of the researchers and organization members. It can also be argued, however, that nonparticipation of "subjects" or lack of involvement of researchers only changes the form of contamination, it does not eliminate it (43, 57). If workers are suspicious of the purposes and use of research data, they are not likely to provide valid responses.

Given that there is no control group or random assignment of subjects in this study, and there are factors within the organization and industry that we are not able to control, questions can be raised about threats to internal validity and the ability to determine causality. It has been argued elsewhere that there is a need to reexamine the issue of causality, and that there are methods other than formal control groups appropriate for conducting valid and reliable organizational research (15, 43, 51-52, 75-78). Several of these alternative approaches that have been used in the present study include the use of statistical control techniques (79-81) and a time series design (51, 75) in order to rule out alternative hypotheses and to increase confidence that hypothetical conditions are associated with desired outcomes. In addition to these responses to the issues of control and causality, it is important to recognize that in any field research within an organization, numerous changes can occur (e.g., layoffs, changes in product line, personnel changes) that are beyond the researchers' ability to control, and may affect the outcomes being studied in both a control group as well as an experimental group. Here again, the need for ongoing monitoring and documentation of the multiple events that occur during the research period is apparent.

Finally, although action research has the aim and potential to be an empowering process, there are constraints on the types of changes that can be accomplished. Experience has shown that there are situations in which "participation" becomes synonymous with manipulation or cooptation (52). Even where meaningful changes are carried out by workers at the shop floor level, the opportunity for influence may not extend to higher decision-making levels within the organization. As Elden states, "one could question how realistic it is to expect an existing power structure to allow itself to be fundamentally transformed" (54, p. 266). This critique suggests the need for strategies in addition to action research in order to achieve more large-scale, organizational changes. The labor legislation and industrial relations policies in Sweden and Norway aimed at democratizing working life are promising examples of such strategies (52, 64).

CONCLUSIONS

The intent of this chapter was to provide a detailed description and rationale for a longitudinal action research project aimed at overcoming some of the weaknesses in the field, and at reducing occupational stress and strengthening psychosocial factors that may mediate the negative effects of stress on health and quality of worklife. In addition to the possible benefits of this effort for individual employees and the organization as a whole, our purpose in this project is to contribute to a better understanding of the following areas: the strengths and weaknesses of an action research design carried out in an organizational setting; the relationship over time between psychosocial factors and the stress process (especially the role of and mechanisms through which social support and participation in and control over decision-making have their effects); the combined use of quantitative and qualitative research techniques; the impact over time of multiple interventions on the factors in the stress process; and the nature of and how to overcome methodological issues and limitations that are frequently faced in the study of occupational behavior and change.

As discussed throughout this chapter, there are several indications that the relatively unique aspects of this study (i.e., action research approach, longitudinal study design, and use of multiple data collection and intervention methods) have contributed to their desired effects. Some of these indications are

1. The active involvement of employees in the action research process increased the quality and applicability of the survey instrument and the response rate.
2. The combined use of qualitative and quantitative data collection techniques has yielded convergence on key findings and more in-depth understanding of numerous issues.

3. The process has generated a focus on major problem areas that are similar to those discussed in the existing literature, are of immediate relevance to the organization, and necessitate diverse interventions to meet identified needs.

We attribute much of these accomplishments to our adherence to the strengths of the action research approach, e.g., close collaboration between and active involvement of researchers and organization members; emphasis on action and research; obtainment of an "inside" understanding of participants' attitudes and needs; and transfer of ownership and control of the process to the organization members themselves. Whether or not this comprehensive approach totally meets its intended goals, we think the potential is great for making a contribution to both action and research—a joint endeavor that has often been neglected.

Acknowledgments — The present research and researchers owe both intellectual and personal debts to Bertil Gardell. The synthesis of research and action embodied in this work has been heavily influenced by what Bertil Gardell wrote and did in these regards. His personal influence on members of the research team has quickened and deepened our understanding of the need for such a synthesis and the ways in which it might be achieved. We wish to thank members of the research team and the worksite Stress and Wellness Committee for their important contributions to this project. We are grateful to Sue Andersen for her competent work in preparing this manuscript.

REFERENCES

1. Holt, R. R. Occupational stress. In *Handbook of Stress: Theoretical and Clinical Aspects*, edited by L. Goldberger and S. Breznitz. Free Press, New York, 1982.
2. House, J. *Work Stress and Social Support*. Addison-Wesley, Reading, Mass., 1981.
3. House, J. S., and Cottington, E. M. Health and the workplace. In *Application of Social Science to Clinical Medicine and Health Policy*, edited by L. Aiken and D. Mechanic. Rutgers University Press, New Brunswick, N.J., 1986.
4. Kasl, S. V. Epidemiological contributions to the study of work stress. In *Stress at Work*, edited by C. L. Cooper and R. Payne. Wiley, Chichester, 1978.
5. Kasl, S. V. The challenge of studying the disease effects of stressful work conditions. *Am. J. Public Health* 71: 682–684, 1981.
6. Levi, L. *Preventing Work Stress*. Addison-Wesley, Reading, Mass., 1981.
7. Fielding, N. G., and Fielding, J. L. *Linking Data*. Sage, Beverly Hills, 1986.
8. Ingersoll-Dayton, B. Combining Methodological Approaches in Social Support Research. Paper presented at the Annual Meeting of the American Psychological Association, August 1982.
9. Reichardt, C. S., and Cook, T. D. Beyond qualitative versus quantitative methods. In *Qualitative and Quantitative Methods in Evaluation Research*, edited by T. D. Cook and C. A. Reichardt. Sage, Beverly Hills, 1979.
10. Fielding, J. E. Health promotion and disease prevention at the worksite. *Annu. Rev. Public Health* 5: 237–265, 1984.
11. McLeroy, K. R., et al. Assessing the effects of health promotion in worksites: A review of the stress program evaluations. *Health Educ. Q.* 11: 379–402, 1984.
12. Murphy, L. R. Occupational stress management: A review and appraisal. *J. Occup. Psychol.* 57: 1–15, 1984.
13. D'Aunno, T. A., and Price, R. H. Methodology in community research. Part II: Analytic and action research approaches. In *Psychology and Community Change*, edited by R. H. Kitteller, et al. Dorsey, Homewood, Ill., 1984.
14. Pasmore, W., and Friedlander, F. An action-research program for increasing employee involvement in problem solving. *Admin. Sci. Q.* 27: 343–362, 1982.
15. Susman, G. E., and Evered, R. D. An assessment of the scientific merits of action research. *Admin. Sci. Q.* 23: 582–603, 1978.

16. Sutton, R., and Kahn, R. L. Prediction, understanding, and control as antidotes to organizational stress. In *Handbook of Organizational Behavior*, edited by J. Lorsch. Harvard University Press, Boston, Mass., 1984.
17. Cottington, E. M., and House, J. S. Occupational stress and health: A multivariate relationship. In *Handbook of Psychology and Health*, Vol. 5, edited by A. R. Baum and J. E. Singer. Erlbaum, Hillsdale, N.J., 1986.
18. House, J. S. Occupational stress and coronary heart disease: A review and theoretical integration. *J. Health Soc. Behav.* 15: 12–27, 1974.
19. Jenkins, C. D. Psychosocial modifiers of responses to stress. *J. Hum. Stress*, December 1979, pp. 3–15.
20. Karasek, R. A. Job demands, job decision latitude and mental strain: Implications for job redesign. *Admin. Sci. Q.* 24: 285–309, 1979.
21. McLean, A. *Work Stress*. Addison-Wesley, Reading, Mass., 1979.
22. Beehr, T. A., and Newman, J. E. Job stress, employee health, and organizational effectiveness. *Pers. Psychol.* 31: 665–699, 1978.
23. Cooper, C., and Marshall, J. Occupational sources of stress: A review of the literature relating to coronary heart disease and mental ill health. *J. Occup. Psychol.* 49: 11–28, 1976.
24. Cooper, C., and Marshall, J. Sources of managerial and white collar stress. In *Stress at Work*, edited by C. Cooper and R. Payne. Wiley, Chichester, 1978.
25. Frankenhaeuser, M., and Gardell, B. Underload and overload in working life: Outline of a multidisciplinary approach. *J. Hum. Stress* 2: 35–46, 1976.
26. Gardell, B. Psychological and social problems of industrial work in affluent societies. *Int. J. Psychol.* 12: 125–134, 1977.
27. Karasek, R. A., et al. Job decision latitude, job demands, and cardiovascular disease: A prospective study of Swedish men. *Am. J. Public Health* 71: 694–705, 1981.
28. Kasl, S. V., Gore, S., and Cobb, S. The experience of losing a job: Reported changes in health, symptoms, and illness behavior. *Psychosom. Med.* 37: 106–122, 1975.
29. Katz, D., and Kahn, R. *The Social Psychology of Organizations*, Ed. 2. Wiley, New York, 1978.
30. Schuler, R. S. Organizational stress and coping: A model and overview. In *Handbook of Organization Stress Coping Strategies*, edited by S. A. Sethi and R. S. Schuler. Ballinger, Cambridge, Mass., 1984.
31. Shostak, A. *Blue Collar Stress*. Addison-Wesley, Reading, Mass., 1980.
32. Van Sell, M., Brief, A., and Schuler, R. Role conflict and role ambiguity: Integration of the literature and directions for future research. *Hum. Rel.* 34: 43–72, 1981.
33. Alfredsson, L., et al. Myocardial infarction risk and psychosocial work environment: An analysis of the male Swedish working force. *Soc. Sci. Med.* 16: 463–467, 1982.
34. Caplan, R. D., et al. *Job Demands and Worker Health*. DHEW (NIOSH) Publication No. 75-160. U.S. Government Printing Office, Washington, D.C., 1975.
35. Gardell, B. Autonomy and participation at work. *Hum. Rel.* 30: 515–533, 1977.
36. Israel, B. A., and Rounds, K. A. Social networks and social support: A synthesis for health educators. *Adv. Health Educ. Promotion* 2: 311–351, 1987.
37. Jackson, S. E. Participation in decision making as a strategy for reducing job-related strain. *J. Appl. Psychol.* 68: 3–19, 1983.
38. Karasek, R. A., et al. Job, psychological factors and coronary heart disease. *Adv. Cardiol.* 29: 62–67, 1982.
39. Morris, J. H., Steers, R. M., and Koch, J. L. Influence of organization structure on role conflict and ambiguity for three occupational groupings. *Acad. Management J.* 22: 58–71, 1979.
40. Williams, D. W., and House, J. S. Social support and stress reduction. In *Job Stress and Blue Collar Work*, edited by C. L. Cooper and M. J. Smith. Wiley, New York, 1985.
41. Winnubst, J. A. M., Marcelissen, F. H. G., and Kleber, R. J. Effects of social support in the stressor strain relationship: A Dutch sample. *Soc. Sci. Med.* 16: 475–482, 1982.
42. House, J. S., Umberson, D., and Landis, K. R. Structures and processes of social support. *Annu. Rev. Sociol.* 14: 293–318, 1988.
43. Blumberg, M., and Pringle, C. D. How control groups can cause loss of control in action research: The case of Rushton Coal Mine. *J. Appl. Behav. Sci.* 19: 409–425, 1983.
44. Brown, L. D. Organizing participatory research: Interfaces for joint inquiry and organizational change. *J. Occup. Behav.* 4: 9–19, 1983.
45. Brown, L. D., and Tandon, R. Ideology and political economy in inquiry: Action research and participatory research. *J. Appl. Behav. Sci.* 19: 277–294, 1983.
46. Cunningham, B. Action research: Toward a procedural model. *Hum. Rel.* 29: 215–238, 1976.

47. Kemmis, S. Action research. In *Youth, Transition and Social Research*, edited by D. S. Anderson and C. Blakers. Australian National University Press, Canberra, 1983.
48. Lewin, K. Action-research and minority problems. *J. Soc. Issues* 2: 34–46, 1946.
49. Peters, M., and Robinson, V. The origins and status of action research. *J. Appl. Behav. Sci.* 20: 113–124, 1984.
50. Price, R. H., and Politser, P. E. *Evaluation and Action in the Social Environment.* Academic Press, New York, 1980.
51. Susman, G. I. Action research: A sociotechnical systems perspective. In *Beyond Method: Strategies for Social Research*, edited by G. Morgan. Sage, Beverly Hills, 1983.
52. Elden, M. Sociotechnical systems ideas as public policy in Norway: Empowering participation through worker-managed change. *J. Appl. Behav. Sci.* 22: 239–255, 1986.
53. Brown, L. D., and Kaplan, R. E. Participative research in a factory. In *Human Inquiry*, edited by P. Reason and J. Rowan. Wiley, Chichester, 1981.
54. Elden, M. Sharing the research work: Participative research and its role demands. In *Human Inquiry*, edited by P. Reason and J. Rowan. Wiley, Chichester, 1986.
55. Fals-Bordon, O. Participatory action-research. *Development: Seeds of Change* 2: 18–20, 1984.
56. Tichy, N. M., and Friedman, S. D. Institutional dynamics of action research. In *Producing Useful Knowledge for Organizations*, edited by R. H. Kilmann, et al. Praeger, New York, 1983.
57. Argyris, C. Some unintended consequences of rigorous research. *Psychol. Bull.* 70: 185–197, 1968.
58. French, J. R. P., Jr., Rogers, W., and Cobb, S. Adjustments as a person-environment fit. In *Coping and Adaptation: Interdisciplinary Perspectives*, edited by G. V. Coelho, D. A. Hamburg, and J. F. Adams. Basic Books, New York, 1974.
59. Elden, M. Client as consultant: Work reform through participative research. *Natl. Prod. Rev.,* Spring 1983, pp. 136–147.
60. Paul, B. *Health, Culture, and Community*. Russell Sage Foundation, New York, 1955.
61. Steuart, G. W. The people: Motivation, education and action. *Bull. Acad. Med.* 51: 174–185, 1975.
62. Rogers, E., and Shoemaker, F. *Communication of Innovations: A Cross-Cultural Approach*. Free Press, New York, 1971.
63. Israel, B. A., et al. The relation of personal resources, participation, influence, interpersonal relationships and coping strategies to occupational stress, job strains and health: A multivariate analysis. *Work and Stress,* 1990, in press.
64. Gardell, B. Strategies for reform programmes on work organization and work environment. In *Working Life*, edited by B. Gardell and G. Johansson. Wiley, Chichester, 1981.
65. Frese, M. Stress at work and psychosomatic complaints: A causal interpretation. *J. Appl. Psychol.* 70: 314–328, 1985.
66. Denzin, N. K. *The Research Act.* Aldine, Chicago, 1970.
67. Hugentobler, M., Israel, B. A., and Schurman, S. J. Linking multiple research methods: "The search for truth at the intersection of independent lies." Manuscript, 1988.
68. Cassel, J. The contribution of the social environment to host resistance. *Am. J. Epidemiol.* 104: 107–123, 1976.
69. Castillo-Salgado, C. Assessing recent developments and opportunities in the promotion of health in the American workplace. *Soc. Sci. Med.* 19: 349–358, 1984.
70. Cooper, C. L. Coping with organizational stress. In *Contemporary Organization Development: Current Thinking and Applications*, edited by D. D. Warrick. Scott Foresman, Glenview, Ill., 1985.
71. Allegrante, J. P., and Sloan, R. P. Ethical dilemmas in workplace health promotion. *Prev. Med.* 15: 313–320, 1986.
72. Sloan, R. P. Workplace health promotion: A commentary on the evolution of a paradigm. *Health Promotion Technical Reports.* Teachers College, Columbia University, New York, 1985.
73. Wallack, L. Practical issues, ethical concerns and future directions in the prevention of alcohol-related problems. *J. Primary Prev.* 4: 199–224, 1984.
74. Gottfredson, G. D. A theory-ridden approach to program evaluation: A method for stimulating researcher-implementer collaboration. *Am. Psychol.* 39: 1101–1112, 1984.
75. Cook, T. D., and Campbell, D. T. The design and conduct of quasi-experiments and true experiments in field settings. In *Handbook of Industrial and Organizational Psychology*, edited by M. D. Dunnette. Rand McNally, Chicago, 1976.

76. Gardell, B., and Gustavsen, B. Work environment research and social change: Current developments in Scandinavia. *J. Occup. Behav.* 1: 3–17, 1980.
77. Lawler, E. E., III. Adaptive experiments: An approach to organizational behavior research. *Acad. Management Rev.* 2: 576–585, 1977.
78. Taylor, R. N., and Vertinsky, I. Experimenting with organizational behavior. In *Handbook of Organizational Design*, Vol. 1, edited by P. C. Nystrom and W. H. Starbuck. Oxford University Press, New York, 1981.
79. Blalock, H. M., Jr. Theory building and causal inferences. In *Methodology in Social Research*, edited by H. M. Blalock, Jr., and A. B. Blalock. McGraw-Hill, New York, 1968.
80. Lord, F. M. Elementary models for measuring change. In *Problems in Measuring Change*, edited by C. W. Harris. University of Wisconsin Press, Madison, Wis., 1963.
81. Nurick, A. J. Participation in organizational change: A longitudinal field study. *Hum. Rel.* 35: 413–430, 1982.

PART 4

Diffusion of the
Psychosocial Work
Environment Model

Workplace Democracy and Worker Health: Strategies for Implementation in the United States

Steven Deutsch

A considerable body of literature demonstrates the contribution made to workers' health by reorganization of work to effect employee participation and democracy at the workplace. The key challenges remain of how best to implement such reforms and promulgate strategies for change. In this chapter, the author seeks to contribute to this goal.

A review of the literature on workplace democratization and worker health will suggest the foundation for action. Scandinavian approaches will be detailed to suggest some exemplary programs. The peculiarities of the Norwegian and Swedish labor relations system, reliance upon centralized bargaining and legislative reform, will be discussed, including problems and limitations of this approach.

Strategic planning for intervention and change in U.S. workplaces is predicated upon the presence and strength of unions, a highly decentralized system of labor relations, the existing system of work environment laws, and the emergence of new political coalitions working for change. One of the most critical factors in the work environment is the application of new technologies, and it is here that some of the more interesting efforts to expand employee participation to obtain worker health and well-being have taken place. Some lessons and possible directions for the future complete the discussion.

THE CONNECTION BETWEEN WORKPLACE DEMOCRATIZATION AND WORKER HEALTH

A tradition of research on employee involvement and work reform was built in England and in Scandinavia during the 1960s, but it was only in the 1970s that work reform became prominent on the U.S. scene (1). The relationship between the European and U.S. research and practice modes in the 1970s accelerated, and the impact of research in Europe was increasingly felt in the United States by the end of the decade. Inquiries about work stress and the psychosocial and physiological health effects of stress multiplied on both sides of the Atlantic throughout the 1970s. That research figured prominently in the work environment legislation in Norway and Sweden and formed a foundation for work reform efforts in the United States as well (2, 3).

The demonstrable evidence marshalled by researchers in Scandinavia was persuasive concerning the negative consequences of job stress on worker well-being (4, 5). This was matched by studies in the United States, which not only identified critical sources of stress, but noted occupations that were especially vulnerable to stress. As a result of the work by the National Institute for Occupational Safety and Health (NIOSH) and many private investigators, considerable publicity was given to the known high-stress occupations such as air traffic controllers and clerical workers. Research identified sources of stress that are critical for worker health. Added to the physical stress agents, such as noise and heat, were the adverse effects of shift work, highly repetitive tasks, overbearing supervision, work load factors, and issues of technological control at the workplace. The key variables of amount of demand upon the worker and the degree of control over the job seemed critical in anticipating the stress factors and health outcomes (5, 6). In summary, the 1970s witnessed a large increase in research on job stress and a growing ability to identify sources, severity, and outcomes of stress on the job.

By 1980 work stress appeared increasingly on professional occupational health agendas, joining the concerns of acute trauma, cancer, respiratory disease, and other primary sources of workplace health and safety problems. Social isolation on the job, a factor often exacerbated by the application of new technologies, was recognized as a problem, particularly since social support was demonstrated as critical in controlling and reducing personal stress (7). By the early 1980s a sufficient body of research had been accumulated to lead the head of the World Health Organization Stress Lab to make an explicit point of the linkage between workplace health and reduction of stress on the one hand and worker participation on the other (6). In short, the healthy organization is one in which conscious efforts are made to create environments of employee involvement and active engagement. Activation of the workforce was noted as contributing to a reduction in workplace health and safety problems (8). This research conclusion had an impact on enlightened managers, trade unions, and the research community involved in employee training and workplace reorganization efforts. In the United States these efforts remained voluntary and dependent upon the existence of an active union and enlightened management, while in Scandinavia the research conclusions led to legislated reforms and more direct action.

SCANDINAVIAN APPROACHES

Scandinavia leads the world in research on occupational stress, and more importantly, the research evidence has been used in social policy and workplace reform. The rich tradition of research in Norway and Sweden has been most instructive for the international research and policy community (9). It is especially noteworthy to observe how the research shaped the 1977 Norwegian Work Environment Act and the 1978 Swedish Work Environment Act (2). In the case of Norway, the Act was explicit in identifying the issues of technology and work organization and employee participation as critical for improved worker health. Section 12 of the Act is worth noting:

NORWEGIAN WORKER PROTECTION AND WORK ENVIRONMENT ACT OF 1977

SECTION 12

Planning the Work

1. General requirements

Technology, organization of the work, working hours and wage systems shall be set up so that the employees are not exposed to undesirable physical or mental strain and so that their possibilities of displaying caution and observing safety measures are not impaired.

2. Arrangement of work

The individual employee's opportunity for self-determination and professional responsibility shall be taken into consideration when planning and arranging work.

Efforts shall be made to avoid undiversified, repetitive work and work that is governed by machine or conveyor belt in such a manner that the employees themselves are prevented from varying the speed of the work. Otherwise efforts shall be made to arrange the work so as to provide possibilities for variation and for contact with others, for connection between individual job assignments, and for employees to keep themselves informed about production requirements and results.

3. Control and planning systems

The employees and their elected union representatives shall be kept informed about the systems employed for planning and effecting the work, and about planned changes in such systems. They shall be given the training necessary to enable them to learn these systems, and they shall take part in planning them.

The strategy of implementation of research findings into legislative directives was carefully developed in the Norwegian case and serves as a challenging model for other nations (8). Similarly, in Sweden, a conscious strategy in the 1970s used legislation in gradual steps to reform the workplace and the system of employee involvement (10). The Work Environment Act, modified in 1978, was linked to the 1977 Law on Codetermination in which employees and their representatives were to be engaged in work design, task allocation, application of new technologies, and overall work environment factors. The legislative mandates were predicated upon the research literature, which gave ample evidence that worker activation contributed to improvements in the work environment and therefore benefited all—the workforce, management, and the society.

In both Norway and Sweden at the end of the 1970s there was considerable expectation that the reform efforts would lead to reduced injuries and illnesses at the workplace and that active involvement by the workforce would lead to a gradual reorganization of workplaces along the lines of a participatory model that would shape the design and implementation of new technologies, systems of supervision, overall work organization, and the approach to the work environment. A holistic approach to the work environment was, in fact, one of the major contributions from Scandinavia to the rest of the industrial world. Elsewhere, job safety and health largely focused upon physical and chemical hazards and little primary attention was given to psycho-social factors, stress, technology, and other parts of the work environment affecting workers' health and well-being (3).

The problems in the 1980s have made it obvious that the expectations were overly optimistic, albeit the approaches in Norway and Sweden to work environment improvement seem very much on the right track and serve as excellent models for the world. There has been a highly centralized system of labor-management relations in these countries, especially in Sweden which has a small amount of public ownership, like the United States but unlike Norway. While the labor relations system in the mid-1980s has become increasingly decentralized, the emphasis upon centralized agreements and leadership from the employer and labor federations has characterized the system until recently (11). This system led to a substantial commitment to work environment improvement, a massive effort for the Joint Industrial Safety Council to give the 40-hour "Better Work Environment" course to hundreds of thousands of workers, and the development of local workplace and regional occupational health centers. A problem is that a centralized model may lead to only modest shop-floor activation since there is some tendency to assume that the central unions will handle things. This has, to some extent, been the experience in Sweden, and the amount of local workplace participation is judged to be modest in comparison with the legislative mandate. While the achievements in Sweden in the work environment area far exceed those of the United States (12), the observer's impression at Swedish places of produc-tion is that there is less active involvement than in organized U.S. workplaces. For the future, one of the challenges for Swedish and Norwegian trade unions is to gain greater active participation by the rank and file members on the job; for the United States the issue is one of having more workers protected by labor agreements and obtaining contracts and new legislative protection that go further toward protecting workers' health.

Although there are challenges in the Norwegian and Swedish contexts and some of the optimism of the late 1970s has been transformed into the realism of the late 1980s, the Scandinavian approach in many ways is exemplary and serves as an inspira-tion for reform efforts elsewhere. In the case of Canada, it is clear how much the influence of Norway and Sweden has affected legislative and policy reform (13). The contributions of the Scandinavian model must be reiterated here. First, a holistic conception of the work environment includes factors beyond the traditional physical and chemical hazards. Second, the application of research on job stress and psycho-social sources of ill-health to the work environment laws is something absent from the U.S. Occupational Safety and Health Act of 1970. Third, a major commitment is made to employee training on work environment improvement, including physical and chemical hazard recognition and abatement along with ergonomics, stress, technology, and other factors. Fourth, employers and unions work toward a joint solution and a process of continuous work environment improvement. Finally, there is a large commitment of major economic and human resources to work environment improve-ment, including research, training, intervention strategies, labor inspectorate, and occupational health services, and in a multitude of institutions and active union programs.

THE CONTEXT FOR WORK ENVIRONMENT REFORM
IN THE UNITED STATES

The labor relations and political context of the United States is in great contrast to that in Sweden and Norway. The system is predicated upon voluntary unionization and free collective bargaining, in contrast to those countries, like those in Scandinavia, which have relied heavily upon legislative reforms to affect decision-making on the job (14). The United States, along with Canada, England, and Australia, follows a model relying upon a decentralized system of voluntary collective bargaining (15). There were 178,000 separate labor-management contracts in 1978 in the United States, albeit less than 1 percent of these covered almost one-third of all unionized workers (16). Since the establishment of the National Labor Relations Act in 1935, government has played a growing role in wage, health, nondiscrimination, and other forms of worker protection, as well as a system of mediation and an active labor law court system. While reform relies primarily upon the private and voluntaristic mode, it is a tripartite system involving government, though to a considerably lesser degree than in the Scandinavian countries and other nations.

In recent years a number of critical shifts have altered the labor relations context and increased the demand for a more active governmental role in the economy. First, the application of new microelectronic technologies has profoundly affected systems of production both in manufacturing and in the service industries, as well as in public employment. The impact has been felt in terms of job dislocation, changes in job skill demands and training, work organization, job tasks, and the work environment (17–19). This has been a major change in the U.S. and world economic scene, and in a later section we will explore some of the specific consequences of new technology at the workplace. Second, massive structural changes have occurred in the economy, reflecting the global competition and reorganization. This is seen in the substantial decline in employment in automobile, steel, electrical appliances, wood products, and other industries. From 1979 to 1984 over 11 million U.S. workers lost their jobs as a result of plant closures and mass lay-offs due to global competition, corporate restructuring, and technological change (20).

In this context of technological and corporate change and new global economic challenge, a shifting emphasis in some quarters of the labor relations community is stressing a cooperative posture to maximize the benefits of the technology and increase productivity to meet the competitive challenge (17, 21, 22). The theme is echoed by some in management, labor, and government. It stresses a cooperative labor-management approach to increase the adaptation of new technologies, to improve production systems and efficiency, and to build in active employee involvement. Along with this, it is argued, must be a more engaged government working in concert with labor and management, as is the case in the United States' competitor nations (23). This line of argument will most likely be successful in many quarters of the economy and, perhaps, in shaping governmental policy and reform efforts into legislative actions. At the same time it must be noted that a parallel mood of active anti-unionism has been thriving in the United States, rejecting the logic of unionism and collective bargaining or power-sharing in decision-making. This "war on labor" is a significant part of contemporary labor relations in the United States and exists alongside a movement for cooperative union-management efforts for mutual benefit.

The decline in employment in the industrial sectors has affected a workforce consisting of largely unionized workers, thus having a major impact on the labor movement. There continues to be some growth of unionization among public employees, now unionized at about twice the rate of those in the private sector. Union growth in the service sector of the economy has been more modest. The labor force has grown to approximately 45 percent female, and 30 percent of union members are women. Only about 8 percent of clerical workers, most of whom are women, are organized. As a result of these trends, the percentage of the U.S. labor force belonging to unions has dropped from the high of about 35 percent to the present rate of about 18 percent. Thus less than one in five workers is under the protection of a collectively negotiated contract specifying hours, wages, and working conditions. Reform affecting all workers must, therefore, go beyond the obvious limitations of collective bargaining.

The influence of foreign reforms affecting worker participation and work environment has been felt in the United States since the beginning of the 1970s, because of the internationalization of the economy and the large number of U.S. multinational firms engaged in production abroad, and the movement of managers and trade unionists across national boundaries. The successes in implementing legislative reforms in Scandinavia, Germany, and elsewhere in the 1970s along with voluntary labor-management participation schemes were brought to the attention of the labor relations practitioners in the United States. By the beginning of the 1980s, a significant number of worker participation programs were in operation, and considerable pressure built for extension of such reform efforts (24). Achievements in Scandinavia, in particular, were accentuated in the labor relations literature and in the field of work environment and occupational stress.

Sweden and Norway weathered the economic challenges of the 1980s much more successfully than did the other nations of Europe or North America. New agreements between the employers and unions were negotiated, emphasizing the need for adopting new technologies and for joint efforts to enhance efficiency in production. The strength of the labor movement and the participatory character of the Norwegian and Swedish labor systems were given credit by many for the flexibility and ability of those economies to shift in production, and for making use of new technologies to meet international global competition. That experience is reflected in the views of some in the U.S. labor and management community as well as policy makers (22, 23).

NEW TECHNOLOGIES AND THE WORK ENVIRONMENT

As noted earlier, the application of microelectronics has been a major source of change at the workplace since the late 1970s. The early "Detroit automation," important in the 1950s and 1960s, was largely limited to mass-production and assembly manufacturing production. In contrast, the silicon chip made the new microelectronic technology highly flexible and inexpensive; hence, it has been applied in manufacturing and service sectors, in the largest factories and the smallest offices. Perhaps one-half of U.S. jobs will be applying microelectronic technology by 1990.

The hazards posed by the new technology cover a wide range of known concerns. Within the United States there is the reality of a permanent high level of unemployment and an economy in which approximately one in five workers in 1987 experienced some involuntary unemployment. Technological change, international competition, and changing markets and corporate structures have produced a high level of anxiety in the workforce. Job loss and feelings of job insecurity have produced very substantial health problems, which have been widely documented in the literature. Depression, suicide, mental illness, spouse and child abuse, alcoholism, obesity, and a wide range of health problems including cardiovascular and gastrointestinal diseases are the result of unemployment and fear of job loss (25).

Each year, 3,000 new chemicals are introduced into U.S. industry, and in the "high-tech" industries such as electronics, many health problems have been linked to the solvents and chemicals used in production, some of which are evidently reproductive hazards and neurotoxins of considerable potency (26). Lasers, biotechnologies, new synthetics, and other features of the new technology contain a number of health hazards, and the evidence is only beginning to accumulate.

Noting the five leading occupational hazards listed by NIOSH—cancer, cardiovascular disease, respiratory diseases, acute trauma injuries, and muscular-skeletal problems—it becomes self-evident that technological change at the workplace poses some threats. NIOSH estimates that 15 to 20 percent of the workforce is at risk for muscular-skeletal problems. Ergonomic problems exist in the areas of manufacturing and increasingly in automated offices where video display terminals (VDTs) are in use.

Perhaps 15 million Americans work with VDTs, making the issue of potential health effects of working with these terminals significant. A growing amount of evidence demonstrates the ergonomic and vision problems, which have been known for some time, the dermatological and reproductive hazards, and especially, the stress hazards (27–32). Unions and health advocates have referred to VDTs as "the asbestos of the 80s," meaning that the issue of job health problems associated with the millions of workers—overwhelmingly female—operating VDTs is slowly emerging, like the slow awareness and serious attention given to asbestos in the 1940s and 1950s as millions of construction, shipyard, and other workers were exposed to a highly toxic substance.

The new microelectronic technology has been used to eliminate tasks that involve health hazards, such as spray painting, welding, and various tasks with repetitive motion and cumulative trauma leading to carpal tunnel syndrome. On the other hand, new technologies have caused many ill effects at the workplace. Poorly designed new-technology work stations have caused carpal tunnel and other ergonomic problems, and there are new hazards with robots (18, 19, 33–37). The design of industrial and office systems has the potential for increasing work load factors and placing workers in greater social isolation while being electronically monitored (38, 39). Furthermore, computer-aided production has led to more continuous operation, especially in manufacturing but also in services. This has meant more shift work, another demonstrable source of stress and a contributor to worsened health and safety on the job (6).

The significance of occupational stress was raised during the 1970s and emerged as a health concern of major importance. Research evidence and growing workers' compensation claims for stress-related illness have placed job stress high on the list of concerns in occupational health (3, 28, 40, 41). The new technologies, with their capabilities for pacing and monitoring work, have considerable potential for contributing to stressful work environments. Employees working on VDTs have given voice to growing numbers of adverse health effects, including job stress (42). Enlightened managers have recognized that involvement of the workforce can reduce health and safety problems for VDT workers (43).

The workplace of today and in the future will increasingly use microelectronic technologies, and the issues of stress and adverse health effects are important for those concerned with improvements in the work environment.

STRATEGIES FOR REFORM

Solving the work environment problems induced by new technology requires a multiplicity of strategies. These include increased awareness and involvement by employees and more active strategies by unions to cope with job stress and the myriad of health hazards in the work environment.

Many have argued that workers must have the basic right to know, right to participate, and right to refuse unsafe and unhealthy work (3). To achieve good work environments, workers need to be active participants and engaged in workplace learning. The process of education and worker activation has been underscored especially by Scandinavian work psychologists and health and labor educators with influence on researchers and worker educators in other countries (44).

The premise of the work by Gardell and other action researchers has been to engage workers in the activity and to have constant interplay between those in the workplace and those attempting to intervene and improve the work environment and study the change process (5, 8). This approach to research and the use of research for policy-making has been a most important contribution and one that will serve as a continuing model for others. It stresses the democratization of the research process itself, as well as the connection between workplace participation and healthy work environments (2, 5).

The challenge of new technology for trade unions has focused importantly upon job security. Job loss or fear of such is a major source of stress and harms health. The contraction of basic manufacturing and the expansion of service sector employment is a pattern in all industrial societies. Chronic high unemployment is endemic to all but a few industrial societies such as Sweden, Norway, and Japan. Thus, unions must deal with strategies for job protection, job creation, and adequate retraining and skills building (15).

The Norwegian Work Environment Act of 1977 gave a clear mandate for the union and workers to be involved in technology questions. This has been a useful model for researchers, work environment reformers, and trade unionists elsewhere. The lesson is clear: workers and their representatives must have influence over the design and implementation of technological change and the work environment. Although union involvement at the appropriate level of decision-making on technology questions is essential, thus far U.S. unions have achieved only modest gains (45).

The first line of action in the United States must be in the collective bargaining arrangement. Unions have exchanged specific ideas about protections related to technology and worker health questions, including the sharing of ideal and actual contract clauses. The Machinists' union has developed a "Technology Workers' Bill of Rights," which formulates a comprehensive strategy for dealing with technology. Gaining protection for job security, retraining rights, guaranteed health and safety linked to new technologies, and other such concerns must be addressed. The issue of initial design of the technology and its implementation is equally important and should form part of future strategic orientations. By the late 1980s considerable sophistication has developed in U.S. trade unions concerning technology matters and appropriate content for negotiated agreements. The problem remains that few ideal contracts have been signed and improvements are very gradual.

The limitations of collective bargaining are due to the imbalance of power, the treatment of technology and work environment issues as permissible rather than mandatory conditions of bargaining, and the fact that only one-fifth of U.S. employees are organized. For these reasons unions have worked in coalition with health professionals, environmental and women's organizations, and others to promote new state job health and safety standards, protective state legislation on plant closings, workers' "right to know" what hazards they are exposed to in the workplace, VDT worker protection, and other such concerns. A similar coalition has pressured the federal government for more research and more active policies to set standards for VDTs and to uniformly inform workers of hazards (19). This lobbying and legislative effort is likely to increase in the next few years as the coalitions strengthen and reforms are implemented. In West Virginia at the unions' urging, the state government passed a law placing restrictions on monitoring telephone employees, although it was later repealed. The issue of electronic monitoring as a job stress and health issue has received considerable attention in the past few years, making reform efforts through legislative action likely (38).

In addition to collective bargaining and legislative reform efforts, in recent years there has been an expansion of worker education on health and safety, technology, participative systems at work, and the connection between these (3). Unions, university labor educators, health professionals, and others have noted the ability of labor-management health and safety committees or joint quality of working life committees to push beyond the limits typically set. This has the potential to make a clearer connection between employee involvement, work environment, and technology issues (45). Worker education is a cornerstone for building effective implementation strategies for worker participation and improved workplace health environments.

CONCLUSIONS

Substantial evidence makes it apparent that increased involvement of workers and their representatives in work environment improvement is beneficial for worker health. The process of work reform is achieved through varying strategies, including legislation, collective bargaining, and informal labor-management relations. Important lessons may be learned from the Scandinavian experiences of connecting workplace hazards, new technologies, job stress, and democratization of the workplace. The legislative approach used in Norway and Sweden cannot be applied directly to the U.S. setting. In the United States, participative management and increased employee involvement has come through collective bargaining and the informal labor-management process (24). However, the factors motivating employers and unions and health professionals derive very much from the research and experience in Norway and Sweden.

A convincing body of research demonstrates that worker activation leads to improved job safety and health (5, 6, 8). Stress reduction is even more specifically related to worker participation. This not only should serve as a motivator for concerned managers, but should also inspire unions.

Programs stressing employee wellness have been a significant development in the U.S. management community in the past few years. In some of these programs stress reduction linked to the work environment has been important. Good management leads logically to a participative mode in which the workforce is actively engaged in the technological and other features of the work environment (46). This comes from research that makes the connection between worker participation and worker health apparent. When health professionals and enlightened managers take the lead in democratic work reorganization plans, they should be lauded.

The reality of U.S. labor relations demands that the union movement not only must work with health professionals and participatory management personnel, but must also aggressively push for work democratization as part of a larger strategy to ensure worker health. The labor movement historically has sought to represent all working men and women, and with only one-fifth of the workforce organized, it will be ever more critical to build coalitions and use the political and legislative process for reform as an adjunct to collective bargaining.

REFERENCES

1. Health, Education and Welfare. *Work in America*. MIT Press, Cambridge, Mass., 1987.
2. Deutsch, S. Work environment reform and industrial democracy. *Work and Occupations* 8(2): 180-194, 1981.
3. Deutsch, S. Extending workplace democracy: Struggles to come in job safety and health. *Labor Studies J.* 6(1): 124-132, 1981.
4. Gardell, B. Psychosocial aspects of industrial production methods. In *Society, Stress and Disease, Vol. IV, Working Life*, edited by L. Levi, pp. 65-75. Oxford University Press, London, 1979.
5. Gardell, B. *Work Organization and Human Nature: A Review of Research on Man's Need to Control Technology*. Swedish Work Environment Fund, Stockholm, 1987.
6. Levi, L. *Preventing Work Stress*. Addison-Wesley, Reading, Mass., 1981.
7. House, J. *Work Stress and Social Support*. Addison-Wesley, Reading, Mass., 1981.
8. Gustavsen, B., and Hunnius, G. *New Patterns of Work Reform: The Case of Norway*. Oslo University Press, Oslo, 1981.
9. Gardell, B., and Gustavsen, B. Work environment research and social change: Current developments in Scandinavia. *J. Occup. Behav.* 1(1): 3-17, 1980.
10. Albrecht, S., and Deutsch, S. The challenge of economic democracy: The case of Sweden. *Economic and Industrial Democracy* 4(2): 287-320, 1983.
11. Hammarström, O. Swedish industrial relations. In *International Comparative Industrial Relations*, edited by G. Bamber and R. Lansbury, pp. 187-207. Allen & Unwin, London, 1987.

12. Kelman, S. *Regulating America, Regulating Sweden: A Comparative Study of Occupational Safety and Health Policy*. MIT Press, Cambridge, Mass., 1987.

13. Sass, R. Alternative policies in the administration of occupational health and safety programs. *Economic and Industrial Democracy* 8(2): 243-257, 1987.

14. Deutsch, S. Voluntaristic and constitutional approaches to worker participation. *Comparative Labor Law* 2(2): 110-121, 1977.

15. Deutsch, S. International experiences with technological change. *Monthly Labor Rev.* 109(3): 35-40, 1986.

16. Windmuller, et al. *Collective Bargaining in Industrialized Market Economies*. International Labour Office, Geneva, 1987.

17. Cyert, R. M., and Mowery, D. C. (eds.). *Technology and Employment*. National Academy Press, Washington, D.C., 1987.

18. U.S. Congress Office of Technology Assessment. *Computerized Manufacturing Automation: Employment, Education and the Workplace*. U.S. Government Printing Office, Washington, D.C., 1984.

19. U.S. Congress Office of Technology Assessment. *Automation of America's Offices: 1985-2000*. U.S. Government Printing Office, Washington, D.C., 1985.

20. U.S. Congress Office of Technology Assessment. *Technology and Structural Unemployment: Re-employing Displaced Adults*. U.S. Government Printing Office, Washington, D.C., 1986.

21. President's Commission on Industrial Competitiveness. *Global Competition: The New Reality*. U.S. Government Printing Office, Washington, D.C., 1987.

22. U.S. Department of Labor. *Economic Adjustment and Worker Dislocation in a Competitive Society*. U.S. Government Printing Office, Washington, D.C., 1986.

23. Marshall, R. *Unheard Voices: Labor and Economic Policy in a Competitive World*. Basic Books, New York, 1987.

24. Deutsch, S., and Albrecht, S. Worker participation in the United States: Efforts to democratise industry and the economy. *Labour and Society* 8(July–September): 241-269, 1983.

25. Roberts, M. Workers without jobs. *AFL-CIO American Federationist*, March 25, 1985, pp. 1-12.

26. U.S. Congress Office of Technology Assessment. *Reproductive Health Hazards in the Workplace*. U.S. Government Printing Office, Washington, D.C., 1985.

27. DeMatteo, R. *Terminal Shock: The Health Hazards of VDTs*. NC Press, Toronto, 1985.

28. Stellman, J., and Henifin, M. *Office Work May be Dangerous to Your Health*. Pantheon, New York, 1983.

29. Smith, M. J., Carayon, P., and Miezio, K. VDT technology: Psychosocial and stress concerns. In *Work with Display Units*, edited by B. Knave and D.-V. Widebäck, pp. 695-712. Elsevier Science Publishers, New York, 1987.

30. Bradley, G. Effects of computerization on work environment and health. *Occup. Health Nursing* 31(11): 35-39, 1983.

31. Slutzker, P. Ergonomics in microelectronic office technology. *Occup. Health Nursing* 33(12): 610-614, 1985.

32. Tabor, M. Worker health in the automated office. *Occup. Health Saf.* 52(4): 22-26, 1983.

33. Brown, I. Ergonomics and technological change. *Ergonomics* 28(9): 1301-1309, 1985.

34. International Labor Office. *The Effects of Technological and Structural Changes on the Employment and Working Conditions of Non-Manual Workers*. ILO, Geneva, 1981.

35. International Labor Office. *New Technologies: The Impact on Employment and the Working Environment*. ILO, Geneva, 1983.

36. U.S. Congress Office of Technology Assessment. *Preventing Illness and Injury in the Workplace*. U.S. Government Printing Office, Washington, D.C., 1985.

37. National Institute for Occupational Safety and Health. *Request for Assistance in Preventing the Injury of Workers by Robots*. NIOSH, Cincinnati, 1984.

38. U.S. Congress Office of Technology Assessment. *The Electronic Supervisor: New Technology, New Tensions*. U.S. Government Printing Office, Washington, D.C., 1987.

39. Nussbaum, K., and duRivage, V. Computer monitoring: Mismanagement by remote control. *Business and Society Rev.* 56(Winter): 16-20, 1986.

40. International Labor Office. *Automation, Work Organization and Occupational Stress*. ILO, Geneva, 1984.

41. National Institute for Occupational Safety and Health. *Potential Health Hazards of Video Display Terminals*. NIOSH, Cincinnati, 1981.

42. Stellman, J. M., Klitzman, S., and Gordon, G. C. Work environment and the well-being of clerical and VDT workers. *J. Occup. Behav.* 8(2): 95-114, 1987.
43. Chapnick, E.-B., and Gross, C. M. Evaluation, office improvements can reduce VDT operator problems. *Occup. Health Saf.* 56(7): 34-37, 1987.
44. Deutsch, S. Worker learning in the context of changing technology and the work environment. *Learning at Work: A New Approach to The Learning Process in the Workplace and Society*, edited by H. Leymann and H. Kornbluh. Gower Press, Aldershot, England, 1988.
45. Deutsch, S. New technology, union strategies and worker participation. *Economic and Industrial Democracy* 7(4): 529-539, 1986.
46. Minter, S. High tech: Its implications for safety management. *Occupational Hazards*, December 1984.

CHAPTER 17

Occupational Health, Stress and Work Organization in Australia

Leigh Deves and Robert Spillane

In Australia, occupational health has emerged as a major "quality of work life" issue, particularly since the introduction of state legislation from the 1970s. This legislation is designed to secure and promote more humane working environments by accommodating the physiological and psychological needs of employees. Furthermore, legislation is intended as a comprehensive replacement for a fragmented and anachronistic regulatory system based in the "social conscience" of the 19th century. But although occupational health is an acknowledged issue on the Australian industrial agenda, there is little evidence of constructive improvements in the quality of work life. This experience seems paradoxical in the context of historical and contemporary influences on Australian industrial life which might be expected to have facilitated work reform. Some of these factors include:

- A tradition of research into the related concepts of stress, fatigue, and monotony at work that dates from the early 1900s.
- Recent research studies into the physiological and psychosocial aspects of stress in several occupational groups which have provided guidelines for work reform consistent with principles derived from earlier Scandinavian research (1).
- Substantial increases in the number of workers' compensation cases in which "occupational stress" is considered a major cause of health problems.
- The introduction of occupational health legislation that places the onus upon employers to provide for employee well-being at work.

Over the past decade, the legitimacy of local reform strategies and the (unintended) consequences of action have generated widespread debate. Conflicting ideological positions, clashes between expert witnesses in litigation proceedings, and unpalatable recommendations from government advisory bodies have characterized the Australian occupational health scene, particularly in respect to the controversial phenomenon known as Repetition Strain Injury (RSI). This phenomenon, which reached epidemic proportions in the 1980s, has been interpreted according to various models that support ideological interests within a highly charged industrial environment. Before proceeding to analyze this phenomenon, an outline of Australian industrial relations is especially indicated.

INDUSTRIAL RELATIONS IN AUSTRALIA

The nature and conduct of industrial relations have been shaped by a history of sustained intervention by federal and state governments. Since the turn of this century, the settlement of industrial disputes has been dominated by tribunals established by legislation. The explicit purpose of the tribunals is the prevention and resolution of industrial conflict at the request of either or both parties in dispute through the processes of conciliation and, if necessary, compulsory arbitration. In a historical context, the legislation provided substantial support for a fledgling union movement which grew from covering 6.1 percent of the labor force in 1901 to approximately 55 percent by the 1980s.

Critics of the arbitration system highlight a legacy of unintended consequences that, it is argued, render the system archaic and incapable of meeting the demands of industrial life in the 1980s. Significant among these criticisms are:

- Restrictive and/or conservative interpretations of legal concepts that protect "managerial prerogatives," thereby providing shelter for "embattled" management, unable or unwilling to deal directly with unions that seek to broaden the industrial agenda.
- A fragmented union movement, plagued by demarcation disputes, that is organized along craft or industry lines, which inhibits consideration of local factors. Efforts to consolidate continue to be resisted strenuously.
- The ease of access to the arbitration process discourages direct negotiation between parties that maintain extreme and antagonistic stances throughout the process. Australian managers and union delegates are therefore relatively inexperienced in consultative and negotiating methods at the company level.

Critics of arbitration advocate widespread reforms that favor broadening the industrial agenda, direct consultation and negotiation between management and labor, and the introduction of worker participation at various levels of organizational decision-making. Although the general ideals of industrial democracy have been endorsed publicly by Australian political parties, managers, and unions, work practices have not changed significantly. A fundamental problem is the lack of consensus about the principles and organizational arrangements necessary to accommodate industrial democracy (2).

One aspect of Australian work life in which the unions have made concerted efforts to expand employee influence concerns occupational health. Australian managers' interests in industrial democracy and occupational health lie primarily in the link between motivation and productivity. Whereas unions have invoked a notion of social justice, the views of management are based firmly on psychological premises and incorporate the paternalism characteristic of the American organizational development movement. Management initiatives center largely on motivational techniques for the individual, team-building, and communication exercises designed to "enhance the attitudinal, behavioral and relational aspects of getting tasks agreed to and effectively accomplished" (3, p. 18). Union perspectives that emphasize joint consultation and participation in decision-making processes are treated with considerable suspicion by management because they are perceived to be "associated with unwelcome political and ideological overtones [which represent] an attack on their ownership and property rights" (4, p. 14).

Politically, successive governments have not been prepared to legislate in favor of any work reform model. Even the Australian Labor Party, which assumed Federal Government in 1983, has forestalled indefinitely traditional social and work reforms expected by the labor movement in favor of macroeconomic concerns. Burdened by deteriorating economic circumstances, the Labor Party has demonstrated a preparedness to implement strategies advocated by economic rationalists and opposed by social-welfare reformists—a substantial shift in political ideology. In particular, it has acted to deregulate selected industries that had previously enjoyed high levels of government protection (e.g., finance, transport) and is moving cautiously toward the (partial) privatization of major public organizations. These examples suggest that economic recovery is to be achieved through private sector operations; industrial practices that inhibit economic performance will be rejected. Although the full economic impact of such strategies is yet to be determined, the implications for the future conduct of industrial relations are far-reaching. Industrial democracy, it would seem, is a "fair weather" concept that currently occupies low priority.

Despite recommendations for sweeping reforms that have emerged from recent inquiries into Australia's system of industrial relations, Australian work organizations remain firmly based on the principles of scientific management with liberal doses of the American human relations movement. Industrial democracy, viewed as an organizational strategy through which substantive and broadly based work reforms can be attained, remains an ideal.

OCCUPATIONAL HEALTH

Arguably the most significant change to occur in Australian work life in recent years has been in the area of occupational health and safety. Alongside other quality of work life issues, such as equal employment opportunity, occupational health and safety has generated considerable discussion in the public and private sectors. The introduction of comprehensive legislation governing health and safety at work has contributed significantly to these developments.

Occupational health and safety is primarily a state government responsibility; each state has its own legislative and administrative machinery dealing with the preventive and compensatory aspects of occupational health and safety. During the late 1970s, several state governments commenced reviews of their armory of preventive legislation. In New South Wales (NSW) for example, a commission of inquiry into occupational health—known as the Williams Report—reported to the Labor Government in 1981, following two years of investigation (5). The Williams Report was indebted to the British Robens Report of the early 1970s (6). Unsurprisingly, common conclusions were reached on several issues concerning the nature, coverage, and administration of legislation and the conflictual nature of occupational health and safety. The Report was critical of the regulatory system in NSW, particularly:

- The inadequacy of existing laws in preventing occupational accidents and ill-health.
- The lack of cohesion between existing laws, which were not only voluminous but also fragmented in subject matter, and differing administrative philosophies that resulted in discrepancies in application.
- The lack of protection given to a large proportion of the workforce despite the plethora of legislation.
- The conflictual nature of occupational health and safety practices in which "management and labour regularly steer collision courses, without much attention being given to the causes of conflict between them, and no means of remedying and resolving their differences" (5, p. 10).
- The preparedness of the trade union movement to compromise the health and safety of members by accepting financial incentives (e.g., danger money) as compensation for dangerous work conditions and practices.

The major recommendations of the Commission were incorporated in the NSW Occupational Health and Safety Act (1983), which is seen as providing a comprehensive and unifying regulatory base.

Clearly, the NSW Act is intended as a preventive law since it aims to "secure the health, safety and welfare of persons at work [by promoting] an occupational environment . . . which is adapted for their physiological and psychological needs" (7, p. 120). By extending the concept of health to include the notion of "psychological well-being," the Act conforms broadly to the conventions of the International Labor Organization and also to workers' compensation statutes in which "psychological illness" has enjoyed the same legal status as organic disease. Employee influence has been recognized formally by the Act, which enables the appointment of elected "employee representatives" to occupational health and safety committees. Workplace committees have review and investigative functions; however, their power is limited to recommendations. Disputes unable to be resolved within the local committee structure can be referred to the government inspectorate for arbitration that is binding upon the committee for legal purposes. Arguably the most sensitive part of the Act is the section that imposes a general and *absolute* duty upon employers to ensure the health, safety, and welfare of workers, breach of which renders them liable to criminal prosecution.

Legal critics have been quick to point out the anomalies, inadequacies, and inappropriateness of the legislation. Outstanding amongst these has been Merritt (8), who, although supportive of a legislative framework to facilitate prevention or limitation of occupational injury or disease, has questioned the foundations of local occupational health and safety legislation, particularly those laws that have adopted a "Robens style" approach. She argues that Australians have become over-reliant upon the law to provide answers to problems that are not of a legal nature or making. The unquestioning commitment to the law as a first rather than last resort, symptomatic of the general conduct of industrial relations in Australia, has worked to the detriment of educative measures as the preferred strategy (8, p. 17):

> The legislation can and should, in at least the majority of situations, provide guidance as to what society expects, and can feasibly expect, in the quest for safe and healthy workplaces. We must redouble our efforts to provide that guidance and to provide education as to how safe and healthy workplaces can be provided. But, insofar as legislation is not the *best* way to do that, or insofar as, in some cases, it is not possible to do that by legislation *at all*, we do not solve the problem by turning the criminal law into an arbitrary and unpredictable avenue of punishment.

For Merritt, the question is not so much one of employer obligation but rather knowing what is to be complied with and also the means of compliance.

Operational concerns have been raised by both management and the labor movement. At one extreme, management argues that this type of legislation is tyrannical. It represents an unwarranted invasion of managerial prerogatives and of the employment relationship, which, with the workers' compensation system, will bring industry to its knees under an avalanche of union demands and impractical codes and standards imposed by an unsympathetic government bureaucracy. Traditionally, management has favored self-regulation and adhered to "minimum standards," reasonably secure in the knowledge that the chance of prosecution by inspectors was negligible. If Australian managers find the legislative approach adopted in recent years a bitter pill to swallow, they have largely themselves to blame.

At the other extreme, the trade union movement also has found little to eulogize in the legislation. Their argument is premised on the belief that reforms needed to create more humane working conditions are contingent upon the ability of the union to extend employee influence by participation in corporate decision-making processes. To the extent that the occupational health and safety laws in general curtail this influence, by restricting the functions and power of local workplace committees to demand changes in work practices for example, changes are seen as cosmetic and substantive work reforms are unlikely to be achieved. This has led some unions to seek greater rights and powers for employee representatives, such as the right to inspect, obtain information, issue prohibition notices, and initiate prosecutions, with or without the sanction of workplace committees. In short, it is argued that the legislation is a sham which, although providing for consultation, has not "ushered in any 'brave new world' of participative industrial democracy" at the level of operations (9, p. 125).

Occupational stress has also become a crucial industrial medico-legal issue. Cases before industrial tribunals have utilized the concept of "stressful working conditions" in support of changes to work practices, while stress is thought to be a major cause of ill-health or even death (10). For compensation purposes, stress-related diseases are not confined to somatic disorders but may include "mental" illnesses, such as neurotic and psychotic conditions. Furthermore, the law provides for compensation in cases where (pre-) existing physical or psychological conditions have been "aggravated," "accelerated," or "exacerbated," or have "deteriorated" in the course of employment that has been deemed a contributory factor. Consequently, managers and union officials are expected to have knowledge of the symptoms of stress, the conditions likely to produce these symptoms, and methods for ameliorating them. Understandably, managers and unions have adopted different attitudes to occupational stress. Furthermore, confusion continues to confront researchers and practitioners because of ill-defined theories and methodological difficulties in the study of occupational stress, work environments, and illness.

One strategy that has sought to place the debate about occupational stress on a more secure foundation is psychophysiological assessment of work behavior. Studies applying this methodology have been completed for shiftworkers (11), clothing workers (12), aircraft cabin crew (13), and bank officers (14). These studies have demonstrated a physiological cost attached to work that may be deleterious to health, thus suggesting the need to reduce stress through job redesign. However, recent experiences in the application of occupational health strategies point to important difficulties.

The Repetition Strain Injury phenomenon in Australia uncovered an inherent danger in the use of occupational health as a strategy to achieve work reform. Whereas stress research has provided guidelines for constructive work reform that emphasize autonomy, participation, and control at work, the RSI phenomenon has resulted in coercive work practices and has generated considerable industrial litigation. This phenomenon emphasizes the problems that arise when moral conflicts are interpreted as medical problems.

REPETITION STRAIN INJURY

It would be difficult to overstate the impact the RSI phenomenon has had on Australian work life. In terms of magnitude and emotional reactions, RSI has had no peer in the history of occupational health in this country. The phenomenon was, for example, held accountable for the near collapse of compensation systems, skyrocketing insurance premiums, industrial disputes, protest marches, parliamentary questions, "unfair" work dismissals, redesigned work stations, etc., and it was also the subject of numerous public inquiries. Apart from Repetition Strain Injury it has been called tenosynovitis, an occupational neurosis, an epidemic, malingering, and a (regional) pain syndrome. It has been attributed to a host of factors that include magnesium deficiencies, fluoride excesses, female hormones, postural complaints, muscle fatigue, stress, and many others. More "colorful" expressions such as Kangaroo Paw, Golden Wrist, and the relabeled acronym Retrospective Supplementary Income, highlight the peculiarity and prevalence of this phenomenon, which has been described as "an Australian disease [that] has become the largest and most prolonged such epidemic in history" (15).

Incidence

Prior to the late 1970s, RSI was unknown in occupational medicine. Process workers, in particular, did suffer from known musculoskeletal disorders, especially inflammatory conditions (e.g., tenosynovitis). However, compensation statistics indicate that the numbers were low and had been relatively static for many years. Statistically, the "epidemic" commenced around 1978, when substantial increases in the number of registered compensation cases started, and continued well into the 1980s. The increases could not be explained easily by changes in the size or composition of the workforce, the nature of the work process, or the compilation of official statistics. Table 1 provides evidence of the increases in compensation statistics in NSW, where the number of new "musculoskeletal" cases grew from about 980 in 1978-79 to 4,550 in 1983-84—a remarkable and unparalleled increase of some 360 percent. By 1983-84, these cases represented 28.5 percent of total disease cases in NSW compensation statistics.

Large organizations, particularly in the public sector, and other Australian states recorded similar increases, though direct comparisons are difficult owing to variations in collating conventions. Unofficial estimates place the national total in excess of 20,000 workers, which is probably not an exaggeration given that almost 4,000 cases were recorded in the Australian Public Service in the December 1985 quarter; 87.3 percent received compensation and 0.3 percent were refused. Other outstanding features of the "epidemic" have been:

- The dominance of females, who account for 60 to 65 percent of the NSW totals, which probably reflects the high proportion of women in jobs that involve repetitive tasks (e.g., typing, machining).
- The change in incidence pattern. No longer were these injuries associated exclusively with process work, as clerical staff working in traditionally "safe" white-collar areas began reporting "injuries" in increasingly large numbers.
- An incidence pattern inconsistent with exposure to repetitive tasks. Some organizations or work divisions remain relatively "unscathed" whereas others report not only a large incidence, but a pattern suggestive of a "contagious" element, in that workers are affected in quick succession.

Table 1

New cases of musculoskeletal diseases in NSW,
1970-71 to 1983-84[a]

Year	Males	Females	Total
1970-71	240	400	640
1971-72	310	450	760
1972-73	230	500	730
1973-74	300	640	940
1974-75	490	580	1,070
1975-76	320	410	730
1976-77	300	370	670
1977-78	310	420	730
1978-79	360	620	980
1979-80	710	1,020	1,730
1980-81	820	1,400	2,220
1981-82	1,100	1,750	2,850
1982-83	1,200	1,950	3,150
1983-84	1,600	2,950	4,550

[a]Source: Adapted from NSW Compensation Statistics cited by NOHSC (17).

Perspectives on RSI

An outstanding feature of the debate about these musculoskeletal complaints, relabeled under the generic term RSI, has been the lack of agreement amongst the "experts" about the nature, causes, and prevention of the phenomenon, which understandably created confusion and fear in the minds of employers, faced with "outbreaks" of RSI and rising compensation premiums, and workers who are considered "at risk" by exposure to repetitive tasks. Spillane and Deves (16) have outlined the four major perspectives invoked to account for the upsurge in RSI, which may be summarized briefly.

Medical Model: Workers suffer a diagnosable physical condition that requires medical intervention. Prevention entails removal from and subsequent modification of the precipitating cause(s), which are biomechanical in nature. This model was endorsed by the National Occupational Health and Safety Commission (NOHSC) in its 1985 report (17), which was criticized extensively because it ignored the influence of psychosocial factors and gave RSI a medical legitimacy that was unwarranted owing to the absence of *clinical signs* necessary to sustain a disease or injury interpretation. In the overwhelming majority of RSI cases, perhaps as many as 90 percent according to medical experts (18, 19), diagnosis is based exclusively on *symptoms*, mainly complaints of pain.

Psychiatric Model: Lucire (20) argued that, in the absence of clinical signs, workers are not physically injured but rather suffer *a conversion or a somatization disorder*, phenomena that closely mimic physical problems and are beyond voluntary control. Recovery rests upon resolution of "intrapsychic conflicts," which may or may not be work related. This model drew vehement criticism from the labor movement on ideological grounds because it discounts occupational factors (e.g., repetitive tasks) as primarily causal.

Malingering Model: Workers are not suffering any affliction, either physical or psychological. Rather they are perceived as pursuing a conscious and subjectively rational strategy to attain concessions in the form of compensation, sick days, etc. This view "caused a public furore for it simultaneously impugns the motives of the worker and the diagnostic skills of the medical profession. Nonetheless it is not unknown for people to feign illness to achieve personal ends" (16, p. 45).

Patienthood Model: This model characterizes RSI as a *social* phenomenon that is best understood by focusing upon the behavior of workers in terms of the social role of *patienthood* (21). Complex and diverse psychosocial factors, rather than any physical sensation per se, underpin the decision to complain, albeit symbolically. For example, in a large comparative study, Spillane and Deves (22) found that RSI reporting was correlated significantly with "adverse" personal experiences at work, such as a lack of autonomy over work practices, dissatisfaction with the physical work environment, and poor interpersonal relationships with superiors. Similar psychosocial factors have been identified in studies of "mass psychogenic illness" in occupational contexts (23). According to the patienthood model then, RSI may be seen as a broad movement that provides a convenient and socially acceptable medium through which discontent about the nature and conditions of work can be communicated symbolically, thereby facilitating personal coping.

To understand more fully the RSI phenomenon, it is necessary to give an account of the social processes that led to and maintained this "epidemic."

Pain, discomfort, and functional disorders of a transient nature have long been recognized as occupational hazards. In Australia, problems of this nature have attracted mild interest and applied research conducted by occupational physiologists. In 1961, Perrott (24) and Peres (25) conducted independent studies and commented on the prevalence of these sorts of simple muscle complaints, particularly amongst process workers. Medical intervention was required rarely, and the problems were generally overcome by rest and prevented by adopting uncomplicated changes to work practices—for example, simple task modifications, training, rest pauses, etc. Later researchers studied similar problems based on complaints about pain at work (26, 27). In the small minority of cases the problem was diagnosed as a known disorder, such as tenosynovitis, which has been associated with occupational use and is usually relieved by conservative medical treatment. For the majority of "ill defined symptom complexes," to use the term Ferguson (25) employed in 1971, the advice offered by earlier researchers was confirmed. However, psychosocial factors both in and beyond the work environment were also thought to be important in the incidence, persistence, and prevention of these complaints.

What can be deduced from the work of these early researchers is that the symptoms of pain and discomfort at work were, by their estimates, widespread, and that amelioration of these problems was relatively simple and did not require extensive medical intervention. But despite the prevalence of these complaints in industry, there were not *large numbers of people entering the medical system for protracted periods or seeking claims as compensation for "damage."* Nor were the complaints the subject of industrial conflict at the local level or any other forum in industry. Workers were experiencing pain and discomfort, their actions were constructive personally and occupationally, and were directed toward *overcoming* their symptoms and assumed causes. They were neither inclined nor encouraged to adopt the helpless and dependent role of patienthood. But neither did workers seek to use their personal experience of pain and discomfort in a political arena, despite the availability of this line of redress, either because their problems were dealt with appropriately at the local level or because they risked penalties for complaining. Prior to the RSI phenomenon, then, pain and discomfort experienced at work were not considered, for better or worse, a major personal or industrial issue. The problems arose and were dealt with locally.

This historical situation provides a stark contrast to the strategies adopted in the 1980s by the principal actors, supported by various advisers. What has changed is not the bodily processes—workers continue to face pain and discomfort—but *behavioral strategies*, which changed from consultation and cooperation to confrontation and stand-offs fought out in circumstances that extend well beyond the local level. Both parties invoke the advice of counsel (medical, legal), not in a spirit that has led to constructive resolution of work issues but rather to justify an adversarial stance.

In the absence of diagnosable clinical signs to substantiate the notion of a somatic disease or injury (e.g., tenosynovitis), workers are accused of malingering or attempting to shirk work responsibilities, or are labeled mentally ill (e.g., occupational neurosis attributable to "intrapsychic conflicts" that have little, if anything, to do with the work environment). Having had their motives impugned and personal experiences devalued, workers are understandably threatened by such allegations and, as might be expected, are encouraged to retaliate by a union movement keen to establish a new power base in occupational health and safety. Retaliation occurs through medical certification, and RSI sufferers are judged ill and removed from the workplace for indefinite periods.

Armed with certification, workers have medically sanctioned access to a compensation system that, in Australia, does little to encourage recovery and penalizes people who actively seek to regain health. Personal activity is further discouraged on the advice of trade unions because insurance companies, facing large payouts and hard pressed to justify additional premiums, are known to employ private investigators whose evidence, admissible in industrial courts, may prove embarrassing to the plaintiff. Faced with the prospect of jeopardizing their claim, workers have little choice but to adopt the patient role and assume a state of helplessness and dependency. It is from this state that psychological problems (e.g., depression, anxiety, etc.) associated with RSI emerge, but importantly, as secondary or "iatrogenic" consequences (28) and not as necessary or sufficient causal mechanisms, as has been claimed. Such secondary conditions may require further "medical" (i.e., psychiatric) intervention. The nature of the processes involved in this industrial context rather than an "injury" per se may account for the large-scale persistence of symptoms beyond the time that could be reasonably expected for pain and discomfort.

The fact that RSI is not and never has been medically recognized for clinical purposes but has come to be granted legitimacy in Australia begs explanation. In 1985 the NOHSC report on RSI offered the following definition: "RSI is a soft tissue disorder caused by the overloading of particular muscle groups from repeated use or maintenance of constrained postures" (17, p. 51). This definition overlooks the fact that RSI is a residue constructed from the process of differential diagnosis and was formerly called pain and discomfort. The term was *invented* in the early 1980s as a matter of medical convenience by physicians specializing in occupational health. It was never intended for diagnostic purposes, nor for use in any proceedings allied to or arising from the clinical function (e.g., litigation). By employing the term RSI, contemporary practitioners ignored the warnings of earlier researchers, such as Perrott, who explicitly disapproved the use of such terms because he believed that they may serve only to inhibit the search for or conceal the true nature of lesions. Shorthand terms may reflect short-sighted medical practice.

That the term escaped from this limited context to gain widespread acceptance in medicolegal proceedings is not attributable to any conspiracy but to injudicious medical practices in a highly charged industrial environment. The trade union movement, understandably concerned by management's reticence about the concept, sought to secure it through workers' health centers by referring to RSI as a "crippling" disease of "epidemic" proportions (29). Management's efforts to substitute malingering or psychiatric interpretations served only to heighten unions' concerns. Subsequent government reports by bodies such as NOHSC further institutionalized the concept of RSI by the issuance of dicta and codes of practice that failed to take adequate account of the social context and processes involved in the RSI phenomenon. Furthermore, the guidelines offered by NOHSC with the ostensible aim of reforming work practices throughout industry involve establishing work routines, standardizing work practices, and scrutinizing workers. These guidelines, apparently destined for legislation, are almost the complete antithesis of the principles of work reform that emerge from research into occupational stress, which emphasize *employee* control of job demands.

The real victims of the RSI phenomenon are both employees and employers. By failing to take constructive and local action in the first instance and by allowing important issues to go unresolved and escalate into significant industrial disputes leading ultimately to government intervention, both parties have foregone an important opportunity to work cooperatively toward the reform of work practices and conditions.

Spillane and Deves (16) have argued that RSI is a "medical myth" to indicate that this phenomenon is a socioindustrial movement and not a medical epidemic. This movement has been built upon a changing set of attitudes and behaviors toward the experience of pain and discomfort in an occupational setting that captures the fears, traditions, and prejudices of Australian industrial life and leads to a redefinition of self from a state of health to one of illness and patienthood. To the extent that few escape happily from the medicolegal system and that more coercive and heteronomous work practices have been implemented, the RSI phenomenon has proved detrimental to both the individual and Australian society.

CONCLUSIONS

The current state of occupational health in Australia is a product of the traditions and practices apparent in the broader industrial context, and many lessons still need to be learned by all parties. The addiction to the legal system and adversarial strategies continues to haunt. The efficacy of solutions, sometimes novel, to industrial issues is contingent upon negotiated settlements at the local level—a process that is best served by joint consultation and cooperation between the principal parties. The view that economic factors must always assume priority is unnecessarily parochial because it assumes that economics and work reform, through occupational health and safety, are mutually exclusive or antagonistic concepts. Work reform provides an opportunity to reinforce economic objectives, and thus the two concepts can be complementary. The recent use of the medical model in the RSI phenomenon has proved illuminating but has had unfortunate consequences. By medicalizing moral conflicts in work relationships, the attainment of more humane working environments has had a significant—but, one hopes, temporary—setback.

REFERENCES

1. Frankenhaeuser, M. Coping with job stress—a psychobiological approach. In *Working Life: A Social Science Contribution to Work Reform,* edited by B. Gardell and G. Johansson, pp. 213-233. Wiley, New York, 1981.
2. Lansbury, R. D., and Spillane, R. *Organisational Behaviour: The Australian Context.* Longman Cheshire, Melbourne, 1983.
3. Industrial Democracy Project Team. *The Democratization of Work in Australia,* Working Paper No. 2. Australian National University, Canberra, 1983.

4. Davis, E. M., and Lansbury, R. D. Democracy and control in the workplace: An introduction. In *Democracy and Control in the Workplace*, edited by E. M. Davis and R. D. Lansbury, pp. 1–29. Longman Cheshire, Melbourne, 1986.
5. *Report of the Commission of Inquiry into Occupational Health and Safety in New South Wales* (Williams Report). NSW Government Printing Service, Sydney, 1981.
6. *Report of the Committee on Safety and Health at Work, 1970–72* (Robens Report). Secretary of State for Employment, England, 1972.
7. Merritt, A. *Australian Occupational Health and Safety Laws*, Ed. 2. CCH Australia Ltd., Sydney, 1986.
8. Merritt, A. Rethinking occupational health and safety legislation–a re-appraisal of the Robens style of prescription for health and safety at work. Unpublished, University of New South Wales, 1987.
9. Creighton, B. Worker participation in occupational health and safety: "Applied" industrial democracy? In *Democracy and Control in the Workplace*, edited by E. M. Davis and R. D. Lansbury, pp. 108–132. Longman Cheshire, Melbourne, 1986.
10. Spillane, R. Stress at work: A review of Australian research. *Int. J. Health Serv.* 14(4): 589–604, 1984.
11. Wallace, M. (ed.). *Shiftwork in Australia*. Brain-Behaviour Research Institute, La Trobe University, Bundoora, Australia, 1983.
12. Romas, N., et al. The effects of automation and piecework on urinary catecholamine responses. *J. Occup. Health Safety Aust. N.Z.* 3(5): 515–523, 1987.
13. Bassett, J., and Spillane, R. Urinary cortisol excretion and mood ratings in aircraft cabin crew during a tour of duty involving a disruption in circadian rhythm. *Pharmacol. Biochem. Behav.* 27(3): 413–420, 1987.
14. Bassett, J., Marshall, P., and Spillane, R. The physiological measurement of acute stress (public speaking) in bank employees. *Int. J. Psychophysiol.* 5: 265–273, 1987.
15. Lucire, Y. RSI: When emotions are converted. *Safety in Australia*, February 1986, p. 8.
16. Spillane, R., and Deves, L. RSI: Pain, pretense or patienthood? *J. Industr. Relations* 29: 41–48, 1987.
17. National Occupational Health and Safety Commission. *Interim Report of the RSI Committee*. Australian Government Publishing Service, Canberra, July 1985.
18. Lowy, A. What is RSI? Submission to National Occupational Health and Safety Commission, Sydney, July 1985.
19. Owen, R. R. Instrumental musicians and RSI. *J. Occup. Health Safety Aust. N.Z.* 1(2): 135–139, 1985.
20. Lucire, Y. Neurosis in an Occupational Setting. Paper presented at RSI: Medical Mythology, Social Impacts, November 1985.
21. Szasz, T. *Insanity: The Idea and Its Consequences.* Wiley, New York, 1987.
22. Spillane, R., and Deves, L. Psychosocial correlates of RSI reporting. *J. Occup. Health Safety Aust. N.Z.* 4(1): 21–27, 1988.
23. Colligan, M. J., and Murphy, L. R. Mass psychogenic illness in organisations: An overview. *J. Occup. Psychol.* 52(2): 77–90, 1979.
24. Perrott, J. W. Anatomical factors in occupational trauma. *Med. J. Aust.* 1: 73–82, 1961.
25. Peres, N. J. C. *Human Factors in Industrial Strains*. Tait Publishing, Melbourne, 1961.
26. Ferguson, D. Repetition injury in process workers. *Med. J. Australia* 2: 408–412, 1971.
27. Welch, R. The causes of tenosynovitis in industry. *Industr. Med.* 41(10): 14–16, 1972.
28. Illich, I. *Limits to Medicine*. Marion Boyars, London, 1976.
29. Walker, J. A crippling new epidemic in industry. *New Doctor* 13: 19–21, 1979.

CHAPTER 18

The Implications of Work Organization for Occupational Health Policy: The Case of Canada

Robert Sass

BACKGROUND

Labor legislation is under provincial jurisdiction in Canada. As a result, each province and territory has its own occupational health and safety legislation. In addition, the federal government has laws that pertain to its own employees as well as employees of industries under its jurisdiction. Despite this diversity, occupational health and safety laws were passed in most jurisdictions during the 1970s that had the effect of broadening traditional health and safety concerns. This was achieved through the promulgation of statute and regulations that gave workers the formal legal right to participate in work environment matters. More specifically, they were given the right to know about hazardous chemicals, to participate with management through joint health and safety committees, and, under certain conditions, to refuse work believed to be unsafe.

The Province of Saskatchewan was the first to legally establish joint health and safety committees in 1972, and the following year passed an amendment that gave workers the right to refuse dangerous work. This approach was thereafter adopted by each provincial federation of labor, and in time, became part of public policy.

Saskatchewan policy in the early 1970s paralleled developments in Scandinavia with regard to the inclusion of worker rights pertaining to work environment matters in statute. By the mid-1970s, Scandinavian research and legal developments became the rationale for 17 new amendments to the Saskatchewan Occupational Health and Safety Act in 1977, and for new health and safety committee Regulations in 1981.

SCANDINAVIAN INFLUENCES

The empirical basis for the 1970s' extension of worker rights in workplace health and safety, and for the unions' demand to extend the legal definition of health and safety to encompass the broader concept of the "work environment," emanates primarily from Scandinavian research developments, especially the research of Bertil

Gardell and his associates (1). These researchers have contributed enormously to public policy matters not only in Scandinavia, but in Canada as well. Their empirical research findings directly influenced the approach taken by the Saskatchewan government to work environment matters. Gardell's investigations of the effects of job characteristics on the well-being of workers both on and off the job contributed in shifting the emphasis of public policy from the "medical" model to the nature of work (job design and the organization of work). Of particular importance was his research finding that workers in low-status, low-control jobs developed less problem-solving ability than the same category of workers in "better" jobs (2). The Scandinavian research, combined with Scandinavian legislation, established a framework in which work environment reforms were developed in Canada. It became more obvious to many Canadian health and safety "activists," as well as to the leadership of the Saskatchewan Occupational Health and Safety Branch, that industrial democracy and effective worker participation in work environment matters represented a necessary approach and long-term strategy for achieving a healthier and safer work environment. More specifically, it became apparent that the democratization of workplace decision-making, so that workers can influence their work environment, held out the greatest promise for the betterment of working conditions. Many recognized this alternative and advocated further worker rights in health and safety in both statute and collective bargaining.

This approach challenged the prevailing "conventional wisdom" regarding public health and safety policy in Canada. The reformers made continuous reference to the Swedish and Norwegian legislative framework as part of an attempt to legitimate a rights-based approach to workplace health and safety. Specifically, they referred to Section 12 of the Norwegian Work Environment Act (1977), which relates to how work is arranged, including the following: the nature of tasks and physical problems, working alone, work organization concerns, shift work, wage payment systems, work routines, boring and monotonous work, authoritarian leadership patterns, and lack of participation by workers, especially as a result of the introduction of new technology.

These issues covered by the Norwegian legislation are all legitimate items for union negotiation in Sweden under the Codetermination Act (1978). However, they are generally beyond the scope of Canadian occupational health and safety legislation so that workers are unable to raise these concerns through the mandatory health and safety committees.

In 1981, Saskatchewan regulations first introduced the term "work environment" as part of the workers' right to know about hazardous substances in their place of work. The regulation reads (3; emphasis added):[1]

> Every employer shall ensure that the worker representatives on the committee or, where there is no committee, the workers are kept fully informed of any information in the employer's possession concerning the *work environment* and the occupational health and safety of workers at that place of employment.

[1]This regulation was proclaimed effective May 17, 1981, pursuant to the Occupational Health and Safety Act, Section 13.

The above regulation has "work environment" concerns preceding "occupational health and safety" in order to demonstrate public policy direction. At the same time, an experimental Work Environment Board (WEB) was established in one of the major provincial crown corporations, the Potash Corporation of Saskatchewan (P.C.S.) (4). The WEB was composed of a parity of representatives of the three certified trade unions, the Director of Mining, and managers from each of the four mines of P.C.S. The WEB also negotiated a Work Environment Fund to assist financially with all work environment matters, including psychosocial considerations (5).

As a result of this experiment, there was agreement between the Saskatchewan Minister of Labour and the chairperson of the Workers' Compensation Board to transform the existing joint occupational health and safety committees into WEBs with the power to negotiate monies from the employers for a "work environment fund" as well as to receive monies from the Workers' Compensation Board. Therefore, workers would have money to do their own occupational health research, bring in their own "experts," and visit other plants to see varied and alternative technical solutions to the problems they identified. This money would also activate the health and safety committees at each of the mine sites.

The transformation of joint occupational health and safety committees into WEBs, with a worker majority and control over a work environment fund to finance research appropriate to worker needs, was intended to be the next phase in the Saskatchewan program. This program had begun a decade earlier with three worker rights: to know, to participate, and to refuse dangerous work based upon a belief. This policy direction occurred after the chairperson of the P.C.S. Work Environment Board, who was also Director of the Occupational Health and Safety Branch, met with Bertil Gardell in 1979. At that time Gardell's advice was to study the Norwegian Work Environment Act more carefully. Gardell believed the Norwegian legislation to be more appropriate to the Saskatchewan situation than the Swedish Codetermination Act, which required that work environment matters be negotiated by an intermediate body. He favored the whole range of "work environment" issues being handled by the mandatory joint occupational health and safety committees which were legislated in Saskatchewan since 1972. These committees had become institutionalized in every place of employment with ten or more workers, and the legitimate items for these committees to deal with should legally be extended to work organization and job design issues. This approach would keep the identification of problems and solutions closer to the shop floor and to those concerned about the resolution.

Gardell noted that work environment issues were difficult to regulate. Therefore, public policy could offer only general guidelines, while the committees could make the actual content concrete. His advice became the basis for a long-term policy direction of the Saskatchewan Occupational Health and Safety Branch, and the rationale for the 1981 Health and Safety Regulations.

In April 1982, after the proclamation of the Saskatchewan health and safety regulations and the adoption of policies suggested by Scandinavian developments, the Saskatchewan government was defeated by the Progressive Conservative Party and these developments came to an end. The defeat of the social democratic government in Saskatchewan reflected a growing conservative political trend throughout Canada. Nonetheless, there have been some initiatives in workplace health and safety, most notably in the area of workers' right to know about hazardous substances. The federal government did pass "catch-up" legislation in the area of worker rights (to know, participate, and refuse) in March 1986, and in June 1987 passed legislation pertaining to the provision of information to workers and appropriate labeling of hazardous materials. Ontario, the largest province in Canada, had already amended its Occupational Health and Safety Act so as to require all suppliers and employers to label "hazardous materials," to provide workers and the public with information of the dangers of such materials, and to provide training to workers on how to use the information in the "hazardous substances inventory" (6).

The Ontario legislation goes farther than the requirements of the federal legislation and incorporates many of the provisions adopted in Saskatchewan in 1981 regarding labeling of chemicals in the workplace and the establishment of a registry of chemicals. In June 1987, the Ontario Ministry of Labour set up a bipartite committee of labor and management to examine existing chemical standards, having adopted the American Conference of Governmental and Industrial Hygiene standards earlier that year. The present government in Ontario is seeking ways to increase labor's participation in the administration and direction of the occupational health and safety program.

There is, at the same time, increasing concern among workers and unions about the negative effects of stressful work environments on employee health. Canadian researchers have been sensitive to this growing concern, especially during the 1980s, when legislative initiatives were minimal and enforcement and compliance of existing standards was negligible.

Canadian studies increasingly reported on the relationship between job characteristics as "stressors" and health and mental health problems. Coburn (7) found that workers with high levels of work alienation due to the performance of repetitive, boring, and unchallenging tasks with little decision-making power tended to report lower job satisfaction and worse mental and physical health. The Canadian Labour Congress investigated the impact of video display terminals on employee health (8). There have been "stress" studies of Quebec fish-processing plants (9), air traffic controllers (10), nurses (11), postal workers (12), and other occupations (13). To a large extent, Canadian studies in the 1980s supported the earlier Scandinavian research and have increased trade union awareness of many potential workplace stressors and of the problems associated with increasing demands put on a worker who lacks control to influence the work environment.

The Canadian legislative reforms of the 1970s and the present public policy efforts to make information more accessible to workers have not altered the balance of power between managers and workers at the workplace in any meaningful way. Worker members on joint health and safety committees in all Canadian jurisdictions are advisory and have no legislative authority to enforce penalties for violations of regulations or to veto the introduction of machinery or new work processes or practices. There is a growing interest by unions throughout Canada to follow the Swedish or Western Australian example by extending worker rights so that a worker representative on the committee is able to stop any unsafe work. This authority is given to the worker inspectors under a collective agreement provision in the uranium mines at Elliot Lake in Northern Ontario.

CANADIAN WORKPLACE ILLNESS AND INJURY TRENDS

The incidence of worker illness and injury rate worsened during the decade of reform. Despite increased government intervention during the 1970s, and greater public awareness of the dangers, there were 1,208,000 occupational injuries in 1980 (52 percent above the 1971 level). When the increase in the labor force is accounted for, accidents per employed worker still rose by 16 percent. At the end of the decade, some 5,000 workers were injured each day, compared with just over 3,000 ten years earlier. The study also found that estimates of total costs in 1980 stood at over $6.7 billion, a rise of 320 percent in the ten years. This represents 2.3 percent of the gross national product and $5,560 per claim or $745 per employed worker. Even after adjustment for inflation, costs doubled from 1971 to 1980 (14).

Charles Reasons (15) estimated that in 1975, occupational disease and injury was the third largest killer in Canada, higher than motor vehicle accidents. Table 1 indicates Canadian death rate by cause.

Canada's poor record in this area reflects serious deficiencies in the major public policy instruments designed to prevent industrial injury and disease. The major policy instruments are statute and regulations, standard-setting, workers' compensation legislation, enforcement and compliance procedures, collective bargaining, and the ultimate sanction of prosecution by the courts (16). These policy instruments reflect a particular kind of economic "utilitarianism" in which health and safety issues are

Table 1

Canadian death rate by cause, 1975[a]

	No. of deaths	Rate, per 100,000 population
Heart disease[b]	56,970	250.0
Cancer	33,998	149.0
Occupational death[c]	8,265	48.3
Motor vehicle accident	5,896	25.9
Pneumonia	5,454	23.9
Suicide	2,808	12.3
Cirrhosis of liver	2,725	12.0
Peptic ulcer	735	3.2
Murder	633	2.8

[a]Sources: *Canada Yearbook*, 1978–79, Ministry of Supply and Services, Ottawa, Ont.; *The World Almanac and Book of Facts*, 1980. Newspaper Enterprise Association, Inc., New York, 1980.

[b]Heart disease deaths will include many work-related causes, in whole or in part, such as short-term and long-term physical and emotional stress and toxic pollutants. While this probably runs into thousands, no reliable estimates are available.

[c]This total includes adding 25 percent to the deaths reported by workmen's compensation (because compensation covers approximately 75 percent of the Canadian workforce) and 20 percent of the cancer deaths in Canada in 1975 (because the conservative scientific estimate is that at least 20 percent of cancer deaths are occupationally related). The base population includes those 15 years and older.

consistently "traded-off" for economic considerations and market values. For this reason, legislated worker rights in this area are basically "weak rights."

Since the late 1970s in Canada, we have witnessed the "triumph" of *economic* utilitarianism and the strengthening of management prerogatives and property rights in the employment contract. Worker rights in work environment matters have been eroded during the 1980s and represent, at best, a "weak" instrumental right without regard to the fact that workdays lost through work injuries and illness continued to climb during the decade of the 1970s (17) (Figure 1).

WORKER RIGHTS AS "WEAK RIGHTS"

While a strong empirical argument can be made for meaningful worker participation in decision-making in work environment matters, resistance to this approach by both employers and regulatory agencies in Canada is evident in all jurisdictions. Employers have opposed the granting of meaningful worker rights in health and safety primarily because they view work environment matters as an essential component of management prerogatives.

Management rights under common law explicitly vest the employer with sole control over the business and management of its affairs. The individual contract of employment at common law emphasizes the limited nature of the parties' relationship

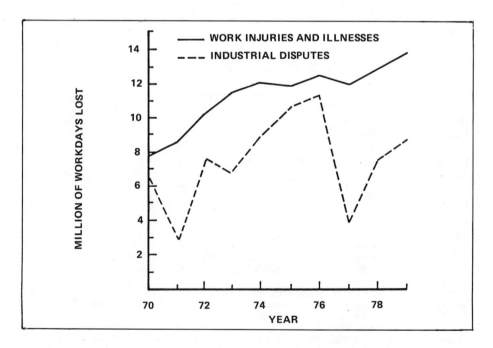

Figure 1. Workdays lost through work injuries and illness, and through industrial disputes in Canada, 1970–79. Sources: Work injury and illness, Labour Canada; industrial disputes, *Strike and Lock-Out Statistics*, 1980 (17).

to each other while reserving full authority of direction and control to the employer. The result is, of course, limited rights for workers.

In effect, the employment contract is primarily a legal device for guaranteeing management the unilateral power to make rules and exercise discretion. Even under a collective bargaining regime, all the initial decisions remain the employer's prerogative. According to Harry Glasbeek, these decisions include the following: "how much to invest, where to do so, what products shall be made, what amount, what quality, what processes are to be used, what *substances* are to be employed" (18, pp. 73-74; emphasis added).

In essence, employer freedom of disposition with respect to capital is the supreme legitimizing principle of private ownership, and includes the rights not to use, to destroy, or to alienate capital ("flight of capital"), and the right to buy, to organize, and to control the labor of others.

Collective agreements and statutory regulations do not limit management rights to any significant degree. The effect of the industrial relations regime is to establish general rules and procedures that must be followed in exercising the rights of ownership. In Canada today, it is generally accepted by arbitrators that the rights to "manage and operate the enterprise, assign work, determine work methods, procedures and equipment, schedule production, and direct the workplace" are reserved to management, and it is not unusual for unions to withdraw entirely from management decisions at this level (19).

Management's resistance to increased worker participation in decision-making is based upon economic considerations, primarily the values associated with efficiency. Additionally, worker rights in health and safety are seen both as irrelevant to the reduction of the frequency and severity of accident rates and the incidence of industrial disease, and as an infringement upon management rights and prerogatives. In both instances, however, the literature suggests the opposite. A vast body of empirical research confirms the positive correlation between worker involvement and productivity. After an extensive review of the literature on this issue, Bruce Stokes (20) found that "ample experience exists to quell most fears that employee involvement in day to day company decisions leads to declining economic efficiency," and that (20, p. 33):

> A 1975 National Science Foundation survey of 57 field studies of worker participation experiences in the United States found that four out of five reported productivity increases. A 1977 study by Dr. Raymond Katzell of New York University of 103 U.S. worker productivity experiments confirmed these findings. Karl Frieden, in a 1978 study for the National Center for Economic Alternatives, concluded that, 'the scientific rigor of many of the studies on workers' participation is less than ideal.' However, a clear pattern emerges . . . supporting the proposition that increases in workers' participation results in improvements in productivity.

Even the Trilateral Commission's Task Force on Industrial Relations, an important management research body, admitted that "nothing in the literature suggests that participation significantly harms productivity" (20, p. 33). At the same time, "weak" worker rights to control work processes are a major contributor to both increased adverse stress and a worsening of accident rates. By contrast, meaningful worker participation and control have a positive effect on worker health and safety (21-23). Nevertheless, there is strong management resistance in Canada against widening existing "partial" worker rights in industry. While worker participation is generally viewed as a "political" goal, it is also a means to come to grips with bad working conditions (24).

Despite growing evidence for the efficacy of worker participation in workplace health and safety, all major political parties in Canada—Liberal, Progressive Conservative (Tory), and the New Democratic Party (social democratic)—accept the notion that productive organizations must be based upon efficiency, and therefore all public policy decisions pertaining to the employment contract must be grounded upon a liberal utilitarian concept of justice and not upon democratic criteria. In effect, all labor policy is based upon a goal-oriented utilitarianism that views existing worker rights as instrumental in furthering economic efficiency and productivity.

The existing worker rights to know, participate, and refuse are frequently traded off in the application of cost-benefit analysis. Utilitarian policy views "equity (justice) versus efficiency" as an appropriate trade-off and as a commonsense ethical and legal principle. This approach denies workers any fundamental right in the area of workplace health and safety, so that all worker rights are derivative or defeasible rights that can readily be defeated either by the courts or by public policy makers.

While many argue that there is sufficient evidence to demonstrate that worker participation in decision-making raises productivity and reduces accidents, their arguments are rejected out of hand by both managers and government officials. Participatory democracy or "strong" worker rights as an instrument most consistent with equality, liberty, and freedom in the employment relation has never penetrated the liberal utilitarian criteria of justice. The existing approach justifies hierarchy as the proper organization principle for industry, and therefore the structure of command enshrines strong management prerogatives.

The utilitarian goal of "the greatest good for the greatest number," often expressed as the "social good," overrides any "independent" or strong right for workers, including the right to strike, especially in the public sector. It also forecloses the consideration that this right is a necessary condition of the wider social good. Consequently, the present public policy thrust of the federal government, the Province of Ontario, and the smaller provinces toward making occupational health information more accessible to the major industrial relations "actors" (labor and management) represents a focus upon a "weak right."

The "right to know" is derived from the workers' right to participate. It is an instrumental right that facilitates worker participation on joint health and safety committees. It is an important right for workers and extends its equivalent in civil society and the political realm into the economic sphere. Still, the right to information and knowledge about hazards does not permit the worker to act upon it in the same way as the legal right to participate and refuse. The latter are "deeper" rights whereby a worker becomes a moral agent rather than a mere moral subject without the capacity to act. The "right to know" must be accompanied by the right to participate and, more importantly, the right to refuse dangerous work. The Director of Health and Safety for the Canadian Auto Workers Unions indicated that it required "mass refusals" by De Haviland auto workers to get the appropriate information in the first instance (25).

Under the Saskatchewan Occupational Health and Safety Act there is a requirement and a duty to provide workers and committees with appropriate health and safety information. As former Executive Director of the Branch within the Department of Labour, I believe that the "right to know" is crucial in strengthening worker involvement on the mandatory joint committees. However, I soon learned from worker "activisits" on the committees that the research articles and data sheets pertaining to specific problems in their place of work were interpreted by "professionals" employed by management. Oftentimes, worker members on the committees felt incompetent and inadequate to challenge these interpretations or, for that matter, to question a study that was contrary to their actual experiences in handling certain substances. Management generally favored the "right to know" policy, felt more reserved about "effective" health and safety committees or the workers' right to participate, and definitely opposed the worker's "right to refuse" dangerous work.

This management perception was further reinforced when I presided as chairperson of the tripartite "Information Utility Committee" of the Canadian Centre of Occupational Health and Safety. This federal crown corporation was set up in the late 1970s to provide labor and management with occupational health and safety information. I posed a question to the management member on the "Information Utility Committee" responsible for developing a strategy to disseminate information to labor and management: why did he favor the provision of health and safety information to workers? He responded by saying that information from a *tripartite body* with labor representation was "necessary to combat the environmentalists and certain labor leaders *using* occupational health and safety as a public issue against industry," and that it was difficult for management to bring forth information contrary to studies used by labor because it would be viewed as biased or "tainted" (26). Generally, unions put forward a recent study showing a causal relationship between a particular chemical and symptom or illness. With the Canadian Centre of Occupational Health and Safety's data bank, managers can access studies with contrary findings bringing into question a single study or the union's concern.

The "right to know," while necessary, is not sufficient. It is an instrumental and a "weak" right in practice. While it is true that "knowledge is power," worker experiences suggest, especially in the area of workplace health and safety, that knowledge is potential. The ability for concerted action is power.

When workers on committees are backed by "strong" trade unions, they are more effective in confronting the "accident-prone worker" and "careless worker" myths which shift environmental problems in industry to workers. Further, the committees are not as easily threatened by the large volume of occupational health studies and data sheets, and the role of company "experts." They are also better prepared to organize a refusal for what they perceive or "believe" to be dangerous work. The primary work group and crews in workplaces represent a community of interest, sentiment, principle (egalitarianism), and activity. Canadian positivist law does not recognize group or communal rights, only individual rights. Nonetheless, these communal rights exist. Where there is a high degree of communality and solidarity within the primary work group or local union, workers are better able to defend their existing legal rights and, possibly, minimize the deterioration of their working conditions. Rationalization and increased efficiency (speed-up and understaffing, etc.) often threaten and offend the social character of work and further individuate the worker. Because of Canadian legislation and strong management prerogatives, the defense of a healthy and safe work environment has been, more or less, hopeless.

Effective committees in Saskatchewan invariably reflected a group association (community), capacity and competence to deal with managers regarding work environment matters, and a high level of group/worker participation in shop floor affairs. One could categorize this as a form of plant citizenship. Group association undeniably enhances the prospects of "effective advocacy," which can therefore be regarded as the value that ultimately supports the protection of the group.

There is no systematic relationship between the worker's right to know or to refuse dangerous work. If association is to be linked with the worker's right to know, to participate, and to refuse, then the linkage must depend upon the intercession of a group value to ensure efficacy of these rights in the promotion of worker health, and safety and the development of a truly human environment. Such an environment is one that promotes growth and self-respect, and conditions that foster competence— the deeper meaning of the "right to know."

The Canadian experience under the "three worker rights" suggests that when you bring labor and management representatives with unequal competence together in joint health and safety committees, you widen rather than narrow the "power" relationship or gulf between the adversaries.

In his studies on "power," Dr. Mark Mulder (27) found that joint consultative committees can be used to the advantage of the party with greater knowledge (so that knowledge is potential power), enabling that party to influence the other. Since management tends to have professional advisory staff (medical or engineering), they can more readily "manipulate" the direction of the committee (27). This was a common occurrence in Saskatchewan during the 1970s.

Mulder (28) also states that "when there are relatively large differences in expertise (expert power) between members of a social system, an increase in participation of the less expert will not lead to a reduced power differential between members, but to its opposite." Further, Mulder states (28, p. 12):

> This great expertise (expert power) of managers and specialists represents potential power. Those with the expertise must communicate with the less powerful to influence them effectively and to realize their power. Thus, when there are large differences in expert power, the introduction of greater participation provides the more powerful with an opportunity to exercise their influence over the less powerful, and thereby makes their power a reality.

Mulder's observation coincides with my experience of many joint health and safety committees in Saskatchewan. Although this imbalance was not manifest in all committees, I have found it to be accurate as a general observation. In part, Mulder's observation accounts for the present public policy thrust in Canada based upon the "right to know." Employers in Saskatchewan, and those who are on the Board of Governors of the Canadian Centre for Occupational Health and Safety, strongly favor the computerization of information as a technical advance. As first chairperson of the Centre's information committee which manages this information, I was unaware of the actual information provided or put out by the computer. The committee never discussed the *content* of information, only the technical aspects of its distribution. Nor has there been a study of the practical effects of the information for unions and workers in Canada. Has this computer-hype primarily benefited managers and professionals? Has it been a management tool against labor? Is this why government funds are available on both the provincial and federal level?

Furthermore, has the "computer thing," with its emphasis on information—materials, data safety sheets, chemical formulas, reference to scientific articles—redirected attention away from the concept of the "work environment," which was of growing interest during the late 1970s and early 1980s? These are questions that need to be asked and studied.

There are, however, some extremely positive developments in the area of occupational health and safety. The recent refusal of workers at DeHaviland Corporation in Toronto to work in an unhealthy environment is an example. The workers are members of the Canadian Automobile Workers Union, which has a well-developed occupational health and safety training program. The Director of Health and Safety for the union, Jim Gill (25), recently stated that in auto plants, his union is attempting to shift health and safety from the personnel and industrial relations department of the company to the plant maintenance departments. There has been a similar attempt by a large local in Saskatchewan.

The relocation of company plant health and safety into plant maintenance departments makes sense in Canada since plant maintenance is organized to solve problems and, unlike personnel and industrial relations departments, does not view unions as adversaries whose "victory" represents a management loss.

RETRENCHMENT OF MANAGEMENT RIGHTS AND RESISTANCE TO WORK ENVIRONMENT REFORMS

Canadian federal and provincial governments represent a major barrier to the creation of a work environment primarily shaped by workers. Labor policy in Canada is based on certain assumptions of an idealized marketplace of small producers or individualistic maximizers of economic wealth. Thus, the instruments of public policy are basically utilitarian, and when they are applied to industry and the employment contract, they conceal libertarian property rights. The increasing acceptance of cost-benefit analysis in standard-setting and a deregulated laissez-faire approach to workplace health and safety are examples of an economic utilitarian policy.

The present conservative political climate has eroded the fragile worker rights that had been developing since the early 1970s. With the economic recession in the mid-1970s, economic values such as efficiency and production activity became more dominant, leading to the erosion of worker rights in health and safety, and the lack of enforcement of existing standards. Workers, therefore, were forced to sacrifice their health and safety to maintain productivity by relaxed standards.

The major political parties in Canada accept the hypothesis that productive organizations are based upon efficiency and that therefore, as stated, all public policy decisions pertaining to the employment contract are grounded upon a liberal utilitarian concept of justice and not upon democratic criteria.

This liberal theory neglects the tension or link between the political and economic spheres of social life. Participatory rights of workers in decision-making in industry are rejected and the employment contract is viewed as a "private contract" of free and equals, assuming workers are analogous to enfranchised citizens in civil society or the political realm. The utilitarian theory of justice is premised on a dichotomy between the political and economic spheres, and the essence of the employment relationship is the employers' direct control over the employees. Meaningful worker participation in work environment matters represents a direct challenge to private ownership and to the employers' control right, which defines the social relations in production. The present structure of command is inconsistent with the conception of the work environment as a community of equals who grow and develop as persons involved in their future.

A deep conception of the work environment implies that workers in the workspace compose a community of sentiment (29)[2] (the primary work group) and a community of principle (31) based upon the enhanced notion of the person rather than the individual, as well as a community of interests. The worker as a person, rather than an individuated factor of production, is a social entity that can more effectively exercise rights in concert with other persons as a practical matter (32). According to Staughton Lynd, the historical experiences of workers foster a solidarity ethnic and "the binding together of individual workers who are alone too weak to protect themselves" (32, p. 1423). Liberal rights consciousness excludes the possibility of construing human freedom as self-expression and growth in and through community. Canadian policymakers virtually refuse to conceive of work as an expression of human meaning or of the collective bargaining process as an experience in participatory self-management.

In the case of the work environment, existing worker rights "to know, participate and refuse" belong to individual employees rather than to *workers* in a work setting consistent with the social nature of production. The very language of "rights" afforded workers in law is permeated with possessive individualism and rests upon a claim based on liberal contractualism which emerged with commercial law and private property. An individual worker, therefore, has only legal claim against an employer rather than an entitlement as a member of a moral community that prescribes standards of conduct and care. The liberal conception of worker rights in workplace health and safety is based upon a worker's claim against other persons. Rights are merely personal properties; it is "our" rights, "their" rights, "his" or "her" rights that support a worker's claim for compensation for hazardous and dangerous work, and injury.

An alternative conception of rights would be grounded on an obligation to provide for human needs (33), and the right to a healthy and safe workplace is among these. This obligation goes beyond the present law, which treats worker rights as possessions that can be bargained or traded away. In this regard, health and safety would be treated as an "inalienable" right—such as the rights to life, liberty, and security— which we do not own in the same way as we own material possessions or private property. After all, worker health and safety are a basic and inalienable human

---

[2] A description of a "community of sentiment" is given by Hume (30).

right which is not to be traded, sold, or treated as a negotiable item in commercial contracts. This approach requires the development of an "ethics of the work environment."

What is urgent for the wider social good in Canada is a thinking through of an ethical framework that grounds a concept of justice, in the obligation to satisfy worker needs, such as friendship, capacity, equality, and community in the workspace. This approach would oppose the existing liberal rights–based doctrine which presupposes the option of assisting or not assisting the victims of hazardous working conditions. When it comes to worker health and safety we need a "politics" of health and safety obligation that, by necessity, facilitates special consideration for worker activation in work environment matters (34).

The concept of the work environment as a community based on universal principles of justice is inconsistent, for instance, with the minute subdivision of labor, and the exploitation and domination of workers according to management "rights" derived from ownership. The present organization of work is the historical product of a dynamic of interaction between technology and class relationships in the work environment. The result, at least in Canada, is the control of the workplace and worker by managers. This requires the absence of a *polis* in the workplace for workers as citizens to deal with work environment matters. From an ethical perspective, there is no "public" or "collective" morality in the employment contract, nor any distinction between technology and morality. This is evident when we observe the manner in which "new" technology is introduced without guidelines, or as an "experiment," and without thought to the effect upon the emotional or economic insecurity of the workforce.

The direction of industry is totally nihilistic and without moral or ethical purpose. The very language of industrial relations is hidden in the technological reduction of meaning to instrumental reasoning, or means reasoning reflecting the underlying assumption that "time is money." Herein, the "fate" of workers is never known, they simply become unemployed, and this is justified by the utilitarian "greater good" of efficiency and pursuit of Canada's competitive position in the international market. This satisfies the notion that "progress" is the inevitable outcome of our productive abilities and efforts, and presumes that generalized worker "anxiety" and insecurity are a separate matter. In part, this is what makes the present language of industrial relations and occupational health and safety both superficial and meaningless. We need a new language with which to talk intelligently and meaningfully about the work environment. This is especially true in the case of the workers' right to know, participate, and refuse. For instance, if the mandatory joint health and safety committees are to be effective, the relationship between workers and managers should be characterized by "dialogue" rather than the present "monologue" reflecting the unequal power relations in work. An ethical conception of the work environment based on obligation to needs would entail possibilities for the exercise of freedom that were necessary and sufficient to satisfy workers' innate psychosocial requirements for autonomy and competence. This would require the extension of rights-based norms to the situation in which workers relate to other workers and to their managers, and vice versa, with mutual respect. In a truly ethical work environment, this requires a relationship of partnership as the proper organization of industry.

Aristotle held that people joined naturally in the partnership of the *polis*, the purpose of which was to provide the conditions of the good life—the life of freedom, of political action, and of virtuous activity (35, 36). An ethics of the work environment demands the creation of a *polis* within the workspace, and the citizenship of workers in the workplace. I believe that this condition would revitalize the notion of a political space in civil society, which Hannah Arendt (37) argued is shrinking and thereby creating the modern preconditions of totalitarianism.

I have attempted to outline only some of the conditions and characteristics of the work environment, and to argue that an ethics of the work environment requires a politics of participation and self-determination based on community and competence. I also maintain that Canada's political parties view such a conception of the work environment as an aspiration, at best, but not a practical possibility. Even the social democratic New Democratic Party (of which I am an active and committed member) is unable, in spite of its direct affiliation with local unions, to translate the progressive extension of workers' capacity to govern their working and personal lives, as well as their social histories, into public policy programs. The political ideology of Canada takes the desirability of maintaining the basic institutional contours of the liberal capitalist social order as given and unquestioned.

This ideology is supported by collective bargaining law that legitimizes unnecessary hierarchy and domination in the workplace (38), and is reinforced by workplace health and safety legislation. Consideration of an ethics of the work environment would, at least, develop a coherent theory of worker rights and conditions for solidarity and mutal aid, rather than the acceptance of liberal labor law thinking which justifies and rationalizes workers' consent of and participation in their own domination.

Along the lines of Staughton Lynd, I have argued that the labor movement represents the best hope for this development and long-term strategy because "more than any other institution in capitalist society, the labor movement is based on communal values . . . and its central historical experience is solidarity" (32, p. 1423).

I am trying to articulate the somewhat inchoate reasoning that seems to lie behind deep public attitudes and legislators' thinking, and that sometimes reflects a bigotry toward the worker. Their defense of liberal utilitarianism is merely a defense of the productive and economic activities of corporations. They do not consider the full range of a corporation's activities and they give insufficient attention to the moral status of the corporation's existence. I am referring not only to the workers' lack of decision-making in job design and work organization questions, or to their lack of control over safety issues and levels of in-plant pollution, but also to the resulting risks of environmental pollution, which affects all of us. Finally, I mean to articulate a concern for the political power of productive organizations.

Unfortunately, these issues remain rather low on the Canadian political agenda. There is no demand or activity regarding the much watered-down conception of the work environment that was developing within the trade union movement in the late 1970s.

Meaningful reforms require worker and union participation in strategic corporate decision-making and planning as a long-term policy, one that goes beyond "consumption politics" to "production politics." Lacking this, any consideration of healthy working conditions for workers, including social and psychological factors resulting from what was believed to be the most "efficient" design of the work environment, is either neglected or simply not understood by the majority of the mandarins of government bureaucracy. They appear to be enraptured by technological advances and the idea of an ever-expanding economy, which they could then manage. They display no awareness of the fact that there are workplaces where human rights are denied on a daily basis because workers do not have the freedom to offer "political" resistance to their own disenfranchisement and dehumanization. The technocrats see the necessity of their actions as progressive, without suspecting that such developments may undermine democracy, freedom, and social justice in society as a whole.

In conclusion, there exists a need for an alternative public policy that increases workers' possibilities of sharing in the control of the work environment and activates workers to reform their working conditions so as to improve their health and safety. This requires the "piercing" of existing management prerogatives, and of their traditional right of control over the labor process, and the planning of work so that a more democratic form and organizational structure begins to take shape.

Acknowledgments — The author would like to thank Professor Harley Dickinson, Department of Sociology, University of Saskatchewan, and Dr. Gary A. Lewis, Toronto-based writer and author of *News from Somewhere: Connecting Health and Freedom at the Workplace* (Greenwood Press, 1986), for their valuable comments.

REFERENCES

1. Gardell, B. Scandinavian research on stress in working life. *Int. J. Health Serv.* 12(1): 31–41, 1982.
2. Gardell, B. Psychosocial aspects of industrial production methods. *Department of Psychology Research Report*, No. 47. University of Stockholm, Stockholm, 1979.
3. *Revised Regulations of Saskatchewan*, Chapter 0-1, Reg. 1, Order in Council 567/81, dated April 14, 1981.
4. Bobiash, D. Industrial democracy in the Canadian potash industry. *Raw Materials Report* (Berlings, Arlov, Sweden) 4(1): 43–57, 1985.
5. Work Environment Board Agreement, Potash Corporation of Saskatchewan, Saskatoon, Saskatchewan, 1981. Unpublished.
6. The Ontario Occupational Health and Safety Act, 1979, S.O. 1979, Section 17.
7. Coburn, D. Work alienation and well-being. In *Health and Canadian Society*, edited by D. Coburn et al. Fitzhenry and Whiteside, Toronto, 1981.
8. *Towards a More Humanized Technology: Exploring the Impact of Video Display Terminals on the Health and Working Conditions of Canadian Office Workers*. Canadian Labor Congress, Ottawa, 1982.
9. Messing, R., and Reveret, J. P. Are women in female jobs for their health? A study of working conditions and health effects in the fish processing industry in Quebec. *Int. J. Health Serv.* 13(4): 636–648, 1983.
10. MacBride, A. High-stress occupations: The importance of job components versus job categories. In *Current Issues in Occupational Stress: Research and Intervention*, edited by R. J. Burke. York University, Faculty Administrative Studies, Downsview, 1984.
11. Leatt, P., and Schneck, R. Sources and management of organizational stress in nursing sub-units in Canada. *Organizational Studies* 6: 55–79, 1985.
12. Lowe, G. S., and Northcott, H. C. *Under Pressure: A Study of Job Stress*. Garamond Press, Toronto, 1986.

13. Grayson, J. P. The closure of a factory and its impact on health. *Int. J. Health Serv.* 15(1): 69–93, 1985.
14. Brody, B., Rohan, P., and Rompre, L. Les accidents industrielles au Canada: Le portrait d'une de'cienne. *Relations Industrielles* 40(3): 545–566, 1986.
15. Reasons, C. Occupational health: Material and chemical aspects. In *Human Resource Management: Contemporary Perspectives in Canada*, edited by K. M. Srinivas, p. 459. McGraw-Hill Ryerson Ltd., Toronto, 1984.
16. Sass, R. Workplace health and safety: Report from Canada. *Int. J. Health Serv.* 16(4): 565–582, 1986.
17. *Strike and Lockout Statistics.* Labour Canada, Ottawa, Ont., 1980.
18. Glasbeek, H. J. The contract of employment at common law. In *Union-Management Relations in Canada*, edited by J. Anderson and M. Gunderson. Addison-Wesley, Don Mills, Toronto, 1982.
19. Swan, K. P. Union impact on management of the organization: A legal perspective. In *Union-Management Relations in Canada*, edited by J. Anderson and M. Gunderson, p. 280. Addison-Wesley, Don Mills, Toronto, 1982.
20. Stokes, B. Worker participation—Productivity and the quality of work life. *Worldwatch Paper*, No. 25, December 1978, p. 33.
21. Cronin, J. B. Cause and effect? Investigations into aspects of industrial accidents in the United Kingdom. *Int. Law Rev.* 103(2): 95–115, 1971.
22. Powell, P., et al. *2000 Accidents: A Shop Floor Study of Their Causes Based on 42 Months Continuous Observation.* National Institute of Industrial Psychology, London, 1971.
23. Nichols, T., and Armstrong, P. *Safety or Profit: Industrial Accidents and the Conventional Wisdom.* Falling Wall Press, England, 1973.
24. Dickinson, H. D., and Strobbe, M. Occupational health and safety in Canada. In *Sociology of Health Care in Canada*, edited by B. S. Bolaria and H. Dickinson. Harcourt Brace Jovanovich, Toronto, 1989.
25. Gill, J., Director of Occupational Health and Safety, Canadian Auto Workers Union. Conversation with the author, February 8, 1988.
26. Bingham, E., Safety Director, Imperial Oil of Canada, Province of Alberta, Hamilton, Ont. Conversation with the author, 1980.
27. Mulder, M. Power equalization through participation? *Administrative Sci. Q.* 16(1): 31–38, 1971.
28. Mulder, M. Reduction and Power Differences in Practice, p. 11. Paper presented at the seminar "European Contributions to Organization Theory," Fontainbleau, France, May 13–15, 1975.
29. Shue, H. *Basic Rights: Subsistence, Affluence, and U.S. Foreign Policy.* Princeton University, Princeton, N.J., 1980.
30. Hume, D. *Treatise of Human Nature*, Book III. Selby-Bigge, London.
31. Dworkin, R. *A Matter of Principle.* Harvard University Press, Cambridge, Mass., 1985.
32. Lynd, S. Communal rights. *Texas Law Rev.* 62(8): 1417–1441, 1984.
33. Weil, S. Human personality. In *Two Moral Essays*, edited by R. Hathaway Traus and R. Rees. Pendle Hill, Wallingford, Pa., 1981.
34. Gustavsen, B., and Hunnius, G. *New Patterns of Work Reform: The Case of Norway.* Universitetoforlaget, Oslo, 1981.
35. Aristotle. *The Politics of Aristotle*, edited and translated by E. Baker. Oxford University Press, New York, 1958.
36. Aristotle. *Nichomachean Ethics*, translated by M. Oswald. Bobbs-Merrill, Indianapolis.
37. Arendt, H. *The Human Condition*, pp. 52–53. University of Chicago Press, Chicago, 1958.
38. Klare, K. Labor law as ideology: Toward a new historiography of collective bargaining law. *Indust. Relations Law J.* 450: 450–481, 1981.

APPENDIX

Bibliography of International Publications by Bertil Gardell

Bertil Gardell published about 130 books, articles, chapters, and reports. The items listed below represent his international production. Among his major publications in Swedish are his doctoral thesis, "Produktionsteknik och arbetsglädje" (Technology, Alienation and Mental Health) in 1971, "Arbetsinnehåll och livskvalitet" (Job Content and the Quality of Life) in 1976, "Sjukvård på löpande band. Ett forskningsprojekt om sjukhusets vård- och arbetsorganisation" (Assembly-line health care. A research project on the organization of care and work in the hospital) with Rolf Å. Gustafsson in 1979, and "Medbestämmande och självstyre. En lokal facklig strategi för demokratisering av arbetsplatsen" (Co-determination and autonomy. A local trade union strategy for democracy at the workplace) with Lennart Svensson in 1981.

1963

1. Gardell, B. Social implications of automation in Sweden. Swedish Council for Personnel Administration, No. 7. Stockholm, 1963.
2. Gardell, B. Reaction du personnel de la compagnie Alfa Laval au transfert de leur usine. Séminaire international mixte sur la mobilité géographique et professionnelle de la Main-Doeuvre, O.C.D.E. Castelfusano 19–22 novembre, 1963.

1966

3. Gardell, B. Plant relocation, personnel planning, and employee reaction. *Personnel Administration* 29(5): 41–44, 1966.

1967

4. Gardell, B. The individual, environment, and productivity. *Journal of Methods–Time Measurement* 12: 18–21, 1967.

1971

5. Gardell, B. Alienation and mental health in the modern industrial environment. In *Society, Stress and Disease. Vol. 1. The Psychosocial Environment and Psychosomatic Diseases,* edited by L. Levi, pp. 148–180. Oxford University Press, London, 1971.

1973

6. Gardell, B. Job satisfaction among forest workers. Summary of a social psychological study. Reports from the Psychological Laboratories, No. 385. University of Stockholm, 1973.
7. Gardell B. Quality of work and non-work activities and rewards in affluent societies. Reports from the Psychological Laboratories, No. 403. University of Stockholm, 1973.

1974

8. Gardell, B. The effects of technology on man. Secretariat for Future Studies. Man in the communications system of the future, pp. 47–55. Swedish Cabinet Office, Stockholm, 1974.
9. Gardell B. Autonomy and participation at work. Reports from the Department of Psychology, No. 422. University of Stockholm, 1974.

1975

10. Gardell, B. Technology, alienation and mental health. Summary of a social psychological research programme of technology. Reports from the Department of Psychology, No. 456. University of Stockholm, 1975.
11. Gardell, B. The compatibility-incompatibility between organization and individual values: A Swedish point of view. In *The Quality of Working Life, Vol. 1: Problems, Prospects, and the State of the Art*, edited by L. E. Davis, et al., pp. 317–326. The Free Press, New York, 1975.
12. Gardell B. Zur Qualität von Werk- und Freizeittätigkeiten und ihrer Anerkennung in Wohlstandsgesellschaften. In *Planvolle Steuerung des Gesellschaftlichen Handelns*, edited by J. K. H. W. Schmidt, pp. 173–190. Westdeutscher Verlag, Opladen, 1975.
13. Gardell, B. Overload—Underload—Lack of Self Control. An interdisciplinary approach to understanding and preventing occupational stress. Paper presented to The International Committee on Occupational Mental Health. Conference on Psychosocial Stressors in the Work Environment. Identification, Research Strategies, Control and Prevention. Stockholm, August 25–27, 1976.

1976

14. Gardell, B. Psychological and social problems of industrial work in affluent societies. Reports from the Department of Psychology, No. 474. University of Stockholm, 1976.
15. Gardell, B. Technology, alienation and mental health. Summary of a social psychological study of technology and the worker. *Acta Sociologica* 19(1): 83–92, 1976.
16. Frankenhaeuser, M., and Gardell, B. Underload and overload in working life. A multidisciplinary approach. Reports from the Department of Psychology, No. 460. University of Stockholm, 1976.
17. Frankenhaeuser, M., and Gardell, B. Underload and overload in working life: Outline of a multidisciplinary approach. *Journal of Human Stress* 2: 35–46, 1976.

18. Gardell, B. Reactions at work and their influence on nonwork activities: An analysis of a sociopolitical problem in affluent societies. *Human Relations* 29: 885–904, 1976.
19. Gardell, B. Man in the production system—the worker. Proceedings of the XVIth World Congress of the International Union of Forestry Research Organization. International Union of Forestry Research Organization, Vienna, 1976.

1977
20. Gardell, B. Autonomy and participation at work. *Human Relations* 30: 515–533, 1977.
21. Gardell, B. Psychological and social problems of industrial work in affluent societies. *International Journal of Psychology* 12: 125–130, 1977.

1978
22. Gardell, B. Arbeitsgestaltung, intrinsische Arbeitszufriedenheit und Gesundheit. In *Industrielle Psychopathologie*, edited by M. Frese, S. Greif, and N. Semmer. Verlag Hans Huber, Bern, Stuttgart, Wien, 1978.

1979
23. Gardell, B. Psychosocial aspects of industrial production methods. Reports from the Department of Psychology, Suppl. 47. University of Stockholm, 1979.

1980
24. Gardell, B., and Gustavsen, B. Work environment research and social change. Current developments in Scandinavia. *Journal of Occupational Behaviour* 1: 3–17, 1980.
25. Gardell, B. Production Techniques and Working Conditions. The Swedish Institute Fact Sheets, No. 256, 1980.
26. Gardell, B . Autonomy and participation at work. In *The Study of Organizations*, edited by D. Katz, R. Kahn, and J. C. Adams, pp. 284–298. Jossey Bass, San Francisco, 1980.

1981
27. Gardell, B. Scandinavian research on stress in working life. Reports from the Department of Psychology, Suppl. 52. University of Stockholm, 1981.
28. Gardell, B., and Johansson, G. (eds.). *Man and Working Life. A Social Science Contribution to Work Reform*. Wiley, Chichester, 1981.
29. Gardell, B. Strategies for reform programmes on work organization and work environment in Sweden. In *Man and Working Life. A Social Science Contribution to Work Reform*, edited by B. Gardell and G. Johansson, pp. 3–13. Wiley, Chichester, 1981.
30. Gardell, B. Psychosocial aspects of industrial production methods. In *Society, Stress and Disease, Vol. 4. Working Life*, edited by L. Levi, pp. 65–75. Oxford University Press, New York, 1981.

31. Frankenhaeuser, M., Levi, L., and Gardell, B. Work stress related to social structures and processes. In *Research on Stress and Human Health*, edited by G. R. Elliot and C. Eisdorfer, pp. 95–117. Springer Publishing Co., New York, 1981.

1982

32. Gardell, B., Aronsson, G., and Barklöf, K. The working environment for local transport personnel. Summary of a research project. Research Unit for the Social Psychology of Work. Reports from the Department of Psychology, No. 31. University of Stockholm, 1982.

33. Gardell, B., Aronsson, G., and Barklöf, K. The Working Environment for Local Public Transport Personnel. The Swedish Work Environment Fund, Stockholm, 1982.

34. Gardell, B. Worker participation and autonomy: A multilevel approach to democracy at the workplace. In *Yearbook of Organizational Democracy: Organizational Democracy and Political Processes*, Vol. 1, pp. 353–387. Wiley, Chichester, 1982.

35. Gardell, B. Worker participation and autonomy: A multilevel approach to democracy at the workplace. *International Journal of Health Services* 12(4): 527–558, 1982.

36. Gardell, B. Scandinavian research on stress in working life. *International Journal of Health Services* 12(1): 31–41, 1982.

1985

37. Gardell, B., Henriksson, J., and Mächs, A. The Ekerö project. A research project on a local nursing home designed by its patients and staff. In *Work and Health in the 1980s. Experiment of Direct Workers' Participation in Occupational Health*, edited by S. Bagnara, R. Mitisi, and H. Wintersberger. Sigma Bohn, Berlin, 1985.

1986

38. Frankenhaeuser, M., Levi, L., and Gardell, B. The characteristics of the workplace and the nature of its social demands. In *Stress, Health and Performance at Work*, edited by S. Wolf and A. J. Finestone, pp. 54–67. PSG Publishing Company, Littleton, Massachusetts, 1986.

1987

39. Gardell, B. Efficiency and health hazards at work. In *Health Care Systems in the Workplace*, edited by J. C. Quick, R. S. Bhagat, J. E. Dalton, and J. D. Quick, pp. 50–71. Praeger Scientific Publishers, New York, 1987.

40. Gardell, B. Work organization and human nature. A review of research on man's need to control technology. The Swedish Work Environment Fund, Stockholm, 1987.

1988

41. Johansson, G., and Gardell, B. Work-health relations as mediated through stress reactions and job socialization. In *Topics in Health Psychology*, edited by S. Maes, C. D. Spielberger, P. Defares, and I. Sarason, pp. 271–285. Wiley, New York, 1988.

Contributors

GUNNAR ARONSSON has been a research psychologist at the National Institute of Occupational Health, Solna, Sweden, since 1983, where he is now a professor. He worked for nine years at the Department of Psychology of the University of Stockholm in an interdisciplinary research group headed by Professors Bertil Gardell and Marianne Frankenhaeuser. Dr. Aronsson was project coordinator of a study on the work environment of bus drivers. He obtained his Ph.D. in psychology in 1985 and has published research articles on psychological and psychophysiological stress reactions in relation to technology and work organization. He is editor of the book *Work Demands and Human Development* (1983), and author of *Occupational Psychology: Stress and Qualification Perspectives* (1987), both in Swedish.

STEVEN DEUTSCH is director of the Center for the Study of Work, Economy and Community and professor of sociology at the University of Oregon. He has written on the topics of work democratization, work environment improvement, and new technology at the workplace. He has acted as consultant to the National Institute of Occupational Safety and Health, the U.S. Congress Office of Technology Assessment, the National Academy of Sciences, several American unions, and most recently the Work Research Institute, Oslo, and the Swedish Ministry of Labor reviewing the Swedish Center for Working Life.

LEIGH DEVES is a lecturer at the School of Business, Nepean College of Advanced Education, Sydney, Australia. He has worked in the Navy and as a psychologist in several government organizations, where he gained experience in operations planning. He received an honors degree in psychology from the University of New South Wales in 1978 and an M.B.A. from Macquarie University in 1986. His research interests and publications are in the fields of occupational health with particular reference to the study of the Australian phenomenon known as Repetition Strain Injury, work performance, and the design of work organizations.

MARIANNE FRANKENHAEUSER is professor and head of the Psychology Division at the Karolinska Medical School in Stockholm. She is also affiliated with the Department of Psychology at the University of Stockholm. She received her Ph.D. from the University of Uppsala, Sweden, in 1959. Dr. Frankenhaeuser's background is in experimental psychophysiology and stress research. In the early 1970s she and Dr. Bertil Gardell started a long-term research collaboration. The aim of their joint program was to integrate social and biological psychology in the study of stress, coping, and health at the workplace. This has remained the focus of her research as Principal Investigator (1983–1989) in the J. D. and C. T. MacArthur Foundation Network on Health and Behavior. In 1989 she was appointed foreign member of the U.S. National

Academy of Sciences. Important publications include "Behavior and Circulating Catecholamines" (*Brain Research*, 1971): "Psychoneuroendocrine Approaches to the Study of Emotion as Related to Stress and Coping" (in *Nebraska Symposium on Motivation 1978*, University of Nebraska Press, 1979); and "A Psychobiological Framework for Research on Human Stress and Coping" (in *Dynamics of Stress*, Plenum Press, 1986).

BERTIL GARDELL was, until his death in 1987, professor of work psychology and director of the Research Unit for the Social Psychology of Work at the University of Stockholm in Sweden. An overview of his career appears in the Introduction, and a bibliography of his international publications can be found in the Appendix.

ROLF Å. GUSTAFSSON received his Ph.D. in sociology at Gothenburg University in 1988. For ten years he collaborated with Bertil Gardell at the Psychology Department of the University of Stockholm. Their studies concerned, among other things, working conditions in hospital care and user influence in the planning of health care systems. Gustafsson's doctoral thesis was a historical-sociological analysis of the organization of medical care in Sweden. He is presently working at the Swedish Center for Working Life.

BJÖRN GUSTAVSEN is a professor at the Swedish Center for Working Life in Stockholm, a part-time research fellow at the Work Research Institute in Oslo, and a visiting professor at the University of Oslo. He has been a research fellow as well as director of the Work Research Institute. He graduated in law from the University of Oslo in 1964 and received his Ph.D. in sociology from the same university in 1972. His main field of action research involves reform programs in which research contributes to the creation of broad changes in working life. These involve worker participation in the design and execution of strategies in which a number of parameters ranging from legislation to workplace action are linked to each other in multilevel approaches. Dr. Gustavsen has written several books and some hundred papers, of which about half are in English, about theoretical and practical issues emerging from this type of effort.

ELLEN M. HALL is on the faculty of the Division of Behavioral Sciences and Health Education, Department of Health Policy and Management, at The Johns Hopkins University School of Hygiene and Public Health. Dr. Hall also holds an appointment as a visiting scientist at the Swedish National Institute for Psychosocial Factors and Health. She has worked in the occupational health field since the early 1970s and has held positions at the Environmental Protection Agency and the Occupational Safety and Health Administration. She has also directed the activities of a number of international unions in the areas of health hazard evaluation and worker education. In Sweden, where she received her Ph.D., she has held research positions at the University of Stockholm's Research Unit for the Social Psychology of Work and at the Karolinska Institute's Department of Psychosocial Environmental Medicine. At present, her research activities include a study of the effects of total life stress on women's health, and the impact of gender-dependent career trajectories on work stress exposure over the life course.

JAMES S. HOUSE is professor and chairperson of the Department of Sociology and research scientist in the Survey Research Center of the Institute for Social Research, the Institute of Gerontology, and the Department of Epidemiology at the University of Michigan. He obtained his Ph.D. in social psychology from the University of Michigan in 1972, and previously was on the faculty in the Department of Sociology at Duke University. His research has focused on the relationship between occupational stress and health and the determinants of both social stress and social support. He is currently involved in a major national survey study of productive activity, stress, and health in middle and late life, and in an action research project on occupational stress and health.

BARBARA A. ISRAEL is an associate professor in the Department of Health Behavior and Health Education, School of Public Health, University of Michigan in Ann Arbor. She has a doctorate in public health from the University of North Carolina at Chapel Hill. She is the principal investigator of the action research effort described in her chapter in this book. Dr. Israel has written extensively on the integration of theory and research concerning social networks and social support with health education practice. Her research interests and involvements include occupational stress and health; participation and control; social networks and social support; organizational, community, and social change; and community-oriented approaches to health promotion and primary care.

GUNN JOHANSSON is professor of work psychology in the Department of Psychology at the University of Stockholm. Her collaboration with Bertil Gardell started shortly after she obtained her Ph.D. in psychology at that university in 1973. She then coordinated a long-term research program initiated by Professors Marianne Frankenhaeuser and Bertil Gardell. Dr. Johansson's research interests and involvements concern psychosocial work conditions, stress, and health, including studies of job dimensions such as mental workload, autonomy, and individual control; levels of computerization; and underutilization of abilities. She has studied these conditions within a multidisciplinary approach applying behavioral as well as physiological and neuroendocrine methods in the laboratory and in the field.

JEFFREY V. JOHNSON is an assistant professor of behavioral sciences in the Department of Health Policy and Management at The Johns Hopkins School of Hygiene and Public Health. He also holds joint academic appointments in The Johns Hopkins University's Department of Environmental Health Sciences in the School of Public Health; in the Department of Medicine in the School of Medicine; and in the Department of Sociology in the School of Arts and Sciences. Dr. Johnson has developed research collaborations with a number of Swedish Institutes where he has held visiting appointments, including the National Institute for Psychosocial Factors and Health, the Karolinska Institute's Department of Psychosocial Environmental Medicine, the National Statistical Bureau, and the Department of Psychology at the University of Stockholm. He received his doctorate in behavioral sciences from The Johns Hopkins University in 1986. Prior to his graduate training Dr. Johnson served an apprenticeship and worked as a journeyman in the printing industry. His research has focused on the relationship between collectivity and control in the work environment and the impact of these factors on cardiovascular disease risk. Over the past six years, he has contributed to and led a research group that has focused on the social epidemiology of social networks and social support, unemployment and depression, and work stress and cardiovascular disease, and is presently developing and testing a theoretical model of life-time occupational stress exposure.

ROBERT KARASEK is an associate professor of industrial and systems engineering at the University of Southern California in Los Angeles, and has previously taught at

Columbia University. He received a Ph.D. in industrial sociology and a masters degree in civil engineering from Massachusetts Institute of Technology, a masters degree in architecture from the University of Pennsylvania, and a B.A. from Princeton University. He has published research in the *American Journal of Public Health, Administrative Science Quarterly,* and *Ergonomics,* and is coauthor with Tores Theorell of *Healthy Work: Job Stress, Productivity, and the Reconstruction of Working Life* (Basic Books, 1989). He does research on psychosocial job structure, stress, and cardiovascular illness, sponsored by the U.S. National Institute of Occupational Safety and Health; on the impact of social networks on the development of worker skills; and on new models of creative work organization.

LENNART LENNERLÖF is professor of psychology and head of the work psychology unit at the research department of the National Swedish Board of Occupational Safety and Health. He received his Ph.D. from Lund University and worked for ten years as managing director of the Swedish Council for Personnel Administration. He has published several books and articles on psychological aspects of work organization, leadership, work environment, and technology. He is a member of the National Committee of Psychological Science of the Royal Swedish Academy of Sciences. Currently, he is manager of a national program on computerization and the work environment.

MICHAEL MARMOT, M.D., Ph.D., is a physician and professor of community medicine at Middlesex Hospital and University College of London. He obtained his academic degrees in Australia and from the University of California, Berkeley, and has held his present position since 1985. The majority of his publications have been in the field of cardiovascular epidemiology. Dr. Marmot has been involved in committee work concerned with the prevention and control of cardiovascular disease for the World Health Organization, the European Community, and the International Society and Federation of Cardiology.

ROBERT SASS is director of the Labor Studies Program at the University of Saskatchewan in Saskatoon, Canada. Between 1972 and 1982 he was executive director of Occupational Health and Safety and Associate Deputy Minister of Labor in the Saskatchewan Department of Labor.

SUSAN J. SCHURMAN is interim director of the Labor Studies Center and co-director of the Joint Labor-Management Center, Institute of Labor and Industrial Relations, University of Michigan. She is completing a doctorate in higher, adult, and continuing education. She is co-principal investigator of the action research project described in her chapter. Both her practice and research interests center on improving the quality of the work environment and working life. She has done extensive work with unions and companies aimed at increasing workers' influence in decisions.

ROBERT SPILLANE is an associate professor of occupational psychology at the Graduate School of Management, Macquarie University, Sydney, Australia. He received a bachelor of commerce degree with honors in applied psychology from the University of New South Wales in 1972, and a Ph.D. in the social psychology of work from Macquarie University in 1978. His publications are in the fields of industrial relations, organizational behavior, occupational health, and stress. He has published two books: *Organizational Behaviour: The Australian Context* (with R. D. Lansbury; Longman Cheshire, 1983) and *Achieving Peak Performance* (Harper & Row, 1985). He has completed a third book: *The Management Entertainers: Management Training as Entertainment* (1987). In 1981 he sponsored the visit to Australia of Bertil Gardell, whose work and friendship inspired the research reported in his chapter.

LENNART SVENSSON received a Ph.D. in sociology at the University of Lund, Sweden, in 1985. He is a research associate in the Swedish Center for Working Life and is a consultant to several trade unions. His research has concerned trade union organizations, work organization in health care work, and the decentralization of community services, with special focus on the problems involved and methods used in introducing industrial democracy, both in the private and the public sector.

S. LEONARD SYME is professor of epidemiology at the School of Public Health at the University of California, Berkeley. Before this, he worked in the U.S. Public Health Service both at the National Institutes of Health in Bethesda, Maryland, and in the Heart Disease Research Field Station in San Francisco. He received his Ph.D. in medical sociology at Yale University in 1957. Dr. Syme is a co-author of *Social Stress and Cardiovascular Disease* and *Social Support and Health*, and has written articles on psychosocial factors in coronary heart disease as well as on environmental approaches to disease prevention and health promotion.

TORES THEORELL, M.D., Ph.D., is a physician and professor of health care research at the National Institute of Psychosocial Factors and Health in Stockholm, Sweden. He also holds an appointment as a Senior Research Associate at The Johns Hopkins School of Public Health. After eleven years in clinical medicine (Department of Medicine, Seraphimer Hospital) he worked at the Department of Social Medicine, Huddinge Hospital, for two years. He has worked at the National Institute of Psychosocial Factors and Health since 1980. He has collaborated extensively with Robert A. Karasek (Karasek and Theorell: *Healthy Work*, Basic Books, New York, 1990) as well as with clinicians (for instance de Faire and Theorell: *Life Stress and Coronary Heart Disease*, Warren Green, St. Louis, 1984) and has published mainly within epidemiology and stress physiology.

GUNNELA WESTLANDER, Ph.D., is a professor of psychology and health and head of the Division of Social and Organizational Psychology at the National Institute of Occupational Health, Stockholm, Sweden. She started her work in this field in 1966 as a research assistant to Bertil Gardell, who at that time held an appointment with the Swedish Council of Personnel Administration. During the 1970s, her research interests were the relationships between work and leisure, differences in working conditions for men and women, and health perspectives of organizational changes. During the 1980s her studies have focused on the implications of new technology. Among Dr. Westlander's recent publications are *Government Policy and Women's Health Care: The Swedish Alternative* (The Haworth Press, New York, 1988).

Index